# The
# Gynecological
# SOURCEBOOK

## Other Books by M. Sara Rosenthal

*The Breast Sourcebook* (2nd ed., 1999)

*The Breastfeeding Sourcebook* (2nd ed., 1998)

*The Fertility Sourcebook* (3rd ed., 2002)

*50 Ways to Fight Depression Without Drugs* (2001)

*50 Ways to Manage Type 2 Diabetes* (2001)

*50 Ways to Manage Ulcer, Heartburn and Reflux* (2001)

*50 Ways to Prevent and Manage Stress* (2001)

*50 Ways to Prevent Colon Cancer* (2000)

*50 Ways Women Can Prevent Heart Disease* (2000)

*The Gastrointestinal Sourcebook* (1997, 1998)

*The Hypothyroid Sourcebook* (2002)

*Managing PMS Naturally* (2001)

*The Natural Woman's Guide to Preventing Diabetes Complications* (2002)

*The Pregnancy Sourcebook* (3rd ed., 1999)

*The Thyroid Sourcebook* (4th ed., 2000)

*The Thyroid Sourcebook for Women* (1999)

*The Type 2 Diabetic Woman* (1999)

*Women and Depression* (2000)

*Women Managing Stress* (2002)

## SarahealthGuides™

These are M. Sara Rosenthal's own line of health books written by herself and other health authors. SarahealthGuides™ are dedicated to rare, controversial, or stigmatizing health topics you won't find in regular bookstores. SarahealthGuides™ are available only at online bookstores such as Amazon.com. Visit sarahealth.com for upcoming titles.

*Living Well with Celiac Disease,* by Claudine Crangle (2002)

*Living Well with Ostomy,* by Elizabeth Rayson (2003)

*Thyroid Eye Disease,* by Elaine Moore (2003)

*Stopping Cancer at the Source* (2001)

*The Thyroid Cancer Book* (2002)

*Women and Unwanted Hair* (2001)

# The
# Gynecological
# SOURCEBOOK

**Fourth Edition**

M. Sara Rosenthal, Ph.D.

**McGraw·Hill**

New York   Chicago   San Francisco   Lisbon   London   Madrid   Mexico City
Milan   New Delhi   San Juan   Seoul   Singapore   Sydney   Toronto

The McGraw-Hill Companies

**Library of Congress Cataloging-in-Publication Data**

Rosenthal, M. Sara.
    The gynecological sourcebook / M. Sara Rosenthal.—4th ed.
        p.    cm.
    Includes bibliographical references and index.
    ISBN 0-07-140279-9
    1. Gynecology—Popular works.    I. Title.

  RG121.R76    2003
  618.1—dc21                    2002041486

1 2 3 4 5 6 7 8 9 0  DOC/DOC  2 1 0 9 8 7 6 5 4 3

ISBN 0-07-140279-9

Interior design by Rattray Design

McGraw-Hill books are available at special quantity discounts to use as premiums and sales promotions, or for use in corporate training programs. For more information, please write to the Director of Special Sales, Professional Publishing, McGraw-Hill, Two Penn Plaza, New York, NY 10121-2298. Or contact your local bookstore.

The purpose of this book is to educate. It is sold with the understanding that the author and publisher shall have neither liability nor responsibility for any injury caused or alleged to be caused directly or indirectly by the information contained in this book. While every effort has been made to ensure its accuracy, the book's contents should not be construed as medical advice. Each person's health needs are unique. To obtain recommendations appropriate to your particular situation, please consult a qualified health care provider. The herbal information in this book is provided for education purposes only and is not meant to be used without consulting a qualified health practitioner who is trained in herbal medicine.

This book is printed on acid-free paper.

# Contents

# Acknowledgments

I WISH TO thank the following people (listed alphabetically), whose expertise and dedication helped to lay so much of the groundwork for this book: Gillian Arsenault, M.D., C.C.F.P., I.B.L.C., F.R.C.P.; Pamela Craig, M.D., F.A.C.S., Ph.D.; Masood Kahthamee, M.D., F.A.C.O.G.; Debra Lander, M.D., F.R.C.P.; Gary May, M.D., F.R.C.P.; James McSherry, M.B., Ch.B., F.C.F.P., F.R.C.G.P., F.A.A.F.P., F.A.B.M.P.; Suzanne Pratt, M.D., F.A.C.O.G.; Wm Warren Rudd, M.D., F.R.C.S., F.A.C.S., colon and rectal surgeon, founder and director of The Rudd Clinic for Diseases of the Colon and Rectum (Toronto); and Robert Volpe, M.D., F.R.C.P., F.A.C.P.

William Harvey, Ph.D., L.L.B., University of Toronto, Department of Philosophy, whose devotion to bioethics has inspired me, continues to support my work and makes it possible for me to have the courage to question and challenge issues in health care and medical ethics. Irving Rootman, Ph.D., director, University of Toronto, Centre for Health Promotion, continues to encourage my interest in primary prevention and health promotion issues. Helen Lenskyj, Ph.D., professor, Department of Sociology and Equity Studies, Ontario Institute for Studies in Education/University of Toronto, and Laura M. Purdy, Ph.D., have been central figures in my understanding the complexities of women's health issues and feminist bioethics.

Meredith Schwartz, my editorial and research assistant, worked very hard to make this book come into being. And finally, Judith McCarthy, my editor at McGraw-Hill, championed this project and saw how important it was for all things gynecological—West to East—to come together in one book.

# Introduction

IF YOU HAVE a copy of my book *The Gynecological Sourcebook*, in its third or an earlier edition, it's time to throw it out and read *this* one instead; this is the book *you* asked me to write!

While there are a myriad of women's health books available, few are devoted solely to gynecological health—and few gynecological health books present both alternative and conventional Western medical approaches. But women today straddle healing systems and routinely incorporate a variety of approaches to stay well below the belt.

## Balanced Gynecology

Based on hundreds of letters and E-mails I have received since 1994, when the first edition of *The Gynecological Sourcebook* was published, the contents of this current edition reflect what women are asking for: *complete information from West to East on all things gynecological*. Women are frustrated by gynecological books that "take up space" with breast health, pregnancy, and infertility, since there are numerous books devoted solely to these topics. Books covering the topics women really need good information on remain sparse, and the popularity of *The Gynecological Sourcebook* was due to its coverage of topics that generally receive minimal treatment in other books: fibroids, gynecological cancers, women and HIV, abortion, female genital mutilation, and the range of gynecological infections that plague women, such as chlamydia (now linked to heart disease), herpes (on the rise with no end in sight), yeast (frequently experienced by diabetic women), and pelvic inflammatory disease (the main cause of infertility in women). Information is also sparse when it comes to uterine health, cervical health, and ovarian health, as well as "complete picture" coverage of birth control.

This book reflects a combination of what's new in gynecology plus my accumulated knowledge as a women's health journalist, scholar, and health promoter in all matters below the belt. As a feminist sociologist and bioethicist, I firmly believe that medical jargon continues to be a barrier to women's health choices. As a woman, I am frustrated that so many of our parts are medicalized and pathologized, and that treatments are aimed at creating a cycle of dependence on the medical system.

Here you'll find "gynie-speak" translated into plain language. Each chapter gives you the full picture from a conventional perspective. Then, under "What to Eat," you'll find all the information you need to complement, supplement, or manage various gynecological conditions through diet and nutrition. Under "Flower Power," you'll find all the herbal information you need to complement, supplement, or manage a condition. And finally, under "How to Move," you'll find how movement, pelvic exercises, healing arts, touch therapies, and good ol' fashioned stretching and aerobics can complement or manage various conditions. (Bet you didn't know belly dancing could prevent pelvic prolapse.) Divided into four key sections, this book can be your "speculum" and guide you through your gynecological issues, from your first period to your last.

# The Women's Health Care Movement and Your Rights

The women's health care movement upon which most of today's women's health care is modeled has amassed a host of alternative or complementary systems of healing that aids in gynecological health and well-being, and which can be combined with diet and lifestyle modification or herbal therapies.

Women have been healing each other, birthing each other (through midwifery), and sharing ingenious reproductive health remedies and recipes since the beginning of time. It's called girl talk in lay terms, but fancier terms refer to women healing through oral tradition or narratives. Women can connect on a number of health issues through online chat rooms and health forums. The most renowned women's health book and "bible," *Our Bodies, Ourselves*, which is a standard in women's health information, was not created by doctors at all—male *or* female. It was created through girl talk!

The Boston Women's Health Book Collective grew out of a course, by and for women, about health, sexuality, and childbearing. This small group of women met regularly to discuss aspects of women's health, particularly their frustrations with doctors. When they realized that the "personal was political," in that each of their experiences mirrored the state of women's health at that time, each woman in the group took a topic, such as abortion or rape, made that the focus of her research, and then brought back what she had learned to the larger group.

*Our Bodies, Ourselves*, which has been revised several times throughout the last thirty years and has sold more than four million copies, still reflects women's own self-knowledge about their health and is just as relevant today as it was when the first edition came out in 1970. Says Gloria Steinem:

> I was part of that small demographic slice of people most likely to get the best health care information. As a journalist, I was even in a position to research what I didn't know. Yet what "best" meant in those largely prefeminist days was whatever limited information the medical establishment considered appropriate—for patients in general and for women in particular.

When women realized that their bodies were their business, the grassroots women's health movement started health care reform in the 1970s. No longer acceptable were the lack of health information provided, abuse of medical procedures, the lack of good birth control information, or being told that natural female processes were diseases. Women were tired of not being in control of their bodies.

"Well-women" clinics run by ordinary women were springing up all over North America in the mid-to-late 1970s. Knowledge gained about their own bodies by simply looking at the cervix at different stages proved that much of what women were being told about their health status "down there" was false. For example, one women's clinic discovered that although gynecologists told women who had a tipped, or retroverted, uterus that they were abnormal, it was, in fact, the most common shape of uterus. Several community-based self-help programs also changed the delivery of women's health care.

The women's health movement extended into patients' rights and bioethics. In a very general way, bioethics rests on four basic umbrella principles: respect for persons, beneficence, nonmaleficence, and justice. You can challenge your doctor on any of these principles and use the following information to launch a complaint to your state medical board if you feel your rights have been ignored.

## *Respect for Persons (a.k.a. Patient Autonomy)*

Respect for persons (sometimes called patient autonomy) means to respect that each person is, in fact, a human being with full human rights. That means he or she has a right to be fully informed about all things involving his or her care, his or her body, or things being done to his or her body (e.g., if you're pregnant, you have the right to know about everything that affects the fetus you're carrying)—and a right to make his or her own decisions about care based on accurate information.

A health care provider has a duty to respect your personhood, wishes, bodily integrity, and health care preferences. Information, counseling, and informed consent (see "What Is Informed Consent?") are all crucial aspects of care supporting this principle. Here are some examples of when your health care provider is ignoring the principle of respect for persons:

- You are given no information about your condition, and your doctor refuses to answer or address your questions.
- You refuse a certain treatment or procedure after being fully informed of all the risks and benefits of that procedure, but your health care provider tries to force or coerce you into having the procedure anyway, which does not respect your choice.
- You request a referral to a specialist, and your doctor ignores your request.
- You do not speak English, and your doctor refuses to speak to a translator you've appointed.
- Your doctor forces a feeding tube up the nose of your ninety-two-year-old mother, who suffers from severe dementia, over your express objections as her appointed decision maker.
- Your confidentiality (see "What About Confidentiality?") is breached in some way.

## *What Is Informed Consent?*

Many of you have heard the term *informed consent* but may not truly understand what it means. To uphold the principle of respect for persons, you have the right to accurate and full information about your health so you can make an informed decision about your health care. You cannot even know to refuse a procedure if you are not given this information first. This is known as informed consent. In order for informed consent to take place, three things have to happen:

- *Disclosure:* Have you been provided with relevant and comprehensive information by your health care provider? For example, your health care provider must give you the following: a description of the treatment and its expected effects (e.g., covering duration of hospital stay, expected time to recovery, restrictions on daily activities, and scars), information about relevant alternative options and their expected benefits and relevant risks, and an explanation of the consequences of declining or delaying treatment. Have you been given an opportunity to ask questions, and has your health care provider been available to answer them?
- *Capacity and competency:* Do you understand information relevant to a treatment decision and appreciate the reasonably foreseeable consequences of a decision or

lack of decision? Do you understand information and appreciate its implications? Do you understand what's being disclosed, and can you decide on your treatment based on this information?

- *Voluntariness:* Are you being allowed to make your health care choice free of any undue influences? To answer the question, you need to take into consideration factors such as pain or manipulation (when information is being deliberately distorted or omitted).

Other barriers to informed consent include:

- language barriers
- wide gaps in knowledge (when you're not a doctor, how informed can you really be unless you go to medical school?)
- health care provider bias (when your health care provider makes assumptions about your intelligence or character and tailors the information to those assumptions)

## *What About Confidentiality?*

No matter how confidential you think your health care records are—or the information you disclose to your health care provider—your medical records are, in fact, *not* confidential. Following are the questions you must ask your health care provider if you're concerned about confidential information getting into the wrong hands:

1. *Who owns this information?* For example, if you test positive for a particular cancer gene or HIV, does your health care provider have a duty to report this information to anyone other than yourself? If you're placed on antidepressants, do you want this information to get out? Can you bar your physician from disclosing this information? And what about employers who demand that you have routine physicals?
2. *How will this information be used?* Can your health status information be used by employers or health insurers as tools of discrimination? In the 1970s, for example, African Americans who tested positive for sickle cell anemia were denied jobs by major airlines and were forced to pay higher insurance costs.
3. *How will your health status affect other family members?* If you test positive for a particular cancer gene, for example, do you have to disclose this information to your children? Ought you? Should they be tested? And what are the consequences involved?

## *Beneficence and Nonmaleficence*
## *(Doing Some Good and Doing No Harm)*

Beneficence (pronounced "be-ne-fi-cents") means that the health care provider must strive to maintain or promote the well-being of a patient and avoid harming that patient. At the same time, the health care provider must also strive not to inflict harm or evil on a patient (this is known as nonmaleficence). In other words, a health care provider has a duty not to kill a patient as well as a duty not to refrain from aiding a patient.

In order to promote the well-being of patients and avoid harming them, therapies, treatments, or diagnostic tests that involve risks to a patient's health need to be weighed against potential benefits. Here are some examples of when your health care provider is ignoring beneficence:

- Your doctor is recommending you try an experimental therapy that has not yet been proven to work better than a standard therapy and that has unknown risks.
- You are given a drug or therapy and not provided with information on side effects or potential risks.
- You are in a drug study that involves some people taking a "dummy pill" (called a placebo) and some people taking a real pill. In this case, you may continue to suffer from an ailment needlessly if you are taking the dummy pill, rather than being offered a standard therapy that will help your ailment.
- Your health care provider breaches your confidentiality (see earlier discussion).

## *Justice*

This means that the health care provider and/or system has to ensure that all people have the same access to health care services (e.g., hospital beds, medicine, treatments, clinical trials, health care providers, preventive care, etc.), regardless of their ability to pay, gender, ethnicity or race, physical or mental ability, age, or any other factors, such as behavior or lifestyle.

For there to be justice or fairness, all people should have equal access to health care services and resources. Being just or fair means all lives and interests are of equal importance and must be given equal weight. As well, a health care provider has a duty to provide the same standard of care and options to all patients, regardless of income, education, or race. Here are some examples of when the health care system—or your individual health care provider—is ignoring justice:

- when some people have more access to resources than other people because of privilege and wealth

- when your health care provider places a greater value on some patients than on others
- when poor women have babies with lower birth weights and more complications at birth than affluent women because the poor women have less access to good prenatal care
- when an HIV-positive person is refused health care service by a health care provider who fears HIV
- when certain groups of people die of curable diseases because they don't have the same access to screening for that disease as other groups of people have
- when vulnerable populations (e.g., the elderly, the mentally ill, people in developing countries, or certain ethnic groups) are selected for dangerous or risky medical experiments because they are perceived as being "expendable"

## *Problems with "Doing the Right Thing" for Patients*

If one of the aforementioned principles is ignored, you can be put in jeopardy, which would make the health care provider negligent. But in many circumstances it isn't always clear what "the right thing" to do is, and it isn't always possible to do the right thing. Here are some examples:

- When people are unconscious, it's impossible to inform them and ask them about their wishes. (In this case, someone close to the unconscious patient may make decisions on his or her behalf.)
- When people are not competent to make their own decisions, it's difficult to inform them. (Here, again, someone close to the incompetent patient makes the decision.)
- When the benefits of certain medications or therapies have to be weighed against certain risks, it's difficult to know what to do and to know what's in the patient's best interests.
- When health care providers are faced with limited resources, such as funding for research, organs for transplant, or even hospital beds, it's difficult to decide who should get the funds, organ, or bed.
- When participating in a drug study (known as a placebo-controlled study), some people will end up taking a dummy pill—and their condition will not be treated. Is this the right thing to do?

Whose life is worth saving? Whose life is worth risking? And who decides? These are all common, everyday questions and situations that health care providers face.

## *Legal Duties of Health Care Providers*

Whether health care practitioners are considered to be trained in a conventional or an unconventional manner, charging a fee for services ought to imply that there are standards of competence their patients or clients have a right to expect. Any health care professional who earns a salary is bound by tort law to uphold standards of care. Moreover, due awareness is a duty of all health care practitioners. This means that they have a duty to stay educated, informed, and up-to-date on all aspects of legally enforceable duties of care to patients and their families, colleagues, and staff members. Health care providers have a basic duty to diagnose, treat, manage, or care for a health problem. They also have a duty to counsel you about potential harms you may be doing to yourself through medications you're taking, bad habits or other practices, or harms from outside forces beyond your control, such as environmental factors. And finally, when medical records need to be transferred or copied to a third party, health care providers have a duty to disclose potentially sensitive or stigmatizing information to that party, as well as to you.

It's important to remember that I am not writing this book from an ivory tower—I have researched and written the book *I* need, too. Let me know what you think, and keep in touch. You can visit me online at sarahealth.com.

# PART I

# Understanding the Basics

# 1

# Southern Exposure

THIS CHAPTER IS designed to give you the basics on your reproductive system, discussing some of the more common anatomical anomalies that women can face. Natural methods of health maintenance for the female system are discussed under "What to Eat," "Flower Power," and "How to Move."

## The Female Reproductive System

Our reproductive system is a complex yet efficient baby machine. The point of all our parts is to produce a baby rather than to serve our social schedules or careers! If you understand that producing a baby is the sole purpose for our reproductive organs, the entire system makes a lot more sense.

### The Key Hormones

Also called the master gland, the pituitary gland, situated in your brain, keeps track of your age, begins your reproductive cycle at puberty, controls your body during pregnancy, and ends your cycle at menopause. All this requires a multitude of parts and hormones that work together. The hormone that jump-starts the entire reproductive process is called follicle-stimulating hormone (FSH). FSH then stimulates the growth of little capsules, or follicles, containing the eggs. As they grow, they produce the hormone estrogen. When estrogen levels are high, the pituitary gland shuts off FSH and turns on luteinizing hormone (LH). When LH peaks, you ovulate. Technically, this means that the follicle bursts and spits out an egg;

the follicle is now an empty sac, and the egg travels through the fallopian tube, awaiting fertilization.

But this is not the end of the follicle. Once empty, it transforms into something called the corpus luteum and starts producing a hormone called progesterone, formerly referred to as luteum, hence the name luteinizing hormone. In Latin, *luteus* means "yellow." When the follicle bursts, it grows larger in size and turns yellow, becoming luteinized. In fact, corpus luteum literally means "yellow body." Meanwhile, progesterone is often referred to as the pregnancy hormone; literally meaning "pro-pregnancy," it is the hormone responsible for preparing the lining of the uterus for pregnancy. An excess of progesterone is known to increase appetite and fatigue, lower libido, and cause acne. See the sidebar in Chapter 21 to learn what progesterone normally does in the body. If the egg happens to get fertilized, it produces human chorionic gonadotropin (HCG; the root word here is *gonad*). HCG makes sure that progesterone levels are kept high until the placenta takes over the production. By this time, a baby is well in the making.

If the egg doesn't get fertilized, the progesterone levels drop off, the uterus sheds its lining and disposes of all that "product," and the whole cycle starts over again. More information on the menstrual cycle is provided in Chapter 2.

## Estrogen and the Ovaries

Situated on either side of your uterus, some five inches below your waist, the ovaries are organs about the size and shape of an actual small chicken egg. If you drew the capital letter Y, the base of the Y would be your uterus, and the arms of the Y would be your fallopian tubes. If you drew a circle behind each arm of the Y, toward the top, that would be where your ovaries are located. The ovaries have two functions in life: to make eggs (encased in follicles) and to make hormones. When the pituitary gland sends FSH to the ovary, the follicles start "growing" and, in turn, begin pouring estrogen into the bloodstream.

Estrogen does more than simply nourish the ovulation cycle. It's responsible for developing and maintaining the female sexual organs and for generally aiding in the growth of tissue. For example, it stimulates cellular division, especially in the base layers of the mucous membrane of the mouth, skin, nose, urethra, vagina, and breasts. Estrogen is also responsible for the retention of water and salt, hence weight gain. It makes the secretion of the sebaceous glands more fluid, which helps to prevent acne. See the sidebar in Chapter 21 to learn what estrogen is supposed to do in our bodies.

An important point is that ovulation may occur from the same ovary in successive cycles. When an ovary is removed, the other one takes up the slack, and you'll get regular periods. In addition, your ovary can produce, as we all know, more than one egg every month. If more than one egg is fertilized, you'll have a multiple pregnancy. The complex hormonal and menstrual cycle is covered more in Chapter 2.

Ovarian cysts, endometriosis, scarring, polycystic ovary disease, and ovarian cancer are usually the culprits when there's a problem with your ovaries. See Chapter 4 for more on ovarian health and Chapter 13 on endometriosis.

## *The Key Parts*

The hormones alone cannot make a baby—you need a few parts.

### The Fallopian Tubes

Fallopian tubes don't really do anything except connect your ovaries to your uterus. Think of them as a chauffeur or shuttle service. When the follicles on the ovary burst and release the egg, the egg jumps down the tube and takes advantage of the shuttle service. Peristaltic (wavelike) contractions of the tube help the egg down. If the egg is fertilized in the outer third of the fallopian tube—the section nearest the ovaries—the fertilized egg will continue down the tube and implant itself in the lining of the uterus. This is pregnancy. Sometimes the egg doesn't quite make it to the uterus. It gets confused and starts to grow inside the fallopian tube. This is called a tubal or ectopic (misplaced) pregnancy. If this happens, the tube can burst, which is very dangerous. Although the tube would need to be removed in this case, with today's technology many ectopic pregnancies are diagnosed prior to rupture and the tube can be salvaged. The remaining fallopian tube will then service only one ovary.

The egg's fallopian tube journey takes about six and a half days. Pregnancy can occur only if the sperm meets the egg at precisely the right moment. If the sperm misses the egg at the entrance of the fallopian tube, that's it. The sperm can't fertilize the egg once the egg hops off the tube into the uterus.

The fallopian tubes don't solely exist to chauffeur the egg from the ovary to the uterus; they also chauffeur sperm from the uterus to the ovary, where the egg is presumably waiting at the top. The sperm will swim up both fallopian tubes, forced to guess which ovary is active that particular month. That's another reason why there are so many millions of sperm each time. Half of them die swimming up the wrong tube.

Cancer in the fallopian tubes is uncommon. The tube is susceptible to infection, particularly bacterial infections that can lead to pelvic inflammatory disease, discussed in Chapter 10. Another tubal problem, as previously mentioned, is that of an ectopic or tubal pregnancy. In this case, the tube may need to be surgically removed but can often be salvaged. When certain sexually transmitted diseases (STDs) are left untreated, the tubes can take the worst beating, which can lead to infertility. See Chapter 10 for more details on STDs.

Finally, there can be a structural problem with the tubes, where the tubes are blocked or not hollow. For example, fallopian tube torsion can occur, which is quite rare.

## The Uterus

The uterus, or womb, is more like a vessel or receptacle than an organ. In the past, it was believed that the uterus didn't produce any hormones at all, although it was 100 percent controlled by them. But current research suggests this isn't the case. The most important aspect of the uterus is its lining, called the endometrium. (This is where the disease endometriosis gets its name, discussed in detail in Chapter 13.)

The endometrium is in a constant state of flux. At each stage of the menstrual cycle, the endometrium is also at a different stage. When estrogen is first produced at the beginning of the ovulation cycle, the endometrium grows, thickens, and forms glands that will secrete embryo-nourishing substances. These glands also increase the uterine blood supply. This happens when progesterone is secreted by the corpus luteum after ovulation. At this point the environment of the endometrium changes to one that is secretory (meaning "nourishing," or "filled with secretions"). It is only in this kind of environment that a fertilized egg can survive.

Basically, the endometrium's function is to prepare itself as a shelter for a fertilized egg, just in case there is one. It never knows when a fertilized egg is on the way, so it's always ready. Estrogen and progesterone are produced only for about twelve days. If conception doesn't occur, the estrogen and progesterone levels will drop, and the arteries and veins in the uterus pinch themselves off. The nourishment to the endometrium is cut off, and the endometrium sheds. The bottom third of the endometrium lining remains intact and forms a new lining. Then the whole cycle starts again.

A common problem that originates in the uterus is fibroids. Fibroids are benign growths inside the uterus that cause extreme discomfort and are often the culprit behind heavy periods, hemorrhaging, clotting, and severe cramps. Often fibroids cause no symptoms and can coexist peacefully within your uterus. Symptoms, diagnosis, and treatment for both symptomatic and symptomless fibroids are discussed in detail in Chapter 14. Endometrial hyperplasia (overgrowth of uterine lining), which can predispose you to uterine cancer, is probably next on the list. Irregular bleeding and bleeding after menopause can also take place, warning signs that something is wrong. Abnormal bleeding and endometrial hyperplasia are discussed in Chapter 17.

Chronic diseases such as endometriosis can also develop. Endometriosis occurs when tissue normally lining the uterus grows in parts of the body where it doesn't belong. Usually, this misplaced tissue ends up in the pelvic region—for example, on the ovaries, the tubes, or the outside surface of the uterus. It can be very painful and can cause a host of health problems, including painful periods and infertility.

Miscarriages, abortion procedures (Chapter 12), intrauterine devices (IUDs; Chapter 8), and surgical procedures such as a dilation and curettage (D & C; Chapter 12) can irritate the uterine lining and cause other uterine problems.

# Hysteria and the Uterus

The uterus has a rich history. Because every human being develops in the womb, uncovering its mystery has been a preoccupation of male physicians for centuries.

Interestingly, the word *hysteria* comes from the Greek word *hystera*, meaning "womb." This is where the term *hysterectomy* (which refers to the removal of the uterus) is derived from. (Hysterectomy procedures are discussed in detail in Chapter 20.)

There is a four-thousand-year-old tradition of viewing hysteria as a disease of the womb. Written medical documents from Egypt date back to 1900 B.C. The oldest of these documents deals specifically with the subject of hysteria and describes it as a disease of women caused by "starvation of the uterus or by its upward dislocation with a consequent crowding of the other organs." The cure was to nourish the hungry organ or return it to its original home; you see, the womb was believed to have "wandered." The Greeks retained this association and named this peculiar condition after the word *womb*, and the legacy remains. The word *hysteria*, then, actually means "wandering uterus."

Why did the womb wander? It was believed at that time that when the womb was barren, it became vexed and aggravated. It would therefore wander throughout the body, blocking respiratory channels and causing bizarre behavior. Hysteria was viewed as a normal physiological reaction that occurred when the uterus was out of sync.

Then there was the "suffocation" theory. In 1603 Edward Jorden published the first English-language work on hysteria, based on his experience as an "expert" medical witness in a witchcraft trial. In that trial he had proposed that the victim was suffering from a hysteria brought on by "natural causes." Amazingly, he believed that the afflicted womb caused suffocation. The womb gave off noxious vapors throughout the body that caused the victim to choke to death.

Later, in the seventeenth century, the focus on the origins of hysteria shifted from the uterus to the brain. Hysteria graduated to a disease of the mind and was considered a behavioral and psychological disorder. It never lost its sexual roots, though. Physician William Harvey maintained that hysteria was caused by a sexual overabstinence when "the passions are strong." Philippe Pinel, considered a psychiatric "innovator" in the eighteenth century, described hysteria as one of the "genital neuroses of women." Slowly, the theory of sexual abstinence evolved into a theory of sexual repression. By the nineteenth century, just before Freud's time, the medical community felt it was experiencing an "epidemic" of hysteria. Wilhelm Griesinger, a German doctor, insisted that "all local diseases of the uterus, ovaries, and vagina are likely to be followed by hysteria, which then may gradually progress into insanity." Freud then advanced the theory to far more sophisticated levels, proposing that repressed memory of traumatic experiences was the origin of hysterical behavior.

The term *hysterical* remained in the medical vernacular from the fourth century B.C. until 1952, when the American Psychiatric Association finally stopped using it. Hysteria was listed as the most common women's disease, next to fevers, and was thought to be a disease caused by sexual dissatisfaction (or longing) commonly diagnosed in virgins, young widows, and nuns, who were discouraged from the terrible sin of masturbation. Marriage was considered a cure, but clearly, it failed to cure many women. Hysteria was also thought to plague women with more "passionate" natures. In fact, Galen called it a disease of sexual deprivation.

In her book *The Technology of Orgasm: Hysteria, the Vibrator, and Women's Sexual Satisfaction*, author Rachel P. Maines meticulously documents the standard treatment for hysteria by physicians: manually stimulating the clitoris during the office visit and bringing the "hysterical" patient to orgasm. This treatment was documented as early as the first century A.D. and continued well into the twentieth century. In fact, bringing women to orgasm was the bread and butter of many physicians from the time of Hippocrates until the 1920s. In the late nineteenth century, it was documented that 75 percent of the female population required these treatments. Vibrators were invented by physicians as a medical device to save time, since apparently so much of it was spent with patients who (ahem) "came once a week" for these treatments. In short, normal sexual fulfillment became a medical treatment for women. Eventually, the vibrator evolved as a consumer sexual product, putting into the hands of women, as Maines says, the "job nobody wanted." Thus much of the symptoms of sexual dissatisfaction, which characterized hysteria, simply disappeared as we learned more about the function of the clitoris and the fact that most women cannot reach orgasm during intercourse without direct clitoral stimulation.

## The Cervix

The cervix is perhaps the most forgotten organ, but it's an extremely important pelvic player. It is located deep inside the vagina and is actually the neck of the uterus. In fact, the word *cervix* clinically means "neck." The entrance into the uterus through the cervix is very small, about the diameter of a very thin straw. No tampon, finger, or penis can possibly go through it. Yet it is capable of expanding enough to allow a baby to pass through!

When a woman is not pregnant, the best way to describe the cervix is as the "gate-keeper" to the reproductive organs. If you've never had children, the "virginal" cervix will feel like the tip of your nose. If you've had children, it will feel more like the tip of your chin. The cervix, however, has gained more importance as a vital gynecological organ in the last twenty years and will become a widely discussed piece of gynecological equipment in the near future.

As the gatekeeper, the cervix fields all visitors wanting access into the uterus. It greets sperm, bacteria, and viruses alike. It's therefore the part most vulnerable to hostile visitors: sexually transmitted diseases such as HIV (human immunodeficiency virus). Certain STDs, among a host of other things, can cause the cells on the lining of the cervix to change, which can lead to cervical cancer. However, a Pap smear can help detect precancerous changes on the cervix before they do any damage. See Chapter 3 for more information on diagnosis and treatment of precancerous cervical cell changes and Chapter 18 for more information on cervical cancer.

## The Vagina

If the cervix is the gatekeeper, the vagina is the gateway. This gateway is actually a balanced ecosystem. It is an efficient, self-maintaining environment with built-in protective devices that keep it healthy, moist, and clean. The two most important devices the vagina has are its acid-base balance and cervical secretions. A healthy vagina is lightly acidic, ranging from about 4 to 5 on the pH scale (1 is most acidic, 14 is most alkaline). The vagina's acidity discourages infections by bacteria and other organisms. Friendly bacteria called *Lactobacillus acidophilus* help keep the vagina acidic and resistant to infection; *L. acidophilus* can be taken as supplements or found in natural foods such as yogurt.

Mucus secretions that come from the cervix wash and lubricate the vaginal walls. The vagina also produces its own secretions during sexual excitement. Normal vaginal secretions have a mild, slightly musky odor and fluctuate between a clear, egg-white consistency during ovulation to a creamy, milky-white consistency after ovulation.

The vagina has three functions: to fend off unwanted bacteria, to play host to the penis, and to expel the contents of the uterus, which consist of the uterine lining and a baby. To do this, the vagina, like the endometrium, is in a continuous state of flux. Its environment changes to accompany circumstances such as sexual activity, hormonal levels (as in menopause), labor, and menstruation.

Basically, what goes wrong in the vagina usually has to do with what goes in it! This includes a long list of garden-variety bacteria that can come from just about anywhere: fingers, vibrators, or penises that are already carrying an infection or are fresh from the anus after anal intercourse. Toilet habits are also a source of bacteria. For example, if you wipe from back to front, you could introduce fecal material into your own vagina. Using a washcloth on your vagina can transfer germs from your washcloth to your vagina.

Perfumed tampons, colored toilet paper, vaginal sprays, and chemicals (such as hair care products) that you use in the shower can cause an irritation in the vaginal area. But most often when there is a problem, a vaginal infection is present. These infections range from yeast infections (diet often predisposes certain women to yeast infections) to bacterial infections such as bacterial vaginosis and parasitic infections such as trichomoniasis. Symptoms vary from unusual discharge and odors to itching, redness, and burning. Treatments also vary depending on what you have. Oral antibiotics are usually prescribed, and antifungals can be given in the form of creams or ointments. Diagnosis (examination and swabbing) and treatment of vaginal infections, viruses, and STDs are covered in detail in Chapters 6 and 7.

Insufficient amounts of hormone can cause vaginal dryness and irritation. Like any other organ or body part, the vagina is also vulnerable to cancer. Incidence of vaginal cancer is low compared to that of other kinds of cancers. Vaginal tumors and cancer are discussed in detail in Chapter 18.

### The Vulva

The vulva refers to your outer genitals—everything you can actually see. Many women think the vulva is one of the many outer genitals, such as the vaginal lips. But it is simply a general term that refers to a whole collection of outer parts.

On your vulva you'll find the mons (the area above your genitals that is covered with pubic hair), the clitoris (a sexual organ made of erectile tissue that, when stimulated, leads to orgasm), the urinary opening, the outer and inner lips of the vagina, the vaginal opening, the perineum (the area of skin that separates your anus from your vagina), and finally the anus. In the same way that your face is a collection of parts—eyes, nose, mouth, and so forth—your vulva is a genital face.

Some women suffer from extreme sensitivity in this area, known as vulvodynia, discussed more in Chapter 6.

## Close Cousins

Your reproductive organs share space with your urinary system, which is part of gynecological health.

### The Bladder and Urethra

Although the bladder and urethra are not considered gynecological per se, they both affect, and are affected by, gynecological health. When women suffer from afflictions such as urinary incontinence or urinary tract infections, their overall gynecological health can suffer as a result. Conversely, when women develop gynecological infections or are not practicing good gynecological hygiene, bladder infections can result.

The urethra is a tube that connects the bladder to the outside. The main function of the urinary tract in women is to transport urine (the body's liquid waste) from the kidneys safely out of the body. Urine travels from the kidneys to the bladder, which is a collapsible bag, of sorts, for holding urine. The bladder functions like a holding tank. The urine flows from the bladder through the urethra to the outside. Little girls often make the common mistake of thinking that they're peeing out of their vaginas.

A woman's urethra is two inches long, while a man's is ten inches long. Obviously, this creates huge differences between male and female urology. The woman's urethra is like a corrugated tube with a large surface area that can stretch and flatten out during childbirth to allow the baby's head to pass through the vagina. Women have a muscle, or sphincter, located in the wall along the whole length of the urethra that acts like an on-off valve. This muscle allows control over the timing of urination. Urologists used to think that women didn't have this external sphincter and unknowingly ruptured this muscle when they performed urethral dilations to stretch open the urethra. (This operation is rarely performed now.)

When a woman urinates, the urethra is positioned perfectly so that the urine flows out over the outer and inner vaginal lips, over the area between the vagina and rectum, and finally over the rectum itself. The problem with this setup is that the urethra, vagina, and rectum share a very small space. Bacteria that normally inhabit the rectal and vaginal areas can gain access to the urethra and make their way into the bladder. When this happens, you develop a bladder infection.

Bladder infections are nasty. They are often not caught or are misdiagnosed. They are frequently caused by normal intercourse but can also be caused by high-risk sexual behavior, for example, anal intercourse immediately followed by vaginal intercourse (see Chapter 9). Other causes include pelvic surgery, such as a hysterectomy (discussed in Chapter 20), and diaphragms. Bladder infections and urinary tract infections are discussed more thoroughly in Chapter 5.

# Anatomically Incorrect

Certain cultural surgeries as well as congenital disorders can alter the normal female anatomy.

## *Female Genital Mutilation*

Until recently, most Westerners were ignorant of a practice called female circumcision by some and, more accurately, female genital mutilation (FGM) by others. More than 130 million girls and women have undergone FGM, and approximately 2 million procedures are performed annually on girls under the age of eleven. The procedure is carried out in Western countries among immigrants from African countries, and it is estimated that the number of girls at risk or who have already been mutilated is 168,000 in the United States, 42,000 in France, and 10,000 in Britain.

The World Health Organization (WHO) adopted the term *female genital mutilation* in 1996 to describe four variations on the procedure. (See the next section.) In 1997 the WHO, the United Nations Children's Fund (UNICEF), and the United Nations Population Fund (UNFPA) defined FGM as including "all procedures that involve partial or total removal of the external female genitalia or other injury to the female genital organs, whether for cultural or other nontherapeutic reasons."

FGM is currently illegal in Europe and the United States; in Canada it is considered child assault. For this reason, international medical authorities have rejected the idea of doctors performing the procedure to prevent physical complications. Cultural groups that carry out the practice typically send their daughters, who may be born in the West, back to their native countries for the procedure.

## The Details

There are various types of FGM that depend on cultural history and practices. Types 1 and 2 constitute about 80 percent of all FGM. The term *sunna* means "tradition" in Arabic, but in English it refers to the removal of the prepuce and/or the tip of the clitoris. This is type 1. A more dramatic procedure, known as clitoridectomy, or excision, involves removing the entire clitoris, complete with prepuce and glans as well as the nearby labia. Known as type 2, this is the procedure most commonly used in Egypt. The most dramatic procedure (type 3) is known as infibulation (a.k.a. pharaonic circumcision), which literally means "to fasten with a clip or buckle." This is practiced widely in Sudan and Somalia. Not only are the clitoris and adjacent labia removed, but the remaining parts of the vulva are sewn together with catgut or thread. Only a tiny hole is left, out of which urine or menstrual blood can barely pass. On her wedding night, an infibulated woman is cut open so that she may have intercourse, only to be sewn together again to prevent infidelity. Often the groom opens his bride with a double-edged dagger. In some cases, the woman is cut open and sewn back together each time she and her husband are separated.

Type 4 includes all other procedures that mutilate or tamper with the female genitalia—for example, pricking, piercing, or incision of the clitoris or labia; cauterization by burning of the clitoris and surrounding tissues; scraping (angurya cuts) of the vaginal orifice; cutting (gishiri cuts) of the vagina; introduction of corrosive substances into the vagina to cause bleeding; or insertion of herbal substances into the vagina with the aim of tightening or narrowing it.

Perhaps if this procedure were performed by a qualified surgeon under general anesthesia, the trauma of FGM would not be as horrific. Egypt has only recently outlawed FGM unless it's performed in a hospital by a trained doctor or nurse. Apparently, though, more tissue is removed when anesthesia is used. Unfortunately, most FGM is performed without any anesthesia by barbers and uncertified midwives. Common surgical instruments used are razor blades, scissors, kitchen knives, and pieces of glass, which can cause severe complications and often death. And because these instruments are not sterile, FGM is a major cause of blood-borne viruses, particularly HIV and AIDS, which are rampant in areas that practice FGM. Death resulting from shock, hemorrhage, or infection is not uncommon.

## The Side Effects

FGM carries with it a laundry list of harsh long-term side effects. Sexual frigidity, genital malformation, and delayed menarche are the norm. This is followed by a lifetime of chronic pelvic infections, recurrent urinary tract infections, kidney stones, infertility, and HIV infection, as well as more limited contraceptive options. Sores, ulcers, and scarring are also common problems. Many women who have been mutilated avoid seeking medical care out of shame.

A smorgasbord of obstetric complications also accompany FGM. The fetus of a mother who has undergone FGM is at greater risk of developing an infectious disease or having its head crushed due to a damaged birth canal. An infibulated mother needs to have her birth canal further opened in order to deliver vaginally, or she must have a cesarean section to avoid suffering from obstructed labor.

A cyst can also develop at the site of the clitoris, known as an epidermal clitoral inclusion cyst. This is commonly seen with type 3 FGM.

## Secondary Consequences

FGM has also been linked, not surprisingly, to psychological problems such as sexual phobias, lack of libido (often causing premature ejaculation in partners), and depression. Socioeconomic problems linked to FGM include a high divorce rate, drug abuse (apparently males will often use narcotics to try to sexually pleasure their mutilated wives), as well as personality problems ranging from rebellion to psychiatric disorders.

## Cultural Pressures

Some of the most ardent supporters of FGM are women themselves who have been raised to believe that unless FGM is practiced, a girl is unclean and, hence, unmarriageable. Many believe that if an intact girl's clitoris comes in contact with a penis, the man will die. Other myths revolve around family honor, witchcraft (the intact woman is vulnerable to spells), virginity, and faithfulness.

The more common excuse for continuing the practice of FGM is simply custom. Mutilated or circumcised women tend to promote FGM for the sake of custom; in other words, it's difficult to accept the fact that they suffered for no good reason. However, many altered women also seek to abolish FGM and want to prevent the practice from continuing. The current literature suggests that in order to abolish FGM, mothers considering FGM for their daughters need to be more educated than the fathers since it is the female community that carries out the circumcision.

Many critics sum up FGM as a legal form of terrorizing women away from sexual pleasure. Indeed, from a male perspective, the following myths have been upheld by centuries as a way of justifying FGM: it prevents uncleanliness or "bad smells," disease, nymphomania, vaginal cancer, masturbation, and homosexuality; and it protects a woman's morality, chastity, and honor.

## Religious Pressures

Islamic cultural and religious pressure to continue FGM boils down to a famous debate between Muhammad and Um Habibah, an exciser, or circumciser, of female slaves. When Muhammad asks her if she is currently practicing female circumcision, she replies, "Unless it is forbidden and you order me to stop doing it." Muhammad then gives her some tips on improving her craft. This passage has come to be known as "the exciser's narration." It is the Islamic equivalent of the Abraham/Isaac sacrifice tale from the Old Testament, and many religious leaders cite this passage when defending FGM as a cultural practice, comparing it to male circumcision in Jewish tradition. Critics argue, however, that in order to draw an accurate comparison, the ceremony of male circumcision would have to involve removing the entire penis, not just the foreskin.

## Where Is FGM Practiced?

Most of the girls and women who have undergone genital mutilation live in twenty-eight African countries; its reported prevalence stands at 90 percent or more in Djibouti, Eritrea, Sierra Leone, and Somalia. The practice can also be found in the Middle East (including Egypt, Oman, the United Arab Emirates, and Yemen), in Asia (including Indonesia, Malaysia, Sri Lanka, and India), and among immigrant groups in Australia, Canada, Europe, New Zealand, and the United States.

## FGM American-Style

North America has a hidden history regarding FGM. Well up until the 1940s, for example, FGM was often used as a "treatment" for women who were declared insane, unruly, or just plain temperamental. This treatment was based on the writings of Freud, who insisted that the clitoris was a very dangerous part of the female anatomy. In his book *Sexuality and the Psychology of Love*, Freud states that the "elimination of clitoral sexuality is a necessary precondition for the development of femininity."

The North American trend of FGM was inspired in Europe. One common type of chastity belt was constructed by passing rings in the labia and vulva and then wiring them shut or closing them with a lock. In Russia the Christians widely practiced infibulation to ensure virginity, citing the teachings from the New Testament. And even today it's been reported that some Paris hospitals perform a peculiar surgery where the clitoris is disengaged and pulled back inside the vagina to add to women's sexual pleasure.

## Ambiguous Genitalia

More attention is beginning to be paid to the problem of ambiguous genitalia, which means that a female child can be born as one of the following:

- a true hermaphrodite (ovary plus testicle)
- a female pseudohermaphrodite (discussed further on)

This can happen if the external genitalia are made more masculine from intrauterine exposure to male hormones for some reason.

A true hermaphrodite is born with both ovarian and testicular tissue. There can be a testicle on one side and an ovary on the other, a set of both on each side, or a combination of ovotestes with either a testicle or an ovary. Ambiguous genitalia is considered to be a pediatric emergency where corrective surgery can resolve the problem. Usually this individual is genetically female with the X chromosome and can be surgically altered into a female.

When girls are born with ambiguous genitalia, the condition most commonly takes the form of female pseudohermaphroditism, which accounts for 70 percent of all cases. These little girls will be born with a normal uterus, fallopian tubes, ovaries, and an upper vagina.

Gender assignment is based on a number of factors, including genotype (the chromosomal pattern), gonads (are there testes or ovaries?), phenotype (is there a penis or a vagina?), and hormonal makeup (are hormones secreting estrogen or androgen?).

There are hundreds of anatomical anomalies, including bifid vaginas (two vaginas) and so forth. This book does not cover anomalies or gynecological problems representing less than 1 percent of the population; instead, the book is devoted to the more common issues surrounding gynecology.

# What to Eat

Diet and gynecology are intricately linked. Unfortunately, the experience of being female affects diet, and hence our reproductive organs, dramatically. The right diet for maintaining reproductive health is a balanced diet: 40 percent carbohydrates, 30 percent protein, and 30 percent fat. Yes, we need to have fat in our diets in order to function properly!

As most women reach adolescence, their eating habits become wound around how they feel about their bodies. Eating disorders are rampant among young women, meaning that starving, bingeing, and purging habits can begin. Overeating can also become out of control. A third of the women in North America believe they are overweight, even though their body weight is normal for their size, height, and age. Not surprising, 90 percent of all eating disorders are diagnosed in women. One in nine women between the ages of fourteen and twenty-five have an eating disorder, but this is certainly an underreported problem. A *New York Times* poll found that 36 percent of girls aged thirteen to seventeen want to change their looks; at least 10 percent of girls fourteen and older suffer from eating disorders.

The most serious eating disorder is food refusal (anorexia nervosa). Young women use food refusal as a way to regain control in their lives. In anorexia, the person's emotional and sensual desires are channeled through food. These desires are so great that the anorexic fears that once she eats she'll never stop since her appetite/desires will know no natural boundaries; the fear of food drives the disease. Many experts also see this eating disorder as an addiction to perfection; the sense of control the eating-disordered woman gains through this behavior is the drug. Women may also become martyrs in their refusal of food, feeling more in touch with their lives and their bodies through the suffering that comes with starvation.

Anorexia can completely retard the reproductive system and prevent women from beginning menstruation. Or it can result in long bouts of no menstruation, having long-term consequences that can affect future fertility and pregnancies and can lead to earlier menopause and more severe osteoporosis.

Binge eating, also known as compulsive eating, can lead to obesity, which can cause a range of estrogen-related conditions, including fibroids, endometrial hyperplasia, and risks for more cancers.

In this case, many women will turn to food as a comfort during times of stress or when other things are missing in their lives, such as sexual satisfaction, love, or other sensuous aspects of life.

Following are traits that make up the typical profile of a compulsive eater:

- eating when you're not hungry
- feeling out of control when you're around food, either trying to resist it or gorging on it

- spending a lot of time thinking or worrying about food and your weight
- always feeling desperate to try another diet that promises results
- having feelings of self-loathing and shame
- hating your own body
- being obsessed with what you can or will eat or have eaten
- eating in secret or with "eating friends"
- appearing in public to be a professional dieter who's in control
- buying cakes or pies as "gifts" and having them wrapped to hide the fact that they're for you
- having a "pristine" kitchen with only the "right" foods
- feeling either out of control with food (compulsive eating) or imprisoned by it (dieting)
- feeling temporary relief by not eating
- looking forward with pleasure and anticipation to the time when you can eat alone
- feeling unhappy because of your eating behavior

Most people eat when they're hungry. But if you're a compulsive eater, hunger cues have nothing to do with when you eat. You may eat for any of the following reasons:

- to satisfy "mouth hunger"—the need to have something in your mouth, even though you are not hungry
- to prevent future hunger ("better eat now because later I may not get a chance")
- as a reward for a bad day or bad experience or to reward yourself for a good day or good experience
- because you think it's the only pleasure you can count on
- to quell nerves
- because you're bored
- because you've got to eat now since you're "going on a diet" tomorrow (hence, the eating is done out of a real fear that you will be deprived later)
- because food is your friend

Food addiction, like other addictions, can be treated successfully with a twelve-step program.

A balanced diet will ensure that you are getting all the essential nutrients you need for your mental, physical, and reproductive health. The following tells you where to find various nutrients from natural sources:

- *Bioflavonoids:* Found in citrus pulp and rind. Herbal sources: buckwheat greens, blue-green algae, elderberries, hawthorn fruits, rose hips, horsetail, and shepherd's purse.

- *Boron:* Found in organic fruits, vegetables, and nuts. Herbal sources: all organic weeds including chickweed, purslane, nettles, dandelion, and yellow dock.

- *Calcium:* Found in milk and dairy products, leafy greens, broccoli, clams, oysters, almonds, walnuts, sunflower seeds, sesame seeds (e.g., tahini), legumes, tofu, softened bones of canned fish (sardines, mackerel, salmon), seaweed, whole grains, whey, and shellfish. Herbal sources: valerian, kelp, nettles, horsetail, peppermint, sage, uva-ursi, yellow dock, chickweed, red clover, oatstraw, parsley, black currant leaf, raspberry leaf, plantain leaf/seed, borage, dandelion leaf, amaranth leaves, and lamb's-quarter. Depleted by coffee, sugar, salt, alcohol, cortisone enemas, and too much phosphorus.

- *Carotenes:* Found in carrots, cabbage, winter squash, sweet potatoes, dark leafy greens, apricots, spirulina, and seaweeds. Herbal sources: peppermint, yellow dock, uva-ursi, parsley, alfalfa, raspberry leaf, nettles, dandelion greens, kelp, green onions, violet leaves, cayenne, paprika, lamb's-quarter, sage, peppermint, chickweed, horsetail, black cohosh, and rose hips.

- *Chromium:* Found in barley grass, bee pollen, prunes, nuts, mushrooms, liver, beets, and whole wheat. Herbal sources: oatstraw, nettles, red clover, catnip, dulse, wild yam, yarrow, horsetail, black cohosh, licorice, echinacea, valerian, and sarsaparilla. Depleted by white sugar.

- *Copper:* Found in liver, shellfish, nuts, legumes, water, organically grown grains, leafy greens, seaweeds, and bittersweet chocolate. Herbal sources: skullcap, sage, horsetail, and chickweed.

- *Essential fatty acids (EFAs), including GLA, omega-6, and omega-3:* Found in safflower oil and wheat germ oil. Herbal sources: all wild plants contain EFAs. Commercial sources: flaxseed oil, evening primrose, black currant, and borage.

- *Folic acid (B factor):* Found in liver, eggs, leafy greens, yeast, legumes, whole grains, nuts, fruits (bananas, orange juice, grapefruit juice), and other vegetables (broccoli, spinach, asparagus, Brussels sprouts). Herbal sources: nettles, alfalfa, parsley, sage, catnip, peppermint, plantain, comfrey leaves, and chickweed.

- *Iron:* (Heme iron is easily absorbed by the body; nonheme iron not as easily absorbed so should be taken with vitamin C.) Heme iron is found in liver, meat, and poultry;

nonheme iron is found in dried fruit, seeds, almonds, cashews, enriched and whole grains, legumes, and green leafy vegetables. Herbal sources: chickweed, kelp, burdock, catnip, horsetail, althea root, milk thistle seed, uva-ursi, dandelion leaf/root, yellow dock root, dong quai, black cohosh, echinacea, plantain leaves, sarsaparilla, nettles, peppermint, licorice, valerian, and fenugreek. Depleted by coffee, black tea, enemas, alcohol, aspirin, carbonated drinks, lack of protein, and too much dairy.

- *Magnesium:* Found in leafy greens, seaweeds, nuts, whole grains, yogurt, cheese, potatoes, corn, peas, and squash. Herbal sources: oatstraw, licorice, kelp, nettles, dulse, burdock, chickweed, althea root, horsetail, sage, raspberry leaf, red clover, valerian, yellow dock, dandelion, carrot tops, parsley, and evening primrose. Depleted by alcohol, chemical diuretics, enemas, antibiotics, and excessive fat intake.

- *Manganese:* Found in seaweeds and any leaf or seed from a plant grown in healthy soil. Herbal sources: raspberry leaf, uva-ursi, chickweed, milk thistle, yellow dock, ginseng, wild yam, hops, catnip, echinacea, horsetail, kelp, nettles, and dandelion.

- *Molybdenum:* Found in organically raised dairy products, legumes, grains, and leafy greens. Herbal sources: nettles, dandelion greens, sage, oatstraw, fenugreek, raspberry leaf, red clover, horsetail, chickweed, and seaweeds.

- *Niacin (B factor):* Found in grains, meats, nuts, and especially asparagus, spirulina, cabbage, and bee pollen. Herbal sources: hops, raspberry leaf, red clover, slippery elm, echinacea, licorice, rose hips, nettles, alfalfa, and parsley.

- *Nickel:* Found in chocolate, nuts, dried beans, and cereals. Herbal sources: alfalfa, red clover, oatstraw, and fenugreek.

- *Phosphorus:* Found in whole grains, seeds, and nuts. Herbal sources: peppermint, yellow dock, milk thistle, fennel, hops, chickweed, nettles, dandelion, parsley, dulse, and red clover. Depleted by antacids.

- *Potassium:* Found in celery, cabbage, peas, parsley, broccoli, peppers, carrots, potato skins, eggplant, whole grains, pears, citrus, and seaweeds. Herbal sources: sage, catnip, hops, dulse, peppermint, skullcap, kelp, red clover, horsetail, nettles, borage, and plantain. Depleted by coffee, sugar, salt, alcohol, enemas, vomiting, diarrhea, chemical diuretics, and dieting.

- *Pyridoxine (vitamin $B_6$):* Found in baked potato with skin, broccoli, prunes, bananas, dried beans and lentils, and all meats, poultry, and fish.

- *Riboflavin (vitamin $B_2$):* Found in beans, greens, onions, seaweeds, spirulina, dairy products, and mushrooms. Herbal sources: peppermint, alfalfa, parsley, echinacea, yellow dock, hops, dandelion, ginseng, dulse, kelp, and fenugreek.

- *Selenium:* Found in dairy products, seaweeds, grains, garlic, liver, kidneys, fish, and shellfish. Herbal sources: catnip, milk thistle, valerian, dulse, black cohosh, ginseng, uva-ursi, hops, echinacea, kelp, raspberry leaf, rose buds and hips, hawthorn berries, fenugreek, sarsaparilla, and yellow dock.

- *Silicon:* Found in unrefined grains, root vegetables, spinach, and leeks. Herbal sources: horsetail, dulse, echinacea, corn silk, burdock, oatstraw, licorice, chickweed, uva-ursi, and sarsaparilla.

- *Sulfur:* Found in eggs, dairy products, plants of the cabbage family, onions, garlic, parsley, and watercress. Herbal sources: nettles, sage, plantain, and horsetail.

- *Thiamine (vitamin $B_1$):* Found in asparagus, cauliflower, cabbage, kale, spirulina, seaweeds, and citrus. Herbal sources: peppermint, burdock, sage, yellow dock, alfalfa, red clover, fenugreek, raspberry leaf, nettles, catnip, watercress, yarrow, brier, and rose buds and hips.

- *Vitamin A/beta-carotene:* Found in liver, fish oils, egg yolk, whole milk, butter; beta-carotene in leafy greens and yellow and orange vegetables and fruits. Depleted by coffee, alcohol, cortisone, mineral oil, fluorescent lights, liver "cleansing," excessive intake of iron, and lack of protein.

- *Vitamin $B_6$:* Found in meats, poultry, fish, nuts, liver, bananas, avocados, grapes, pears, egg yolk, whole grains, and legumes. Depleted by coffee, alcohol, tobacco, sugar, raw oysters, and birth control pills.

- *Vitamin $B_{12}$:* Found in meats, dairy products, eggs, liver, and fish. Depleted by coffee, alcohol, tobacco, sugar, raw oysters, and birth control pills.

- *Vitamin C:* Found in citrus fruits, broccoli, green peppers, strawberries, cabbage, tomatoes, cantaloupe, potatoes, and leafy greens. Herbal sources: rose hips, yellow dock root, raspberry leaf, red clover, hops, nettles, pine needles, dandelion greens, alfalfa, echinacea, skullcap, parsley, cayenne, and paprika. Depleted by antibiotics, aspirin and other pain relievers, coffee, stress, aging, smoking, baking soda, and high fever.

- *Vitamin D:* Found in fortified milk, butter, leafy green vegetables, egg yolk, fish oils, butter, liver, skin exposure to sunlight, and shrimp. Herbal sources: none—not found in plants. Depleted by mineral oil used on the skin, frequent baths, and sunscreens with SPF 8 or higher.

- *Vitamin E:* Found in nuts, seeds, whole grains, fish-liver oils, fresh leafy greens, kale, cabbage, and asparagus. Herbal sources: alfalfa, rose hips, nettles, dong quai, watercress, dandelion, seaweeds, and wild seeds. Depleted by mineral oil and sulfates.

- *Vitamin K:* Found in leafy greens, corn and soybean oils, liver, cereals, dairy products, meats, fruits, egg yolk, and blackstrap molasses. Herbal sources: nettles, alfalfa, kelp, and green tea. Depleted by x-rays, radiation, air pollution, enemas, frozen foods, antibiotics, rancid fats, and aspirin.

- *Zinc:* Found in oysters, seafood, meats, liver, eggs, whole grains, wheat germ, pumpkin seeds, and spirulina. Herbal sources: skullcap, sage, wild yam, chickweed, echinacea, nettles, dulse, milk thistle, and sarsaparilla. Depleted by alcohol and air pollution.

# Flower Power

Essential oils, from plants (mostly herbs and flowers), can do wonders to maintain the female system naturally. All oils listed in this section and throughout this book can be used in a diffuser (a ceramic pot with a tea light underneath and a bowl of water on top, into which the oils are dropped; a lightbulb ring also works), in a hot bath (you can drop the oils directly into the hot water), or as a massage oil (you need a "carrier" base oil such as olive, jojoba, carrot seed, grape seed, or sweet almond). You can also mix certain oils into a nonscented moisturizer and apply to your face (neroli, lavender, ylang-ylang, and rose all make for excellent facial oils). Twelve drops of oil in any of these methods is the average "dose." When oils are applied directly to the skin, two drops is the average.

In general, the following essential oils are considered essential for the female system, in terms of balancing hormones and offsetting a number of discomforts: bergamot, clary sage, lavender, nutmeg, ylang-ylang, clove, fennel, geranium, and sage. Applying any of these directly to the soles of the feet is a good way to feel the effectiveness faster. Many of the herbs discussed in this book can be used as tinctures or infusions.

# How to Make an Herbal Tincture

A tincture is a multipurpose liquid brew made from fresh plants steeped in alcohol (not vinegar), which makes them heavily alkaline. You may drink it or bathe in it. Tinctures can be made with fresh plants and herbs or with dried roots, seeds, and berries. Follow these steps to make a good tincture:

1. Take the fresh or dried plant and chop it up coarsely. Do not wash.
2. Put the choppings into a glass jar and fill with 100-proof vodka.
3. Seal the jar tightly and label it with the date and name of the plant.
4. Open in six weeks. It can be used for at least a year.

**Proportions for Fresh Plants**
Use 1 ounce (30 gm) of fresh plants per 1 ounce (30 ml) vodka.

**Proportions for Dried Plants**
Use 1 ounce (30 gm) of dried plant material per 5 ounces (150 ml) vodka.

# How to Make an Herbal Infusion

An infusion is a strong tea or a brew that does not keep longer than about three days. An infusion is a large amount of dried (not fresh) herbs or plants brewed for a long time. You can use a pot or a teapot to make an infusion. You may drink the infusion hot, room temperature, or chilled. You can add milk to infusions and sweeten them with sugar, honey, or sugar substitutes. You can bathe in infusions as well or use them as rinses for your hair or skin.

**Directions**
When using roots or bark, add about 1 ounce (30 gm) to 1 pint (500 ml) water and steep for eight hours.
When using leaves, add about 1 ounce (30 gm) to 1 quart (1 liter) of water and steep for four hours.
When using flowers, add about 1 ounce (30 gm) to 1 quart (1 liter) of water and steep for two hours.
When using seeds or berries, add about 1 ounce (30 gm) to 1 quart (1 liter) water and steep for thirty minutes.

# How to Move

In order to maintain reproductive health, daily movement, in the form of walking and stretching, is important. The maintenance exercises that follow are recommended for improving general health and well-being, rather than to combat specific health problems.

## *Deep Breathing*

Deep breathing helps to calm the nervous system, relaxes the small arteries, and permanently lowers blood pressure. It also helps to improve oxygen flow throughout your body, vital for the proper functioning of your reproductive system. Some of these exercises are modeled after yoga practices. (See "Yoga.")

- *Abdominal breathing:* Lie down on a mat or on your bed. Take slow, deep, rhythmic breaths through your nose. When your abdominal cavity is expanded, it means that your lungs have filled completely, which is important. Next, slowly exhale completely, watching your abdomen collapse again. Repeat six to ten times. Practice this morning and night.

- *Extended abdominal breathing:* This is a variation on the abdominal breathing exercise. When your abdomen expands with air, try three more short inhalations. This is akin to adding those last drops of gas in your tank when your tank is full. Then after you exhale in one long breath, don't inhale just yet. Take three more short exhales.

- *Abdominal lift:* Stand with your feet at about shoulder width, bend your knees slightly, bend forward, exhale completely, and brace your hands above your knees. Then lift your abdomen upward while holding your exhalation. Your abdomen should look concave. Stand erect again and inhale just before you feel the urge to gasp. Greer Childers, in her video "Body Flex," demonstrates this technique very well.

- *Rapid abdominal breathing:* This is abdominal breathing done at a fast speed so it feels as though your inhalations and exhalations are forceful and powerful. Try this for twenty-five to one hundred repetitions. Each breath should last only a second or so, compared to the ten to twenty seconds involved in regular deep abdominal breathing.

- *Alternate nostril breathing:* Hold one nostril closed, inhaling and exhaling deeply. Then alternate nostrils. This is often done prior to meditation and is thought to balance the left and right sides of the brain.

## Meditative Stretching

Stretching improves muscle blood flow, oxygen flow, and digestion. The natural desire to stretch is there for those reasons. The following stretches will help relieve stress and improve tranquility. Many of these are classic yoga postures, too.

- While sitting or standing, raise your arms above your head. Keep the shoulders relaxed and breathe deeply for five seconds. Release and repeat five times.

- Gently raise your shoulders in an exaggerated "shrug." Breathe deeply and hold for ten seconds. Relax and repeat three times.

- Sit cross-legged on the floor with your spine straight and neck aligned. Focus on your breath, letting it gently fill your diaphragm and the back of your rib cage. On the inhalation, say "so," and on the exhalation, say "hum." Voicing the breath in this manner will keep you focused and relaxed. Continue with "so-hum" until you feel at ease. (This is the Lotus position.)

- Sit on your heels. Bring your forehead to the floor in front of you. Breathe into the back of the rib cage, feeling the stretch in your spine. Hold as long as it's comfortable.

- Stand tall and find a point across the room at which to focus your gaze. Place the heel of one foot on the opposite inner thigh. Float your arms upward until your palms are touching. Breathe deeply and hold for five seconds. Release and repeat on the other side.

- Lie on your back with palms facing upward, feet turned gently outward. Focus on the movement of your breath throughout your body.

- Lie on your belly, with arms at your sides. Bend your legs at the knees and bring your heels in toward your buttocks. Reach back and take hold of your right and then your left ankle. Flex your feet if you're having a hard time maintaining this position. Inhale, raising your upper body as far off the floor as possible. Lift your head, completing the arch. Your knees should remain as close together as possible (tying them together might help here). Breathe deeply and hold for ten to fifteen seconds.

## Eastern Movement

All ancient, non-Western cultures, be they in native North America, India, China, or Japan, believed that there were two fundamental aspects to the human body. There was the actual physical shell (clinically called the corporeal body) that made cells, blood, tissue, and so on, and then there was an energy flow that made the physical body come alive. This was known as the life force, or life energy. In fact, it was so central to the view of human function that each non-Western culture has a word for life force. In China it is called *qi* (pronounced "chee"). In India it's called *prana*, and in Japan it's called *ki*, while the ancient Greeks called it *pneuma*, which has become a prefix in medicine having to do with breath and lungs.

Daily exercises that help stimulate the life force energy, which is considered vital to maintaining our reproductive organs, include yoga and qi gong (pronounced "chee kong"). Most fitness and wellness centers offer classes in yoga and qi gong.

## Yoga

Yoga is not just about various stretches or postures but is actually a way of life for many. It is part of a whole science of living known as Ayurveda. Roughly three thousand years old, Ayurveda is an ancient Indian approach to health and wellness that has stood up quite well to the test of time. Essentially, it divides up the universe into three basic constitutions, or "energies," known as doshas. The three doshas are based on wind (vata), fire (pitta), and earth (kapha). These doshas also govern our bodies, personalities, and activities. When our doshas are balanced, everything functions well, but when they are not balanced, a state of disease (dis-ease, as in "not at ease") can set in. Finding balance involves changing your diet to suit your predominant dosha (foods are classified as kapha, vata, or pitta, and we eat more or less of whatever we need for balance); practicing yoga, a preventive health science that involves certain physical postures and exercises; and meditating. Essentially, yoga is the exercise component of Ayurveda. It involves relaxing meditation, breathing, and physical postures designed to tone and soothe your mental state and physical state. Many people benefit from taking introductory yoga classes or even by following along with introductory videos. This book will list assorted yoga postures that aid with the various conditions that are discussed.

## Qi Gong

Every morning, people of all ages gather at parks throughout China to do their daily qi gong exercises. These exercises help get your life force energy flowing and unblocked. Qi gong exercises are modeled after movements in wildlife (such as birds or animals) and movements of trees and other things in nature. The exercises have a continuous flow, rather than the stillness of a yoga posture. Using the hands in various positions to gather in the *qi*, move the *qi*, or release the *qi* is one of the most important aspects of qi gong movements.

One of the first groups of qi gong exercises you might learn are the seasons: fall, winter, spring, summer, and late summer (there are five seasons here). These exercises look more like a dance with precise, slow movements. The word *qi* means "vitality," "energy," and "life force"; the word *gong* means "practice," "cultivate," and "refine." The Chinese believe that practicing qi gong balances the body and improves physical and mental well-being. These exercises push the life force energy into the various meridian pathways that correspond to organs. It is the same map used in pressure point healing. Qi gong improves oxygen flow and enhances the lymphatic system. Qi gong is similar to tai chi, except it allows for greater flexibility in routine. Qi gong is difficult to learn from a book or video. The best place to learn qi gong is through a qualified instructor. You can generally find qi gong classes through the alternative healing community. Check health food stores and other centers that offer yoga or tai chi classes.

# 2

# Menstrual Health

THIS CHAPTER SERVES as a refresher course on the menstrual cycle and explains some of the common menstrual cycle problems women have, along with ways to remedy them. Safety and environmental issues surrounding menstrual products are discussed in the section "What to Wear for Your Period."

The first period, clinically known as menarche, is probably one of the most powerful psychological, sociological, and physiological occurrences in any woman's life. It is her rite of passage. Once we begin our menstrual cycle, we enter into a completely different physiological phase: our reproductive years.

Even today, many young women don't understand what the menstrual cycle is; they feel shame, fear, anxiety, and depression about their first periods, and as a result, they have very negative experiences. Sometimes the negative experience of the first period has to do with painful periods and cramping (discussed later in this chapter), but often the negative experience is linked to false information about what the period actually is and what it means. The negativity of menstruation is then reinforced when we become sexually active. For example, many men are repulsed by the menstrual flow and refrain from petting or having intercourse with menstruating women.

There is also a negative mythology about menstruation that traces all the way back to the book of Genesis. The phrase *the curse*, for example, comes from the story of Adam and Eve. In a nutshell, Eve's punishment for biting the apple—the forbidden fruit from the Tree of Knowledge—was to be cursed with painful childbirth ever after. The historical and completely erroneous translation is that the period is a monthly reminder to women that it is *they* who kicked man out of paradise.

Unfortunately, the negative mythology and imagery associated with menstruation are both a cultural reaction to it as well as a patriarchal one. Until the twentieth century, very little was understood about the menstrual cycle, and nothing was known about hormones. Menstruation was thus seen as a mysterious enigma, and the emotional premenstrual signs leading up to menstruation were feared, branded as a kind of hysteria by the male medical profession. Since women have been living in a patriarchal society for so many centuries, they, too, have become quasi believers in the "evils" of menstruation, believing that medicating and masking our cycles is appropriate.

# The Moon Cycle

A normal menstrual cycle is actually more like a moon cycle. Interestingly, the only event in human life that corresponds to the lunar calendar is menstruation. Time itself was probably first measured by the moon's phases. One of the problems with the current English calendar is that the months don't coincide exactly with the solar year. In our current system, the months were made to fit by Gregory XIII, who gave them an arbitrary number of days unrelated to the moon calendar. So our calendar actually puts us *out* of sync with the moon.

The word *menstrual* comes from the Latin word *mens* meaning "month"; the word *month* comes from the root word *moon*. The Greek word for moon is *mene*, while menstruation actually means "moon change." (In some dictionaries, the root word for month and menstruation is *measure*.) The point of all this is to simply establish that a far more accurate and positive interpretation of menstruation was recorded in our history through language.

Countless other languages and cultures link menstruation to the moon as well. German peasants literally refer to menstruation as "the moon," while the French term for menstruation is *le moment de la lune* ("the moment of the moon"). The Mandingo, Susus, and Congo tribes also call menstruation "the moon," while in parts of East Africa, menstruation is thought to be *caused* by the new moon. The Papuans believe that the moon has intercourse with girls, triggering their periods; the Maori call menstruation "moon sickness"; the Fuegians call the moon "The Lord of the Women." Clearly the belief that the lunar cycle is identical to the menstrual cycle is universal. There is even some remarkable physical evidence that connects the moon to menstruation even more; for example, the cervix, *metra* in Greek, referring again to the word *measurement*, and also called the "meter of a woman," changes color, size, and position during menstruation. In fact, when it's viewed with a speculum (an instrument doctors use to open up the vagina), the cervix has been said to resemble a globe. Even in pregnancy, the embryo is shaped like the moon; the embryo starts out round and full, and as it becomes a fetus, it curves like the half-moon.

All this evidence suggests that women are perhaps far more in tune to the natural rhythms of the universe than they think. Meanwhile, comprehending the similarities between the menstrual and lunar cycles is crucial in order to understand what a healthy, normal menstrual cycle really is. Women are also in tune with other women's cycles; two women living together will often synchronize cycles. The rhythmic timing of menstruation also provides women with a sense of their own timing, other than just daylight.

## What Is "Normal"?

It's more accurate to call a menstrual cycle a "hormonal cycle" because that is in fact what the menstrual cycle is. The menstrual cycle is driven by a symphony of hormones that trigger each other, stopping and starting, flooding and tapering in a regular rhythm each month. Every woman's hormones dance to a different tune—but rarely does the menstrual cycle correspond to the English calendar.

Low levels of sex hormones are continuously produced during a woman's reproductive years. But it is the continuous *fluctuation* of hormones that establishes the menstrual cycle and the understandable premenstrual symptoms (described in the section "Premenstrual Signs and Symptoms").

The main organs involved in the cycle are the hypothalamus (a part of the brain), the pituitary gland, and the ovaries. The hypothalamus is like the omniscient figure, watching over the cycle and controlling the symphony of hormones from above. It tells the pituitary gland to start the hormonal process, which signals the ovaries to "do their thing." The hypothalamus is sensitive to the fluctuating levels of hormones produced by the ovaries. When the level of estrogen drops below a certain point, the hypothalamus turns on FSH-RF (follicle-stimulating hormone–releasing factor). This stimulates the pituitary gland to release FSH. FSH triggers the growth of ten to twenty ovarian follicles, but only one of them will mature fully; the others will start to degenerate sometime before ovulation. As the follicles grow, they secrete estrogen in increasing amounts. The estrogen affects the lining of the uterus, signaling it to grow or proliferate (proliferatory phase). When the egg approaches maturity inside the mature follicle, the follicle secretes a burst of progesterone in addition to the estrogen. This progesterone-estrogen combo triggers the hypothalamus to secrete more FSH-RF—this time with LH-RF (luteinizing hormone–releasing factor). These releasing factors signal the pituitary gland to secrete FSH and LH simultaneously. The FSH and LH levels peak and signal the follicle to release the egg. (This is ovulation.)

To simplify this process, think of it like a thunderstorm. The lightning that precedes the storm is the hypothalamus, sending out FSH-RF. The thunder that follows is the pituitary gland, answering with FSH. Then the rain starts, lightly at first. The ovaries, which are beginning to grow follicles and trickle estrogen and progesterone into the bloodstream, are the rain. This light rain goes on for a few minutes until suddenly, two bright bursts of lightning ignite the sky—the hypothalamus again, this time sending out two releasing factors, FSH-RF and LH-RF. Then, *bang, bang*—the pituitary gland answers the lightning, sending out FSH and LH simultaneously. The intensity of the rain increases, and it starts pouring—the follicles burst, and estrogen and progesterone pour out into the bloodstream, which is when you ovulate. Slowly the rain dies down, as hormonal levels taper off until the storm stops. It is at this point that you menstruate.

Under the influence of LH, the follicle changes its function and is now called a corpus luteum, secreting decreasing amounts of estrogen and increasing amounts of progesterone. The progesterone influences the estrogen-primed uterine lining to secrete fluids that nourish the egg (the secretory phase). Immediately after ovulation, FSH returns to a normal, or base, level, and the LH decreases gradually, as the progesterone increases. If the egg is fertilized, the corpus luteum continues to secrete estrogen and progesterone to maintain the pregnancy. In this case, the corpus luteum is stimulated by HCG, a hormone secreted by the developing placenta. If the egg isn't fertilized, the corpus luteum degenerates until it becomes nonfunctioning, at this point called a corpus albicans. As the degeneration progresses, the progesterone levels decrease. The decreased progesterone fails to maintain the uterine lining, which causes it to shed. Then the whole thing starts again.

The first period usually starts about the middle of puberty, at about eleven or twelve years of age. The first few periods are sporadic, and it's not uncommon for periods to be irregular for a couple years. A woman continues having her period until she's about forty-eight or forty-nine years of age, at which point the period starts to get sporadic again, tapering off as menopause sets in. Few cycles are absolutely twenty-eight days. Where does that number come from? Twenty-eight is only an average representing the cycle length of thousands of women added together and divided by the number of women. It is therefore a statistical average, not a figure that refers to the typical number of days in a woman's cycle. Menstrual cycles range anywhere from twenty to forty days, and the bleeding lasts anywhere from two to eight days, with four to six days being the average.

There's a big difference between your own cycle and a calendar month, however. When you tell your doctor that your period starts on the fifteenth of every month, for example, you're actually stating the impossible. Since the number of days varies per month, unless you were consistently irregular, you wouldn't begin menstruating exactly on the fifteenth of each month.

Finally, it's important to count the first day of bleeding as day 1 of your cycle. Many women count the first day of clear discharge after their periods as day 1, but this is not as accurate. What's the difference? Since ovulation always takes place roughly fourteen days before your period, five days off in your counting could radically interfere with your family planning. Secondly, if you're on the Pill, the first day of bleeding is *always* counted as day 1. If you're planning to go on or off the Pill, your cycle is more accurately tracked by using the same counting method. Thirdly, doctors always count the first day of bleeding as day 1 of the cycle.

Many of us assume that our menstrual flow is strictly blood, but this is not so. The menstrual fluid is made from a variety of ingredients: cervical and vaginal mucus, degenerated endometrial particles, and blood. The fluid does not smell until it makes contact with the bacteria in the air and starts to decompose.

# Irregular Cycles: Metrorrhagia

One of the most common gynecological problems is an irregular menstrual cycle. But before you jump to the conclusion that you're irregular, it's important to remember that being regular doesn't mean your cycle is the same number of days each time. One month your cycle may be twenty-nine days, and the next month it may be thirty-one days. This is still considered the norm. It's also normal to be lighter one month and heavier the next. So long as you're menstruating every twenty to forty days, it's a sign that you're ovulating. Another common misperception about irregular cycles is the belief that unless you have a period every four weeks (again, the statistical average) you're irregular. This is not true. Some women menstruate every three weeks, which is normal for them; some menstruate every five weeks, which is normal for them. The only time you should be concerned is if your period consistently yo-yos: three weeks, then four weeks, then five weeks, then three weeks, and so on. When this happens, it's usually a sign that you're not ovulating regularly. This is common in young girls after they first begin menstruating. If your period only jumps around once or twice a year, there isn't anything to worry about. Occasional stress is usually the culprit when this happens.

## *When You've Skipped a Period*

Women may skip a period from time to time and then experience a heavier flow with their next period. This is extremely common. Women who are trying to get pregnant, however, often fear that this is a mild miscarriage—so mild that it simply feels like a heavy period. This is usually not the case. Although it's possible for a pregnancy not to take and instead to expel in the menstrual flow, it's rare and occurs in less than 1 percent of women. If this were to occur, it would be so early a pregnancy that the term *miscarriage* would be inappropriate; it would simply be a pregnancy that wasn't yet established, technically called a blighted ovum. Skipping one period, in most cases, is caused by stress. The flow is heavier after a skipped period because the estrogen has been building up in the endometrium longer, and there is more lining than usual that needs to be shed. In essence, you would have built up two cycles' worth of lining, so the flow is naturally heavier than normal.

It's also common to skip a period altogether and not experience a heavier flow the next time around. This means you actually skipped an ovulation cycle and had not produced a lining in your endometrium that would support a pregnancy. In this case, there wasn't a lining to shed. It's not unusual to skip one or two periods a year; it is unusual to skip them more often than that, however.

## Causes of Irregular or Missed Cycles

The number-one cause of irregular or skipped periods is emotional stress. The typical scenario is worrying that you might be pregnant and then actually missing your period *because* you're worried. Other stress-related situations revolve around career changes, job loss, a death in the family, moving, exams, and overwhelming workloads. It's not really understood why stress can cause you to miss a cycle, but a missed cycle is considered a protective mechanism, a sort of prehistoric parachute in the female body. The body senses the stress level and decides somehow to stop ovulation for that month, preventing a "stressed" pregnancy.

Overdieting and overexercising can also affect your cycle. For example, sudden weight loss could cause you to miss your period or cause a long bout of irregular cycles. Overexercising can also cause you to miss your period, and it's actually not unusual for female athletes to stop menstruating when they're in training.

Another cause of irregular cycles could be a thyroid disorder of some sort. The thyroid gland regulates your metabolism by secreting thyroid hormone. When the gland is overactive (and secretes too much thyroid hormone), known as hyperthyroidism, you can either miss periods or have a much longer cycle than normal. Meanwhile, your period is shorter, with a scanty or light flow. On the flip side, when the gland is underactive (and doesn't secrete enough hormone), known as hypothyroidism, your cycles can become shorter, while the period itself is longer, with a much heavier flow than normal. Thyroid problems occur in about one in twenty women. If a thyroid problem is the cause of your menstrual irregularity, this is easily remedied. Once your thyroid problem is treated, your periods will simply return to normal. For more information, see my book *The Thyroid Sourcebook for Women*.

Finally, irregular cycles may be normal for your age. For example, it often takes young women several years before they establish a regular menstrual cycle, and many times young women will be put on oral contraceptives to regulate their periods. Then, women older than forty could begin menopause at any time, and irregular cycles may be a sign of perimenopause, discussed more in Chapter 19.

# No Menstrual Cycle: Amenorrhea

There is such a thing as having no menstrual cycle. These days, however, if you don't begin menstruating by the age of eighteen, there's usually a hormonal imbalance that is easily remedied with hormonal supplements or oral contraceptives. If you are regularly menstruating and are between twenty and forty, it's unusual to simply stop menstruating. If this does occur, an eating disorder, such as anorexia nervosa (food refusal), is the most common cause, triggering a protective mechanism in the body. When the female body is malnourished, it stops ovulating because it can't sustain a pregnancy. One doctor told me about an aboriginal tribe in Australia that demonstrates this unique protective mechanism. Women of that particular tribe only menstruate at certain times of the year, when the food cycle is abundant.

Athletes, again, may experience amenorrhea, and either an overactive or underactive thyroid gland, just described, can cause it. (If this is the case, once your thyroid problem is treated, you'll begin menstruating again.) In all other cases of a stopped or stunted menstrual cycle, progesterone supplements will remedy it. Natural progesterone therapy is discussed in Chapter 21.

## *The Need to Bleed*

Today, women have to deal with having more periods in their lifetime than women did in the past, due to fewer pregnancies and a longer life cycle. Also, in the past century, women have experienced a radical change in their diet, environment, stress levels, and career and family expectations. Understandably, the accumulated effect of all these factors has affected the hormonal cycle of women, which, of course, affects the menstrual cycle.

Again, it's fine to skip a period once in a while or experience some occasional fluctuation. But if you've missed more than two consecutive periods and you know for certain that you're not pregnant (either confirmed by a pregnancy test or the absence of any sexual activity), then you should investigate having your period induced through a natural progesterone supplement, which will kick-start your cycle again. It's dangerous to go longer than three months without "a bleed"; if the uterus isn't regularly "cleaned out," your risk of uterine cancer can increase. See Chapter 17 for more information.

# Heavy Flow: Menorrhagia

If you have an extremely heavy flow, it may be normal for you. This is known as primary menorrhagia, which means that your flow has been heavy since you first began menstruating. If this is the case, there isn't anything to worry about. You should regularly (every six months) have your blood levels checked, however, because consistent heavy flows could cause anemia. In fact, the number-one cause of anemia is a heavy menstrual flow.

If a lighter flow slowly develops into a continuous heavy flow, this is known as secondary menorrhagia. When this happens, as long as you're having annual pelvic exams and biannual blood tests, you shouldn't be concerned. If, however, your flow suddenly becomes unexplainably heavy, see your doctor. This kind of menorrhagia may signify other problems, such as fibroids, tumors, and so on. Flows are considered dangerously heavy if you need to change your pad or tampon every hour.

## A Word About Clots

A clot looks like a tiny sample of raw liver or raw oyster and often comes out with a heavy menstrual flow. Clots are normal and do not mean you're hemorrhaging. Blood naturally clots, and often when you're sleeping during a heavy period, the blood will collect in clots and expel in the morning. The only time you need to worry about clots is if you're passing them after your period is over, passing them with a prolonged period, passing them midcycle, or passing them while you're pregnant. (Similarly, if you're bleeding at all during these times, you should see a doctor.)

## When You Experience Abnormal Heavy Bleeding

Abnormal heavy bleeding is when your bleeding is suddenly heavy or significantly heavier than what your normal menstrual flow "pattern" is. In fact, it is your own perception of what's heavy that's more important than your doctor's perception. And good doctors will try to get you to describe your impression of "heavy" and have you compare it to your normal pattern. If your doctor tries to determine exactly how much blood you've lost, this is a waste of time for both of you.

Clinically, an abnormally heavy menstrual flow is defined as being more than 80 cc of blood lost per cycle. But studies show that many women who complain of an abnormally heavy flow have lost much less than that. In fact, a more "scientific" measurement is to simply take inventory of the number of pads and tampons you're going through and compare that with your normal pattern.

## But Why Is It Suddenly So Heavy?

Your age has a lot to do with your menstrual flow. In fact, teenaged women and women approaching menopause will have similar cycles, often characterized by changes in flow.

Women between the ages of twenty and forty will have (or should have!) regular patterns that do not fluctuate that much from period to period.

If you are under twenty and are noticing heavy bleeding, ask your doctor to check you out for a blood coagulation disorder known as van Willebrand's disease or for platelet disorders, such as thrombocytopenia or thromboasthenia.

Most of the time, however, abnormal heavy bleeding is caused by some sort of hormonal disorder, which can be investigated by a reproductive endocrinologist.

If you're over forty, abnormal heavy bleeding is usually caused by what's known as the anovulatory period. Here, you make estrogen in the first part of your cycle, but for some reason (often unknown) you just don't ovulate. Therefore, you do not produce progesterone and you develop an unusually thick uterine lining, which is expelled during your period. This translates into abnormally heavy bleeding.

No matter how old you are, one of the chief culprits of abnormally heavy bleeding in women is often high doses of acetylsalicylic acid (ASA), or aspirin. So if you're fighting off headaches or other ailments before your period, you may want to use an alternative pain reliever.

Sometimes your contraception method can affect your menstrual cycle. For instance, an IUD (intrauterine device) or hormonal contraception can sometimes trigger heavy bleeding. See Chapter 8 for more details. Changes in exercise patterns (usually less exercise) can also affect your menstrual flow.

## *What Your Doctor Should Rule Out*

If you notice abnormal bleeding either during or between periods, make sure your doctor rules out the following: hyperthyroidism or hypothyroidism (an over- or underactive thyroid gland), ovarian cysts, abnormal tissue within your uterus, and endometriosis (discussed in Chapter 13). Your doctor should also perform a pelvic exam as well as a transvaginal ultrasound. The latter is a procedure where a dildo-shaped transducer with a condom on it is inserted into your vagina by the ultrasound technician. Transvaginal ultrasound produces much sharper images than abdominal ultrasound. And, of course, your doctor should be ruling out symptoms of possible sexually transmitted diseases.

See the "Flower Power" section for natural remedies used to treat abnormal heavy bleeding. Natural progesterone therapy is also helpful in regulating flow and cycles (see Chapter 21). A less invasive traditional medicine approach may be taking a nonsteroidal anti-inflammatory drug (NSAID), which will reduce your menstrual flow. A common prescription NSAID is naproxen sodium (Anaprox). The usual dose is 275 milligrams (mg) two to four times a day.

If none of these treatments help, you should be evaluated for more serious conditions, such as endometriosis.

# Painful Periods: Dysmenorrhea

Primary dysmenorrhea means that you've always had painful periods—ever since you started menstruating. Secondary dysmenorrhea means that your periods have become more painful with time. In either case, painful periods are common. Cramps are simply caused by uterine contractions, which is how the lining is pushed out; some uteri contract more than others. It is also believed that cramps may be caused by low levels of calcium. Drinking alcohol or eating lots of eggs, meat, and dairy foods can worsen menstrual cramps.

There are a number of herbal supplements (see "Flower Power") that can help regulate your cycle and reduce heavy flows, thereby lessening cramping as well. That said, many women turn to traditional medicine for severe cramps. Taking an analgesic such as ibuprofen before your period starts can really help; this will also reduce flow. Oral contraceptives also reduce cramping and flow, which is known as one of the noncontraceptive benefits. For more information on oral contraceptives, see Chapter 8. It's also important to recognize the difference between normal cramping and unusual, debilitating pain during your periods. Often the culprit behind severe pain during your period is endometriosis, a serious disease affecting women in their reproductive years, which until recently was widely undiagnosed. See Chapter 13 for more details.

# Periods on Oral Contraceptives

It's common for younger women in particular to be placed on oral contraceptives as a way of controlling their cycles. If you are uncomfortable with taking an oral contraceptive solely for cycle control and are using another method of birth control, there are natural ways to control your cycle, which are discussed further on under "Flower Power." If you're happy on an oral contraceptive, as long as you don't smoke and don't have any adverse health problems that oral contraceptives can complicate, you can be on them for a long time if you're regularly monitored by a doctor. There are two kinds of oral contraceptives: combination (which contain synthetic estrogen and progestin, a synthetic progesterone) and progestin-only (which contain no estrogen). Oral contraceptives are said to have noncontraceptive benefits that include a reduction in ovarian cysts, ovarian cancers, endometrial cancers, and, of course, premenstrual discomforts. That's because oral contraceptives stop ovulation. Women who have never breast-fed or been pregnant stand to benefit the most from noncontraceptive benefits as pregnancy and breast-feeding are designed to give your ovaries a natural break from ovulating.

When you have your period while taking combination oral contraceptives, it is a chemically induced period called withdrawal bleeding. On some progestin-only contraceptives, you may also shed the uterine lining once a month. If you're on Depo-Provera, your periods will be less frequent. Periods while on the Pill, as many of us know, are a dream come true: relatively mild cramps, medium-to-light flow, and punctual to the point where you can set your watch by them. For more information on oral contraceptives, see Chapter 8.

## *Periods After Oral Contraceptives*

Many women are surprised to find that when they go off oral contraceptives, their menstrual problems return. Women whose cycles were irregular before taking oral contraceptives will continue to have irregular cycles after going off them; women who suffered from painful periods before will probably have painful periods after. And so on. Oral contraceptives are only a temporary panacea for menstrual cycle problems.

Often women will remain regular when they go off oral contraceptives. This is usually because when the women initially went on oral contraceptives, they were younger and had less mature ovulation cycles. Ovulation cycles do mature as we get into our twenties and thirties, which is why the cycles will normalize. But often, as just mentioned, the original cycle—however flawed—returns. Frequently, not only will your original cycle return (many women actually forget what their true cycle was like), but it can take up to six months for your ovulation cycle to kick in and return to normal. If you're planning to get pregnant, allow at least that much time. Doctors will tell you to wait until you get two natural periods before you try to conceive, which is fine—but don't panic if you don't conceive by your third, fourth, or fifth cycle. There is a delusion that as soon as we go off oral contraceptives we'll get pregnant. This is just not true. Couples having intercourse every other day can sometimes wait a year before conception actually takes place.

# What to Wear for Your Period

In the early 1990s, women began to be much more aware of products that harmed the environment. For example, washable diapers are now back in vogue as a way to reduce our trash. Menstrual products became the focus of much debate when it was learned that plastic tampon applicators are commonly washed up on beaches all over North America because the plastic does not break down in sewage treatment plants. (Many women flush them even though they are meant to be disposed of in the garbage, which just means more garbage.) For these reasons, women are encouraged to use applicator-free tampons (there are many brands).

## *Green Periods*

Reducing "period trash" can mean two things: reducing back-end garbage or improving front-end cleanliness, which involves reducing the amount of chemicals used in the initial manufacture of menstrual products, thereby helping to reduce environmental exposure to contaminants overall. Green menstrual products are also safer for women, reducing our exposure to bleaches and other questionable chemicals and ingredients currently in use to make our pads and tampons "clean and white" so we feel psychologically cleaner around our periods.

Reducing back-end garbage involves choosing a reusable product, such as washable pads. There are now a few companies that produce washable pads made from organically grown cotton that is undyed and unbleached, reducing both garbage and chemical usage. Check out the following:

- Gladrags: Visit gladrags.com.
- Lunapads: Visit lunapads.com.
- Mama Elle: For information, send E-mail to mamaelleproducts@yahoo.ca or phone 819-424-1291.
- Many Moons: Visit pacificcoast.net/~manymoons.
- Pandora Pads: Visit pandorapads.com.

Alternatives to pads are tampons, but there are safety issues revolving around tampons (which I'll discuss further on) that require you to use unbleached tampon products—even if you don't care about the environment! There is also the new menstrual cup, which is shaped like a small diaphragm that sits just under your cervix (no applicator or creams necessary) and catches the flow. The Keeper is a cup that you remove and wash. Another brand, Instead, gives you disposable cups, which does not solve the garbage problem but does solve the safety problem for women who want an alternative to tampons. (See the next section, on tampons.)

Improving front-end cleanliness by reducing the amount of chemicals used in the manufacture of pads and tampons involves using menstrual products made from natural materials that don't form chemical by-products. All of the reusable pads are made from organic cottons that do not involve the use of pesticides or other toxins. Nonbleached tampons are another way to go. These can be purchased at any health food store, as well as most drugstores now. Popular brands include Eco Yarn, Terra Femme, Natracare, and Organic Essentials.

## *What You Ought to Know About Bleached Tampons*

Women use a lot of tampons. Just in North America alone, more than eighty-five million women use tampons; the average woman may use as many as 16,800 tampons in her lifetime, and if she is on hormone replacement therapy after menopause, that figure may jump up to as many as 24,360 tampons in her lifetime.

Since 1980 there has been a lot of press questioning the safety of tampons. The first reports that tampons may not be safe surrounded toxic shock syndrome, which I discuss further on. The most shocking tampon revelations arose from an independent study in 1991, which found that tampons usually contained one of the following additives: chlorine compounds, absorbency enhancers (which can be toxic), natural and synthetic fibers (such as cotton, rayon, polyester, and polyacrylate), deodorant, and fragrance.

The main concern over tampons is the bleaching of the product, which produces dioxin, a chemical the Environmental Protection Agency and the International Agency for Research on Cancer say probably cause cancer. (For more information on environmental carcinogens, see my book *Stopping Cancer at the Source*, which can be ordered from sarahealth.com.) The extent to which dioxins are in tampons has been a source of debate, but since dioxin is a by-product of chlorine-bleaching processes used in the manufacture of paper products, including tampons, sanitary pads, panty liners, and diapers, it stands to reason that tampons do contain dioxin. There are bleaching processes that do not produce dioxin, but unfortunately, the paper manufacturers (which produce the raw materials used in tampons) use either elemental-chlorine or chlorine-dioxide bleaching processes, which we know do produce dioxin. The Food and Drug Administration (FDA), however, insists that the raw materials used to produce tampons now involve chlorine-free bleaching processes, but it also says that "some elemental chlorine-free bleaching processes can theoretically generate dioxins at extremely low levels, and dioxins are occasionally detected in trace amounts."

As a result, women have been unwittingly exposed to more dioxin than most men because of their use of tampons and other menstrual products. According to the FDA, "State-of-the art testing of tampons and tampon materials that can detect even trace amounts of dioxin has shown that dioxin levels are at or below the detectable limit. No risk to health would be expected from these trace amounts." But trace amounts of dioxin are not considered safe by most environmental groups and women's health groups.

The questioning of tampon safety led the U.S. Congress to introduce in 1999 the Tampon Safety and Research Act, which has yet to be passed. The purpose of this bill is to research the ingredients used to make tampons, such as dioxin, synthetic fibers, and other additives, and to investigate the true health effects and whether these ingredients place women at risk for cervical cancer, endometriosis, infertility, ovarian cancer, breast cancer, immune system deficiencies, pelvic inflammatory disease, and toxic shock syndrome.

## *What About Asbestos?*

Some women's groups have published that U.S. tampon manufacturers add asbestos to their products to promote excessive menstrual bleeding in order to sell more tampons. This isn't that crazy a claim, considering that the tobacco industry added substances to cigarettes to make them more addictive. The FDA maintains that the asbestos charges are purely rumor and that there is no evidence that asbestos is used in tampons. Nonetheless, to confirm or negate such claims, it's important that independent studies are done on tampons.

## Who Regulates Tampons?

Tampons are considered medical devices and as such should be regularly assessed, tested, and monitored as vigorously as bandages or heart valves. But they're not. The U.S. government has determined that the FDA has not adequately investigated the safety of tampons because of the FDA's reliance on safety data provided by the tampon manufacturers rather than independent peer-reviewed scientific studies on the safety of the products. And tampon manufacturers do not make their data available to the public. This is how the tobacco industry escaped as long as it did with not disclosing all the ingredients in cigarettes. In Japan, however, there are strict tests that the government applies to tampon manufacturing and testing. No level, including trace levels, of dioxin is considered acceptable by European health authorities or the World Health Organization.

Aside from toxic shock syndrome, there are other problems tampons can cause. Because tampons actively absorb menstrual blood and do not differentiate between blood and vaginal mucus, the skin that lines the vaginal walls dries up. That can lead to microulcerations and infection. Artificial fibers such as rayon, which most brand-name bleached tampons contain, are abrasive; when the tampon expands, it can cause tiny cuts and embed pieces into the vaginal tissue. To read information directly from the FDA on tampons, see www.fda.gov/bbs/topics/consumer/con00116.html or www.fda.gov/fdac/features/2000/200_tss.html. Keep in mind, though, that many health experts do not feel the FDA's take on tampon safety is accurate or acceptable. But it's worth a read.

## Tampon Hygiene Rules

Tampons should therefore never be used between periods, during pregnancy (to absorb mucus, for example), or when you already have a vaginal infection. In the United States, to help tampon shoppers compare absorbency from brand to brand, packages use terms that determine thickness, such as *junior*, *regular*, *super*, and *super plus*.

Many women with extremely heavy flows are in the habit of using more than one tampon at the same time. If you're among them, get out of the habit. The second one can "get lost"—pushed up so high in your vagina, you can't retrieve it yourself. The general rule with tampons is to change them every four to six hours. Official warnings state that tampons left for twelve to eighteen hours may put you at risk for toxic shock syndrome.

## Toxic Shock Syndrome (TSS)

Toxic shock syndrome is a group of symptoms caused by a bacterium already present in the vagina that adheres to the tampon. The bacterium then starts producing a toxin that attacks other parts of the body. The initial symptoms of TSS are fever, nausea, vomiting,

## Menstrual Websites

Women are taking ownership over their periods on the Internet. The following are some interesting menstrual websites offering other interesting links.

Blood Sisters: Visit bloodsisters.org/bloodsisters.
Museum of Menstruation and Women's Health: Visit mum.org.

For further reading on menstrual products, check out *Whitewash: Exposing the Health and Environmental Dangers of Women's Sanitary Products and Disposable Diapers—What You Can Do About It*, by Liz Armstrong and Adrienne Scott.

diarrhea, sore throat, and dizziness. Other symptoms include a sunburnlike rash, peeling of the skin (especially on the hands and feet), and low blood pressure. All of these symptoms are, of course, vague and can be attributed to a host of other diseases. So if someone has TSS, she can easily be misdiagnosed, particularly if she has only a few symptoms. These days, TSS caused by tampon use is considered pretty rare now that we have warnings about it in tampon packaging. The Centers for Disease Control and Prevention reports a great reduction in tampon-related TSS. For example, in 1997 only 5 confirmed tampon-related TSS cases were reported; in 1980 there were 814 cases. The higher the tampon's absorbency, the greater the risk of TSS regardless of whether the tampon is made with rayon or the purest, most organically grown cotton.

## Premenstrual Signs and Symptoms

Virtually all women in their childbearing years have premenstrual signs (as opposed to "symptoms," which make our normal hormonal changes sound like a disease). As we age, our premenstrual signs can become more severe, especially as we approach perimenopause, a term that means "around menopause," which usually occurs when we're somewhere in our mid-to-late forties. (See Chapter 19.) Premenstrual signs occur roughly fourteen days before your period and disappear when, or just after, you get your period. The main questions are: Ought premenstrual signs be treated? Is it right to think of these signs as a disease or disorder, medicating them with antidepressants, tranquilizers, water pills, or synthetically produced hormones? (Even if you are the one who wants your doctor to prescribe medication for your premenstrual changes, you should still consider these questions.)

Traditionally, women's complaints about premenstrual signs have been either viewed as psychological or written off as part of the biological lot of women. Many women have difficulty admitting they suffer from them for fear of compromising their position in the workplace. But virtually all women experience some premenstrual signs. It's how you experience these signs and how severely they affect you that determines whether these premenstrual signs warrant remedying through natural means or, in the extreme, through medical interventions, such as harsh medications or synthetic hormones.

Some 90 percent of women who menstruate experience premenstrual signs of some sort. Of this group, half will experience the more traditional premenstrual signs, such as breast tenderness, bloating, food cravings, irritability, and mood swings. These signs, for many women, are often perceived as a sign that their bodies are "in tune" or "on schedule" and that all is well. In other words, these signs are natural markers of a healthy menstrual cycle. If you fall into this group, you may find that moderately adjusting your diet, or adding one or two of the dietary or herbal supplements discussed further on, can dramatically improve your premenstrual discomforts.

About 35 to 40 percent of menstruating women experience the same signs of the first group, but in a more severe form. In other words, these women have really tender breasts, so sensitive that they hurt if someone just lightly touches them. These women have severe bloating to the extent that they gain about five pounds before their periods. Instead of just food cravings, these women may suddenly find that they have voracious appetites. Instead of just being irritable, these women may find that they become impossible to be around. And so on. Even these more severe signs are considered to be very normal experiences. If you fall into this group, you may find that more rigorous dietary adjustments, supplements in combination with herbal remedies, and increased physical activity can dramatically decrease your level of discomfort. You may also benefit from ruling out other causes for your discomforts and may even want to explore natural progesterone supplements.

Roughly 3 to 10 percent of menstruating women (the latest statistics hover around 3 to 4 percent) suffer from incapacitating discomforts that affect their ability to function. These women experience discomforts that interfere with their quality of life, such as profound mood swings, sudden or unexplainable sadness, irritability, sudden or unexplainable anger, feelings of anxiety or being on edge, depression, hopelessness, self-deprecating thoughts, and a range of physical discomforts, such as tender breasts, bloating, and so on. In the psychiatric literature, even women with hysterectomies and oophorectomies (removal of their ovaries) were found to experience these symptoms. It is considered sound and good medicine to offer this group of women antidepressants as a treatment for their premenstrual syndrome (PMS), even though incapacitating discomforts can still be managed through natural remedies. If you fall into this group, it's important to first rule out other causes for your physical and emotional discomforts, such as stress or an underlying depression that has social causes and has more to do with your life's conditions. Or determine if you may be having reactions to other synthetic hormones or medications you are taking, which get aggravated by fluctuating hormones around the time of your period. Next, take a long hard look at your diet and activity patterns. Adjusting your diet, adding supplements and herbs, and becoming more active can really make a difference. Finally, you may benefit from natural progesterone supplements, which I discuss in Chapter 21. I urge you to consider synthetic hormones, antidepressants, antianxiety agents, and other medications as a very last resort. These are strong medications that carry a long list of side effects.

PMS is understandably a complex topic that I felt demanded a separate book. For more information, please consult my book *Managing PMS Naturally*.

# What to Eat

Most women will want to use diet and nutrition to control premenstrual discomforts, which can range from emotional to physical discomforts. One of the first dietary rules is to keep blood sugar levels stable, which experts on PMS believe is essential in order for the progesterone receptors to function properly. Premenstrual discomforts worsen when progesterone receptors are not functioning, which causes the progesterone symptoms of bloating, cravings, and so on.

## *Vitamins and Minerals*

There is so much solid evidence on the benefits of vitamins and minerals in improving PMS that the American College of Obstetricians and Gynecologists, in April 2001, revised its recommendations on PMS to include them. Keep in mind, though, that once you're eating more regularly and eating the right balance of a variety of foods (see Chapter 1), you may not need further supplements.

### Vitamin $B_6$

This is an old standby that has raised some controversy. Most studies on vitamin $B_6$ conclude that up to 100 mg per day can improve PMS-related depression in particular. But at high doses, there are disturbing side effects, known as neurotoxicity or nerve damage, which include the feeling of pins and needles in the arms and legs or of an electric current running through the arms, supersensitivity or burning of the skin, muscle weakness, numbness, shooting pains, and generalized itching. Some $B_6$ side effects can easily be mistaken for PMS: headaches, irritability, tiredness, depression, and puffy eyes. So please approach $B_6$ supplements with caution and do not exceed the 100 mg per day dosage.

## Calcium

Adding 1,200 to 1,500 mg calcium daily has been shown in several clinical trials to significantly improve PMS. When progesterone receptors are blocked by low blood sugar levels or adrenaline, not enough progesterone can get to the cells, which means that important bone-building cells called osteoblasts are not being produced. This may explain why calcium supplements help.

Four glasses of milk is equal to about 1,200 mg calcium. In one study, women on calcium supplements for three months found that most of their PMS problems improved, with the exception of fatigue and insomnia.

When you're trying to increase calcium in your diet, you should avoid foods that cause you to use up or "pee out" calcium, such as alcohol or coffee.

*Maximizing Calcium Absorption.* Calcium is best absorbed in an acidic environment. To increase acidity, do any of the following:

- Drink lemon juice in water with or after your meal.
- Add two tablespoons (30 ml) apple cider vinegar and two tablespoons raw honey or blackstrap molasses to one cup (250 ml) water, and drink with or after your meal.
- Use calcium-rich herbal vinegars in your salad dressing.

*Calcium Greens.* A number of leafy greens also provide calcium:

- One serving of broccoli, kale, turnip greens, or mustard greens contains about 200 mg calcium.
- One cup cooked collards, wild onions, lamb's-quarter, or amaranth greens contains about 400 mg calcium.
- The following greens are not high-calcium sources but rather are high-iron sources: spinach, Swiss chard (silver beet), beet greens, wood sorrel, and rhubarb.

*High-Calcium Sources.* Some of these you probably already know about, and others you might not:

- tahini
- soy or tofu (not all tofu contains calcium—check labels)
- oats/oatmeal
- seaweeds
- sardines

- yogurt
- nettles
- dandelion leaves
- dried fruit (65 mg calcium is in three small figs, a handful of raisins, four dates, or eight prunes)
- corn tortillas (high in calcium because they are made with lime)

*Calcium-Rich Herbs.* A big mug of infusion using any of the following herbs is equal to 250 to 300 mg calcium. Add a big pinch of horsetail and increase the calcium by 10 percent.

- nettles
- sage
- chickweed
- red clover
- comfrey leaf
- raspberry leaf
- oatstraw

The Uni-Tea Company makes a calcium-rich tea called FemininiTea, which contains raspberry leaves, nettles, ginger, licorice, chamomile, sarsaparilla, rosemary, rose petals, yellow dock, uva-ursi, dong quai, peony, lavender, and angelica. You can find this product in some health food or natural food stores.

*Calcium in Dairy Products.* The highest-calcium dairy product is live-culture yogurt (from milk without hormone and antibiotic residues). Yogurt also strengthens the digestive system, boosts the immune system, eases the nervous system, and helps prevent vaginal infections. Yogurt is much lower in fat than other dairy products, in case you want to stay heart healthy. In fact, 25 percent (350 to 400 mg) of your 1,500 mg daily calcium requirement can come from one cup (250 ml) of yogurt, which is equal to one cup of milk, one ounce (30 gm) of hard cheese, or one-half cup (115 gm) of ricotta cheese. One cup of soy milk yields 80 mg calcium, and one cup of almond milk yields 165 mg calcium.

*Calcium Supplements.* If you can't get enough calcium in your diet, there are always supplements: 500 mg magnesium (not citrate) with calcium. Calcium supplements are more effective in divided doses. Two doses of 250 mg, taken morning and night, actually provide more usable calcium than a 500-mg tablet. New research also shows that the amount of calcium absorbed from calcium citrate supplements is consistently higher than the amount absorbed from calcium carbonate supplements. Popular supplements include:

- *Calcium-fortified orange juice:* This is easier to digest and absorb than other supplements.
- *Calcium citrate in tablet form:* Crushed tablets are better absorbed.
- *Calcium gluconate, calcium lactate, and calcium carbonate (if chewable):* You can take 1,500 mg daily of one of these.

### Magnesium

Some studies are showing that small amounts of magnesium (no more than 200 mg per day) help to reduce water retention and bloating. Magnesium is found in leafy greens, seaweeds, nuts, whole grains, yogurt, cheese, potatoes, corn, peas, and squash. Herbal sources include oatstraw, licorice, kelp, nettles, dulse, burdock, chickweed, althea root, horsetail, sage, raspberry leaf, red clover, valerian, yellow dock, dandelion, carrot tops, parsley, and evening primrose.

### Vitamin E

There are some studies showing that a dose of 400 International Units (IUs) of vitamin E per day is also useful in improving cramps and breast tenderness. To get vitamin E out of food sources, the key word is *color.* Vitamin E is highest in nongreen vegetables. The richer the color, the more E you get. Beets, carrots, yams, and so on, are all good sources. Otherwise, you can take a supplement. Vitamin E is also found in nuts, seeds, whole grains, fish-liver oils, fresh leafy greens, kale, cabbage, and asparagus. Herbal sources of E include alfalfa, rose hips, nettles, dong quai, watercress, dandelion, seaweeds, and wild seeds.

# Flower Power

Many women rely on traditional medicine to help regulate their cycles or to cope with heavy flows and cramps. Regulating the cycle, one of the keys to reducing premenstrual discomforts, can be done through natural means.

## *For Irregular Cycles*

First, it's been found that both regular orgasms (through self- or partnered stimulation) and pelvic floor exercises can help maintain regular periods. For irregular cycles, including amenorrhea, the following are reportedly helpful:

- *Raspberry leaf:* Best as an infusion (see Chapter 1 for directions), raspberry leaf nourishes the ovaries as well as the uterus and helps with erratic periods.

- *Dong quai compound:* As a tincture, this warms, regulates, and gently heals the entire reproductive system—especially useful if your irregular cycles are accompanied with premenstrual discomforts. (Note: dong quai can aggravate fibroids.)

- *Liferoot blossoms:* As a tincture, five drops taken daily helps tone the reproductive hormones, ovaries, uterus, adrenals, liver, and pituitary gland.

- Vitex: As a tincture, this helps with irregular periods. Use one dropperful in a small glass of water two or three times daily for six to eight weeks after every irregular period.

- *Cinnamon bark* (Cinnamon zeylanicum): This invigorates the blood, helps regulate the menstrual cycle, and helps with very heavy flows as well, especially during perimenopause. Sip a cup (250 ml) of infusion, use five to ten drops of tincture once or twice a day, gnaw on a cinnamon stick, or simply sprinkle cinnamon on everything.

## Estrogen Herbs

The following herbs help promote estrogen production, help stabilize infrequent periods, and may reduce the severity of estrogen-loss discomforts during perimenopause:

- alfalfa and red clover flowers or leaves
- black cohosh roots
- hops (female flowers)
- licorice roots
- sage leaves
- sweetbrier hips or leaf buds
- pomegranate seeds
- any herb containing flavonoids

## Progesterone Herbs

The following herbs help promote progesterone production and help stabilize too-frequent periods, which can occur as you approach perimenopause:

- chaste tree *(Vitex)* berries
- sarsaparilla roots

- wild yam roots
- yarrow flowers and leaves

## *For Menstrual Cramps*

The following herbs are helpful in relieving cramps. Many have an antiprostaglandin effect, which is why they work.

- black yaw
- blue cohosh
- cinnamon
- cloves
- cramp bark
- evening primrose
- false unicorn root
- feverfew
- flaxseed
- garlic
- ginger
- hops
- meadowsweet
- motherwort
- red raspberry
- thyme
- wild yam
- yarrow

## *For Heavy Flows*

If you're coping with very heavy menstrual flows, then it's important to consume roughly 2 mg iron from herbs or foods while the bleeding persists. This will help to prevent anemia. Iron is best in small doses throughout the day, rather than in one big gulp. Coffee, black tea, soy protein, egg yolks, bran, and calcium supplements over 250 mg can also impair iron absorption. Bleeding can be aggravated by aspirin, Midol, and larger doses of ascorbic acid (vitamin C supplements) because they thin the blood. In general, foods rich in bioflavonoids and carotene such as the following will help decrease blood loss:

- *Dandelion leaves:* This is the best source of usable iron, containing roughly 30 gm iron per ounce.

- *Yellow dock root:* An alcohol or vinegar tincture is best: twenty drops of alcohol tincture or three teaspoons (15 ml) vinegar, taken in tea or water, gives you 1 mg of iron.

- *Lady's mantle* (Alchemilla vulgaris): This alchemical weed controlled heavy bleeding in virtually all of more than three hundred women in a recent study.

- *Wild yam root:* As a tincture, twenty to thirty drops daily for the two weeks before your period can help reduce flow.

- *Cinnamon bark:* See earlier, under "For Irregular Cycles," for how to take it.

- *Shepherd's purse:* Commonly used to stop bleeding or reduce flow, it is available dried and as a liquid extract. It can cause heart palpitations in large doses and should not be taken with an anticoagulant.

## For Dealing with Odor

Because we are conditioned to feel unclean during our periods, we are tempted to cover up odor with feminine deodorant products. The odor is normal and natural, and the commercial deodorants sold can irritate your vaginal ecosystem. There are natural ways to deal with the odor, which I discuss below. Furthermore, never use commercially scented tampons or pads; they can cause irritations and infections due to the chemicals used in them.

Don't douche—ever. Douching rids your vagina of friendly bacteria, which are very important for maintaining its ecosystem. Douching is never recommended after menstruation, even though many women practice it. As long as you regularly bathe, your vagina and uterus are self-cleaning and will do everything that's necessary on their own. Finally, avoid perfumed or colored toilet paper. Again, the perfumes can irritate your vagina and cause infections.

## Natural Ways to Deal with Menstrual and Vaginal Odor

The cheapest natural "odor eater" during your period is baking soda. Simply bathe in about a cup of baking soda per tubful.

Aromatherapy is a wonderful way to smell good below the belt. Purchase essential oil in any health food store. Make sure the label reads "100% essential oil" or "pure essential oil." Fill your bathtub, and add about six to eight drops of the oil in the bath. A ten-to-twenty-minute soak in the tub is all you need. Essential oils can be used for all kinds of health problems, including the full range of premenstrual discomforts, allergies, fatigue, depression, and so on. Depending on the health problem, there are other ways to apply the oils, such as to the soles of the feet or via a diffuser. But for vaginal odor, sit in a tub! Here are the best oils to have on hand during your period. You can combine them for a real treat, or just use them as single "shots" in the tub.

- *Lavender:* This is the most useful oil to have on hand as it not only nourishes the female reproductive system and improves vaginal health, but it is also a natural anti-depressant and sleep aid.

- *Geranium:* This also nourishes the female reproductive system and has a strong floral scent.

- *Ylang-ylang:* This nourishes the female system and acts as an antidepressant as well as an aphrodisiac! (Try it, you'll like it.)

- *Rose:* This nourishes the female system and also acts as an antidepressant.

If you don't have a bathtub you can use, dilute the oils in a bowl of warm water and take a washcloth or cotton ball to apply as a wipe around the vaginal area. This can be done after bowel movements, too, to keep your rectal area nourished and clean.

### *For Cramps*

The following oils are recommended to relieve cramps, in order of best known: clary sage, cypress, chamomile (Roman), geranium, jasmine, and lavender. Also recommended are peppermint, sage, tarragon, and thyme, but it's best to apply these to the soles of the feet as they're very strong.

## How to Move

Performing the maintenance exercises discussed in Chapter 1 is vital for maintaining cycle control. The following yoga postures are also helpful for menstrual cramps:

- The Butterfly
- Squatting Posture
- Knee and Thigh Stretch
- Chest Expander

- Supine Knee Squeeze
- Fish Posture
- Legs Up
- Pose of Tranquility
- The Crocodile
- Star Posture
- Spread Leg Stretch
- Child's Pose
- Pelvic Stretch
- The Camel
- Lying Twist
- Side Leg Raise
- Half Moon
- Spinal Twist

Many women also find that acupuncture and reflexology help alleviate menstrual cramps. See Chapter 16 for more information.

# 3

# Cervical Health

THE CERVIX IS the opening to the womb. It's the part of your uterus that extends into your vagina, and it's also vulnerable to cancer. In fact, many of our grandmothers and great-grandmothers died from cervical cancer, and until the 1940s cervical and uterine cancer killed more women than any other gynecological cancer, including breast cancer. But thanks to an accidental discovery by Greek physician George Papanicolaou, millions of women worldwide are spared from cervical and uterine cancer.

While doing research on the menstrual cycle of guinea pigs for a genetics experiment in 1917, Dr. Papanicolaou noticed that he could see cellular changes in vaginal tissue and fluid obtained from the guinea pig. This gave him the idea to obtain vaginal fluid samples from a woman who had uterine cancer. If his theory was correct, then one could actually see cancer cells in the vaginal fluid. And if that proved true, one could routinely check the vaginal fluid for the presence of abnormal cells before they had a chance to develop into cancer. Well, he was right. He could indeed see the woman's cancer cells in her vaginal fluid. Though it was too late to save her, it was not too late to save her daughters and many other women from this sort of cancer. At last, a painless way to screen for cervical cancer (which advances into uterine cancer) was discovered. In 1943 a paper that Papanicolaou coauthored, "Diagnosis of Uterine Cancer by the Vaginal Smear," received international attention, and by 1948 the Pap smear, as it was dubbed, became a widespread cervical cancer screening method. Unfortunately, women still develop cervical cancer (currently, 160,000 women worldwide die each year from cervical cancer), though not nearly as many as in the pre-Pap days.

# Cervical Cancer: An STD

Women's sexual attitudes and behaviors have changed since 1943. Studies are finding that cervical cancer rates in North America are starting to rise again, particularly in younger women. One reason may be that many women are simply not going for Pap smears as often as they should be. Women who have unprotected sex are at risk for a sexually transmitted disease called human papillomavirus (HPV), which causes not only genital warts but cervical cancer. Monogamous women can also be vulnerable to HPV if their partners are promiscuous. Based on research led by the Johns Hopkins University School of Medicine, men may bring home HPV, which is now found in 97 percent of all cervical cancers. Studies show that certain HPV strains predispose you to invasive and noninvasive cervical cancer. Some studies also show that genital herpes is associated with an increased risk of cervical cancer. HPV has also been found to be linked to prostate cancer in men. Women at the greatest risk for cervical cancer are those who are immune suppressed, discussed further on in this chapter.

HPV is the most common STD in North America; 10 to 46 percent of all sexually active women are infected at any given point in time, depending on the population evaluated. HPV infection is what is widely accepted as the cause of cervical cancer. In 2001, 12,900 women in the United States had cervical cancer diagnosed, and 4,800 died of the disease. Roughly 700,000 cases of cervical dysplasia (precancer) are detected every year in the United States.

As of this writing, a successful vaccine against HPV-16—one of the most notorious strains of HPV—has been developed. HPV-16 is most commonly associated with cervical cancer. In a fall 2002 study, published in the *New England Journal of Medicine*, women who had not been exposed to HPV-16 were vaccinated against it. They were observed for a long period of time to see whether they would develop cervical precancer or even signs of HPV infection. The results were astounding: 100 percent of the women who were vaccinated against HPV-16 remained infection-free.

It's important to note that the HPV vaccine is still in testing stages only and is not being widely dispensed. Roughly five years of testing is estimated before we see this vaccine make a dent in cervical cancer occurrence. Logically, young women and teens would be the first group to be vaccinated against HPV since women who were sexually active prior to this vaccine breakthrough may have already been exposed. The development of this vaccine does not mean that women would stop having Pap smears. Indeed, the only way to know whether the vaccine is being successful is to continue to screen women for cervical abnormalities. Also, before the vaccine can be deemed truly "successful," we need to see Pap smear results over a considerable amount of time on the first generation of vaccinated women. We still don't know how long the protection would last nor how frequently women would need to be vaccinated for sufficient protection over their lifetime. For example, if a fifteen-year-old girl received a vaccine this year, researchers would want to follow her for at least ten to fifteen years to see if she ever developed signs of HPV infection. At the time of this writing, HPV vaccine trials on young women are beginning all over the world at major universities. I'll keep you posted in future editions!

## *Symptoms of HPV*

HPV is asymptomatic. A healthy immune system will usually eradicate the virus on its own within six to eighteen months, but you can be reinfected again and again with various strains of HPV. A doctor will often be able to detect genital warts, which HPV causes. HPV can also trigger the cells on your cervix to behave abnormally, often referred to as dysplasia. Fortunately, though, a Pap smear will detect HPV.

## Who's at Risk for Cervical Cancer?

The following are known risk factors for cervical cancer:

1. *Unprotected sex:* A condom will protect you from HPV.
2. *Unprotected sex under age twenty:* Sexually active women under twenty are considered five times more likely to develop cervical cancer because of more cellular activity on the developing cervix.
3. *Unprotected sex using hormonal contraception:* This can predispose you to cervical dysplasia and HPV. Some findings suggest that the use of oral contraceptives may cause a folate deficiency, which puts you at risk for developing cervical dysplasia.
4. *Having another STD or infection:* If you are already infected with another sexually transmitted disease or infection, your immune system remains suppressed, which can predispose you to cervical dysplasia.
5. *Being HIV positive or having AIDS:* You are at very high risk of developing invasive cervical cancer even if you practice safer sex.
6. *Women over age sixty-five:* Again, too many guidelines falsely advise women over sixty-five to stop going for Pap screening. Discuss appropriate screening intervals with your doctor; if you are sexually active, you should be having annual Pap tests.
7. *Women who do not have Pap smears:* Women who live in underserviced areas because of socioeconomic factors are far more likely to develop cervical cancer than women who are regularly screened.
8. *Smoking:* Smokers develop cervical cancer at far higher rates than nonsmokers.

# The Pap Smear

The purpose of a Pap smear, in lay terms, is to get some cells from both the outside of your cervix (exocervix, or portio) and the inside of your cervix (endocervix). The junction that joins both the endocervix and exocervix is called the transformation zone; it is also crucial to get cells from the transformation zone because this is the area where cell abnormalities are most often found. The test is done during a pelvic exam after a speculum is inserted into your vagina to widen the opening. For most women, the Pap smear is quick and painless.

When all the scrapings are obtained, your doctor will literally smear them onto a small glass slide and spritz a fixative (a sort of hair spray) onto the slides to hold the samples in place.

Those cells are then sent off to a cytologist (a doctor who specializes in reading cells), who will screen them for abnormalities such as abnormal cell growth, infection, and inflammation. A Pap smear can also detect cell changes on the vaginal wall, which are signs of vaginal cancer. And finally, a Pap smear can pick up yeast and HPV, which, as already mentioned, causes genital warts. In fact, certain people can have HPV without ever developing warts. Certain strains of HPV are more likely to cause cells lining the cervix to change. If an abnormality is found, then the idea is to treat you before anything more serious, such as cervical cancer, has a chance to develop. Other health practitioners besides doctors can also perform Pap smears. Physician assistants, nurse midwives, and nurse practitioners (often referred to as clinicians) often do Pap smears as well.

A Pap test is only used for determining cancer and should not be confused with a "wet prep," in which a long Q-tip is inserted and used to soak up discharge for yeast, trichomoniasis, bacterial vaginosis, or other vaginal infections. A separate swab is used to obtain cultures for chlamydia and gonorrhea. There's a newer test for chlamydia that requires a swabbing inside the cervical canal. When you see your doctor for any kind of irritation, infection, or discharge, this is when you'll be swabbed. A Pap test is not done when there's an infection.

## It's All in the Technique

While some doctors "give great Pap," others do not. In fact, Pap smear technique is one of the most commonly covered stories in general practice magazines. That's because an accurate interpretation of your Pap smear is directly related to the purity of the sample to begin with. Poorly obtained samples can lead to false negatives. As a result, cervical cancers could be missed. Although recent media reports suggest having separate labs analyze your Pap tests, no professional, medical, or federal organization agrees with this approach.

The best way to ensure an accurate sample is to make sure your doctor knows what he or she is doing. Much of the problem has to do with the instrument doctors use to do Pap smears. Currently, no Pap smears should be done without a tool called a cytobrush (which looks like a mascara brush) as well as a small wooden spatula; any other tools, such as cotton swabs, are simply not appropriate. Other ways doctors can taint your sample is by waiting too long to smear the samples onto the slide. Your doctor must transfer your samples (from both the exocervix and endocervix) to one slide, quickly spraying a fixative onto the slide to avoid the common problem of air drying, which is associated with poor interpretation.

## *The Right Steps to a Good Sample*

The following steps are considered the shortest route to a good sample—and the shortest route to an accurate reading:

- Do not douche or use tampons or vaginal medication for at least twenty-four hours prior to your Pap test. Any of these can interfere with the sample.

- Your doctor should do your Pap smear before screening you for any STDs, such as gonorrhea or chlamydia. A long Q-tip is used to obtain cultures when screening for STDs.

- Your doctor should remove excessive amounts of vaginal discharge prior to doing the Pap.

- Under no circumstances should your doctor be using a lubricant before the Pap smear. This will interfere with the sample and render it useless.

- Under no circumstances should your doctor perform a Pap smear during your period. This will interfere with the sample.

- Repeat Pap smears must be at least two to four weeks apart.

- Your doctor should be using a cytobrush and wooden spatula to obtain samples from both the exocervix and endocervix, as well as from your vaginal walls. Recent studies show that by doing it this way, the yield of the sample (high-quality cells you can accurately read) improves sevenfold.

- Your doctor should not be performing a Pap smear if you have a lot of pus discharge, a sign of infection. Ask your doctor during the exam if any unusual discharge is present, and question your doctor if he or she continues to perform the Pap smear in the presence of unusual discharge.

- In general, avoid Pap smears during pregnancy. If for some reason you're having a Pap smear done while you're pregnant, you may experience some slight spotting, but this should not jeopardize your pregnancy.

- To transfer your sample onto a slide from the wooden spatula, your doctor should smear the sample with a single stroke using moderate pressure to thin out clumps of cells and mucus. Too much force or manipulation will damage cells and interfere with appropriate interpretation. To transfer material from the cytobrush, your doctor should roll the bristles across the slide by twirling the brush handle.

- If you think you're at risk for genital warts, caused by HPV, or you are a "DES daughter," you need to have your doctor take additional smears from suspicious areas. (Note: DES stands for diethylstilbestrol, an estrogen-containing drug prescribed to some women between 1941 and 1971 to prevent miscarriage. Any daughter born to a mother who took DES runs a higher than normal risk for reproductive organ abnormalities, cervical and vaginal cell changes, and cancer. For more information visit desaction.org, the website of DES Action.)

Most Pap test errors have to do with a poorly collected or preserved sample. Detection error occurs when abnormal cells on the Pap slide are missed or misinterpreted. Again, using a fixative solution to preserve the sample is now the gold standard for preparing Pap slides for interpretation.

Special software now approved by the FDA, such as AutoPap Primary Screening System or TriPath Imaging, uses computerized images that help to interpret Pap slides more accurately.

## How Often Should You Have a Pap?

The Pap smear determines only the condition of the cervix. It's done once a year because that creates a greater likelihood of picking up changes in the cervix. Cervical cancer can take up to ten years to develop. So if you have a Pap test once a year and it does happen to come back positive (meaning only that something fishy was detected, not that you have cancer), you'll be treated for your condition before it has the chance to develop into cancer.

Experts recommend that screening begin at age eighteen, or earlier if you are having sexual intercourse. All women, regardless of their sexual preference or partners, should have regular Pap smears. Pap smears should be repeated once a year if they're normal, and more often (to be determined by your doctor) if they are abnormal. Annual Pap smears should continue throughout your life span. But even women who no longer have a uterus benefit from what is known as a vaginal cuff smear because cells lining the area have been known to change. And women who are no longer sexually active are still susceptible to cervical cancer. If you're over sixty-five, some guidelines stipulate that you can stop having Pap smears so long as your previous two smears within the last ten years were negative; other guidelines stipulate that if you have had four normal Pap tests within ten years before age seventy, you can stop being screened. Most experts strongly advise you to discuss screening frequency with your health care provider—life does not stop at seventy for most women these days!

If you answer "yes" to any of the following questions, you must have an annual Pap smear:

- Have you ever been diagnosed with genital warts (a.k.a. venereal warts, or condyloma), caused by HPV?

- Have you had more than one sex partner in the past three years?

- Have you had a new sex partner since your last Pap smear?

- If you're in a monogamous relationship, is it possible that your partner has been unfaithful?

- Do you smoke? (Recent epidemiological studies have identified smoking as a major risk factor for cervical cancer. In other words, more smokers get cervical cancer than do nonsmokers. Apparently, nicotine is detected in the cervical mucus of smokers, which can trigger abnormal cell growth. Sorry, ladies—it's just one more reason to quit smoking!)

## If You're HIV Positive

Here is an official warning to all HIV-positive women: you must have frequent Pap smears throughout the year. HPV, which I discussed at the beginning at this chapter, turns lethal when it meets HIV. Women who are HIV positive are thirty times more likely to develop cervical cancer when HPV is detected than are women who are HIV negative. In fact, many experts feel that when HPV is found on the Pap smear of an HIV-positive woman, this qualifies as an AIDS-defining diagnosis, which is discussed more in Chapter 11. If you are HIV positive, and so far have had clear Pap smears, you must also request at least one examination per year using colposcopy (discussed a little later in this chapter). In fact, the first and only AIDS-defining illness exclusive to women is invasive cervical cancer, which was added to the list of AIDS-defining illnesses by the Centers for Disease Control and Prevention (CDC) on January 1, 1993.

### If You're Immune Suppressed for Other Reasons

You don't have to have HIV to be immune suppressed. You could be undergoing chemotherapy treatment for a variety of conditions, or you may be fighting an illness that leaves you immune suppressed. Regardless of the reason, be sure to request regular Pap smears. Studies show that HPV as well as abnormal Pap smears are far more prevalent in immune-suppressed women than in the general population.

### If You've Had a Hysterectomy

Once your cervix is removed, you should continue to have cells from your vaginal walls checked periodically for abnormalities, and you should continue to have annual pelvic exams, particularly if you still have your ovaries. Older women who have undergone a total hysterectomy for diseases other than cervical cancer are not at risk for cervical cancer and don't have to be screened. But some women may have undergone a hysterectomy in which the cervix is retained. If you have had any kind of genital tract cancers, suffer from repeated vaginal infections, and are sexually active, you should probably continue to have vaginal cuff smears after hysterectomy.

## Getting Positive or Negative Results

If your Pap smear comes back negative, then it was normal, or clear. If it comes back positive, it can mean a whole bunch of things. The Pap test may have picked up an infection, such as HPV, herpes, or yeast, which can cause inflammation of the cervix, known as cervicitis. In this case, your doctor will treat and repeat. Your doctor will first treat the infection and then ask you to repeat the Pap smear to make sure the infection has cleared up. After you're treated, the usual pattern is to have a Pap smear every six months for up to two years, then annual Paps after two normal smears. Otherwise, you'll go on to colposcopy.

Cervicitis can also be a sign of pregnancy or may result from a miscarriage or an abortion, the use of certain medications, as well as hormonal changes. In other words, you can have cervicitis without the presence of an infection. Depending on where you live, there are two ways your Pap test results will be classified. In the United States, the most current systems are the Bethesda System and the CIN Grading System. (See Table 3.1.) Prior to 1993 some regions in North America, as well as outside the continent, may still have been using the older, Papanicolaou classifications.

The Bethesda System is considered a far more valuable reporting system because it actually describes what's going on instead of slotting your sample into a class system ranging from 1 to 5. The Bethesda System also evaluates the adequacy of the sample in the first place, helping to cut down on the number of false negative test results, caused in large part

### Table 3.1   *Interpreting Pap Smear Results*

| Description | CIN Grade | Bethesda System |
| --- | --- | --- |
| normal | normal | normal |
| HPV | HPV | ASCUS |
| atypia | atypia | ASCUS |
| mild dysplasia | CIN 1 | low-grade SIL |
| moderate dysplasia | CIN 2 | high-grade SIL |
| severe dysplasia | CIN 3 | high-grade SIL |
| carcinoma in situ | CIS | high-grade SIL |
| invasive cancer | invasive cancer | invasive cancer |

by bad samples. Nevertheless, both the CIN Grading System and the Bethesda System are in widespread use today. Table 3.1 outlines all the various terms involved in classifying your Pap smear so that you can figure out what the heck is going on!

In the Bethesda System, your Pap smear is classified into various descriptions: "normal"; "atypical squamous cells or glandular cells of undetermined significance" (ASCUS), which means that your Pap smear has picked up something unusual but that nothing may be necessarily wrong; "low-grade or high-grade squamous intraepithelial lesion" (SIL), which means that the cells are growing in an inappropriate manner (a.k.a. CIN [cervical intraepithelial neoplasm] 1, CIN 2, or CIN 3—ranging from mild to moderate to severe dysplasia). A Pap smear will also pick up cervical carcinoma in situ, a precancer, and invasive cervical cancer, which means that your cancer may be limited to the cervix but may be in a more advanced stage.

Essentially, anything short of invasive cervical cancer is really akin to your dashboard emergency indicator light going on while you're driving—there's more than enough time to drive to a service station and fix the problem. Here, the indicator light goes on as a warning to get the problem diagnosed and looked after. When the Pap smear detects invasive cancer, this is more like blowing out a tire on the road—the problem is fixable, but it needs to be tended to immediately before you can drive any farther.

When the Pap smear picks up harmless, abnormal cells, called benign atypia, you'll need to repeat the test in six months' time. Benign atypia usually clears up on its own. If this is the case, you'll simply repeat the Pap test in a year, as you normally would. If benign atypia persists, you'll be referred to a colposcopist.

Occasionally, with mild dysplasia and a clean Pap history, your family doctor or gynecologist may simply choose to repeat the test and see if it clears up on its own. If you have moderate to severe dysplasia, you'll be referred to a colposcopist for further investigation.

Colposcopy is the most common referral in gynecology. The incidence of positive Pap smears has skyrocketed in the last ten years. Not only has sexual behavior changed, but more women are going for Pap tests. As a result, more cervical abnormalities are being picked up because of increased testing. However, death from cervical cancer has dropped dramatically since the test was introduced.

### When They Tell You It's Dysplasia

Dysplasia means that you have abnormal cells on your cervix. This is considered precancer; it's not yet cancer, but it could develop into cancer if something isn't done. On the cervix, new cells are made in the deeper portions of the tissue. As the cells mature, they "rise" to the surface. Abnormal cells are cells that have risen to the top without maturing at all and are, hence, primitive. So when these cells are found in a Pap smear, it's a sign that there's something odd going on. The more abnormal cells found on the surface, the more serious is your dysplasia. When your entire cervical epithelium (the tissue that lines the cervix) is covered with these primitive cells, you have cervical carcinoma in situ—technically cancer, but so early and noninvasive that it's not at all life threatening if caught in time.

Dysplasia is treatable almost 100 percent of the time. In fact, in some cases of mild or moderate dysplasia, the dysplasia may even disappear on its own, but since there's no way of knowing this in advance, all dysplasia is treated.

The abnormal cells in dysplasia can only be detected under a microscope, but they are harmless for the moment. They will not invade any nearby healthy tissue. As you can see from Table 3.1, dysplasia is classified as mild, moderate, or severe, depending on how abnormal the cells appear under the microscope. The more serious the classification, the more chance of that dysplasia developing into invasive cervical cancer. If you are HIV positive, dysplasia is often the first warning that invasive cervical cancer is developing.

In many cases, you may not even have dysplasia, but rather a condition known as metaplasia, which is present in at least 50 percent of all women at some point in their lives. Metaplasia is a process of cellular repair or cellular growth; it's when, for whatever reason, the cells on your cervix are in flux, but they're absolutely fine. They're just in the process of turning from a cocoon state into a butterfly. At any rate, if a Pap smear is done during this process, the Pap report may come back reading "dysplasia."

### When They Tell You It's Genital Warts

Genital warts are caused by the sexually transmitted disease human papillomavirus (HPV), discussed at the beginning of this chapter. There are two distinct shapes that genital warts can take. Cauliflower-shaped warts are called condyloma, or more specifically, condyloma acuminata. Flat warts are simply referred to as genital warts, or venereal warts (genital warts is the more modern vernacular). Genital warts are treated the same way as dysplasia, using one of the therapies discussed later under "Treatment." Once your warts are treated, they will not recur unless you have unprotected sex with a new partner—or with the same partner who infected you the first time. As already discussed, several strains of HPV are directly linked to cervical cancer, which is why your warts need to be treated.

Furthermore, if you have genital warts, you should be screened for HIV if you have any reason at all to suspect that you've been exposed. Again, HPV + HIV = invasive cervical cancer.

### When They Tell You It's Cancer

Pap smears will also detect invasive cervical cancer or cervical carcinoma in situ. Cancer is discussed in detail in Chapter 18.

# Colposcopy

A colposcope is a lighted microscope used to magnify your cervix during an exam. With a colposcope, a doctor can see abnormal areas of your cervix and vagina that cannot be seen with the naked eye. This exam takes about ten minutes to perform. If you've been referred to a colposcopist, chances are you have HPV or dysplasia. Before viewing, the cervix will be stained with vinegar. Because of the frequency of colposcopy, most gynecologists and many family doctors are now upgrading their skills and training so they can perform it. Your colposcopist may at this point want to do a biopsy (described in the next section). Depending on what the colposcopist finds, you may require treatment for your condition, in the form of loop electrosurgical excision procedure (LEEP), laser surgery, cryosurgery, or a type of sloughing cream. (See more detailed discussion later in this chapter.) For mild dysplasia, rather than treat you immediately, your doctor may have you undergo a repeat Pap and colposcopy. When you first meet your colposcopist, ask the following questions:

1. *What did my Pap smear show?* This will tell you whether you have an infection, dysplasia, and so forth. Then you'll be able to better gauge whether the treatment your doctor suggests is reasonable.

2. *Is it possible that the lab report was wrong?* The first citing of poor quality Pap smears was published in 1987, when a *Wall Street Journal* report found that a large majority of Pap smears were sent to cut-rate labs with overworked, underpaid technicians. A large percentage of Pap tests remains inaccurate. You could wind up being

treated for a condition that would have cleared up on its own, or worse, pass your Pap test when you should have failed. Ask your doctor if your Pap smear was analyzed by a lab certified by the American College of Pathologists or American Society of Cytologists. If the answer is no, request a second opinion from a lab that is. Then, if both reports come back the same, you can be sure you're being treated appropriately. Even a properly obtained and properly interpreted Pap smear can be falsely positive or falsely negative. A false positive results because the problem may resolve between the time you have the Pap test and the time you see the colposcopist. The worst problem with a false positive is the anxiety and expense. The danger with a false negative smear is that a significant problem may not be diagnosed and treated. False negatives can result if the abnormality is too high in the cervix for the Pap smear to reach it or if it's not shedding abnormal cells for some reason. Because of the possibility of a false negative, it's best to have regular Pap smears performed. It's unlikely that you'll have two false negatives in a row.

# Biopsy

Once you're comfortable that your Pap smear was analyzed correctly, your colposcopist will most likely do a cervical biopsy. This means that he or she will remove bits of tissue from the cervix, under the guidance of a colposcope. This procedure can take anywhere from five to twenty minutes. It is relatively painless. The tissue samples look like pieces of grain or rice and are obtained with an instrument that looks like a hole puncher. At this point, the colposcopist will also scrape cells from the cervical canal and send them to a pathologist for examination. It is possible to have a negative biopsy with a positive Pap smear. This means that your condition may have cleared up on its own or that your Pap smear is inconclusive. You may not require any further treatment and may be asked to repeat your Pap test again in about three months to see if the condition has cleared up or remains clear. This negative biopsy–positive Pap smear combination is rare, but it does happen. You will most likely have a positive biopsy and will need treatment.

## *Cone Biopsy*

In some cases, your doctor may want to do a cone biopsy, which is a minor surgical procedure done on an outpatient basis. Here, your doctor removes a cone-shaped tissue sample from your inner cervix, or endocervix. This sample is then sent off to a pathologist for analysis. Often a cone biopsy is a way for your doctor to decide whether you need to be treated with one of the therapies discussed next.

# Treatment for Cell Abnormalities on the Cervix

If your biopsy comes back positive, it simply means that you do have cell changes on your cervix. It does not mean you have cancer. There are three kinds of treatment available for cell abnormalities on the cervix: cryosurgery, laser surgery, and sloughing cream. In cryosurgery the lesions or cells on the surface of the cervix are destroyed by freezing via nitrogen gas. With laser surgery the lesions are vaporized with a carbon dioxide laser. With either procedure you may have bleeding and cramping afterward. If you're told that either procedure is painless, it's not true. It really helps to take a nonsteroidal painkiller beforehand.

Another treatment option is an external sloughing cream called 5-fluorouracil (5-FU, or Efudex), which has been used in the past for skin cancers and essentially gives your cervix a "facial." If you choose to use the sloughing cream, you can apply it yourself at home, and you'll need to see the doctor only for Pap tests. You insert the sloughing cream with an applicator, and the surface cells will slough off your cervix. The cream may cause a burning sensation on the outer portions of your vagina or vulva. This can be easily prevented by coating your vulva and outer lips with diaper rash cream; ask your doctor for a recommendation.

In laser surgery your cells are removed with a laser. A newer procedure, known as loop electrosurgical excision procedure (LEEP), involves a thin 5-mm wire, formed into a loop, which is used to remove the suspicious area of your cervix, with the aid of a colposcope. You'll be given a local anesthetic. LEEP is much easier on women than cryosurgery or traditional laser surgery, and success rates after one single treatment are at 95 percent, with very few complications and very little bleeding.

About 95 percent of the time cryosurgery requires only one treatment. Healing from cryosurgery can be unpleasant, especially for women who are overweight, are older, or have had more than one child. Healing after cryosurgery involves a watery discharge that has an odor, which can last about two weeks. Studies have found that the odor and discharge are reported as the most unpleasant part of the healing process.

Treatment for cancer of the cervix is discussed in detail in Chapter 18, but most times you're referred to a colposcopist for a precancerous condition. After a suitable number of clear Pap smears and normal pelvic exams (anywhere from three to six), the person performing the colposcopy will decide when to send you back to the doctor who is handling your basic gynecological care.

Most women can expect a recurrence of dysplasia at some point, particularly if they were treated for a moderate to severe dysplasia; this has to do with the nature of HPV.

## *The Smear Campaign*

Clearly, Pap smears save millions of lives every year on a global scale. With better techniques to obtain samples and interpret slides, Pap smears will continue to become one of the best cancer-screening methods ever invented. However, your role in improving cervical cancer screening is an important one, too. Here are some guidelines to help you become more proactive:

- Keep track of when you have your Pap tests, and ask for copies of your lab reports. Remind your doctor when your next screening should take place; don't wait for your doctor's office to call you.

- If you have never had a Pap test but are clearly due for one, make every effort to get one. If you're scared of the procedure, seek out other women who have them regularly, and find out more about the procedure from them.

- When you're having your Pap smear done, reread the section "The Right Steps to a Good Sample" before you go, so you know what to expect and can question your doctor if necessary.

- Before you leave the office after your Pap smear, find out what the office's policy is when it comes to an abnormal smear. Do they call you? Who does colposcopy if it's necessary? And so on.

- Follow up with your doctor's office exactly one week after you have your Pap smear to get your results. You call them—don't wait. Many offices are in the habit of calling only when there's a problem, but this system can leave you wondering.

- Ask your doctor which reporting system (Bethesda, CIN, etc.) the lab uses to identify your Pap smear. Understanding the local laboratory reporting terminology will really come in handy if your Pap smear comes back abnormal.

- If you're not satisfied with the service you've received from your doctor regarding your Pap smear or with the reporting results, let your doctor know. This is the only way customer service will begin to improve.

## *Stop Smoking*

Smoking can dramatically increase your risk of cervical dysplasia and cancer. Undertake a smoking-cessation program using any of the following:

- *Herbal and homeopathic smoking-cessation aids:* There are many herbal and home-opathic smoking-cessation products available. Some use plant sources to reduce cravings; some work by using natural substances to help you detox. For all the many natural smoking-cessation products, contact your local health food store.

- *Behavioral counseling:* Behavioral counseling, either group or individual, can raise the rate of abstinence to 20 to 25 percent. This approach to smoking cessation aims to change the mental processes of smoking, reinforce the benefits of not smoking, and teach skills to help the smoker avoid the urge to smoke.

- *Nicotine gum:* Nicotine (Nicorette) gum is now available over the counter. It helps you quit smoking by reducing nicotine cravings and withdrawal symptoms. Nicotine gum helps you wean yourself from nicotine by allowing you to gradually decrease the dosage until you stop using it altogether, a process that usually takes about twelve weeks. The only disadvantage with this method is that it caters to the oral and addictive aspects of smoking (i.e., rewarding the urge to smoke with a dose of nicotine).

- *Nicotine patch:* Transdermal nicotine, or the "patch," doubles abstinence rates in former smokers. Most brands (including Habitrol, Nicoderm, and Nicotrol) are now available over the counter. Each morning, a new patch is applied to a different area of dry, clean, hairless skin and left on for the day. Some patches are designed to be worn a full twenty-four hours. However, the constant supply of nicotine to the bloodstream sometimes causes very vivid or disturbing dreams. You can also expect to feel a mild itching, burning, or tingling at the site of the patch when it is first applied. The nicotine patch works best when it is worn for at least seven to twelve weeks, with a gradual decrease in strength (i.e., nicotine). Many smokers find it effective because it allows them to tackle the psychological addiction to smoking before they are forced to deal with the physical symptoms of withdrawal.

- *Nicotine inhaler:* Available only by prescription in the United States, the nicotine inhaler (e.g., Nicotrol Inhaler) delivers nicotine orally via inhalation from a plastic tube. Its success rate is about 28 percent, similar to that of nicotine gum. Like nicotine gum, the inhaler mimics smoking behavior by responding to each craving or urge to smoke, a feature that has both advantages and disadvantages to the smoker who wants to get over the physical symptoms of withdrawal. The nicotine inhaler should be used for a period of twelve weeks.

- *Nicotine nasal spray:* Like nicotine gum and the nicotine patch, the nasal spray reduces craving and withdrawal symptoms, allowing smokers to cut back gradually. One squirt delivers about 1 mg nicotine. In three clinical trials involving 730 patients, 31 to 35 percent were not smoking at six months. This compares to an average of 12 to 15 percent of smokers who were able to quit unaided. The nasal spray has a couple of advantages over the gum and the patch: nicotine is rapidly absorbed across the nasal membranes, providing a kick that is more like the real thing, and the prompt onset of action, plus a flexible dosing schedule, benefits heavier smokers. Because the nicotine reaches your bloodstream so quickly, nasal sprays do have a greater potential for addiction than the slower-acting gum and patch.

- *Alternative therapies:* Hypnosis, meditation, and acupuncture have helped some smokers quit. In the case of hypnosis and meditation, sessions may be private or part of a group smoking-cessation program.

- *Smoking-cessation drugs:* The drug bupropion (Zyban) is now available and is an option for people who have been unsuccessful using nicotine replacement. Formerly prescribed as an antidepressant, bupropion was "discovered" by accident: researchers knew that quitting smokers were often depressed, so they began experimenting with the drug as a means to fight depression, not addiction. Bupropion reduces the withdrawal symptoms associated with smoking cessation and can be used in conjunction with nicotine-replacement therapy. Researchers suspect that bupropion works directly in the brain to disrupt the addictive power of nicotine by affecting the same chemical neurotransmitters (or "messengers") in the brain, such as dopamine, that nicotine does.

# What to Eat

It is well known that immune suppression influences the development of cervical dysplasia. Making sure you get enough of the B vitamins and vitamins C, D, and E, as well as flavonoids, EFAs, calcium, copper, iron, manganese, selenium, vanadium, zinc, and carnitine is essential (see Chapter 1).

The following spices are said to be immune boosters (they stimulate your immune system or strengthen it to help fight viruses and infections):

- garlic (rubbing a cut clove directly onto genital warts has been touted as a homegrown cure for decades, to be used with fresh chickweed)
- turmeric
- onions
- black pepper
- asafetida
- cumin and poppy seeds
- neem flowers
- parsley

# Flower Power

Here's an overview of some of the well-known herbal immune boosters:

- *Echinacea:* Echinacea is not just for colds. This is a flower that belongs to the sunflower family. It's believed that echinacea increases the number of cells in your immune system to fight off diseases of all sorts. It's been considered an herbal remedy for genital warts for decades, along with goldenseal root and garlic.

- *Essiac:* This is a mixture of four herbs: Indian rhubarb, sheepshead sorrel, slippery elm, and burdock root. Essiac is believed to strengthen the immune system, improve appetite, supply essential nutrients to the body, possibly relieve pain, and, ultimately, prolong life.

- *Ginseng:* This is a root used in Chinese medicine, believed to enhance your immune system and boost the activity of white blood cells.

- *Green tea:* This is a popular Asian tea made from a plant called *Camellia sinensis.* The active chemical in green tea is epigallocatechin gallate (EGCG). It is believed that green tea neutralizes free radicals, which are carcinogenic. It is considered to be an anticancer tea particularly for stomach, lung, and skin cancers, to which genital warts can be linked.

- *Iscador (a.k.a. mistletoe):* Iscador is made through a fermentation process using different kinds of mistletoe, a plant known for its white berries. More popular as an antitumor treatment in Europe, Iscador is believed to work by enhancing your immune system and inhibiting tumor growth.

- *Paul d'Arco (a.k.a. Taheebo):* This usually comes in the form of a tea made from the inner bark of a tree called tabebuia. Believed to be a cleansing agent, it can be used as an antimicrobial agent and is said to stop tumor growth.

- *Wheatgrass:* This grass is grown from wheatberry seeds and is rich in chlorophyll. Its juice contains more than one hundred vitamins, minerals, and nutrients and is believed to contain a number of cancer-fighting agents and immune-boosting properties.

# How to Move

Meditative stretching and deep breathing to reduce stress, which can also suppress the immune system, are key. See Chapter 1 for those exercises. The following yoga postures are also recommended:

- The Tree
- Pose of Tranquility
- The Crocodile
- The Plough
- Angle Posture
- Spinal Twist
- Half or Full Shoulder Stand
- Sun Salutations

# 4

# Ovarian Health

COMEDIENNE GILDA RADNER, who died of ovarian cancer, walked around with it for a long time before it was finally diagnosed. Feeling gassy and uncomfortable for months, she was told that her symptoms were gastrointestinal and not to worry. If only Radner had been educated as to the early warning signs of ovarian cancer, she might not have succumbed too early in life to this cancer.

In 2000, ovarian cancer struck approximately twenty-three thousand women in the United States, and approximately fourteen thousand women previously diagnosed with the disease died of it. This places it fifth in order of the five leading cancers that are diagnosed in women in North America: breast, lung, colon, uterine corpus, and ovary. The only well-known risk factors for ovarian cancer are infertility and family history of ovarian cancer. There are conflicting studies showing that fertility drugs, as well as HRT, may also be a factor in ovarian cancer incidence. This chapter is designed to give you all the facts about ovarian health, including noncancerous conditions, as well as everything you need to know to catch ovarian cancer before it progresses to a later stage.

## Ovarian Cysts

Abnormal bleeding and irregular periods can be caused by an ovarian cyst. This is a scary diagnosis, but ovarian cysts are very common and are not cancerous conditions. An ovarian cyst is a fluid-filled lump, just like a breast cyst, but it forms on the ovary. Often ovarian cysts don't even require surgery and just need to be monitored. An ultrasound can tell your doctor whether the cysts are benign.

## *Follicular Cysts*

During normal ovulation, the follicle spits out the egg. When the follicle fails to do this, fluid, hormones, and other guck build up inside the unruptured follicle until a cyst develops. This kind of ovarian cyst is most common in women who are between the ages of twenty and forty. Some women are plagued by follicular cysts, which may keep forming. The symptoms of follicular cysts are different from symptoms of ovarian cancer. They include delayed periods, bleeding between periods, pelvic pain (constant dull ache or sharp jabbing), and cramping, but often there are no symptoms. A full pelvic exam is done first in investigating abnormal bleeding (see Chapter 17). Often follicular cysts are found in a bimanual exam. If your ovary is enlarged by more than two inches, it will immediately be investigated. Your doctor will order a blood test to see how well your ovary is producing hormones. Then he or she will perform an ultrasound scan to see the size and composition of the ovary. Just like an ultrasound can determine fluid-filled lumps in breasts, it can also determine fluid-filled lumps on the ovaries. In the United States sometimes a CAT scan or an MRI is done as well. Follicular cysts are always benign.

The next step in treating follicular cysts depends on your age and the size of the cyst. If you're menstruating regularly and the cyst is small, waiting it out may be the best course of action. However, since most follicular cysts resolve within one menstrual cycle, the first step is simply observation, eliminating the need for expensive tests and treatment. Most go away without rupturing, but these cysts may also rupture on their own. In either case, your menstrual cycle will get back in sync and return to normal. You'll then need to be reevaluated. If you're under thirty, you can be reevaluated in about two cycles (eight to ten weeks). If you're between the ages of thirty and forty, you should be reevaluated after only one cycle (about four to six weeks).

If you are experiencing a lot of pain, are over forty, or have a solid enlargement of the ovary, you'll need to be treated immediately. If the cyst persists after a second evaluation, you'll also need to be treated.

Treatment involves a laparoscopic procedure, which will tell the doctor more about the texture and size of your cyst. Depending on what is found, the cyst might be aspirated on the spot, at which point it will simply collapse and you'll be cured. But if the ovary is unusually large, the cyst is removed and your ovary biopsied via fine-needle aspiration. If no cancerous cells are found, once the cyst is removed, you'll also be cured. Sometimes a condition known as polycystic ovary disease can occur where a woman has numerous follicular cysts, which can be treated. This is also a major cause of infertility.

## *Corpus Luteum Cysts*

After your egg is spit out by the follicle, which then turns yellow and becomes the corpus luteum (an empty shell that produces progesterone; see Chapters 1 and 2), the follicle doesn't shrink like it's supposed to. Instead, the little blood vessels that feed the follicular sac and bleed during ovulation continue to bleed into the empty sac and form a blood-filled cyst. This sounds dangerous, but it isn't. Corpus luteum cysts will often rupture and resolve on their own. If not, the diagnosis and treatment route is the same as for follicular cysts: the blood is aspirated during laparoscopy, and the ovary is biopsied. Sometimes, though, the ovary may be too large or the bleeding too severe. At this point, some doctors may opt to remove the ovary, but this is premature. The bleeding is caused by a stubborn blood vessel that can be tied off, which will stop the bleeding, allowing the cyst to be aspirated and the ovary to remain intact.

## *Dermoid Tumors*

These are not cysts but common benign tumors (making up about 10 percent of benign ovarian tumors). Dermoid tumors are more common in young women but can occur throughout the reproductive years. Prepare yourself—these are really disgusting! What happens here is that the egg begins developing without being fertilized. So these growths develop hair, teeth, cartilage, and fat. Even surgeons are shocked by their appearance. The symptoms and diagnosis process for these tumors are the same as for follicular cysts, and an ultrasound test or even an x-ray can pinpoint dermoid tumors. Teeth often show up in the scans or x-rays!

Many surgeons will do laparoscopic surgery to remove the tumor and leave the ovary intact. Unfortunately, some doctors will just remove the ovary altogether. Because dermoid tumors can be removed while leaving the ovaries intact, your best bet is to seek out a doctor who will not remove the ovary. If you can't find one, contact the Hysterectomy Educational Resources and Services (HERS) Foundation (see Chapters 14 and 20), an organization that has lists of surgeons who perform alternative surgery to hysterectomy and oophorectomy.

# Preventing Ovarian Cancer

Preventing ovarian cancer means, first, understanding your risk profile and going for regular pelvic exams. Second, know the symptoms. Seventy percent of all ovarian cancer is discovered in an advanced stage that does not respond well to treatment. However, if discovered early, it carries an 85 to 95 percent five-year survival rate.

The average woman has a one in seventy risk of developing ovarian cancer in her lifetime. The women at highest risk are those who never have a break from ovulation and who began their cycles earlier than the average twelve and a half years of age. On the flip side, if you had your first child after age thirty-five, you may also be at higher risk. Basically, having lots of kids starting at age twenty-five or younger and breast-feeding them (breast-feeding delays ovulation) will greatly reduce your chances of ovarian cancer. If you're having children beyond age thirty-five, breast-feeding also reduces your chances of ovarian cancer.

Not planning a life like this? Well, don't panic. We now know that oral contraceptives (discussed in Chapter 8) can also protect you from ovarian cancer because they give you a break from ovulation. The longer you are on an oral contraceptive, the greater your protection. A recent study reported a substantially reduced risk of ovarian cancer for women taking oral contraceptives who had a family history of ovarian cancer and who tested positive for the gene mutation linked to ovarian cancer (BRCA1 or BRCA2—the same mutation linked to premenopausal breast cancer). The risk of ovarian cancer decreased by 60 percent in high-risk groups with oral contraceptive use. In fact, oral contraceptives are now thought to be an ovarian cancer prevention drug for women who were previously considering a prophylactic oophorectomy (see further on).

## Genetic Screening for Ovarian Cancer

When you're told you carry a gene for a particular cancer, it means that you have inherited a normal gene that is more vulnerable to attack by certain carcinogens, meaning that it can mutate. Cancers that are considered to be familial (inherited) are cancers that occur in first-degree relatives (parents, siblings, and children). Grandmothers, great-aunts, and paternal relatives are not as crucial in determining familial cancers. Genetic screening can find some of these vulnerable genes, but what does this information mean?

Familial ovarian cancer accounts for a significant percentage of all ovarian cancers. Several inherited genes can cause susceptibility to this cancer, including BRCA1 and BRCA2, also implicated in breast cancer. Women who have these genes are more susceptible to breast and ovarian cancer than those who don't.

If you are BRCA1 or BRCA2 positive, it's estimated, using data from high-risk families, that you are at very high risk of developing ovarian cancer if you have a family history of ovarian cancer. The problem with finding out whether you have a mutated gene that could cause cancer in your body is that it is not necessarily meaningful information. The stress that the information causes could be more damaging to you than the mutated gene. On the other hand, knowing you are vulnerable to certain cancers may help you to make certain decisions, such as going on oral contraceptives or even having a prophylactic oophorectomy.

A wider issue surrounding genetic testing is the fast-approaching future—a future where a long list of genetic information may be compiled about each person. And that means there may be a stigma attached to certain information getting out to people who may not understand what having a certain gene means and who may discriminate against you for having certain cancer genes. This is not an issue that you need to worry about today, but it may be one that will affect your children ten years from now. Now that the Human Genome Project is complete, many more cancer gene tests will be available.

### The Downside of Genetic Testing

Testing for genetic mutations in presymptomatic women who come from high-risk families is producing a registry of confidential information that can perhaps be even more damaging to the future of the affected woman or families than the genetic mutation itself. Some of the following dilemmas regarding testing for the breast/ovarian cancer gene present themselves:

1. *Who owns this information?* It is currently unclear whether a woman who tests positive for a cancer gene mutation can keep the information confidential.

2. *How will this information be used?* The 1997 film *Gattaca* dramatizes the results of a genetically obsessed culture. In this film one's genetic makeup determines one's eligibility for education, employment, and social status, even though the film's protagonist makes it clear that "genoism" (a word in the film, which meant discrimination against people with genetic "defects" or mutations) is against the law. *Gattaca* shows us a world that is not so futuristic anymore—a world where every strand of hair or eyelash serves as one's genetic resume.

   Insurance companies in the United States already practice a form of "genoism," with clauses that prevent people with preexisting conditions from receiving health care insurance. Could insurers in the near future require, for example, BRCA-positive women to undergo a prophylactic oophorectomy as a condition of coverage? Or would health insurance premiums simply become unaffordable for BRCA-positive women or even the families of these women? As for denying employment to BRCA-positive women, while the Equal Employment Opportunity Commission considers genetic discrimination unethical under the 1990 Americans with Disabilities Act, its powers are limited. Given this, what would stop employers from requiring that BRCA-positive women undergo a prophylactic oophorectomy as a condition of hiring?

3. *"BRCA Daughters":* At what point does a mother tell her daughter that she is BRCA positive? At age twenty-one? At sixteen? At birth? While there are guidelines in place that prohibit genetic testing in girls under age eighteen, there is no way to enforce that a BRCA-positive woman withhold her *own* testing results from her daughter. The emotional impact of a daughter knowing that she may carry a "defect" may be

an unfair burden. How will this information affect other decisions this daughter makes, ranging from career choices to contraception methods to childbearing?

Secondly, would BRCA screening become available prenatally? Would BRCA-positive pregnancies be terminated? In India, for example, little girls are aborted because they are viewed as economic burdens on families; in kind, little girls who grow up to be breast/ovarian cancer patients may be viewed as economic burdens.

### Is Getting Tested Harmful?

Well, it can be, depending on how you're interpreting the news or who is interpreting it for you. If you have inadequate genetic counseling (which happens a lot!), critics of genetic testing state that misunderstood genetic information can do enormous damage. It's important to consider the following before deciding to get tested:

- *Testing negative:* Testing negative is never a "true negative," since the test is not an accurate prediction of one's future health. Some women mistakenly interpret a negative result to mean that they will never develop any form of ovarian cancer. If other women in your family are being tested at the same time, the women in the family who test negative may suffer from survivor's guilt if other women test positive.

- *Testing positive:* On the flip side, testing positive is not necessarily a guarantee of ovarian cancer, although there is certainly a greater likelihood of a BRCA-positive woman developing ovarian cancer. The issue of harm should be examined, in the context of whether a still-healthy, presymptomatic woman should sacrifice her emotional health. Women who test positive are more likely to suffer from anxiety, depression, and hopelessness; strained relationships with family members; and even employment and insurance discrimination.

- *Harmful interventions:* Right now, women who test positive for an ovarian cancer gene are recommended for prophylactic oophorectomies, meaning that they will require hormone replacement therapy (HRT) for life, which has now been shown to be potentially harmful as a long-term therapy. This prophylactic surgery asks women to sacrifice their health before showing symptoms of a disease.

## *Prophylactic Oophorectomy*

A prophylactic oophorectomy means removing the ovaries to prevent disease—in this case, ovarian cancer. Women whose mother or sister(s) had ovarian cancer are three times more likely to develop ovarian cancer themselves. Women who have witnessed family members die from ovarian cancer are particularly fearful that they will suffer the same fate and often request prophylactic oophorectomy before it is even recommended. However, the complications that can follow this procedure because of surgical menopause are not always discussed in great enough detail. And in light of changing guidelines regarding HRT, many women considering prophylactic oophorectomy may have to weigh other risks with the perceived benefits. For more on menopausal symptoms and HRT, please see Part IV of this book.

## Ovarian Cancer Symptoms

The symptoms of ovarian cancer are very different than they are for ovarian cysts, comprising more general signs of ill health, such as gas, bloating, and flulike symptoms. Occasionally, vaginal bleeding or even masculine hair growth might be a sign, but these are rare. Sharp abdominal pain or a continuous dull ache could be a symptom of ovarian cancer but usually points to a cyst. Menstrual irregularities are also not a common symptom.

The following are the official signs of early ovarian cancer:

- discomfort in the lower abdomen
- painless swelling or bloating in the lower abdomen
- a feeling of fullness (even after a light meal)
- loss of appetite
- gas and indigestion that can't otherwise be explained
- nausea
- weight loss
- frequent urination
- constipation
- pain during sexual intercourse

Typically, most women with early ovarian cancer won't notice symptoms unless they're on the lookout. Noticeable symptoms occur when the cancer has spread to the abdominal cavity, causing abdominal fullness and early satiety (a sensation of fullness after eating only a small amount). Many women will be sent off to a gastroenterologist to investigate motility disorders, hiatal hernia, or gallbladder disease.

Early ovarian cancer is usually caught by a doctor during a routine pelvic examination where he or she finds an enlarged ovary or mass (in a premenopausal woman) or can actually feel the ovary (in a postmenopausal woman—the ovary shouldn't be "feelable" at this stage). Enlarged lymph nodes around the pelvic region are sometimes a clue as well. In rare cases, brain tumors are the first sign of ovarian cancer. This is why it's so important to have regular pelvic exams. Your doctor can feel for enlarged ovaries or masses by inserting two gloved fingers inside the vagina and simultaneously feeling the outside of your abdomen with the other hand (something akin to fitting your duvet into its cover with your fingers).

Let's invent a rule from now on: if you are over fifty and notice three of the aforementioned symptoms for ovarian cancer, go to your doctor without delay and ask him or her to feel for an enlarged ovary or mass. If this doesn't reveal anything, ask to have a transvaginal pelvic ultrasound to rule out ovarian cancer. When it comes to this kind of deadly cancer, better safe than sorry. If your doctor gives you a hard time, say that you don't want to be another ovarian cancer statistic, and then blame what may be perceived as overcautiousness on this book.

## When the Abdominal Pain Is Caused by the Fallopian Tubes

A rare problem, known as fallopian tube torsion, can cause almost the exact symptoms as ovarian cancer: gastrointestinal symptoms, such as nausea and vomiting, and urinary frequency and urgency with voiding difficulties. This may need to be ruled out if no mass is found when you present with ovarian cancer symptoms.

Women who are at risk for ovarian cancer tend to have one or more of the following characteristics:

- They have a family history of ovarian, uterine, breast, or colon cancer.
- They are between fifty-five and sixty-four years of age.
- They have never been pregnant. (In this case, the risk is twice as likely.)
- They have been diagnosed with breast, intestinal, or rectal cancer. (This appears to increase the risk of developing ovarian cancer.)
- They have been on fertility drugs but have not conceived. (Fertility drugs cause your ovaries to "superovulate.")
- They are exposed to environmental toxins (including in the workplace).
- They experience irregular or no menstrual cycles, ovarian malfunctions, ovarian tumors, or ovarian cysts or have polycystic ovary disease or Turner's syndrome (a genetic disorder).
- They consume a high-fat diet, low in vitamin A.
- They have hypertension or diabetes.
- They are Caucasian or of northern European descent.
- They are living in an industrialized country.

## *Ultrasound Screening*

If you are in a high-risk category for ovarian cancer, once you reach forty, you should request an initial pelvic ultrasound to measure the size of your ovaries, even if you've already had a hysterectomy. Have blood tests done to obtain a baseline reading of your hormone levels. Then go back once a year for a comparative ultrasound and blood test. Any readings or results that veer too far from your first baseline reading can be investigated before it's too late. Canadian researchers have now developed a blood test that can detect ovarian cancer at an early and treatable stage. The test measures the levels of lysoPC, which is significantly increased in women with ovarian cancer. Ask your doctor about the availability of this test.

Unfortunately, ultrasound is not an effective screening method for women who are not in a high-risk group, but you can request it if you notice symptoms. The gastrointestinal-like symptoms of ovarian cancer are simply too vague for mass ultrasound screening to be routinely recommended. However, keep in mind that ultrasound or CA-125 can produce false positive or false negative results.

The CA-125 screening test (also discussed in Chapter 18) can find cancer cell "sheddings" in 80 percent of patients with advanced ovarian cancer. In fact, it is 99.9 percent specific in postmenopausal women, but only 50 percent specific in premenopausal women. The problem is that it doesn't always find ovarian cancer, but it does find other cancers, such as breast, lung, and gastrointestinal cancers. It also can test positive for benign conditions, such as benign cysts and endometriosis, simple menstruation, and pregnancy. Exploration laparotomy is often necessary to diagnose ovarian cancer.

# What to Eat

Adopting a diet that is low in animal fats and free of pesticides will reduce your exposure to excess estrogen and may help to reduce your risk of ovarian cancer, since it is seen in women who consume higher fat diets. You can also make extra estrogen when your liver is not functioning well or you have other nutritional deficiencies or bowel problems.

Taking all the B vitamins in doses of 50 to 100 mg a day as well as an additional 200 mg of $B_6$ a day can help improve liver function. Choline, methionine, and inositol also improve the breakdown of estrogen in the liver. Bitter greens such as endive, escarole, dandelion greens, and radicchio also stimulate liver function. Swedish bitters are another very helpful tonic to stimulate liver action and improve digestion. Supplements such as evening of primrose oil, vitamin E, vitamin C, and bioflavonoids may also help.

If you have an ovarian cyst, you can use diet to help dissolve the cyst. The following are reported to be helpful:

- raw vegetables
- red raspberry leaf tea
- cayenne pepper
- yarrow infusions
- chickweed in a tincture

# Flower Power

To maintain the reproductive system and overall ovarian health, you can use the essential oils listed in Chapter 1 as a daily tonic in a bath.

## *Natural Progesterone*

Natural progesterone can help to balance out excess estrogen in the body. Excess estrogen in the body causes, among other things, increased body fat. Natural progesterone (see Chapter 2) can help to counterbalance excess estrogen.

# How to Move

Aerobic activity, such as that described in Chapter 17, can help to burn fat and hence reduce the estrogen in your body. Practicing the daily exercises described in Chapter 1 is also helpful.

# 5

# Urinary Tract Health

THE URINARY TRACT is not separate from the reproductive tract; what affects one frequently affects the other. This chapter outlines ways to combat the common problems of urinary tract infections and incontinence, as well as prevention measures to maintain urinary tract health. For information on interstitial cystitis, see Chapter 16. For information on uterine prolapse, which can also cause urinary incontinence, see Chapter 15.

## Urinary Tract Infections

Urinary tract infections (UTIs) are among the most common infections in women, accounting for more than eight million office visits per year in the United States. Because they have been traditionally treated with antibiotics, and because of widespread overuse of antibiotics, we are now seeing antibiotic-resistant strains of UTIs, which means that the UTI may recur. The most commonly used antibiotic for UTIs was trimethoprim-sulfamethoxazole (TMP-SMX). Strains of *Escherichia coli*, which account for 75 to 90 percent of cases, are now appearing to be resistant to this antibiotic. *Staphylococcus saprophyticus* accounts for 5 to 15 percent (particularly in younger women), and enterococci and non–*E. coli* aerobic gram-negative rods, such as *Klebsiella* species and *Proteus mirabilis*, account for the remaining 5 to 10 percent of UTIs. *E. coli*–resistant strains occur now in about 20 percent of UTI cases.

### Cystitis

*E. coli* bacteria travel from the colon to the urethra to the bladder, which can cause inflammation or infection of the bladder, known as cystitis. Classic cystitis symptoms include a

81

painful or burning sensation coming from inside the urethra (known as dysuria, meaning "painful urination," as opposed to a burning caused by the urine touching an inflamed vagina or vulva), as well as feeling like you have to urinate constantly (some women report that they have to urinate up to sixty times a day), and then finding that almost nothing comes out when you do try. It's estimated that between 10 and 20 percent of all women will experience or have already experienced a UTI of some sort. And 80 percent of women who have had a UTI will have another one within a year.

Other symptoms of UTI may include blood in the urine, known as hematuria, or pus in the urine, known as pyuria. Sometimes cystitis clears up on its own within approximately twenty-four hours. Because of this, wait one day before you see your doctor. If it doesn't clear up, report all your symptoms to your doctor and request a urinalysis (a urine test) to check for an infection. You may also need a urine culture; however, with a typical uncomplicated cystitis symptom, many doctors will treat it without a culture. At this point, your doctor may also perform a pelvic exam to check for the presence of other vaginal infections. For instance, women will often think they have a UTI when it's really bacterial vaginosis (see Chapter 6).

As you already know, a urine sample can be taken during your doctor's appointment. What you might not know, however, is that there is a specific technique involved in getting the "most" out of your urine sample to avoid false positives due to contamination with skin or vaginal bacteria. Ask for the proper materials to do a "clean catch" or get a "midstream" urine sample. This will include a sterile container and some moistened wipes for cleaning the outer vaginal area. To obtain the urine specimen, you may want to sit backward on the toilet and use the toilet lid as a shelf. Wash your hands before you begin and open the container, but do not touch the inside of the lid or the container. Using one hand, spread your vaginal lips apart and don't let go. Use the moistened wipes, wiping front to back one time with each wipe and then dropping it in the toilet. Start the stream of urine, letting a small amount go into the toilet, and then put the container under the stream. It's not necessary to fill the container completely. Put the lid on the container without touching the inside of the lid. At this point you may wash your hands to remove any urine from your fingers. Wipe the outside of the container with a moist paper towel. This may seem elaborate, but it's designed to keep normal vaginal and skin germs out of the culture. If your lab technician doesn't seem to know what a "clean catch" kit is, discuss this with your doctor. An alternative would be to carry your own sanitary wipes with you and follow this procedure.

If the urine culture is negative, meaning that no bacteria are present in your urine, your symptoms may be caused by another infection, probably an STD. In this case, you could be suffering from urethritis rather than cystitis. You would then need to be screened for various STDs and treated accordingly.

A positive culture test means that bacteria are present in your urine. You can also have bacteria in your urine (found during a routine exam) but have no symptoms of a UTI. This is more common in pregnancy. In either case, you'll be treated with an antibiotic.

## Treatment for Cystitis

For a simple case of cystitis with no complications, you'll be prescribed either a single dose or a short-course treatment of an appropriate antibiotic, such as TMP-SXT (Septra) or Macrodantin. If the infection doesn't clear up, you may be prescribed a different antibiotic. After the treatment, you'll need to give another urine sample to make sure the infection has cleared up.

If you're pregnant, diabetic, or elderly, or you have just had a UTI in the past six weeks, you'll be given the same antibiotic or other antibiotics for a longer period of time, ranging from ten to fourteen days. Then a follow-up urine culture will need to be done. If you do happen to suffer from recurrent UTIs, you can do a home urine test on your own, available through any pharmacy in the United States. This test is easy to do and comes equipped with a dip-slide stick that turns color if it's positive.

## Recurrent or Chronic Cystitis

Some women are more prone to cystitis than are others, but the disease is triggered by several behavioral factors that you can control.

Intercourse can trigger cystitis. The term *honeymoon cystitis* refers to a woman who develops cystitis after her sexual "debut." The urethra can become irritated with intercourse, and more bacteria may get inside the urethra, which leads to the bladder. Also, during intercourse many women hold back their urge to urinate. Experts recommend that you empty your bladder both before and immediately after sex. Urinating after sex will also help wash out the bacteria from the urethra. (See Chapter 1 on the structure of the urethra and bladder.)

Diaphragm use is another trigger. Diaphragms that are too large can alter the angle of the bladder neck, making it difficult to empty the bladder completely. You can easily avoid this problem by making sure your diaphragm fits properly (see Chapter 8) and by urinating before you put it in and after you remove it six hours later.

In addition, women in the habit of "holding it in" can be predisposed to cystitis. When you gotta go, you gotta go—don't hold it in. (The classic example is a teacher who can't leave her class to "go.")

Other reasons why you might be prone to cystitis include an obstruction or a blockage, such as a stone anywhere along your urinary tract. This blockage may show up on a kidney x-ray or an intravenous pyelography (IVP). An IVP is an x-ray of your kidney and urinary tract. Iodine dye is injected into you, which makes the x-ray easier to read.

Damage to your lower back area can affect the nerves that go to your bladder. This may prevent you from completely emptying your bladder, creating a breeding ground for bacteria, and it is often a leading cause of chronic or recurrent cystitis. In addition, pelvic surgery such as a hysterectomy can damage nerves to the bladder. In this case, your cystitis bouts would have begun immediately after your surgery.

The general pattern of recurring cystitis is about three infections per year. If you suffer from more than three infections per year, you should consult a urologist. If no specific abnormality is found, prophylactic antibiotics can be used to prevent recurrent cystitis. Since as many as 85 percent of women with recurrent cystitis notice the onset of infection within twenty-four hours after intercourse, postcoital antibiotics are often helpful. Usually, your doctor will get you on a self-treatment regimen for recurrent cystitis. This may involve using a home urine culture test kit (mentioned earlier) and taking one or two doses of antibiotics if the culture is positive.

Here are some tips for women with recurrent cystitis:

1. Never start your antibiotic until you know the results of your urine culture. If you have repeated cystitis symptoms with negative cultures, you may have another condition known as interstitial cystitis, discussed in Chapter 16.

2. Before you start self-treatment, make sure your doctor examines your urine under the microscope to check for blood and pus, which will help in making a more accurate diagnosis.

3. If bacteria show up in your urine more than three times in a row, request an IVP or an ultrasound of your kidneys. You may have kidney stones; if so, your doctor will determine whether they need to come out.

4. Make sure you have a pelvic exam and an evaluation for yeast infection, trichomoniasis, chlamydia, and gonorrhea. Your symptoms could be caused or aggravated by these vaginal infections.

5. If all else fails, you should request a cystoscopy examination. Done under a general anesthetic, a cystoscopy checks your bladder for structural problems.

## *Pyelonephritis*

Pyelonephritis occurs when a bacterial infection has spread to your kidneys, causing inflammation. The symptoms of pyelonephritis are similar to those of cystitis. Usually, you'll have a fever, pain in the flank (the fleshy side of your body between your ribs and hips), nausea, or vomiting in conjunction with cystitis symptoms. A urine culture may distinguish whether you have cystitis or pyelonephritis. To treat this infection, broad-spectrum antibiotics are used for fourteen days; TMP-SXT or ciprofloxacin (Cipro) are the popular ones. With pyelonephritis, you'll need to be hospitalized and treated with intravenous antibiotics if nausea or vomiting is a problem or if you're pregnant. A new urine culture will be taken about forty-eight hours later. If you're still not well after this, further diagnostic procedures, such as an ultrasound test, will be done to get to the bottom of the problem. It will need to be taken care of to prevent more serious or even life-threatening consequences of severe kidney infection, and if you're not referred to a urologist or an infectious disease specialist at this point, request it.

## *How to Take Antibiotics*

Recently, national campaigns in several countries have been funded to teach people how to take antibiotics. That's because antibiotics are dangerous. Not to you, but to the future of humankind. The more antibiotics that are prescribed, the more potential there is for them to be misused, which leads to resistant strains of bacteria that no antibiotic can cure. Studies show that antibiotics are also misprescribed in a variety of scenarios; patients may insist on antibiotics for a viral infection, for example, when antibiotics, by definition, can treat only bacteria. Studies show that 70 percent of patients insist on prescriptions for antibiotics for viral infections; many doctors just give in rather than argue. Antibiotics are also requested as preventive medicine to ward off feared bacteria. This is not what antibiotics were designed to do. Unfortunately, when people take them as "prevention pills," it gives other, friendly bacteria in your body a chance to mutate.

The biggest problem is that people don't understand how antibiotics work and therefore stop taking them as soon as they feel well. As a result, the antibiotic is unable to kill the bacteria it was meant to kill, and the bacteria have time to mutate and resist that antibiotic.

Shockingly, more than 50 percent of people in one survey failed to take their antibiotics as prescribed—even though 75 percent of those surveyed said that they were counseled about how to take their medication.

A contributing factor to the problem are antibiotics prescribed in pediatric medicine. Antibiotics prescribed for the roughly 24.5 million children's ear infections in the United States can also lead to resistant strains of bacteria.

Therefore, it's crucial that you follow these directions whenever an antibiotic is prescribed:

1. Take your antibiotic as prescribed (with meals, at night, or whenever). Don't take four pills a day when you're supposed to take one; don't take your antibiotic once

a day when you're supposed to take it three times a day. In other words, be sure you understand how many pills to take in a day and when to take them. Skipping doses can allow the antibiotic to become ineffective and give your bacteria some time to mutate. Doubling up on a dose is usually not encouraged either.

2. Ask how alcohol, milk, or food will affect the antibiotic. Some foods can weaken the antibiotic and make it ineffective.

3. Finish the bottle. Don't stop taking the antibiotic because you feel better. You're feeling better because the bacteria may be dying; but they're not dead unless the bottle is finished. Many antibiotics must be taken several times a day for ten or more days to do the job, even though you will probably feel better within forty-eight hours.

4. Never take leftover antibiotics from the bottle you didn't finish last year, and never borrow an antibiotic from your sister-in-law's friend's mother or lend it to your brother's friend's sister-in-law!

5. Be prepared for some side effects. Antibiotics kill off friendly bacteria in your body, too, and classically cause vaginal yeast infections. You may also experience nausea, diarrhea, rashes, or a number of other side effects. Ask your doctor what to expect before you fill your prescription. Antibiotics may also affect other medications you're taking and render them ineffective. Oral contraceptives and antibiotics don't mix, for example. You may wind up trading a UTI for a baby if you're not careful.

# Urinary Incontinence

Urinary incontinence refers to the involuntary loss of urine, or involuntary urination, which can lead to physical, hygienic, or psychological distress. Urge incontinence means urine loss that is associated with a strong sense of urgency or frequency or with nighttime urinating (nocturia). This problem affects roughly 30 percent of women in their twenties and thirties, 40 percent of women in their forties and fifties, and 50 percent of women over sixty-five. If you lose urine at times you don't mean to such as when you sneeze, cough, laugh, run, jump, or play sports (stress incontinence) or if you feel an urgent need to go and are unable to reach the toilet in time (urge incontinence), you join about six and a half million other North American women with this problem. More recently, this has been renamed overactive bladder by drug manufacturers.

Incontinence tends to plague women who do a lot of sitting, have had several children, have repeated UTIs, have diabetes, have diseases that affect the spinal cord or the brain (such as Parkinson's disease, multiple sclerosis, or Alzheimer's disease), have a history of bladder cancer, or have had major pelvic surgery such as a hysterectomy. The muscles of your pelvic floor and abdomen get weaker, and your urinary apparatus drops down. On top of this, less estrogen causes the urethra to thin and change, similar to the vaginal changes you experience.

Chapter 1 discussed how the bladder and female urethra work. When we're younger, we have tremendous control over the pubococcygeal muscle. This muscle controls the vaginal opening as well as the urinary opening. Normally, when we feel the urge to urinate, we hold it in until we get to the right place. When we get to the toilet, urine doesn't come out immediately. We relax slightly, then urinate. This relaxing that takes place prior to urination is the relaxing of the pubococcygeal muscle, which also enables us to stop and start our streams. Anyone who's had to have a urinalysis has probably mastered this technique.

Urinary incontinence is categorized into one of four groups: stress incontinence, urge incontinence, overflow incontinence, or irritable bladder. Stress incontinence is when urine leaks out during a sudden movement, such as a sneeze or a cough or even uncontrollable laughing. This can happen to women of all ages and is considered the most common form of incontinence. You may be in the habit of holding it in or simply have aged.

Urge incontinence refers to a sudden, sometimes painful urge to urinate that is so unexpected and powerful you may not always be able to make it to the toilet.

Overflow incontinence occurs in only a small percentage of overall incontinence problems. With no warning, urine suddenly overflows after you change your position (from sitting to standing or vice versa, for example). You may lose just a few drops of urine or enough to require a maxipad. Sometimes these episodes are followed by the urge to urinate a few minutes later, but when you try, nothing comes out. This is a neurological problem where the bladder doesn't contract and empty well. It therefore overflows.

An irritable bladder is a mishmash of all three incontinence symptoms and UTIs. You'll need to see a urologist to sort out what's causing your bladder to behave so erratically. You may also suffer from interstitial cystitis (see Chapter 16).

Overweight women are more likely to experience incontinence because the weight exerts more pressure on the bladder, causing the muscles and urethra to overwork themselves. Try losing weight and see if your bladder function resumes.

## *Treating Incontinence*

Today, most cases of urge incontinence are treated with anticholinergic drugs, such as oxybutynin chloride and propantheline bromide. Immediate-release oxybutynin appears to be more effective in some studies. Nondrug therapies include behavioral modifications and urge suppression. The side effects of drug therapy include dry mouth, decreased tear production, blurred vision, dizziness, and urine retention. In postmenopausal women, estrogen can be very helpful as a treatment for incontinence because it restores the "luster" of your urethra just as it restores the vagina. Estrogen has the same beneficial effect whether in pill, cream, or patch form; more women may prefer the cream in light of new studies regarding potential risks of long-term hormone replacement therapy.

More invasive treatments for incontinence involve surgery that lifts and tightens the pelvic floor or the use of pessaries, a stiff, doughnut-shaped rubber device (which needs to be fitted and sized) that fits into the top of the vagina and holds it up slightly. This raises the neck of the bladder and helps reposition it.

Some women may choose to live with the problem and wear bladder control products.

# What to Eat

If you suffer from cystitis, drinking a sixteen-ounce glass of cranberry juice daily as well as a sixteen-ounce glass of water twice daily has been known to prevent recurrence. If you have an active infection, a sixteen-ounce glass of cranberry juice hourly at the first signs of infection can stop cystitis before it really starts.

Mixing one teaspoon of baking soda in a glass of water and drinking it, when symptoms first appear, can also stop cystitis before it gets a chance to actually start.

Creating a more alkaline diet, by adding fruits, almonds, leeks, barley, and turnips, is also helpful.

Eliminating diuretics such as caffeine and alcohol, or other drugs that may be working as a diuretic, is important, too. Spicy foods can sometimes irritate the bladder, as can some acidic fruit juices (other than cranberry juice). If you suffer from incontinence, avoid the following bladder irritants:

- caffeine
- alcohol
- white sugar
- citrus
- tomatoes
- cayenne
- hot peppers
- iced drinks
- carbonated drinks
- pineapple

Many common drugs trigger incontinence: diuretics, antidepressants, beta-blockers, blood pressure lowering drugs, sleeping pills, and tranquilizers. Also, note that smoking increases your risk of developing stress incontinence by 350 percent.

## Flower Power

If you have an active bladder infection, bearberry (a.k.a. uva-ursi) as an infusion is helpful. Chinese herbs used to treat incontinence are designed to strengthen the kidney *qi*. *Eucommia* bark, dogwood, walnut, Golden Lock tea, or Sextone are often combined with acupuncture. Other herbal remedies that help clear up bladder infections and prevent incontinence include:

- goldenseal
- *Pulsatilla*
- Zincum
- dried teasel (*Dipsacus sylvestris*) roots (boiled with a tablespoon to a cup of water for ten to fifteen minutes; drink daily)
- antispasmodic herbs such as black cohosh, ginger, catnip, and cornsilk (may help with urge incontinence)
- yarrow (*Achillea millefolium*; will help heal bladder infections, incontinence, and heavy periods but may aggravate hot flashes; recommended as a tea or an infusion of the dried flowers as desired, or as a tincture of the fresh flowering tops, five to ten drops, two to three times daily)

## How to Move

The Kegel exercise is very helpful in strengthening the pubococcygeal muscle, thereby strengthening the bladder and helping to prevent incontinence. You can do this convenient exercise in any position, anywhere, anytime: in an elevator, on the subway, in a movie theater, or while you're cooking, eating, or lying down. All you do is isolate the muscle that stops and starts your urinary stream. To isolate it, you can insert your finger into your vagina and try to squeeze your finger with your vaginal opening. Once you've isolated the muscle, just squeeze it five times, then count to five, or squeeze ten and count ten. The key is to keep the muscle in shape. It's that simple, and it really helps. You can also do general exercises to firm up your abdomen and pelvis in conjunction with your Kegel exercises.

Retraining your bladder can help, too. Schedule your toileting to go on a regular schedule, say every sixty to ninety minutes. After three or four consecutive dry days, increase the interval by fifteen to thirty minutes, and keep increasing until you're at every four hours.

Following are exercises you can do as you are urinating, which will help strengthen your bladder muscles:

- Pulse your urine flow by pushing out very strongly, then slackening it off until it's just a dribble, then push out again, and so on. Repeat as many times as possible every time you urinate.
- Empty the bladder completely every time you void by pressing down behind your pubic bone with your fingertips or the flat of your palm.

And here are some other useful exercises:

- Push hard on the very top of your head to relieve urge incontinence on the spot.
- Set out two large shallow basins: one with very hot water, the other with cold. Start by relaxing for three minutes in the hot one. Then lower yourself into the other basin, going up and down, in and out of the icy water for one minute. Repeat three to four times. Do this several times a week.

## Pelvic Floor Trainer

A new product known as Epi-No, which has just received FDA approval, was introduced to the North American market in 2002. This pelvic floor trainer consists of a narrow, naturally shaped silicon balloon, a hand pump, a pressure display, and an air release valve, all connected by a flexible plastic tube. It's designed to gently train the pelvic floor muscles and has been a successful treatment for incontinence, combined with Kegel exercises. For more information, you can visit the website for Epi-No at www.epino.de.

## Yoga

Yoga postures that strengthen the bladder include:

- The Butterfly
- Squatting Posture
- Knee and Thigh Stretch
- Pose of Tranquility
- Star Posture

- Spread Leg Stretch
- The Camel
- The Cobra
- Half Locust
- The Bow
- Side Leg Raise
- Spinal Twist
- Cat Stretch series

# 6

# Common Vaginal Infections

THE DELICATE VAGINAL ecosystem can be easily disturbed. Vaginal infections can be triggered by dozens of daily things, such as your sexual behavior, hormones (including hormonal contraceptives, changes in menstrual cycle), vaginal blood (from your period, irregular bleeding, etc.), anything inserted into the vagina (diaphragm, tampons, strings from an IUD), or medications (antibiotics, douching agents, antifungal agents, spermicides). Studies have even found that women from different races have different vaginal ecosystems, predisposing some groups of women to more vaginal infections than others. This chapter outlines the common vaginal infections women suffer from. The "What to Eat," "Flower Power," and "How to Move" sections offer nondrug therapies for many of these infections, which can be chronic or recurrent.

## Bacterial Vaginosis (BV)

Bacterial vaginosis is a common vaginal infection in which the wrong bacteria flourish due to changes in the vaginal ecosystem that can alter its pH balance. What happens is that the number of normal lactobacilli decreases in the vagina (which can be altered by eating yogurt with live culture), while the number of bacteria flourish (which can be *Gardnerella*, mycoplasmas, as well as anaerobic bacteria such as *Prevotella* and *Mobiluncus*). In other words, it is considered to be a condition where different kinds of bacteria, rather than one specific bacterium, flourish.

No one has any idea what causes BV. It is indeed garden variety, and most experts in the field do not think that a single cause will ever be identified. We do know that BV is not an STD, although it can be transmitted to a partner through sex.

BV causes abnormal vaginal discharge and vaginal odor, and it is considered a nuisance infection. In the past, the term *bacterial vaginosis* did not exist; what we call BV today could have been called nonspecific vaginitis, or *Gardnerella vaginalis* to honor Gardner, the physician who first described BV. In the 1980s it was sometimes referred to as anaerobic vaginitis, anaerobic colpitis, or anaerobic vaginosis. All of these terms have been replaced with bacterial vaginosis. This infection has suffered from too many labels and name changes, as well as disputes within the medical community over which bacterium is indeed responsible for BV. To date, no one actually knows which specific bacterium causes BV, and it has become an umbrella term that could refer to a few different bacterial culprits. Since the treatment is the same—microbial agents (drugs that kill a few different bacteria)—it has become moot to pinpoint exactly which bacterium is causing the problem.

Often there are no BV symptoms. When there are symptoms, they are the same for this infection as for trichomoniasis (see next section), but the discharge is creamier or grayer and very fishy smelling. The treatment is either oral or vaginal metronidazole or clindamycin suppositories. If your partner has it, he should be treated with metronidazole, and if he doesn't, make sure he wears a condom until you're cured. The natural remedies outlined under "What to Eat" and "Flower Power" can also help with BV.

Taking metronidazole (500 mg twice daily for seven days) continues to be a standard therapy recommended for BV. It is successful approximately 80 percent of the time. Sometimes, as an alternate treatment, 300 mg of clindamycin given twice daily for seven days works well, because it also kills anaerobic bacteria. The antibiotic therapy can cause, as a side effect, an overgrowth of yeast in about 20 percent of the women treated for BV. (See further on.) Diarrhea and loose stools can also be common, as bacteria in the colon is sometimes altered by antibiotics.

# Trichomoniasis

Trichomoniasis is caused by a one-cell parasite called *Trichomonas vaginalis*. This parasite is very common in both men and women, and many women have trich organisms inside their vagina without knowing it. In fact, about 50 percent of all women infected with trich are asymptomatic. When there are symptoms, you'll notice itching, irritation, painful intercourse, and thin, foamy vaginal discharge that is yellowish green or even gray in color and has a foul odor. If there is another infection present as well, the discharge can be thicker and whiter.

Trich is diagnosed by swabbing the vaginal discharge and examining it under the microscope. But trich can also cause urinary tract infections, discussed in Chapter 5. Usually, trich is contracted through vaginal intercourse, but it can be passed on by moist towels, bathing suits, underwear, washcloths, and, yes, toilet seats. Emotional stress can cause "friendly trich" to flare up and cause symptoms.

Metronidazole is a drug used to treat trich; it usually works well as a single-dose therapy, but if it doesn't, a repeat dose ought to cure trich once and for all. Generally, if you're taking medication for trich, make sure your partner gets treated as well.

# Yeast Infections

Yeast infections are caused by a yeast known as *Candida albicans*, a type of one-cell fungus that belongs to the plant kingdom. Under normal circumstances, candida is always in your vagina, mouth, and digestive tract. It is a "friendly" fungus. For a variety of reasons, candida will overgrow and reproduce too much of itself, changing from a harmless one-cell fungus into long branches of yeast cells, called mycelia. This is known as candidiasis.

## *Causes*

Generally, any changes to your vagina's normal acidic environment can make you vulnerable to yeast infections. The list of factors that affect your vaginal environment is actually quite long. The most common factor is pregnancy, because it makes the vagina less acidic and increases the amount of sugar stored in the vaginal cell walls. And yeast loves sugar! In fact, diabetic women often suffer from chronic yeast infections because of their blood sugar levels. Sometimes the first sign of diabetes is a stubborn vaginal yeast infection. If you suffer from chronic yeast infections, get screened for diabetes.

Hormonal changes and contraception are other factors. In order to work, hormonal contraceptives change the cervical secretions that bathe the vagina, as discussed in Chapter 8. This can change the vaginal environment drastically and make it vulnerable to yeast. Menopause also causes the cervical mucus to change, which again predisposes you to yeast infections.

Anything that interferes with the immune system will make yeast thrive. Antibiotics, for example, kill not only the harmful bacteria but also the friendly bacteria that are always in the vagina, necessary to fend off infection. If you're prone to yeast infections and your doctor prescribes antibiotics for, let's say, chlamydia, tell your doctor that you're prone to yeast infections before you fill the prescription. He or she can recommend some preventive measures (some of which are discussed later in this chapter) you can take to ward off yeast infections.

Immune deficiency is another common factor that causes yeast infections for the same reasons. In addition to HIV infection (yeast and HIV infection are discussed in Chapter 11), steroid drugs and anticancer drugs and therapies (such as radiation or chemotherapy) also destroy the body's natural immune system, which leaves the vagina vulnerable to yeast overgrowth. Furthermore, whenever you're fighting another infection, your immune system is involved and not as responsive to nipping candidiasis in the bud.

Menstruation is always a factor that affects the vagina. Yeast loves the warm, moist conditions that menstruation provides. Wearing tampons will make the conditions even better for yeast to grow, so avoiding tampons is a good idea if you're suffering from chronic or frequent yeast infections.

A number of overall health factors affect the vagina: stress, fatigue, too much sugar or fruits, anemia, and low levels of thyroid hormone (which will affect your whole metabolism and slow down your menstrual cycle).

Following are guidelines to help you avoid yeast infections:

1. *Don't wear tight clothing around your vagina.* Tight pants, panties, and nylon pantyhose prevent your vagina from breathing and make it warmer and moister for yeast overgrowth. Wear looser pants that allow your vagina to breathe, switch to knee-highs or stockings, or limit your pantyhose wearing to special occasions. Go to bed bottomless to let air into your vagina.

2. *Wear only 100 percent cotton clothing and/or natural fibers around your vagina.* Synthetic underwear and polyester pants are not a good idea. All-cotton underwear and denim, wool, or rayon pants that are loose fitting are fine.

3. *Don't ever use vaginal deodorants or sprays.* These are unnecessary and disturb the vagina's natural environment, which is fully designed to self-clean.

4. *Don't douche unless it's purely for medicinal purposes.* Douching can push harmful bacteria higher up into the vagina, disturb the vagina's natural ecosystem, or interfere with a pregnancy.

5. *Watch your toilet habits.* Always wipe from front to back with toilet paper. When you do it the other way around, you can introduce rectal material and germs into your vagina. After a looser bowel movement, moisten the toilet paper and clean your rectal area thoroughly so that fecal material doesn't stay on your underwear and wind up in your vagina. To be prepared for less hygienic circumstances, consider carrying some moist wipes, the kind that is safe for babies' bottoms.

6. *Don't insert anything into a dry vagina.* Whether it's a penis or tampon, make sure your vagina is well lubricated before insertion. Dry vaginas can be cut during insertion, creating an excellent home for a yeast infection.

7. *Avoid sex "feasting."* After long periods of abstinence, continuous sex can predispose you to yeast infections. This is common in new relationships, when it's as if

two thirsty people are drinking from a well. Basically, the vagina doesn't adjust quickly enough to its new visitor, and its environment is upset. Cuts or abrasions from postabstinence sex are also common.

8. *Avoid long car trips where you'll be sitting on vinyl car seats.* New research indicates that extended periods of time sitting on vinyl seats increase a woman's risk of developing a yeast infection. The vinyl traps moisture and doesn't allow the crotch area to breathe.

## Symptoms

Severe itching and a curdlike or cottage-cheesy discharge are classic symptoms of a vaginal yeast infection. The discharge, interestingly, may smell like baking bread, fermenting yeast, or even brewing beer. The discharge may also be thinner and mucoid. Other symptoms are swelling, redness, and irritation of the outer and inner vaginal lips, painful sex, and painful urination due to an irritation of the urethra. Women who have candidiasis may not have symptoms.

When yeast is in the throat, it is called thrush and usually occurs in immune-deficient women (they may be HIV positive or undergoing cancer treatment). Thrush is unsettling because the mouth and throat are coated with a milky white goop. It can also be present in newborns when yeast-infected mothers give birth. Thrush is treated orally with nystatin drops. Finally, since yeast is present in the intestines, HIV-positive women can develop severe, life-threatening esophageal yeast infections, discussed in Chapter 11.

## Treatment for Single Vaginal Yeast Episodes

Vaginal yeast infections are so common that in the United States, over-the-counter medications such as miconazole (Monistat), terconazole (Terazol), nystatin (Mycostatin and many others), and even an herbal product, Yeaststat, are readily available. Don't ever self-treat without consulting your doctor and confirming that what you have is indeed yeast. Again, by self-diagnosing, you could be misdiagnosing gonorrhea, trich, chlamydia, or bacterial vaginosis for candidiasis. A doctor will confirm yeast by doing a wet prep. Generally, you can treat all yeast infections yourself with the many over-the-counter antifungals available.

In 1990 the FDA approved the labeling of clotrimazole, an imidazole, as the first available over-the-counter drug to treat yeast infections. Other antifungal medications, such as miconazole butoconazole nitrate, have since been switched from prescription-only to over-the-counter status. All of these topical antifungal drugs have a proven cure rate for vaginal yeast infections of 85 to 90 percent. There is no significant difference in the effectiveness or side effects of the various over-the-counter antifungal agents. And now the single-dose therapies are shown to be just as effective as the multiple-dose therapies that last three, five, or seven days.

Other over-the-counter treatments include boric acid. This is really cheap, and you can put it in gelatin capsules and insert it high into the vagina as a suppository. Boric acid can also be used as a douche: two tablespoons to two quarts of lukewarm water once a day for a week (when douching is medicinal, such as in this case, it's fine). Caution: keep boric acid out of your child's reach. It is very toxic if taken orally. Betadine is also helpful. It's a concentrated antiseptic iodine solution that kills yeast, trich, and bacterial vaginosis. Betadine is really messy, however, and stains everything brown. Pregnant women should not use it.

For more severe cases, using a Q-tip to paint the vagina, cervix, and vulva with gentian violet, a purple antifungal stain, does the trick. You'll need to wear a sanitary napkin to avoid dripping the stain onto your clothes. The only time this stain is not helpful is when you're allergic to the stain itself.

## Treatment for Recurrent or Chronic Vaginal Yeast Infections

If you have four or more episodes of vaginal yeast infections per year, you have recurrent yeast infections. You should confirm that the problem really is yeast and not serial infections with different organisms (that is, one month gonorrhea, the next month trichomoniasis, and so on). If you have frequent episodes of vaginal infections, it's especially important to confirm the exact diagnosis. If you seem to always be getting rid of a yeast infection, you suffer from chronic yeast infections. For recurrent episodes, it's important to try to do as much prevention as you can by following some of the dietary guidelines under "What to Eat."

Miconazole in vaginal cream or boric acid in gelatin capsules every night for seven days, then every other night for four weeks, and then monthly during menstruation is one recommended route for recurrent episodes. At the same time, taking one teaspoon of *Lactobacillus acidophilus* powder orally with meals is recommended. Studies have shown that a single 150-mg oral dose of fluconazole with a two-dose regimen given seventy-two hours apart in women with recurrent yeast can also do the trick.

Women who tend to suffer from chronic yeast infections include:

- women on HRT
- women with diabetes
- women who are HIV positive
- women who are immune suppressed due to stress, cancer therapy, or antibiotic therapy
- women who regularly douche or use vaginal sprays

- women who bathe in commercially prepared bubble baths
- women who wear panty liners

# Genital Inflammations

The result of various STDs or vaginal infections, such as yeast, are often inflammations of the vagina, cervix, or vulva. In fact, anything with the suffix *-itis* means that you have an inflammation of some sort, as in tonsillitis, hepatitis, and thyroiditis.

Gynecological inflammations, however, are tricky. In these cases, the inflammations themselves are not the infection; they are only symptoms of an infection. For example, when your doctor tells you that you have vaginitis (inflammation of the vagina), you may think it is the name of an actual infection that's causing your itching or other symptoms. It isn't. It is simply the name of a symptom, which is in turn caused by something else. The purpose of this section is to explain the various causes behind each inflammation and the symptoms characterized by the inflammation itself.

## Vaginitis (or Vulvovaginitis)

Vaginitis, now being called vulvovaginitis (inflammation of the vulva and vagina), is characterized by itching, redness, and a swollen vaginal opening. The three major causes of vaginitis are yeast infections, trich, and bacterial vaginosis. Vaginitis can also indicate the presence of other diseases. In addition, it can be caused by irritation as a result of insufficient lubrication due to hormonal changes that affect vaginal secretions.

Menopausal women frequently complain of vaginitis, which is aggravated by intercourse. Lubricating the vagina artificially should clear up vaginitis caused by dryness. The next time your doctor tells you that you have vaginitis, respond by asking, "And what's causing it?"

## Cervicitis

Again, cervicitis is not a disease in and of itself. Cervicitis is characterized by a swollen, red cervix, which is not usually noticed until a doctor examines your cervix with a speculum. What you may notice is bleeding between periods, bleeding after intercourse and painful intercourse, unusual cervical mucus or tenderness when you touch your cervix for any reason (inserting a diaphragm, for example), or unusual discharge that comes from the cervix. Gonorrhea, chlamydia, pelvic inflammatory disease (PID), and other STDs can all cause cervicitis; these are discussed in Chapter 10. Cervicitis can also result after IUD insertion, abortion, or childbirth. If cervicitis is caused by an STD, it will get better when the STD is treated. If it's the result of childbirth or IUD insertion, it will usually get better without treatment. In any case, you should have a pelvic exam whenever you have cervicitis. A Pap smear should be performed as well as a thorough STD screening to isolate the disease that may be causing the cervicitis.

## Vulvitis

Vulvitis is characterized by an itchy, red, swollen vulva and may include blistering. Diabetic women often suffer from vulvitis because of a sugar imbalance that predisposes them to infection. Postmenopausal women can develop vulvitis because the tissue in this area becomes less elastic, thinner and drier, and more susceptible to irritation. Scratching only makes it worse.

A number of factors cause vulvitis. External irritants, such as allergies to certain fabrics, powders, soaps, or perfumes, are common causes. Oral sex, sanitary napkins, medications, diet, stress, or the presence of STDs or other infections can trigger it.

The best way to deal with vulvitis is to first isolate the cause, especially if it's an allergy or a bacterial infection. If you're predisposed to vulvitis as a result of menopause or diabetes, avoid overcleaning your vulva, and use either Crisco or mineral oil to clean it. Treat your vulva like you would your face: keep it moisturized. Vitamin E oil is a good choice. The extra lubrication will really help.

## Endometritis, Salpingitis, and Oophoritis

Endometritis means "inflammation of the uterine lining (or endometrium)" and is not to be confused with endometriosis. It's caused by a bacterial infection that gets inside your uterus. Salpingitis is an inflammation of the fallopian tubes and is caused by a bacterial infection that invades your tubes. Oophoritis, inflammation of the ovaries, is also caused by bacteria. Like both tubal and uterine inflammations, oophoritis is a manifestation of PID, discussed in Chapter 10.

# Pain

Irritants from the environment, combined with autoimmune responses that affect muscles and nerve endings, can cause chronic gynecological pain.

## Vulvar Pain

A condition that is getting more attention lately is that of vulvar pain, called vulvodynia. One of the conditions causing vulvar pain is vulvar vestibulitis, a condition in which specific points in the vulvar vestibule (the portion surrounding the entrance to the vagina) are inflamed and painful. The pain tends to be on the vulvar skin on either side of the clitoris. Women who suffer from it describe the pain as feeling like grains of sand beneath the skin's surface in these areas. Burning, stinging, irritation, or rawness are the most commonly reported symptoms, but the pain is highly individualized and may vary in terms of location, severity, and duration (it may be chronic or periodic, for example). No one clearly understands the exact cause of this pain, but women who suffer from vulvar pain also tend to suffer from fibromyalgia, interstitial cystitis (see Chapter 16), irritable bowel syndrome, or other autoimmune disorders. Allergies and autoimmunity appear to have some interplay in this problem. Women suffering from vulvar pain usually have vulvitis or vulvovaginitis. Vulvar pain can also accompany herpes (see Chapter 10), cystitis, BV, and dryness in the vagina.

In the absence of another infection, speculated causes of vulvar pain include the following:

- an injury to, or irritation of, the nerves of the vulva
- a localized hypersensitivity to yeast
- an allergic response to environmental irritants
- high levels of oxalate crystals in the urine
- spasms of the muscles that support the pelvic organs

Managing the pain revolves around diet and lifestyle changes. Following are some lifestyle guidelines to help prevent vaginitis, vulvitis, vulvodynia, or vulvar vestibulitis:

- Avoid douching.
- Wear all-white cotton underwear.
- Do not wear pantyhose.
- Wear loose-fitting pants or skirts.
- Remove wet bathing suits and exercise clothing promptly.
- Use dermatologically approved detergent, such as Purex or Clear.
- Double-rinse underwear and any other clothing that comes into contact with the vulva.
- Do not use fabric softener on undergarments.
- Use soft, white, unscented toilet paper.
- Avoid getting shampoo on the vulvar area.
- Do not use bubble bath, feminine hygiene products, or any perfumed creams or soaps.
- Wash the vulva with cool to lukewarm water only.
- Rinse the vulva with water after urination.
- Urinate before the bladder is full.

- Use 100 percent cotton menstrual pads and tampons.
- Avoid chlorinated pools or hot tubs.

## *Vaginismus*

This refers to involuntary painful vaginal muscle spasms that can make intercourse very painful. This is a muscular condition that can be managed with retraining the muscles through a pelvic floor trainer (see Chapter 5).

# What to Eat

Most women can control vaginal infections through diet. Eliminating sugar will help enormously. Reacidifying your vagina is also an important preventive measure. Certain foods will help; check with your doctor or nutritionist. (Note: cranberry juice, associated with reacidifying in the past, is not helpful in preventing yeast infections but is instrumental in preventing cystitis, discussed in Chapter 5.)

If you suffer from severe, chronic yeast infections, in addition to eliminating sugar in your diet you should also avoid the following: honey, maple syrup, molasses, and any foods that contain these; alcoholic beverages; vinegars and foods containing vinegar, such as pickled foods, salad dressings, mustard, ketchup, and mayonnaise; moldy nuts, such as peanuts, pistachios, and cashews; soy sauce, miso, and other fermented products; dairy foods (with the exception of butter, buttermilk, and yogurt); coffee, black tea, or sweetened soda; dried fruits; and processed foods.

Instead, eat more of these foods: whole grains, such as rice, millet, barley, and buckwheat; breads, crackers, and muffins that are yeast-free and preferably wheat-free; raw or cooked fresh vegetables; fish, chicken, and lean meats (organically fed and hormone- and antibiotic-free); nuts and seeds that are not moldy; and fruit in moderation (limiting sweeter fruits).

If you're immune deficient for any reason, you can try strengthening your immune system with the supplements and herbs discussed in Chapter 3.

## *Probiotic Foods*

To maintain the vaginal ecosystem and prevent BV, trich, yeast, and the vulvo-vaginal inflammations that can accompany these infections, eating more "probiotic" foods is key. A probiotic food is defined as a live microbial food supplement that beneficially affects the host animal by improving its intestinal microbial balance. In plain English, this refers to several fermented foods, including yogurt, kefir (a yogurtlike drink), certain edible yeasts, and dietary supplements derived from these foods. You can also buy commercially prepared *Lactobacillus acidophilus*, *Bifidobacterium bifidum*, and *Saccharomyces boulardii*.

It is also important to eat probiotic products when you're on antibiotic therapy for either BV or any STD (discussed in Chapter 10). Generally women suffering from recurrent yeast infections who eat eight ounces of *Lactobacillus*-containing yogurt a day for six months can usually eradicate yeast. Studies have also found that eating probiotic products decreased STD transmission in women on that diet.

If you want to purchase more probiotic products, here are some buying guidelines:

- Be sure the labels say "live, active cultures."
- Do not use products that have expired or do not list an expiration date.
- Avoid products that are not refrigerated.

### For Vulvodynia or Vulvular Vestibulitis

Many vulvodynia self-help groups now recommend a low-oxalate diet to help with symptoms. A low-oxalate cookbook is available from the Vulvar Pain Foundation, at www.vulvar painfoundation.org. A low-oxalate diet is a diet that reduces levels of oxalic acid in the urine. Increased levels can cause kidney stones. It is now believed that increased levels may also cause vulvar pain. Foods that are low in oxalate (0 to 2 mg per serving) include:

- apple juice
- avocado
- bacon
- bananas
- beef (lean)
- Bing cherries
- Brussels sprouts
- cabbage
- cauliflower
- cheese
- eggs
- grapefruit
- green grapes
- jellies
- lamb (lean)
- lemonade or limeade (without peel)
- melons

- milk
- mushrooms
- pork (lean)
- poultry
- preserves
- nectarines
- noodles
- oatmeal
- oils
- onions
- peas (fresh)
- plums
- radishes
- rice
- salad dressing
- seafood
- spaghetti
- white bread
- wine
- yogurt

# Flower Power

Taking regular baths can do wonders to control vaginal infections. Bathing or taking a sitz bath in one of the essential oils mentioned in Chapter 1 or 2 will control odor and help tone the reproductive organs. A natural remedy that may help relieve the symptoms of trich and other vaginal infections, including yeast, is a garlic suppository. Just take an ordinary peeled (but not pierced) garlic clove, wrap it in gauze, and insert it into the vagina for twelve hours; you may repeat every twelve hours as necessary. This is a harmless way to relieve the symptoms.

### More Herbal Yeast Busters
- caprylic acid and myocidin (fatty acids derived from oils that are excellent antifungal agents; two capsules three times a day will help fend off yeast infections)
- citrus seed extract
- biotin supplements
- black walnut hull

- cranberry juice (must be unsweetened), mixed with oatstraw tea (or oatstraw tea on its own)
- echinacea
- garlic
- goldenseal
- grapefruit seed extract
- tea-tree suppositories

# How to Move

Practice the daily maintenance stretches and postures discussed in Chapter 1. Some exercises can cause or aggravate vaginal infections. Avoid exercises that put direct pressure or a lot of friction on the vulva, such as bicycle riding and horseback riding. Instead, try lower-intensity exercises, such as walking. Always remove exercise clothing promptly and use a frozen gel pack wrapped in a towel to relieve any symptoms after exercise.

# PART II

# The Joy of Safety

# 7

# Preventing Sexually Transmitted Diseases (STDs)

THERE'S A DIFFERENCE between preventing sexually transmitted diseases and preventing pregnancy. Preventing STDs involves practicing safer sex and using prophylactic products, such as condoms. Preventing pregnancy (discussed in Chapter 8) does not necessarily mean preventing infection. Common sexual activities include vaginal intercourse, oral sex (fellatio and cunnilingus), deep kissing (French or wet kissing), mutual masturbation (or petting), masturbation, hugging, body rubbing, and massage. Sex toys (dildos, vibrators, flavored gels) are also part of normal sexual activity. This chapter discusses how to remain safe to avoid the spread of STDs.

## What Is Safer Sex?

Safer sex means that you are taking necessary precautions to prevent acquiring a sexually transmitted disease, such as chlamydia or HIV (see Chapter 11). Exchanging blood, semen, vaginal secretions, or breast milk with someone else can infect you with an STD. While few will go to all lengths to protect themselves, adopting a slowed-down sexual repertoire with partners you don't know very well can work wonders. Here's a list of what is safest (with the least safe listed last):

1. French kissing (bleeding gums can be dangerous, however)
2. Oral sex using a latex barrier (this involves covering a woman with a latex barrier, such as a dental dam, a latex condom or latex glove cut open, or nonmicrowavable plastic wrap, or performing oral sex on a man who wears a condom)

109

3. Genital stimulation using latex gloves instead of bare fingers
4. Sharing sex toys with a latex barrier
5. Genital stimulation with no latex barrier
6. Oral sex with no latex barrier
7. Sharing sex toys without a latex barrier
8. Vaginal intercourse with a condom
9. Anal intercourse with a condom (anal intercourse is high-risk behavior and is discussed at length in Chapter 9)
10. Unprotected vaginal intercourse
11. Unprotected anal intercourse

There are good romantic substitutes for sexual activity:

- *Hugging:* Go to different locations: hug in water, rain, moonlight, etc.
- *Full body massage:* Light some candles and use aromatherapy to enhance romance!
- *Shared masturbation:* This can be very erotic.
- *Grinding (or "outercourse"):* This is erotic rubbing while fully clothed.
- *Bathing or showering:* Taking a bath or shower together can be very arousing.
- *Sex toys:* Vibrators and dildos are very enjoyable. Use condoms on the sex toys to stay safe.
- *Dry kissing:* Kissing without using the tongue is safe. Use your tongue elsewhere—earlobes, toes, fingers—as long as there are no cuts, scratches, or sores.
- *Dancing:* Slow dance together in private or public.

## When Is Unprotected Sex Safe?

Presuming no other high-risk factors, if both you and your partner have been tested for HIV infection, are both negative, and are practicing mutual monogamy, then it is safe to resume normal sexual activity without condoms or other latex barriers, such as dental dams. However, if you're not planning to get pregnant, you'll need to use effective contraception anyway (discussed later in this chapter).

If you and your partner are mutually monogamous and have been together since before 1977, you don't have to be tested for HIV infection and can engage in normal sexual activity without condoms. (The year 1977 is considered to mark the beginning of the HIV epidemic in the United States.)

The problem, of course, is that partners lie about monogamy and may stray without your knowledge, or vice versa. It's common for unfaithful spouses to infect their monogamous partners. If you don't trust your partner, then don't have sex without using condoms. Use safer sex to "test" the boundaries of your relationship by getting to know each other better and uncovering common values, history, and so on. The outcome may prove beneficial for both of you. Seeking counseling may also be an option if you're not sure what to do.

# All About Condoms

Mechanical barriers that cover the penis have been used for centuries for protection against both pregnancy and infection, for decoration, and occasionally to produce penile or vaginal stimulation. Such practices can be traced to 1350 B.C., when Egyptian men wore decorative sheaths over their penises. The Italian anatomist Fallopius described the use of linen sheaths in 1564. Protective devices from animal intestines soon followed. There was an actual Dr. Condom (or Conton, according to some sources), who, as physician to King Charles II (1630–85), designed a condom for him. It was not until the eighteenth century, however, that penile sheaths were given the name condoms and became popular forms of "protection from venereal disease and numerous bastard offspring." Casanova (1725–98) was among the first to popularize the condom as a contraceptive, but he was also aware of the protective effect of condoms against sexually transmitted infections. When rubber latex was invented in the 1840s, condoms became mass-produced and were coined rubbers.

Ironically, the early condoms were sold primarily as prophylactics—in other words, as devices to protect against disease. They were available in brothels as well as drugstores, where they were known in slang terms as French letters or capotes. They were also sold in barbershops and other places men frequented. But the quality latex condoms sold today would not become available for several more decades.

## *Choosing and Using a Condom*

Millions of couples currently use condoms for protection against STDs and as a contraceptive. Condoms are the second most widely used reversible contraceptive in the United States after oral contraception. Condoms are available in all drugstores, and you don't need a prescription. There are dozens of brands and colors to choose from. Some are ribbed (enhancing stimulation for the woman), some aren't; some are lubricated, some aren't; some have built-in spermicide, some don't. Basically, as long as the box says "latex" and you check the expiration date on the box, your choice will be fine.

All condoms originally came in one size, and the assumption that one size fits all was challenged only when the United States began exporting condoms to Asian countries and found that they were too large for many Asian men (not to mention Asian American men). Most large international manufacturers now produce two basic sizes, Class I and Class II. In the United States some manufacturers offer the smaller-size condoms, promoting them as fitting "snugger for extra sensitivity" rather than indicating they are for men with smaller penises. The latest *Consumer Reports* study on condoms found that its readers preferred lubricated latex condoms with a reservoir tip. One study tracked 245 couples in which one partner was HIV positive and the other was not. Out of 123 of those couples who used condoms correctly and consistently, none of the healthy partners became infected, but out of the 122 couples who used condoms occasionally or did not use the condom correctly, 12 of the healthy partners became infected. Does this mean that religious use of condoms will prevent HIV infection? Not according to a similar Italian study. Here, out of 171 couples who used condoms correctly and consistently, 3 healthy partners became infected. As for the remaining 134 couples who were inconsistent condom users, 16 healthy partners became infected.

If you've never used a condom before, it does take some practice. The most fumbling comes from putting it on the wrong way, with the lubricated side touching the penis instead of the other way around. You might want to practice first on a shampoo bottle. (Don't use the practice condom for sex. Throw it out.) Following are tips on using a condom:

1. Make sure you keep a supply of condoms in your purse and near your bed (nightstand, decorative box beside your futon, under the bed in a shoebox, or wherever). The oldest excuse partners use for having unprotected sex is not wanting to get out of bed to get the condoms. This ensures that you don't have to!

2. As soon as the penis is erect, open the condom package carefully to avoid tearing the condom. Put the condom on before you insert the penis into the vagina. Either partner can put the condom on. If you're having anal sex, put on two condoms (anal sex is discussed in detail in Chapter 9).

3. Pinch the air from the tip of the condom to leave space for the semen. Air left in the condom will cause it to burst. Unroll it, lubricated side away from the penis, down to the base of the erect penis.

4. Wait until the vagina is lubricated. A dry vagina can cause the condom to fall off or break.

5. Avoid Vaseline and oil-based lubricant products, such as Crisco (which apparently is popular). Use a water-based lubricant, such as K-Y Jelly or Lubafax, to prevent

the condom from deteriorating. For additional protection, use a spermicide containing nonoxynol-9, a spermicidal condom, or a spermicidal foam (such as Delfen).

6. After your partner ejaculates, pull out the penis while it is still hard, holding the base of the condom firmly.

7. Remove the condom, being careful not to spill any semen.

8. Then check the condom for any tears. If it has torn or has come off inside the vagina, insert contraceptive foam or gel immediately. (Always keep contraceptive foam or gel on hand for this reason.)

9. Throw the condom away. Use it only once.

10. Don't store condoms anywhere near extreme temperatures; cars and wallets are bad places.

The best condoms to use share the following three qualities:

- They are latex.
- They are lubricated.
- They are large enough to fit your partner comfortably.

## *The Female Condom*

There is such a device as the female condom, which passed FDA approval in May 1993. The female condom (e.g., the Reality Female Condom) is a variation of the male condom, but instead of fitting over the penis, it lines the inside of the vagina. The disposable condom is made of polyurethane, which is thin but strong (40 percent stronger than the latex used in male condoms). It's also very resistant to rips and tears during use. Its design consists of a soft sheath that is open on one end and closed at the other. It has two soft flexible rings. The ring inside the closed end is used to insert the device and to hold it in place over the cervix. The other ring forms the open edge and remains outside the vagina after insertion. So in addition to lining the inside of the vagina, this condom covers your labia and the base of your partner's penis during intercourse, reducing skin-to-skin contact.

The female condom was originally invented in 1985 by a Danish husband-and-wife team (he is a gynecologist, she is a nurse), Erik and Bente Gregerson. Polyurethane was chosen as a material not only because of its strength and skinlike fit, but also because it is resistant to oils, which means it isn't damaged (unlike latex male condoms) by oil-based lubricants, such as petroleum jelly. It is also suitable for women allergic to latex and is less likely to cause vaginal infections. Polyurethane transmits heat between partners, which gives the material a more sensitive and natural feel. It may also allow more spontaneity since it can be inserted before sex, like a diaphragm. However, you don't need a plastic inserter to fit it, nor do you need a prescription or a fitting for one, and it's available over the counter at most drugstores. Like a male condom, it is intended for one-time use only.

This product is designed as both a safer sex tool as well as a contraceptive. Findings of a six-month study conducted by Family Health International and the Contraceptive Research and Development Program (CONRAD) were published in the December 1994 issue of the *American Journal of Public Health*. CONRAD concluded that the condom was as effective in preventing pregnancy as other barrier methods but had the added advantage of protecting women from STDs. Among the 262 women who took part in the study and used the condom correctly and consistently every time they had sex, the failure rate was 2.6 percent. Of those who didn't use the condom correctly, the failure rate was 12.4 percent—roughly the same failure rate cited for the diaphragm and cervical cap (see Chapter 8).

And what do female condom users have to say? Eighty percent of the women from the CONRAD study said they liked using it, and two-thirds of women in a New York City acceptability study said they liked it, too. Meanwhile, 73 percent of the New York City study participants said they preferred the female condom to the male condom.

Although there are several forms of contraception already available to women, it's important for women to be able to protect themselves from STDs during intercourse without having to rely on male compliance. The female condom is an ideal option if you're looking for both a prophylactic and a barrier method. However, as with any condom, it is critical that you use it consistently and correctly every time you have intercourse in order for it to work. It should never be used when your male partner is wearing a condom; neither will work properly because of the friction this condom combo will generate. Here are the rules, compiled from the Reality instruction pamphlets:

- Never use the female condom if your partner is wearing his own.
- Use more lubricant if the condom rides the penis, the outer ring is pushed inside, the condom is noisy during sex, you feel the condom has slipped out of place, or the condom comes out of the vagina during use.
- Remove the female condom if it rips or tears during insertion or use, the outer ring is pushed inside the pouch, the condom bunches up inside the vagina, or you have sex again.

## *Female Condom Versus Male Condom*

If you're unsure about which condom to use, here's the overall benefit package:

- The female condom can be inserted before you have sex to allow not just for spontaneity but for intercourse before the penis is fully erect.
- You're more "covered" with the female condom, which offers protection from the gamut of STDs ranging from AIDS to trichomoniasis.
- The polyurethane female condom is stronger than the male latex condom.

A second female condom has been developed, known as the Janesway biodegradable female condom. This works as a cotton panty with a latex center. The panty serves as a holder for the latex portion that covers the entire genital area and extends into the vagina.

## *An HIV Repellent?*

Prophylactic foam may soon be available to women. The World Health Organization has recently launched a new global research strategy to develop a safe antimicrobial agent (called a microbicide) capable of inactivating HIV in a woman's vagina. The term *microbial* means "hodgepodge of bacterial and viral infections." If this effort proves successful, you will be able to insert a foam or gel, similar to spermicide, which would not only render HIV inactive but would also prevent HIV from attaching itself to your vaginal walls.

Although certain spermicides have been found to destroy HIV in a test tube and can already protect you from diseases such as gonorrhea and chlamydia, there is still not enough evidence that these spermicides can prevent HIV in actual intercourse. In fact, some studies suggest that spermicides currently on the market may even damage your vaginal walls, making HIV transmission even easier. Therefore, the challenge is to develop a microbicide not only strong enough to kill HIV within the vagina but mild enough so that it will not harm the vaginal walls or the vaginal ecosystem or impair fertility in any way.

# If Your Partner Is a Woman

For too long, women who have sex with other women have been considered at low risk of contracting sexually transmitted diseases. Studies show that roughly 13 percent of women who have exclusively female partners contract STDs. Women can pass infections to one another, especially since many women who have female partners also have had male partners in their past. Safer sex for women involves:

- using a latex barrier or Saran wrap when performing oral sex on another woman
- using sex toys with barriers

# What to Eat

If you're sexually active, drink at least three eight-ounce glasses of water daily to make sure that you urinate frequently, rather than retain urine, which can predispose you to urinary tract infections. Drinking a glass of cranberry juice every day can also help prevent urinary tract infections.

Following a varied, nutritious diet is also important (see Chapter 1), as well as a diet that has probiotic products to prevent vaginal infections, such as yeast (see Chapter 6).

# Flower Power

Bathe after intercourse in one of the essential oils known to tone the female system (see Chapters 1 and 2). Lavender and ylang-ylang are especially good. Bathing will help to clean the vagina without the need for douching.

# How to Move

Practice the exercises discussed in Chapter 1 for overall health maintenance and well-being.

# 8

# Preventing Pregnancy

CURRENTLY, ONE IN eight girls aged fifteen to nineteen gets pregnant each year—78 percent of these pregnancies are unintended. Even today, with all the contraception education available, 36 percent of teenaged girls report they do not use contraception. Preventing pregnancy is still a high priority!

The first contraceptive method, coitus interruptus (pulling out), is referenced in Genesis 38:9. But the first "prescription" for a contraceptive product dates back to 1500 B.C., when a contraceptive tampon is discussed in Ebers Papyrus, a compendium of medical practices. This product was a medicated lint tampon designed "to cause that a woman should cease to conceive for one, two, or three years. Acacia and dates are finely ground with a hint of honey; seed wood is moistened therewith and placed in her vulva." We know today that acacia ferments into lactic acid, a substance still recognized as a spermicide. This chapter outlines all the contraceptive methods available as of this writing. Most of these methods do not protect against STDs and therefore would need to be combined with condoms (see Chapter 7). Many of these methods will be used to treat other hormonal problems, as a means of cycle control. The oral contraceptive is also considered to offer protection against ovarian cancer (see Chapter 4).

## Hormonal Contraception

With the exception of oral contraceptives, which are discussed separately beginning on page 121, there are two other kinds of hormonal contraception available: Depo-Provera and the contraceptive patch, both of which are designed to be used by women. There are still no hormonal contraceptives for men, even though this is the twenty-first century! A third kind of hormonal contraception—the Norplant contraceptive implant—was removed from the marketplace in 2002 due to concerns over the implant procedure and debates over its safety. Pharmaceutical companies are currently developing alternative hormonal implant products.

## Depo-Provera

Millions of women worldwide use Depo-Provera for contraception. Depo-Provera is an injection that works as a time-release progesterone. One injection of Depo-Provera in the muscle of the arm or buttocks protects you against pregnancy for three months. The cost of injection is about $140 annually. The FDA approved Depo-Provera in October 1992, and the contraceptive is manufactured by the Upjohn Company. The active ingredient in Depo-Provera is a synthetic progestin hormone, which is released into the bloodstream. The hormone prevents ovulation and also causes the mucus of the cervix to thicken, making it more difficult for sperm to reach the egg. In addition, the lining of the uterus becomes thinner, making it less receptive to an egg's implanting in it. Depo-Provera is rated as 99 percent effective in preventing pregnancy. The amount of Depo-Provera in the bloodstream is at the highest level just after injection. Over time the level drops, and after three months the level may no longer offer enough protection. It's important to be on time for your next injection and to use a backup method, such as condoms, in the last week before you're due for another shot. If the time between injections is more than fourteen weeks, you should request a pregnancy test before you get your next injection. You can't use Depo-Provera if you either are pregnant or suspect you're pregnant.

You'll need to get your first injection within five days after your period starts. Depo-Provera is effective immediately after the injection. If you have just had a baby and want to wait a while before having your next child, you should get your shot within five days after giving birth if you're not breast-feeding. Otherwise, you'll need to wait six weeks after delivery. If you decide that you want to get pregnant, don't go back for another injection.

Depo-Provera takes at least three months before you can conceive again. Depo-Provera does not accumulate in the body, so fertility may not be affected by the number of injections you have received but may be affected by your age or weight. Until the dosage can be perfected for each individual woman, immediate fertility won't be possible.

### What Are the Side Effects?

The most common side effects of Depo-Provera are irregular periods; there are more days of light bleeding or spotting and of amenorrhea than heavy bleeding. Women also report headache, acne, nausea, weight gain, breast pain, nervousness, dermatitis, change in appetite,

#### Table 8.1   Estrogen-Related Side Effects

| Caused by Too Much | Caused by Too Little |
|---|---|
| splotchy face | bleeding/spotting days 1–9 |
| chronic nasal congestion | continuous bleeding/spotting |
| flulike symptoms | flow decrease |
| hay fever/allergies | pelvic relaxation symptoms |
| urinary tract infections | vaginitis atrophic |
| bloating | |
| dizziness | |
| edema (water retention) | |
| headaches | |
| irritability | |
| leg cramps | |
| nausea/vomiting | |
| vision changes | |
| weight gain | |
| cervical changes | |
| breast cysts | |
| dysmenorrhea (painful periods) | |
| heavy flow and clotting | |
| increase in breast size | |
| excessive vaginal discharge | |
| uterine enlargement | |
| uterine fibroid growth | |
| capillary fragility | |
| blood clots and related disorders | |
| spidery veins on the chest area | |

ovarian enlargement, and abnormal hair growth or loss. These are classic side effects (see Tables 8.1 and 8.2), which are common to hormonal contraceptives in general. The incidence of side effects appears to decrease over time as the progestin dosage levels off. Reports that Depo-Provera can interfere with calcium levels are a concern to health care providers. Women who use this contraceptive need to build calcium reserves for the future.

Weight gain is particularly undesirable; women tend to gain an average of 5.4 pounds during the first year, rising to 13.8 pounds after four years of use. The progestin has also been shown to increase insulin resistance in women, predisposing them to diabetes.

### Table 8.2  Progestin-Related Side Effects

| Caused by Too Much | Caused by Too Little |
|---|---|
| appetite increase | bleeding/spotting days 10–21 |
| depression | delayed withdrawal bleeding |
| fatigue | dysmenorrhea |
| hypoglycemia symptoms | heavy flow and clots |
| weight gain | bloating* |
| hypertension | dizziness* |
| leg veins dilated | edema* |
| cervicitis | headache* |
| flow length decrease | irritability* |
| yeast infections | leg cramps* |
| acne** | nausea/vomiting* |
| jaundice** | vision changes* |
| hirsutism** | weight gain* |
| libido increase** | amenorrhea |
| libido decrease | |
| oily skin and scalp** | |
| rash and pruritus** | |
| edema** | |

Key: * = caused by excess estrogen; ** = caused by excess androgen

## Contraceptive Patch

A new transdermal contraceptive patch (Ortho Evra/Evra), which offers similar protection to a combination oral contraceptive, has been approved. When you wear this patch, the hormones norelgestromin and ethinyl seep through the skin into the bloodstream. Norelgestromin is the primary active metabolite of norgestimate, the progestin used in Tricyclen, a popular low-dose combination oral contraceptive. You wear the patch for one week and apply a new patch on the same day of the week for the next two consecutive weeks, for a total of twenty-one days. You then go the fourth week patch-free; you'll get your period during that week. It's similar to the cycle on oral contraceptives. You wear only one patch at a time, on the buttocks, abdomen, upper torso (front or back, excluding the breasts), or upper outer arm. You can start the patch on a Sunday or simply within the first twenty-four hours after your period starts. Whatever your start day is will remain your start day for new patches. The side effects are exactly the same as they are for oral contraceptives (see further on).

# Oral Contraceptives (OCs)

Oral contraception is about four thousand years old. There is a long history of women orally consuming a wide concoction of "potions" and toxins to prevent pregnancy. Women in China drank mercury to prevent conception. Women in India swallowed carrot seeds as a "morning after" contraceptive in the 1500s. Dried beaver testicle was brewed in a strong alcoholic solution and drunk by women in the backwoods of northern New Brunswick.

Today's modern oral contraceptive pills were developed in the 1930s from the Mexican plant barbasco root, which led to the discovery of steroids, the "flour" of today's oral contraceptives (OCs).

OCs have changed since 1960, when they were first introduced. Back then, early pills contained about 10 mg progestin (norethynodrel) and 100 to 175 micrograms (mcg) estrogen (mestranol)—significantly higher levels of the equivalent estrogens and progestins than found in today's Pill. By the 1970s OCs contained 50 mcg or less of estrogen (ethinyl estradiol). The progestin-only mini-Pill (containing no estrogen) had also been developed.

To reduce the side effects of the pills, such as nausea, headache, and breast tenderness, the estrogen levels were reduced from 50 to 35, to 30, to 20, and newer progestins were reduced as well. The 1980s saw the creation of triphasic pills, which contained increasing amounts of progestin (0.50, 0.75, 1.25 mg levonorgestrel) and phased amounts of estrogen (30, 40, 30 mcg ethinyl estradiol) throughout the cycle (known as triphasic). Older pills were monophasic, producing the same dose of estrogen throughout the cycle. Most high-dose pills (those that contained more than 50 mcg estrogen) were off the market by the late 1980s.

In the late 1990s a new class of OCs hit the market. These contained phased estrogen in low doses, with a low, constant dose of progestin (1 mg norethindrone acetate). Now there are a whole variety of very low-dose OCs, such as Organon's Desogen and Ortho-McNeil's Ortho-Cept, and new low-dose monophasic combination OCs containing 20 mcg estrogen (ethinyl estradiol), such as Pfizer's Loestrin, Wyeth's Alesse, and Berlex Laboratories' Levlite.

OCs work by preventing ovulation and causing the cervical mucus to thicken. It's almost exactly the same as Depo-Provera (which is modeled after OCs), except that with combination OCs, the estrogen causes the uterine lining to thicken, which means that it needs to shed. The difference between combination OCs and the new timed-release hormonal contraceptives is that your periods are induced on OCs. All OCs come in a packet or case containing either a twenty-one-day or twenty-eight-day supply of pills. For the twenty-eight-day pack, the last week of your supply contains only sugar pills; the twenty-one-day supply requires a little more thought. You'll need to remember to start your next pack seven days later. Because you're off the synthetic hormones for seven days, you will get a period, known in clinical-speak as withdrawal bleeding. These periods are incredibly punctual and usually come on exactly the same day at the same time, every month. You'll have less cramping and a briefer, lighter flow. You need to take the pills at exactly the same time every day in order to keep the hormone levels in your body consistent. Some experts do not agree with "taking a break" from the Pill when a woman has her period. A new way to take the Pill nonstop is with a monophasic pill. You should discuss this option and its related health risks with your doctor.

The induced period is what makes OCs so popular. Women who suffer from irregular cycles, painful periods, PMS, or heavy flows may benefit from OCs, as long as they are using them to prevent pregnancy and not STDs. OCs are also known to guard against fibrocystic breast disease, benign ovarian cysts, and pelvic inflammatory disease (PID; discussed in Chapter 10).

The mini-Pill has exactly the same advantages and disadvantages as Depo-Provera because it is the same thing, except it is taken orally. Mini-Pill users will therefore experience irregular menstrual cycles. But these pills are an option for smokers, older women, women who are breast-feeding, and other women for whom traditional pills are a risk. Unless you smoke, are over thirty-five, or have high blood pressure, a heart condition, a personal history of breast cancer, or certain cancers of the reproductive organs, you'll be prescribed one of the low-dose combination pills. Then, if you suffer from too many adverse side effects, your doctor will put you on the mini-Pill.

## The New Rules: From Menarche to Menopause

If you don't smoke and are healthy, you can be on a combination OC from the time of your first period (called menarche) right up until menopause. That's because there are a number of fringe health benefits to OCs, known by clinicians as noncontraceptive benefits. Because OCs prevent ovulation, they will also prevent diseases associated with the ovaries, such as ovarian cancer, ovarian cysts, and endometrial cancer. In fact, if you have no children or no plans to get pregnant and breast-feed, staying on an OC will have the same therapeutic effects on your ovaries as pregnancy and breast-feeding because it will give your ovaries a break. The following are considered clear, undisputed benefits of OCs (note that low-dose OCs offer the same benefits as higher-dose OCs):

- reduced incidence of endometrial cancer and ovarian cancer (see Chapter 4; in women who come from high-risk families, OCs reduced the risk by as much as four times)
- reduced likelihood of developing fibrocystic breast condition
- reduced likelihood of developing ovarian cysts
- lighter periods and more regular cycles, which reduces the chance of developing iron deficiency anemia
- reduced menstrual cramps and PMS

- improvement of androgen-related side effects, such as unwanted facial hair (see Table 8.2)
- improved cholesterol levels (a benefit of some brands)
- protection against colorectal cancer (several studies suggest that OC use lowers the risk of colon cancer, the third leading "killer cancer" in women)
- reduced occurrence of rheumatoid arthritis
- reduced risk of ectopic pregnancy
- decreased risk of PID (see Chapter 10)
- improvement of acne
- preservation of bone mass

At age fifty, you can begin to go off your OC at annual or biannual intervals to see if you're in menopause.

## What Are the Side Effects and Risks of Combination OCs?

Combination OCs now have far less estrogen or progestin than did those of the 1960s and 1970s; women today are exposed to about one-twenty-fifth of the estrogen that they were previously exposed to. However, the side effects of estrogen in OCs are still considerable: nausea, breast tenderness, swelling, increased breast size (which some women enjoy), weight gain, vaginal discharge, headaches, and blood clots. Serious risks include cardiovascular problems, which increase the chances of heart attacks and strokes. A careful family history and personal medical history should be taken by the person prescribing OCs to you. The side effects caused by the progesterone in OCs are increased appetite and weight gain, depression, fatigue, decreased sex drive, acne and oily skin, decreased carbohydrate tolerance, increased risk for diabetes, and increased cholesterol levels. The combination of both estrogen and progesterone can cause headaches, high blood pressure, heart problems, and cervical dysplasia. Both triphasic and monophasic OCs can cause breakthrough bleeding (bleeding between periods). Persistent breakthrough bleeding can usually be treated with supplemental estrogen without stopping the oral contraceptive.

We've all read the long list of risks associated with combination OCs. In general, if you are under thirty-five, don't smoke, and don't have any chronic medical illnesses, then your risk of suffering from any of the "fine print" risks listed on your OC package is low. That being said, here is the fine print:

Blood clots (a.k.a. venous thromboembolisms) are the most common serious risk linked to OCs. Clots can form in the brain and heart, which translates into heart attacks and strokes. Smokers on OCs are more likely to have a heart attack than are non-Pill users who smoke. Because OCs increase the chance of having a heart attack, women on the Pill who don't smoke are more likely to develop heart disease than are non-OC users who don't smoke.

They are also more likely to have a stroke than non-OC users. Women on OCs are also more likely to rupture a blood vessel in the brain than are non-OC users and are more likely to develop a blood clot in the leg or arm, which can mean amputation. They are more likely to suffer a pulmonary embolus, and the risk of blood clots in the lungs is higher. A woman planning to have major surgery will need to discontinue taking OCs about six weeks prior to the surgery.

Studies looking at the newest formulations of OCs found that cardiovascular risks in nonsmokers were far less than with older formulations, and experts today conclude that risk of heart attack in the newest formulations is very small. It's now believed that OCs do not increase the risk of heart attack for healthy nonsmokers who do not have other risk factors for heart disease.

## Will I Get a Blood Clot?

Serious cardiovascular problems linked to OCs are rare in women placed on low-dose pills. Nevertheless, it's important to make sure that you're not already at risk for blood clots. If you have a history of thrombophlebitis, pulmonary emboli, or other cardiovascular diseases, you should not be encouraged to take OCs. Your risk of blood clots also increases if any of the following apply to you:

- you smoke
- you don't exercise
- you are overweight
- you are over fifty
- you are hypertensive or diabetic
- you have high cholesterol

## Breast Cancer Risk

If you are under thirty-five, have no family or personal history of breast cancer, and are not considered at risk for breast cancer due to any other significant factor, OCs will most likely not increase your risk of breast cancer. That's because the combination pills used these days are very low-dose pills. Studies from the 1970s and early 1980s may also not apply to women today because they studied the effects of much higher-dose pills than what women are on now.

That said, the official warnings in your Pill packets will tell you that if you have a mother or sister with a history of breast cancer, a pill containing estrogen can put you at greater risk for developing breast cancer prior to menopause. The warnings will also tell you that if you've been on OCs longer than eight years and/or began them early, you are considered to be statistically more at risk for breast cancer. One U.S. study found that women under thirty-five who used an estrogen-containing pill for more than ten years increased their risk of breast cancer by about 70 percent compared to women who never took OCs. There are also studies that showed no difference between women on the Pill for ten years compared to non-Pill users, as well as studies that showed a decreased risk in Pill users after the age of forty-five (which is potentially very good news).

Since less than 2 percent of all breast cancers are diagnosed in women under thirty-five anyway, the study showing an increased risk really shouldn't rattle you all that much because, in the final analysis, you're looking at a very small number. Instead of one in five hundred women developing breast cancer before thirty-five, that statistic increases it to one in three hundred.

At any rate, if you're concerned about breast cancer and OCs, you may want to ask your doctor about the progestin-only pill (POP), also called the mini-Pill. For the record, women are more at risk for blood clots on OCs than they are for breast cancer, and the risk of unwanted pregnancy before the age of twenty should also be weighed.

Age, of course, is also a factor. Since breast cancer incidence increases with age, using OCs at an older age can also increase your risk. But just like hormone replacement therapy, we don't know whether the increase is only age related or whether OCs truly contribute to the increase. Regardless, you'll still get protection from ovarian and endometrial cancer.

## Estrogen Versus Progestin Side Effects

Many of the side effects of OCs are dose related. In other words, if you go on a lower-dose OC, your side effects will likely disappear. In some cases, you may even require a slightly higher-dose OC—particularly if you have a history of heavy uterine bleeding. Tables 8.1 and 8.2 will help you sort out whether your side effects are caused by too high a dose of estrogen or too high a dose of progestin, the synthetic progesterone that's in combination OCs. Too much progestin is what creates those androgenic side effects, which are basically appearance related (referred to sometimes as nuisance side effects): weight gain, acne, facial hair. The older progestins can cause a complex chemical reaction in the body that basically makes more testosterone available, causing these side effects. In fact, most women who discontinue their OC use will do so because of the androgenic side effects (understandably). The good news is that if you're experiencing androgenic side effects, it's very easy to fix! Simply request a low-dose, triphasic OC with a low-activity selective progestin, which, studies show, does make a difference in reducing side effects.

So when your doctor is prescribing an OC for you, you should ask: what is the estrogen dose? Anything above 30 to 35 mg is considered high. The bottom line is that you should be able to walk out of your doctor's office with the lowest-dose OC possible to prevent pregnancy or, as I like to say, ALAP (as low as possible). In fact, ask your doctor to show you all the OC samples available, and then you play a role in selecting the one you want. For example, the same OC may be available in two different packaging formats; some are more discreet than others.

### Different Physiques Need Different OCs

If you have tender breasts, heavy periods, and clots, request a low-estrogen, full-progestin OC. This is the type of OC that will bring your cycles under control, as discussed in Chapter 2.

If you tend to have acne, oily skin, and unwanted hair (other than underarm and leg hair) and you suffer from PMS and mood swings, request a low-progestin OC.

If you're not getting your period with your OC, this is a sign you need a low-progestin or new-progestin OC.

If you have been unable to tolerate a combination OC, you may want to request an extremely low-dose OC called Minestrin (this delivers 20 mg estrogen).

Although migraine sufferers should stay away from OCs, it's important to note that the side effects vary. In fact, about 33 percent of women on an OC will notice an improvement in migraine headaches; 33 percent will notice no change at all; while another 33 percent will notice that their migraines get worse, which means that the OC is not a good choice.

If you're diabetic, stay on top of your blood sugar levels. OCs can alter your insulin requirements because the progestins used in combination OCs can decrease glucose tolerance and increase insulin resistance.

And finally, if you have high blood pressure and do decide to go on an OC, have your blood pressure checked every three months during your first year on the OC.

Obviously, all these risks are scary. That's why when you begin using OCs, initially you may be given only a three-month supply. Then, if you do suffer any serious or unpleasant side effects, your dose can be reevaluated and your doctor may suggest either the mini-Pill or another form of birth control altogether. If you've been using OCs for more than three months and you don't suffer any serious side effects, you probably never will, but you still have the health risks just described to contend with. When you decide to get pregnant, it takes between three and six months for your menstrual cycle to return to normal. (See Chapter 2 for details on menstrual cycles after using OCs.) Only 1 percent of OC users suffer from infertility. Depending on what you read, some sources will say the risks are greater or less than others, and these statistics vary from country to country and year to year.

Stay away from OCs if you have a history of any of the following:

- blood clots in the legs or eyes
- cardiovascular problems
- heart disease or coronary heart disease

- breast cancer
- liver tumors
- abnormal vaginal bleeding
- migraine headaches
- high blood pressure
- diabetes
- active gallbladder disease
- sickle cell disease
- any major injury to your leg(s) that required a cast (check with your doctor)
- epilepsy (use with caution)
- planned elective surgery within a month (use with caution)

Many doctors feel that this list should be revised to reflect the much lower dose OCs now available.

## Spotting and Bleeding

Spotting is when you notice a slight pink discharge between periods and need to use one pad or tampon per day. This usually stops after a few days, but it is nothing to worry about. Your body is simply adjusting to the hormone content of your OC, which is still effective. If your spotting persists throughout the cycle, it's a sign that you may be on the wrong dose of progestin. Your doctor will simply prescribe another brand if this is the case.

Bleeding while you're on an OC is called breakthrough bleeding (BTB) and is somewhat heavier than spotting, but just as normal. In this case, you may need to use more than a pad or tampon per day. You may experience it for a few days in the first three months at a certain point in your cycle. BTB disappears after about three months. Again, if it persists, talk to your doctor about possibly switching to another brand of OC.

It also makes a difference when in your cycle you're experiencing spotting or bleeding. If your episodes occur at the beginning of your cycle, you probably need more estrogen and less progestin; if the episodes occur at the end of your cycle, you need a stronger progestin.

If you have unprotected sex before or after you stop taking your OC, sudden episodes of BTB or spotting can be a sign that you have chlamydia. Get screened for this. Tetracycline will treat the problem.

Most doctors will probably tell you to wait three months after taking your OC to see if the spotting or bleeding resolves on its own. Of course, if you missed pills or have had vomiting or diarrhea, this can be a factor, too. If the spotting and bleeding persist after three months, your doctor will probably switch you to another brand and in some cases may give you estrogen supplements.

Some doctors are in the habit of telling their patients to take two pills a day until the bleeding stops. This is bad medicine and will put you more at risk for estrogen side effects! Switch doctors before you switch OCs if this is the advice.

## *How to Use Combination OCs*

Following is a set of guidelines for using OCs:

1. There are several ways to start taking your OC; use the method your doctor suggests or the method suggested in the instruction booklet that comes with your OC.

   *Method A:* Start your first pack of pills on the first day of bleeding, when you get your period.

   *Method B:* Start your first pack of pills on the first Sunday after your period begins.

   *Method C:* Start your first pack of pills on the fifth day of your cycle or the fifth day after your period starts.

   *Method D:* Start your pill today if there is absolutely no chance that you could be pregnant.

2. For the first month, use a backup method of birth control. OCs don't take full effect until the second month. Furthermore, use your backup method if you run out of pills, forget to take one, or experience danger signals (see item 9) and, of course, to protect yourself against STDs.

3. Read the pamphlet that comes with your pills. Each pamphlet is FDA approved and tells you about warning signs and risks of your particular brand.

4. If you're on a twenty-eight-day pack, swallow one pill a day until you finish the pack, and then start a new pack immediately. If you're on a twenty-one-day pack, swallow one pill a day until you finish the pack. Wait one week and then start a new pack. You will always start your new pack on the same day of the week every month.

5. Take your pills at the same time every day to keep the hormone levels in your body stable. It doesn't matter what time of day you take them.

6. Check your pack of pills each morning to make sure you took one the day before.

7. If you have bleeding between periods, it probably means you're not taking your pills at the same time every day. If you are taking them at the same time every day and you still have bleeding, see your doctor. Spotting is not serious and will probably go away after your system is accustomed to the OC. If it doesn't go away, the bleeding can be stopped with supplemental estrogen.

8. If you get sick and have either diarrhea or vomiting for several days in a row, use a backup method. You might have expelled the pills before they had a chance to work.

9. To remember the danger signals of OCs, remember the word *ACHES*: Abdominal pain, Chest pain, Headaches, Eye problems, and Severe leg pain are signs to watch out for. Stop taking the pills if you experience any of these symptoms.

Finally, it's important to remember that periods can be scanty when taking combination OCs. Even if your blood is brown and you just spot slightly, this is considered a period.

## When You Forget to Take a Pill

If you forget to take one pill, take it as soon as you remember. Take your next pill at the same time you would regularly take it, even though it may mean taking two pills on the same day. Pregnancy is highly unlikely in this case, but use a backup method of birth control until you finish the pack.

## When You Miss Two Pills in a Row

The more pills you miss, the greater the risk of unwanted pregnancy. The risk also varies depending on when in the cycle you forgot to take your pills. So you must use a backup method of birth control in this scenario, too.

If you forget to take two pills in a row in the first two weeks, take two pills the day you remember and two pills the next day as well. Then take one pill a day until you finish the pack.

If you forget to take two pills in a row in the third week of your cycle, you'll need to adjust your pill schedule depending on the start day. If you're on a Sunday start method, take one pill a day until Sunday. On Sunday discard the rest of the pack and start a new pack. If you're on a day 1 start or a day 5 start, discard the rest of the pack and start a new pack immediately. You might miss your period this month, which is common. But if you miss two periods in a row, get a pregnancy test.

If you miss your two pills in the fourth week (if you're on a twenty-eight-day pack), don't worry about it. They're just sugar pills anyway. Throw out the pack and just start a new one on your regular start day.

If you're on a twenty-eight-day pack, even if you've missed no pills, begin your next pack immediately on the same day of the week that you started your last pack, whether you're having your period or not. If you've missed three or more pills in a row, discard the pack. Use your backup method, and start a new pack the following Sunday, even if you're bleeding.

## Common Questions About OCs

**Q:** *If I'm in a monogamous relationship, when do I need to use a backup method of birth control?*

**A:** As long as you're taking your pills correctly, your chances of getting pregnant are practically zero. You'll need a backup method of birth control if you miss a pill, vomit, have diarrhea, or are taking antibiotics, oral antifungal medications, or other medications that could interfere with your OC's effectiveness.

**Q:** *Exactly how much weight can I expect to gain?*

**A:** The newer OCs on the market are designed to minimize appearance-related side effects, such as weight gain. The latest studies show that women who do gain weight tend to gain less than three pounds. Of course, your lifestyle habits will affect your weight, too.

**Q:** *If I don't plan to get pregnant, when should I take a break?*

**A:** Again, so long as you're on a newer, low-dose OC, you can stay on the pill right up until menopause if you're healthy and you don't smoke. When you reach fifty, your doctor may decide to pull you off your OC to determine if you're in menopause. That means you simply won't get your period after being off the OC. Or your doctor can also check your follicle-stimulating hormone (FSH) levels; if they're high, you're in menopause. At that point, you'll probably need to discuss hormone replacement therapy (see Chapter 21).

**Q:** *What are my OC options if I smoke?*

**A:** Technically, if you're under thirty-five and you smoke, you can still take a combination OC, but you're at greater risk for blood clots, which could lead to a stroke. If you're over thirty-five and you smoke, you should not be on a combination OC, but you may be able to take the progestin-only pill (mini-Pill); that will depend on other health risks you have.

**Q:** *What if I want to get pregnant in a few years?*

**A:** OCs do not interfere with future fertility. When you're ready to get pregnant, finish your pack and wait for at least one natural period before you try to conceive. Use a backup method of birth control while you're waiting.

Your fertility can be affected, however, if you've been having unprotected sex while on your OC and contracted certain STDs, such as chlamydia and gonorrhea.

**Q:** *Is there a safe OC I can use if I'm breast-feeding?*

**A:** The mini-Pill is your best bet because it does not contain estrogen, which may not harm your baby but may dry up your milk. You can start the mini-Pill before your periods return. When planning for another baby, simply go off the mini-Pill and wait for one natural period prior to conceiving.

Many doctors will tell you that the low-dose combination OCs are perfectly safe during breast-feeding; however, you can't change biology. Estrogen can inhibit the hormone prolactin, and vice versa. So even a small amount of estrogen could have an effect on your milk.

**Q:** *Am I more or less likely to get an STD while on an OC?*

**A:** Much more likely if you're having unprotected sex. Because OCs change the consistency of your cervical mucus, some experts believe that this may predispose OC users to certain STDs, such as gonorrhea or chlamydia. Other experts believe that the altered cervical mucus should protect you from STDs because it thickens and becomes more "hostile," and they blame higher STD rates on the theory that OC users have more unprotected sex more often.

## A Word About the Mini-Pill

Follow the same instructions just given for the Pill. You will not be getting regular periods, however, so just keep track of when you do get them. If you go for more than forty-five days without a period, go to your doctor for a pregnancy test, just in case. You'll also need to take your pill religiously at the same time each day. If you're even three hours off, you'll need a backup method of birth control for the next forty-eight hours.

## Oral Contraception for Men

It's astounding, when one considers the progress of medical science and genetic technology, that there still is no oral contraceptive for men. The problem with developing this product is that efforts have been focused on reducing sperm production by manipulating hormone levels. This, however, interferes with the male sex drive and causes female-related side effects, such as the development of breasts.

Gonadotropin-releasing hormone analogs, testosterone, and progestins, alone and in various combinations, have all been studied. As of this writing, a male pill is still several years away from coming to market.

# Emergency Contraception Pills (ECPs)

If you have had sex without using any birth control method, have been sexually assaulted, or have discovered during or after sex that your own method failed (if the condom broke, for example), there is a way to prevent pregnancy using what's known internationally as an emergency contraceptive pill (ECP), which in lay terms is called the morning after pill. Clinical circles refer to this method as postcoital contraception. Recent public health campaigns throughout the world have called upon birth control educators like myself to refrain from using the term *morning after pill* because it is misleading. The term implies that this form of birth control can be used all the time (which it cannot) and that it should be taken only in the morning (which is not true).

## *What Are ECPs?*

In 1974 Canadian gynecologist Albert Yuzpe invented postcoital contraception by prescribing two tablets containing high doses of estrogen and progestin. The first dose was administered within seventy-two hours of unprotected intercourse, followed by a second dose twelve hours later. The Yuzpe regimen was shown to prevent 75 percent of possible pregnancies.

ECP involves taking two pills at once of a higher-than-usual dose of ordinary combination OCs (which contain both estrogen and progestin, or specifically 100 mg ethinyl estradiol and 500 mg norgestrel) within seventy-two hours after unprotected sex. That means if you had sex on a Friday night, you can wait until Monday to take your first two pills. You then wait twelve hours and take two more pills. Experts recommend taking ECPs with an antinausea drug such as Gravol since a sudden hormone increase in your system commonly causes nausea and vomiting. Some women experience breast tenderness as well. You should get your period within ten to twenty-one days of taking ECPs, and your cycle will return to normal thereafter.

Although public health counselors will tell you that ECPs should be taken as soon as possible within the seventy-two-hour window, studies so far have found no significant differences in failure rates of the ECP when it's taken twenty-four, forty-eight, or seventy-two hours after unprotected sex. The approximate 2 percent failure rate is a little above that of a regular OC, but it's still far more reliable than waiting it out. By the time this book is published, there may be specially packaged emergency contraception pills to make the process easier.

ECPs work no differently than regular OCs: they thicken your cervical mucus, making it hostile to sperm; they alter your uterine environment, making it hostile to sperm as well; and they thin out your endometrial lining, making it very difficult for a fertilized egg to implant.

ECPs are not the same thing as chemical abortion, discussed in Chapter 12. They prevent conception instead of inducing miscarriage. This is a big difference, so don't let anybody tell you that you're aborting if you take an ECP.

People confuse ECPs with abortion pills because data from clinical trials suggest that using mifepristone (RU 486) as emergency contraception may be an even more effective way to prevent pregnancy after unprotected sex. These trial results show, simply, that there are fewer side effects with mifepristone than with the current high-dose OC method. Clinical trials have also investigated danazol (discussed in Chapter 13) as a possible ECP. For the moment, only high-dose OCs are prescribed for emergency contraception in North America.

There is another form of emergency contraception touted by some gynecologists: using OCs as suppositories. In this case, a high-dose estrogen-containing OC is placed inside the vagina like a tampon. It apparently stays in place and is absorbed. This reduces the side effects some women experience with the ECP.

## Where to Get ECPs

In September 1998 the FDA approved Preven, an emergency contraception kit. It consists of four birth control pills (each containing 0.05 mg ethinyl estradiol and 0.25 mg levonorgestrel), a home pregnancy test, and a detailed patient information booklet. The booklet instructs you to take the pregnancy test first. If the results are negative, you're then instructed to take two pills within seventy-two hours of unprotected intercourse and the remaining two pills twelve hours after the first two. If the test is positive, you're advised to contact your doctor for more information.

In July 1999 the FDA approved Plan B, a progestin-only ECP kit consisting of two 0.75-mg tablets of levonorgestrel to be taken twelve hours apart, the first one within seventy-two hours of unprotected intercourse. Pilot studies throughout the United States and Canada have made ECPs available through the pharmacist directly, without a doctor's prescription. This has been the most successful way for women to access ECPs. Emergency rooms across the world dispense ECPs. Keep this in mind next time you have an overseas fling. Finally, please do not make a habit of using ECPs. They are for emergencies only. If you've taken ECPs once for reasons other than sexual assault, it's time to read this chapter from beginning to end and choose a reliable form of birth control for your future encounters.

### Who Should Use ECPs

ECPs are a good option if any of the following apply:

- No contraceptive method was used during sexual intercourse.
- A male condom slipped, broke, or leaked.
- A diaphragm or cervical cap was inserted incorrectly, dislodged, removed too early, or torn.
- Two or more of the first seven combined oral contraceptive pills were missed, or four or more pills during the second week were missed.
- One or more progestin-only oral contraceptive pills were missed.
- A female condom was inserted or removed incorrectly.
- "Safe" days while using the rhythm method of contraception were miscalculated.
- Withdrawal did not happen in time.
- An IUD was partially or totally expelled.
- Possible teratogen exposure has occurred (e.g., exposure to isotretinoin, alcohol, cocaine, certain antibiotic classes, and rubella).
- Rape has occurred.

The side effects of ECP can include nausea and vomiting. If you do vomit, you will need to repeat the dose because the drug may not be in your system anymore.

# Intrauterine Devices (IUDs)

IUDs are tiny devices that are fitted inside the uterus. A thin, silky thread hangs down through the cervix, just barely into the vagina, in a tamponlike fashion, to indicate that the device is in place correctly. Some IUDs are shaped like rings, with a thread attached; some are shaped like tiny sewing scissors, with a thread extending from the base; some are shaped like a capital T, with a thread extending from the base; the earlier IUDs were loop shaped. The amazing thing about IUDs is that no one really knows why they prevent pregnancy. The main theory is that as a foreign object in the uterus, it interferes with the sperm's reaching the egg and the egg's implanting itself in the uterus. Its failure rate ranges between 3 and 6 percent. The IUD actually dates back three thousand years. Smooth pebbles were apparently inserted into a camel's uterus to prevent pregnancy during long trips through the desert.

The first IUD was developed in 1909 by a German gynecologist and sex researcher named Ernst Grafenberg. It was a ring-shaped device that wasn't widely used until the 1920s. In 1934 Tenrei Ota, a Japanese physician, came up with another design. Both designs had no strings, and both physicians were reluctant to use the device because of the fear of uterine infection. Once antibiotics were discovered, physicians felt comfortable using the IUD.

The most extensive IUD study was done in Israel between 1930 and 1957, where one doctor reported his success with the 1909 model. The Israeli results were promising, and IUDs were being engineered in the United States by the 1960s. One of the key figures in American IUD engineering was Jack Lippes, a gynecologist from Buffalo, New York. He tried both the Grafenberg and Ota rings but found they were difficult to remove. He ingeniously attached a simple blue string and changed the ring to a loop. The string would allow women to check to see if the device was still in place and would enable the doctor to remove it more easily. This string has been the springboard for IUD engineering ever since. The Lippes Loop became the best-known and most widely used IUD in developing countries outside of China. Currently, eighty-five million women use IUDs, and fifty-nine million of them are in China (where the stringless IUD is still used).

After the Lippes Loop came out, several IUD series were soon developed, including the Saf-T-Coil and copper-bearing IUDs in the late 1960s. In the 1970s a second generation of IUDs was born, and usage shifted toward copper IUDs, which yielded fewer complications, and hormone-containing IUDs, which released progestin into the bloodstream. (Progestasert, a hormone-releasing IUD, was the first widely available IUD in the United States.) By the mid-1970s everyone wanted to get in on the IUD market. Untested devices went out, and IUDs have been followed by lawsuits and controversy ever since.

## The IUD Disaster

The most controversial IUD was the Dalkon Shield, which was banned in 1975 and recalled in 1980. This was a badly designed, untested IUD that was rushed onto the market by the pharmaceutical firm A. H. Robins Company. At that time, IUDs did not require FDA approval. A. H. Robins purchased the rights to the Dalkon Shield from Dr. Hugh Davis in 1970, but the pharmaceutical company didn't conduct any tests on the IUD. Instead, it relied solely on Davis's research, which was faulty. Furthermore, since Davis was both testing and marketing the device himself, he was in violation of professional ethics.

Insertion of the Dalkon Shield was painful, and there was a very high rate of infection among users. This was due to its braided tail, which was a haven for bacteria. As a result, the device was banned in 1975. By 1976 seventeen deaths had been linked to its use, but A. H. Robins took no action until 1980, when it finally recalled the shield, advising physicians to remove it from all users. The company's failure to act quickly resulted in several lawsuits, and A. H. Robins eventually went bankrupt in 1985. As of that date, ten thousand lawsuits had been brought against it. By 1986 several U.S. pharmaceutical companies, fearing the same predicament, discontinued their IUD lines.

In the post–Dalkon Shield era, however, IUDs were—and still are—alive and well throughout the world. The reason why they were virtually banned in the United States had more to do with liability insurance, since U.S. health care is all private. Since the Dalkon disaster, IUDs must now pass FDA approval before they're marketed.

Thirty years ago nearly 10 percent of North American women chose IUDs; since the Dalkon disaster, fewer than 1 percent do so. In contrast, one in five women in Denmark and Germany use IUDs.

## How Do You Get an IUD?

Right now, two other IUDs are also available. The copper ParaGard T 380A device was approved by the FDA in 1984. This is the most widely used IUD worldwide. In December 2000 the FDA approved the levonorgestrel-intrauterine system (LNG-IUS) under the name of Mirena. This device releases 20 mg of levonorgestrel per day over a period of five years.

IUD insertion requires the utmost skill and sensitivity. If your doctor isn't experienced or won't disclose his or her experience, find another doctor who will, or find another contraceptive method. If you want an IUD removed, these same credentials aren't necessary; removing an IUD simply involves pulling on the string. If the device is embedded in the muscle, most gynecologists can remove it. Improper removal can result in perforation, however.

## What Are the Risks and Side Effects?

IUDs increase your risk of pelvic inflammatory disease (PID), an infection in the upper genital tract that can cause infertility. Recent studies show that the risk is highest in the first four months after insertion. Basically, the infection results because the IUD needs to go through the cervix when it's inserted. Bacteria transfer from the vagina to the cervix to the uterus, hitchhiking up the IUD string. You're also at a higher risk of getting PID if you have been exposed to an STD. In other words, STD + IUD = PID! Another potential risk is an ectopic pregnancy, or tubal pregnancy. If you do get pregnant with an IUD in place, an ectopic pregnancy should be ruled out. Since IUDs prevent the egg from implanting in the uterus, the egg decides to stay in the fallopian tube, which is very dangerous. Periods may also be much heavier with IUDs, and you'll either get more severe cramps or develop cramps. Because of this, anemia is common in IUD users. IUDs have also been linked to uterine and cervical cancer, but this area is still murky. About 15 percent of IUD users have them removed because of bleeding, spotting, hemorrhaging, or anemia.

Other complications arise when the IUD partially expels (comes out), which means lots of cramping, painful intercourse, unusual discharge, and spotting. Often, though, expulsion is painless. Lost strings are another problem, making removal difficult. Full-term pregnancies have been reported with an IUD in place, but if you do get pregnant while you have an IUD, there's a 30 percent chance you'll miscarry. If a miscarriage does occur, there's an increased risk of infection. Some of these infections can be fatal. Punctures in the uterus or cervix are another drawback to IUDs and can lead to pelvic infections.

Don't go anywhere near an IUD if any of the following apply:

- You have PID, an active pelvic or vaginal infection, or an STD.
- You suspect you're pregnant.
- You have multiple sexual partners.
- You have hemophilia or a blood coagulation disorder.

In addition, avoid IUDs if you have a history of heavy and/or painful periods, diabetes, any kind of benign or malignant pelvic tumors, or STDs.

If you choose to use an IUD, keep in mind these important guidelines:

1. Insertion can be very painful. Bring along a friend or your spouse. Don't walk home or drive home yourself. Take Advil, Nuprin, or Anaprox before you have it done.

2. Always read the package insert for your IUD. It will tell you about the risks and warning signs for removal.

3. Make sure your doctor shows you how to find the string. Check the string every other day, especially after intercourse. If your string is missing, longer, or shorter, or if you can feel the IUD through your cervix, see your doctor immediately. These are indications that your IUD is not in place correctly. Whatever you do, don't pull on it. Get yourself to your doctor's office as soon as possible. Always use a backup contraceptive when you have string problems.

4. The danger signals for IUDs spell the word *PAINS*: Period problems (lateness, spotting, bleeding in between), Abdominal pain or intercourse pain, Infections of any kind, Not feeling well (fever, chills), String problems (missing, longer, or shorter). See your doctor immediately if you have any of these symptoms.

5. Use a backup method of birth control for the first three months after insertion, just in case. IUDs do not protect you from STDs, and furthermore, exposure to an STD could be aggravated by an IUD. If you are concerned, use a latex condom in conjunction with your IUD.

### New Thoughts About IUDs

In 1974 studies showed that IUD wearers had a ninefold increased risk of PID. Researchers today challenge those studies and wonder if the rise in STD incidence at the time was taken into account, along with the sheer number of Dalkon Shield wearers. When the Dalkon Shield was introduced in 1970, it also coincided with an epidemic of PID in the United States. By 1973 roughly 40 percent of IUDs in use were Dalkon Shields, yet Dalkon Shields also had a 40 percent higher risk of pregnancy failure and miscarriage than competing IUDs. Furthermore, researchers wonder how much of the pregnancy failure rate was due to inexperienced inserters. Another point researchers make is that, believe it or not, the FDA did not recommend removal of an IUD during pregnancy until 1974—which would undoubtedly have had an enormous impact on the high miscarriage rate associated with Dalkon Shield wearers. In other words, while the Dalkon Shield had many faults, is incorrect data to blame for the IUD's current bad rap?

Current studies seem to suggest that PID incidence increases with IUD wearers within a short space of time after insertion. This means that there is probably an STD present at the time of insertion. However, reanalyzed data does not show an increase in PID in long-term IUD wearers. A 1992 World Health Organization study found the following: PID incidence increases in IUD wearers only during the first twenty days after insertion; if you're at low risk for an STD (you have children and are in a monogamous relationship), you can probably wear an IUD; and long-term IUD users have a low risk of PID.

# Barrier Methods

Barrier methods are the oldest type of contraception. They involve simply placing some kind of obstacle inside the vagina that prevents the sperm from entering the uterus. Many women, weary of the risks associated with hormonal contraception and IUDs, are returning to barrier methods.

The second century was alive with contraceptive barriers. In this time period vaginal plugs, tampons, and suppositories were used to prevent conception. These devices were usually made out of sticky things like honey, cedar gum, and oils. Apparently, elephant dung mixed with sodium carbonate was believed to act as a spermicide. Other spermicides used with sponges included lemon juice, vinegar, or a soap solution. Even the Talmud cites "spongy substances" (such as tampons) used by women to prevent pregnancy.

One of the stranger items was the block pessary—a square block with concave sides that was inserted into the vagina with the belief that the concave surfaces fit over the cervix. Other popular items were the wishbone intro-cervical device and the stem plugs of the early 1900s. These were the precursors of the IUD. Some wishbones were made out of 10-karat or 14-karat gold, while the stem plugs were often sewn into the uterine wall to prevent them from expelling. These earlier IUDs were almost always followed by horrendous infections and PIDs, not unlike today's IUDs.

In the past, women in Sumatra molded opium into a cuplike shape and inserted it into the vagina to cover the cervix. Chinese and Japanese women covered the cervix with oiled silky paper. Hungarian women used beeswax melted into small disks. Some barrier devices that have been recorded were particularly ingenious: Casanova recommended women squeeze half a lemon and then insert the lemon rind into their vaginas, fitting it over the cervix. The citric acid from the lemon acted as a spermicide, while the rind served as a diaphragm, covering the cervix. Natural sea sponges have been used since antiquity for contraception and did much the same thing as a contraceptive sponge does today.

Not much has really changed in barrier method designs other than the materials. Barrier methods are also very safe and pose fewer risks to the user. However, unless they're combined with spermicide and a condom, they offer no protection against STDs. The only risk considered significant with barrier contraceptives is that of toxic shock syndrome (TSS), discussed in Chapter 2. TSS occurs in 10 out of every 100,000 barrier users, a very low occurrence rate. The reasons why TSS would occur are the same reasons as for tampon use. Whatever barrier method you decide on, here are some rules to follow that will greatly reduce your risk of TSS:

1. Wash your hands with soap and water before inserting or removing a barrier (diaphragm or cervical cap).
2. Do not leave your barrier in place longer than twenty-four hours (cervical caps can be left in up to forty-eight hours).
3. Don't use your barrier during your period, when you're bleeding for any other reason, or if you have any abnormal vaginal discharge. (The menstrual flow may also break the suction.)
4. After full-term pregnancy, wait six to twelve weeks before using your barrier again. (The cervix may still be dilated.)
5. If you think you may have TSS (see symptoms in Chapter 2), remove your barrier immediately and see your doctor.
6. If you have a history of TSS, choose another method of birth control.

What you might want to know about barrier methods is that they offer protection against cervical cancer or abnormal cervical cell changes. The reason is simple: when the cervix is covered, it's protected!

## *The Diaphragm*

The diaphragm is a dome-shaped cup with a flexible rim that fits over your cervix and rests behind your pubic bone. It looks like a tiny rubber flying saucer. Inserted before intercourse, it blocks the sperm from entering the uterus through the cervix. Rubber diaphragms have been around since the early 1880s and were introduced into the United States by Margaret Sanger. Not much happened to diaphragm technology until the 1950s, when spermicides were introduced and used in conjunction with the diaphragm. Typically, you place spermicidal jelly inside the diaphragm before inserting it. The jelly helps to hold the diaphragm in place. A newer form of spermicide known as Vaginal Contraceptive Film is a 10-by-10-cm square of translucent film containing spermicide, which is easier to insert and cannot be felt by you or your partner. The film lasts about an hour and then simply dissolves.

The most recent development in the history of the diaphragm was the introduction of a new model in 1983. This product incorporates a soft latex flange attached to the rim. The flange is intended to create a seal with the vaginal wall. In addition to the new model, the same manufacturer introduced a spermicide packaged in foil in premeasured amounts for convenient, one-time use and portability. Disposable spermicidal diaphragms are also being developed but haven't yet passed FDA approval.

The failure rate for diaphragms ranges between 10 and 20 percent. This is considerably higher than hormonal methods, but much of the failure has to do with improper use and insertion. Diaphragms come in different sizes and styles. You'll need to be fitted for one by either your family doctor or, of course, your gynecologist. Once you're fitted, you will be given a prescription and can purchase the diaphragm at any drugstore. Then you'll need to go back to your doctor and be shown how to use it by yourself. Sometimes you'll need a plastic inserter, sometimes you won't. Go home and practice and see your doctor one more time before you use it so that he or she can make sure you're putting it in correctly. (See instructions under "How to Use a Diaphragm.")

There are three basic types of diaphragms on the market:

1. The Arcing Spring has a double spring in the rim, which applies pressure against the vaginal walls. It's most suitable for women with poor vaginal muscle tone or mild uterine prolapse. This style tends to flip in place by itself and is almost impossible not to fit correctly. Many physicians recommend this type to new users.

2. The Coil Spring Rim is the most common style in North America. It's suitable for women who have strong vaginal muscles, no displacement of the uterus, and a normal size and contour of the vagina. It can be inserted by hand without an inserter.

3. The Flat Spring Rim has a thin, delicate rim with gentle springs. It's most useful for women who haven't had children.

Before recommending a diaphragm, your doctor should perform a pelvic exam to make sure you don't have any physical abnormalities that would prevent you from using one in the first place. It's important to get a diaphragm that fits well. If it's too small, it will expose the cervix; if it's too big, it will buckle. You should also be refitted if you have gained or lost more than fifteen pounds, have had pelvic surgery, have had a child or an abortion, or found the first fitting uncomfortable. If you just can't get the hang of a diaphragm, it's probably not for you.

## What Are the Side Effects?

Aside from the low risk of TSS, there is evidence that suggests a link between urinary tract infections and diaphragm use. If you have a history of urinary tract infections, don't use a diaphragm. Some women are allergic to rubber or spermicide. Don't use a diaphragm if you have these allergies. Other side effects include an irritation caused by the spermicide, foul-smelling discharge associated with prolonged wearing of the diaphragm, pelvic discomfort, cramps, or pressure on the rectum or bladder (usually caused by poor fit).

There is a benefit to diaphragm use. Women who use a diaphragm have lower rates of STDs and PID. This may be because the diaphragm helps block bacteria from entering the cervix, and the spermicide helps to kill them.

## How to Use a Diaphragm

Hold the diaphragm as if it were a cup. Apply one teaspoon of spermicide in the center, making a circle about the size of a quarter. Spermicide may also be applied to the rim of the diaphragm to ease insertion. Squeeze the diaphragm firmly between your thumb and forefinger into an even fold. This should make it narrow enough to fit inside the vagina. Then assume a comfortable position: stand with one foot on a chair, bed, or toilet seat, squat on the floor, or lie back on the bed with your knees up. Then insert the folded diaphragm into your vagina and push it up as far as it will go. When you release the diaphragm, the rim will regain its round shape and fit around the cervix. When it's in place comfortably, you shouldn't be able to feel it. If you do, take it out and reinsert it. You might also want to incorporate the diaphragm insertion into your foreplay. Partners can insert and check the diaphragm as well.

To remove it, hook your finger or thumb over the rim toward the front, and pull the diaphragm down and out. Use the same position to remove it as you did to insert it. You may also try breaking the suction by slipping a finger between the diaphragm and the sides of the vaginal wall, and then pulling the diaphragm out. Don't panic if you can't get it out at first. It just means you're tensing up. Wait a while and try again. There's no way it can get lost inside your body. You'll need to take it out after twenty-four hours or else you may get a foul smell as the bacteria grow on it. The bacteria can also cause irritations and discharge.

If you use a diaphragm, keep the following in mind:

1. Be sure to use the diaphragm with spermicidal cream or jelly every time you have intercourse.

2. After intercourse, leave your diaphragm in place for at least six to eight hours before removing it. Don't douche during that time (or ever, in fact!).

3. If you are going to have intercourse again after eight hours, wash the diaphragm with mild soap and water, dry it with a clean towel, apply new spermicidal jelly or cream, and reinsert it. Try to remove your diaphragm at least once every twenty-four hours.

4. If you have intercourse more than once within the six- to eight-hour period, you can leave the diaphragm in, but insert more spermicide with an applicator into your vagina each time you have intercourse.

5. Make sure you always have a "diaphragm supply kit" on hand, at home and when you travel: a diaphragm in a plastic case, one or two tubes of spermicidal jelly or cream, and a plastic applicator for inserting extra spermicide.

6. Each time you use your diaphragm, check for holes! Diaphragms wear out after about two years. Hold your diaphragm up to the light to see if there are any defects, and stretch it a little bit. Then pour water into it and see if any water leaks out. If it does have holes, don't use it. You'll need a new one.

7. Your diaphragm shouldn't interfere with normal activities. Urination or bowel movements shouldn't be affected, and you should be able to bathe and shower normally. If it is interfering with these activities, it may not be in properly or might be the wrong size.

8 Keep your diaphragm away from petroleum jelly, which can erode the rubber. For lubricants, try K-Y Jelly, Personal Lubricant, H-R Lubricating Jelly, or Surgilube.

9. Although this may sound like a broken record, diaphragms do not offer any protection against STDs. If this is a concern, you'll need to use a latex condom with it.

### Diaphragm-Like Devices

Two new barrier methods are modeled after the traditional diaphragm but are more convenient. The Lea's Contraceptive and the SILCS (pronounced "silks") intravaginal barrier are both one-size-fits-all. They are made of silicone rather than latex and can be left in place for up to forty-eight hours. Neither of these products is in the United States yet, but they are awaiting FDA approval.

## *The Cervical Cap*

The cervical cap is a small, thimble-shaped cap that blocks only the cervix and not the entire upper part of the vaginal canal, the way a diaphragm does. In essence, the cervical cap is a minidiaphragm with a tall dome. It was actually invented forty-four years before the diaphragm. Dr. Adolphe Wilde of Germany took an individual impression of a woman's cervix and then made a custom-fitted cap out of rubber to wear over it. At about the same time, a New York physician, Dr. E. B. Foote, invented his own version. The cervical cap has always been widely available in Europe. The caps that were popular in North America thirty to forty years ago were actually made out of silver or copper (more recently of plastic) and were left in place for up to four weeks. The caps that are currently available in North America are manufactured in England and are now made of soft rubber.

The same instructions apply to the cap as to the diaphragm. The only difference between the cervical cap and the diaphragm is that the cap doesn't need to be squeezed or folded to fit in; you simply insert the cap with your forefinger and place it over the cervix yourself. You can also leave the cervical cap in for a longer time frame—thirty-six to forty-eight hours instead of twenty-four hours. Because it is smaller, you need far less spermicide inside it.

The device was not widely available in North America until 1988. Although the cap was popular at the beginning of the twentieth century, it lost popularity because it is a little more difficult to fit than a diaphragm (although many women do report that it is easier and less messy than a diaphragm). The main problem with the cap was that it required women to be very comfortable with their bodies. In the early 1970s feminist health organizations lobbied for its return to the U.S. market. By 1976 all contraceptive manufacturers had to provide the

FDA with data on the safety and failure rates of their products. Lamberts Ltd., the British manufacturer of the cap, for some reason failed to provide the necessary data to the FDA. As a result, the FDA put the cervical cap on its Class III list, banning its use. Finally, after much protesting, tests were done, data were provided, and the ban was lifted in 1988. The FDA approved one type of cap, the Prentif cavity-rim cervical cap, for general use. Like the diaphragm, it must be fitted. The cap also has the same side effects and advantages as the diaphragm, except that there's no risk of bladder infections. However, there can be some irritation to the cervical lining if the cap is used improperly. The cap has a failure rate of about 17 percent. Some 6 percent of cervical cap candidates will not be able to find one that fits (shorter or longer cervixes are a problem, apparently). Obviously, as with a diaphragm, until you're using it correctly, use a backup method of birth control.

The only women who shouldn't use the cervical cap are those who have a history of abnormal Pap tests, cervical or vaginal infections, or PID; those who have had a cervical biopsy or cryosurgery within the past six to twelve weeks; those who have an allergic reaction to rubber (plastic caps are also available); and those who have difficulty using it properly.

Cervical cap users will need to follow the general rules given earlier under "Barrier Methods," as well as the instructions outlined under "How to Use a Diaphragm."

Conventional caps can be worn up to forty-eight hours. However, they are made of latex, must be fitted by a provider, and can be difficult to insert or remove. Two new cervical caps made out of silicone are under development; they are both being tested in the United States.

## The Vaginal Contraceptive Sponge

One of the best-loved barrier methods—the Today Sponge—was removed from the market in the mid-1990s because the manufacturer couldn't afford to retrofit its factory after an inspection found that it had contaminated water. In a famous "Seinfeld" episode, the character Elaine, upon hearing this news, buys out the remaining sponges from her drugstore and assesses her partners as "sponge-worthy" to decide whether she can "waste" one of the precious sponges on them. In 1998 Allendale Pharmaceuticals acquired the rights to the Today Sponge, and now it is once again available. The sponge is a good method so long as you are not menstruating or have an active infection. If left in the vagina too long, it can also cause a vaginal infection.

The sponge is one-size-fits-all, which is why women like it so much; they don't need to see a doctor to be fitted. Also, the sponge can be used spontaneously for women who do not want to be on hormonal contraceptives. The sponge blocks the cervix, trapping sperm and releasing spermicides. The sponge can be left in for roughly twenty-four hours.

## *Fertility Awareness*

If you're not using hormonal contraceptives, combining fertility awareness techniques with a barrier method of contraception can work very well. Observing your cervical mucus is the best way of understanding your cycle. This method is sometimes called the Billings method, invented by Evelyn and John Billings, an Australian couple who developed a way of interpreting the changing consistencies of vaginal discharge, which is influenced by the cervical mucus bathing the vaginal walls. All you need to do is observe your toilet paper about twice a day, when you wipe yourself before or after going to the bathroom. Or you can simply insert a finger into your vagina to collect whatever discharge is present.

Here's how it works. After your period finishes, you'll notice several days of no vaginal discharge at all (your "dry days"). Your vagina will still be moist, however, as it always is. Then your mucus days will begin. The discharge starts out sticky, then gradually becomes creamier, wet, and slippery. Finally, on your mucus peak day, the discharge has the consistency of egg white (some women describe it as snotlike) and will be dripping out of your vagina, very evident when you wipe yourself or take off your underwear. This discharge will also be thinner, transparent, and stretchy—you should be able to stretch it between two fingers. This mucus is your "fertility marker." You will be ovulating either just before or just after it appears. The mucus will last for just about two days, then it will begin to get thicker and stickier. These are your postpeak days, also known as your luteal phase. This is when premenstrual symptoms will begin to make an appearance. The mucus will remain on the thicker, sticky side until your period starts. Then the whole phase begins again.

During the peak you'll be most fertile; you may want to abstain from sex during those days or use a backup method of birth control, such as a condom.

# Spermicides

Spermicides are sometimes used as the only contraceptive; this is not a reliable method and should be combined with a barrier method, such as the diaphragm or cervical cap. There is also the belief that spermicides, such as nonoxynol-9, can protect women from STDs, including HIV. There have been a few conflicting studies and reports about this, showing that spermicides may have some effect on bacterial infections. But the experts agree that nonoxynol-9 ought not to be marketed as any sort of protection against STDs without the use of a condom.

Microbicide gels are in development now. These may replace nonoxynol-9 as the gold standard gel, offering protection against a number of bacteria and viruses, such as HIV.

This is still a few years away from being marketed in North America, and trials in developing countries are under way for several types of microbicides.

# Permanent Contraception

Thousands of couples in North America deliberately seek out sterilization, otherwise known as permanent contraception. For couples who have chosen a child-free lifestyle, permanent contraception is an alternative, as it is for couples who already have children and do not want to have any more. Many single adults as well will seek out permanent contraception if they are certain they do not want children. It is also an option for many HIV-positive adults, who fear they would pass on the virus were they to have children.

Two procedures are involved in sterilization: a vasectomy for the man and what's called tubal ligation (tying the tubes) for the woman. Only tubal ligation will be discussed here.

If you're a single woman who wants permanent contraception, the only procedure you should consent to is tubal ligation. Shockingly, and as recently as ten years ago, hysterectomies and oophorectomies were recommended to many women as sterilization procedures. Women were told that having "everything out" would protect them from other problems such as fibroids and cancer. Hysterectomies should never be done for this reason! As discussed in Chapter 20, women need their reproductive organs for all kinds of functions other than pregnancy and childbirth. Tubal ligation is a safe procedure that preserves all of your reproductive functions except for one: having open tubes where the egg and sperm can meet. This procedure requires a general anesthetic, and it should be considered irreversible.

Tubal ligation cuts the fallopian tubes, burns the ends with electrocautery, and blocks them so that the sperm can't get inside to meet the egg. The egg is then absorbed by the body. For this procedure, you'll need the services of a gynecologist trained in microsurgery (laparoscopy and laparotomy) and an anesthesiologist. Although 30 to 60 percent of fallopian tubes can be successfully reconstructed in the event that a woman changes her mind and wants it reversed, there's now only a 12 to 20 percent chance of her ever becoming pregnant. Therefore, this procedure is really irreversible for all intents and purposes. In recent years, newer methods for tubal ligation that do not involve surgery have been developed to make the procedure less complicated for women. The nonsurgical method involves pellets that are inserted through an IUD.

In the past, this procedure involved major abdominal surgery. Today it's done via laparoscopy, just as is any pelvic microsurgery. After you go under a general anesthetic, your bladder is emptied and your vagina and abdomen are cleaned with an antiseptic solution. Your doctor will then make one small incision about one-fourth to one-half inch long, just above the pubic bone. Next, the laparoscope is inserted into the incision and the instrument used to block your tubes is inserted through the telescope. While looking through the laparoscope, the doctor will proceed to block your tubes using cauterization, clips, rings, or bands (these squeeze the tubes together, which successfully blocks them) and may even remove a section of the tube. (There are various procedures your doctor can use, each about as effective as the next.) Ask your doctor to tell you which method is being used and whether the procedure has any chance of reversal. The operation takes about thirty minutes and can be done on an outpatient basis. You can usually go home the same day and resume normal activities after about a week.

After the procedure, the incision is covered with a fairly small bandage. You should refrain from heavy lifting and may need a couple days to recover from the anesthetic. This procedure is effective immediately and does not require you to wait three months. Since this procedure does not affect your menstrual cycle, your periods will resume as usual, and you'll go into menopause naturally. About two in one thousand women will still become pregnant after a tubal ligation; some of these women will have ectopic pregnancies.

Although tubal ligation is a safe procedure, no pelvic surgery is guaranteed to be free of complications—there are potential long-term side effects. Some women report heavier menstrual periods and painful cramps. Some women go into ovarian failure because the surgery may interfere with the blood supply to the ovaries (see Chapter 20). Some women develop scar tissue from the procedure and have pelvic infections or recurrent abdominal pain. A 1989 Australian study showed that sterilized women had 40 percent less estrogen in their systems and 20 percent less progesterone, caused by damage to the ovaries' blood supply.

## *Curious Protection*

Tubal ligation seems to be linked to lower rates of ovarian cancer. An American study recently concluded that women who have tubal ligation have a 70 percent lower risk of developing ovarian cancer than do women who don't have this procedure. This study followed 100,000 married nurses, aged thirty to fifty-five, from 1976 to 1988, but critics point out that it may not have done a good job in ruling out family history and other predisposing factors. If this study's findings are accurate, no one can seem to explain them.

The logical explanation from my own research is that women who have children, especially those women who breast-feed, have much lower rates of ovarian cancer than do those who do not have children or who do not breast-feed. This is due to the fact that women don't ovulate during pregnancy, while breast-feeding delays ovulation even longer. The less you ovulate, the less stress you place on your ovaries, and the less cancer you get. This is the same reason why OCs offer protection against ovarian cancer. And women who have at least one child are the ones usually interested in tubal ligation. So there may not be as much mystery in this study's conclusions as these researchers are suggesting.

# What to Eat

If you're on hormonal contraception, it's important to eat regular, balanced meals (see Chapter 1). Hormonal contraception can cause hypoglycemia, or low blood sugar, as well as insulin resistance. Low blood sugar can cause you to become shaky, irritable, and disoriented. Keeping your blood sugar level stable has to do with understanding carbohydrates—they can be simple or complex. Simple carbohydrates are found in any food that has natural sugar (e.g., honey, fruits, juices, vegetables, milk) and anything that contains table sugar or sucrose. Complex carbohydrates are more sophisticated foods that are made up of larger molecules, such as grain foods, starches, and foods high in fiber. The fiber foods, both soluble and insoluble (an important distinction), such as cereals, oatmeal, or legumes, are important, too, and will help to delay the breakdown of simpler carbohydrates to prevent sugar "rushes" and "crashes."

## *The Glycemic Index*

The glycemic index (GI) shows the rise in blood sugar from various carbohydrates. Therefore, planning your diet using the GI can help you control your blood sugar by using more foods with a low GI and fewer foods with a high GI. This glycemic index, developed at the University of Toronto, measures the rate at which various foods convert to glucose, which is assigned a value of 100. Higher numbers indicate a more rapid absorption of glucose. This is not an exhaustive list and should be used as a sample only. This is not an index of food energy values or calories; some low-GI foods are high in fat, while some high-GI foods are low in fat. Keep in mind, too, that these values differ depending on what else you're eating with that food and how the food is prepared.

**Sugars**
glucose = 100
honey = 87
table sugar = 59
fructose = 20

**Snacks**
Mars bar = 68
potato chips = 51
sponge cake = 46
fish sticks = 38

tomato soup = 38
sausages = 28
peanuts = 13

## Cereals
cornflakes = 80
shredded wheat = 67
muesli = 66
bran = 51
oatmeal = 49

## Breads
whole wheat = 72
white = 69
buckwheat = 51

## Fruits
raisins = 64
banana = 62
orange juice = 46
orange = 40
apple = 39

## Dairy Products
ice cream = 36
yogurt = 36
milk = 34
skim milk = 32

## Root Vegetables
parsnips = 97
carrots = 92
instant mashed potatoes = 80
new boiled potato = 70
beets = 64
yam = 51
sweet potato = 48

## Pasta and Rice
white rice = 72
brown rice = 66
spaghetti (white) = 50
spaghetti (whole wheat) = 42

## Legumes
frozen peas = 51
baked beans = 40
chickpeas = 36
lima beans = 36
butter beans = 36
black-eyed peas = 33
green beans = 31
kidney beans = 29
lentils = 29
dried soybeans = 15

# Flower Power

Natural progesterone (also discussed in Chapter 21) can be used as a contraceptive, although it is tricky!

Don't blame me if you get pregnant, but Dr. Katherina Dalton, who promotes natural progesterone to treat many gynecological problems, recommends the following contraceptive recipe: a daily low dose of progesterone ranging from 100 to 200 mg. Then a progesterone suppository starting with day 8 of the cycle. Then you increase to the "optimum" progesterone dosage (to be worked out with your doctor) at ovulation (and *you'll* have to know when you're ovulating). And then you continue daily progesterone until your period. Sounds a bit confusing to me, which is probably why it fails as a contraceptive in so many women. But if you're gifted with truly understanding your fertility cycle, it may work beautifully. If you want to try this method, combine it with a barrier method of contraception, such as a diaphragm, female condom, cervical cap, and so on.

# How to Move

Practice the exercises discussed in Chapter 1 for overall health maintenance and well-being.

# 9

# High-Risk Behavior

HIGH-RISK BEHAVIOR refers to certain activities that place you more at risk for STDs (such as HIV) than do other activities. Chapter 7 outlined safer sex practices for more usual sexual activity. But many women are involved with activities that are more on the edge, including S/M (sadomasochism), anal sex, fisting, body piercing, and so forth. This chapter discusses some of the more common high-risk activities and provides tips for greater safety.

## Intense Oral Sex

Since the dawning of the AIDS age, oral sex has become far more popular. This is only natural since many believe oral sex is a safe activity. Well, as more research is showing, it is a high-risk activity. Not only is HIV present in semen, pre-ejaculate, vaginal secretions, and menstrual blood, but oral sex today is quite different than oral sex of yesteryear. The mouth, for many, has essentially replaced the vagina or anus as the intercourse orifice of choice, and far more vigorous thrusting is going on these days. In fact, oral sex, which in the 1980s was not considered a major risk factor, has now become a major risk factor in HIV transmission.

HIV can be transmitted during oral sex. One reason has to do with the fact that many people can have bleeding gums or gingivitis (inflammation of the gums) without even realizing it. Dentists insist that many people, even without experiencing obvious symptoms, have gum disease, which will make the gums vulnerable to bleeding. And if you even have a history of gum disease, you can continue to be susceptible to bleeding and open sores. People can also have a variety of mouth sores, caused by biting the tongue or lip, by having chapped, cracked lips, by burning the roof of the mouth, and so on. If you do have gum disease, you are far more susceptible to ulceration or bruising in the mouth or gums.

It's also been found that people who vigorously brush or floss their teeth before or after oral sex (where you've been the recipient) are also at greater risk of contracting HIV. And if your male partner has cuts on his penis, then the risk of HIV is even higher.

What researchers are finding as well is that throat infections can increase your risk of HIV transmission. Other STDs, such as gonorrhea, herpes, and syphilis, can also manifest as throat infections in the first place, if you're engaging in a lot of oral sex. In fact, throat-based gonorrhea, which is generally not tested for, has increased dramatically, particularly in the gay community.

Of course, the safest oral sex involves using a latex male or female condom and a dental dam. If you are not willing to do this, then at the very least you should follow these guidelines:

1. Use your tongue to lick and kiss the penis instead of having the penis thrust into your mouth, which can rub off tissue in the upper palate, allowing semen to enter your bloodstream.
2. Combine oral sex with a hand job when your partner is ready to ejaculate to avoid getting semen in your mouth—especially if you have cold sores, mouth sores, or bleeding gums or if you have just been to the dentist.
3. Refrain from receiving oral sex when you have your period.

# Anal Sex

Statistics show that roughly 35 percent of heterosexuals and 50 percent of the gay community practice anal sex at least occasionally. Whenever anal penetration is taking place, you need three things: lubrication, condoms, and common sense.

Liberal amounts of lubrication are necessary because the rectal wall can be quite sticky and is subject to tearing and developing lesions if not kept lubricated. The anus and rectum are narrow, so lubrication is needed to press inside smoothly.

Condoms are another necessity. Although experienced anal sex performers will try to "clean out the ass," as the vernacular goes, enemas, douches, and other cleaners will not be able to get all the germs and bacteria out of the rectum. The main function of the rectum is to act as a passageway for feces. Feces are not normally stored in the rectum except just prior to a bowel movement. Yet small amounts may remain in the rectum, especially if the feces are not well formed. Anal douching before anal sex will help some people concerned about cleanliness to relax. Without a condom, anal sex can facilitate the transmission of STDs better than any other form of sex; it can also cause urinary tract infections and other bacterial diseases.

As for common sense, the rule in a mutual anal sex encounter is no painful sex. The rectal wall curves and is thin, so long, hard objects can tear your insides. When fingers are going inside, it's key to not wear any jewelry and to keep fingernails short and trimmed. Mutual respect for comfort and pain thresholds is key.

As any doctor who does digital rectal exams knows, when you insert a finger about one-half inch into the anus and press the fingertip against the side, you can feel the two sphincter muscles. There is less than a quarter-inch between them. The external sphincter is controlled by the central nervous system, which you can voluntarily control.

Since the rectum is not straight, penetration is tricky: the short anal canal connects the anal opening to the rectum; the rectum tilts toward the front of the body. A few inches in, it curves back, sometimes as much as 90 degrees. Then, after a few more inches, it swoops toward the front of the body once again. Slow, gentle movements are absolutely essential to avoid damage and tearing.

For extremely detailed information on anal sex (positions, technique, etc.), go to sexuality.org.

Anal sex carries more risks for women than men in heterosexual encounters; during unprotected anal sex, a male can get feces on his penis and then transfer fecal material into the vagina. This can create truly nightmarish vaginal infections.

## Anal-Oral Sex (a.k.a. Rimming)

Without a latex barrier, such as a dental dam, this is a high-risk activity that can introduce fecal matter into the mouth; if there are mouth sores, the oral contact can introduce blood into rectal tears, which is a direct hit for blood-borne viruses such as HIV or hepatitis A (which is spread through oral-anal contact). Intestinal parasites, bacteria, or tiny bugs are usually passed along when fecal matter finds its way into someone's mouth or vagina, most likely through rimming.

## Fisting

Fisting is a form of anal sex in which several fingers or even the entire hand and forearm are inserted into the rectum and sometimes into the lower colon. This, for obvious reasons, is an extremely high-risk activity that carries serious health consequences.

## Safer Anal Sex

If you must have anal sex, here are the rules:

1. Use two condoms and plenty of the proper lubricant (see next rule). Two condoms are necessary in case one condom breaks.

2. *Never* use petroleum jelly (such as Vaseline) as a sexual lubricant. It can erode the condom and cause it to break, and it does not dissolve inside the rectum (or the vagina, for that matter). Use a proper sexual lubricant, such as K-Y Jelly. The lubricant will moisten the orifice and help prevent the tearing of rectal tissue.

3. After anal intercourse, make sure your partner carefully washes and dries his penis, carefully washes and dries his hands, and puts on a fresh condom before continuing. You want to make sure that no fecal material is transferred into your vagina and that no blood from your rectal tears gets inside your vagina.

4. After anal intercourse, reapply lubricant into your rectum to help soothe any irritation that results.

5. Practice follow-up care. If you're engaging in regular anal intercourse, make sure you have a full pelvic exam twice a year. Report any bleeding, pains, or difficult bowel movements you may experience after having anal intercourse.

6. If you're engaging in rimming or fisting, wear latex gloves. Do not use a "finger cot" (i.e., a piece of plastic or latex), as it can fall off.

7. Use only nonmicrowavable plastic wrap for rimming or wrapping fingers. Microwavable plastic wrap has small holes in it to allow the air to escape; this means that HIV can pass through it, too.

## High-Risk Terminology

If you're negotiating high-risk sexual activities with your partner, it's important to understand what is being requested or discussed. Get to know these terms:

*Bondage and domination (B/D):* role-play without pain
*Fisting:* the insertion of a whole hand into the rectum or vagina for sexual stimulation
*Rimming:* oral-anal contact for sexual stimulation
*Sadomasochism (S/M):* the use of pain in consensual sexual acts
*Water sports:* urination for the purposes of sexual pleasure

# Body Piercing

Body piercing is growing in popularity. In various cultures body piercing has been used to identify people of different tribes or clans; to indicate age group or social ranking; as a means of adornment; and, as many pierced individuals claim, to enhance stimulation and sensual pleasure. In a recent survey about who pierces, 79 percent of the respondents were older than twenty-nine and 58 percent were married or in long-term relationships. Body piercing is no longer just an activity of rebellious teens.

In a 2001 survey of female university students, 16 percent had pierced tongues, 6 percent had pierced nipples, 32 percent had pierced navels, 2 percent had pierced genitals, and 1 percent had pierced eyebrows, lips, or cheeks. Additionally, 23 percent of these students wore tattoos. These numbers are high, considering that piercing these areas used to be taboo among mainstream women ten years ago.

Body piercing can be a high-risk activity when it is conducted in unsterile conditions, as is often the case. Because blood is involved, it can spread blood-borne viruses. Even when body piercing is done under sterile conditions, piercing sites can become infected and bleed. Sites that are involved in sexual contact can therefore become breeding grounds for HIV and other blood-borne viruses. Several studies have now concluded that body piercing is a risk factor for hepatitis infection and HIV. Blood service agencies around the world, for example, will typically reject blood donors who are pierced or have tattoos.

## *Piercing Skin During S/M Play*

Piercing the skin is a common ritual during S/M play. Nipples and labias are common sites. Bloodletting, by poking these body parts with needles and razor blades, is not uncommon. Using "metal ass toys," which can be unsterile, is also common. Sometimes dental floss is wrapped around the nipples to cut off blood supply.

If you are engaging in these activities, you must use a sterile cleanser, such as Betadine or another iodine-based cleanser. Soap and water or rubbing alcohol will not sterilize these areas; they only clean in the sense of removing surface oils.

If you are engaging in whipping, which can produce blood, the whipping areas should be sterilized as well.

Anything touching the body, such as clamps, needles, razor blades, and so on, should be sterilized, too.

If you are involved in S/M play, you should follow these rules:

1. Negotiate S/M roles before you start the play. "Bottoms" (i.e., subordinates) should negotiate stop signals to "Tops" (i.e., dominants) beforehand.

2. If you suffer from any health problems (such as diabetes, migraines, muscular problems, and so on), disclose this before you wind up in bondage scenes, scenarios that can put your health at risk.

3. Sterilize all pierced sites, as well as sites to be pierced or whipped, beforehand to reduce transmission of blood-borne viruses.

For extremely detailed information on safer S/M play, consult *On the Safe Edge: A Manual for SM Play*, by Trevor Jacques. It can be ordered at alternate.com.

# Sharing Needles

Sharing needles with anyone is high-risk behavior that can almost assure that you will contract a blood-borne virus, such as HIV or hepatitis. This section is not for people injecting themselves with insulin, but for people who are injecting narcotic or hallucinogenic drugs. This climate also makes it easy to use sex as "currency" for drugs, creating a truly unsafe atmosphere.

## *Safer Sex Rules for IV Drug Users and Abusers*

Even though drug use and abuse are not sexual per se, safer sex practices need to be adopted here as well. Obviously, the first rule is that unless you need to use an IV drug for health reasons (such as diabetes or hemophilia), don't use them. Failing that, here are some safer sex guidelines to live by:

1. Always use clean needles. Never share your needles, and never use someone else's needles. There are needle-exchange programs set up all over the continent. Ask your doctor about where you can go to make sure you're getting clean needles.

2. If you have to share your equipment, clean the equipment between uses by flushing the syringe and needle with bleach and water, then flush it with clean, uncontaminated clear water.

3. If you're taking drugs intravenously for legitimate health reasons, make sure you have regular checkups with your family doctor, and make sure you're using a screened blood product. Don't use any product unless you know for a fact that it's been screened for HIV infection.

4. As a rule, get an AIDS test done every six months (or ask your doctor to recommend reasonable time intervals) to make sure you haven't been infected. HIV can remain dormant for several years before it becomes active. Just because you've had one negative AIDS test doesn't mean you weren't infected with HIV. As an IV drug user, you are in the highest risk category for developing AIDS. So keep getting tested until you're absolutely sure.

5. Avoid having sex with an IV drug user; if you must, then use two condoms and plenty of spermicide. If you are the drug user, always disclose your drug use to your partner, and if you can't abstain from sex, insist on two spermicidal condoms.

# Have You Been Exposed to HIV?

If you've been engaging in any of the activities discussed in this chapter, you are in a high-risk category for being exposed to HIV. Make it a ritual to be tested for HIV every six months. For people in lower risk categories, answering "yes" to any of these questions also necessitates an HIV test.

1. Have you (or any of your partners) had unprotected sex with any of the following:

   - a homosexual man
   - a bisexual man
   - a prostitute (male or female)
   - anyone from central, eastern, or southern Africa or some Caribbean countries
   - anyone believed or known to be HIV positive
   - anyone who has ever been in jail (forced anal sex and IV drug use are common in prison)

2. Have you (or any of your partners) had an unprotected sexual encounter after an HIV test?
3. Have you (or any of your partners) ever had an STD, such as gonorrhea, syphilis, herpes, or genital warts?
4. Have you (or any of your partners) used needle drugs and shared injection equipment?
5. Have you (or any of your partners) ever blacked out from using alcohol or drugs, especially during sex?
6. Did you (or any of your partners) have any transfusions of blood or blood components between 1977 and 1985? (If you had any major surgery between

1977 and 1985, or if you were ever under a general anesthetic in that time span, find out if you were given any kind of transfusion.)

7. Are you a hemophiliac? Did you have unprotected sex with a hemophiliac before 1990?

8. Have you (or any of your partners) received donor semen, donor eggs, transplanted organs, or transplanted tissue?

9. Have you (or any of your partners) ever been exposed to blood in your work setting?

If you answered "yes" to any of these questions, you should be tested for HIV exposure, even if you are as healthy as can be.

Your age is also a factor in HIV infection. Women in their teens and women over forty-five are more vulnerable to HIV. Teenaged women are vulnerable due to an immature cervix, which acts as a less efficient barrier to HIV than does a more mature cervix. After age forty-five when women begin to enter menopause, they experience thinning and drying of their vaginal walls and tissue. In addition to this, the cervical mucus produced by the teenaged and menopausal cervix is simply not as HIV resistant as it is during other times in a woman's reproductive life.

### If You Suspect Your Partner Is HIV Positive

HIV can remain dormant in an infected person for up to ten years or more before any symptoms manifest. There are a number of symptoms you can look out for: weight loss, loss of appetite, fever, sweats or night sweats, skin rashes or pigmented lesions, general dryness of the skin, enlarged lymph nodes below the ear and around the neck, headaches, persistent cold symptoms, whitish or painful lesions around or inside the mouth, persistent cough or shortness of breath, abdominal pain, diarrhea, depression or severe mood changes, cognitive difficulties, bowel or bladder dysfunction (bed-wetting), general muscle weakness, persistent oral yeast infections, persistent or chronic vaginal yeast infections in women for more than a year, and sores around the genitals, such as herpes, which fail to heal within a reasonable time.

## What to Eat

If you frequently engage in anal sex, it's important to have a diet that is high in fiber, to facilitate regular bowel movements without having to rely on laxatives, which can be harsh and make that area more sensitive.

## Cereals and Breads

Most of us will turn to cereals and breads to boost our fiber intake, which experts recommend should be at about 25 to 35 gm per day. Refer to Table 9.1, which lists amounts of insoluble fiber, to help gauge whether you're getting enough. (Insoluble fiber is good not only for colon health but also for your heart.) If you're a little under par, an easy way to boost your fiber intake is to simply add pure wheat bran (which is available in health food stores or supermarkets in a sort of sawdustlike format) to your foods. Three tablespoons of wheat bran is equal to 4.4 gm fiber. Sprinkle one to two tablespoons onto cereals, rice, pasta, or meat dishes. You can also sprinkle it into orange juice or low-fat yogurt. It has virtually no calories. It's important to drink a glass of water with your wheat bran, as well as a glass of water after you've finished your wheat bran–enriched meal.

**Table 9.1   Amounts of Insoluble Fiber in Cereals and Breads**

| Cereals | Grams of Insoluble Fiber |
| --- | --- |
| *(based on ½ cup unless otherwise specified)* | |
| Fiber First | 15.0 |
| Fiber One | 12.8 |
| All-Bran | 10.0 |
| oatmeal (1 cup) | 5.0 |
| Raisin Bran (¾ cup) | 4.6 |
| Bran Flakes (1 cup) | 4.4 |
| Shreddies (⅔ cup) | 2.7 |
| Cheerios (1 cup) | 2.2 |
| cornflakes (1¼ cup) | 0.8 |
| Special K (1¼ cup) | 0.4 |
| Rice Krispies (1¼ cup) | 0.3 |

| Breads | Grams of Insoluble Fiber |
| --- | --- |
| *(based on 1 slice)* | |
| rye | 2.0 |
| pumpernickel | 2.0 |
| 12-grain | 1.7 |
| 100% whole wheat | 1.3 |
| raisin | 1.0 |
| cracked wheat | 1.0 |
| white | 0 |

Keep in mind that some of the newer high-fiber breads on the market today have up to 7 gm fiber per slice. Table 9.1 is based on what is normally found in typical grocery stores.

## Fruits, Beans, and Veggies

Another easy way of boosting fiber content is to eat more fruits, beans (or legumes), and vegetables. Table 9.2 shows measurements for insoluble fiber found in fruits, beans, and vegetables. Some of these numbers may surprise you!

**Table 9.2  Amounts of Insoluble Fiber in Fruits, Beans, and Vegetables**

| Fruit | Grams of Insoluble Fiber |
| --- | --- |
| raspberries (¾ cup) | 6.4 |
| strawberries (1 cup) | 4.0 |
| blackberries (½ cup) | 3.9 |
| orange (1) | 3.0 |
| apple (1) | 2.0 |
| pear (½ medium) | 2.0 |
| grapefruit (½ cup) | 1.1 |
| kiwi (1) | 1.0 |

| Beans | Grams of Insoluble Fiber |
| --- | --- |
| *(based on ½ cup unless otherwise specified)* | |
| green beans (1 cup) | 4.0 |
| white beans | 3.6 |
| kidney beans | 3.3 |
| pinto beans | 3.3 |
| lima beans | 3.2 |

| Vegetables | Grams of Insoluble Fiber |
| --- | --- |
| *(based on ½ cup unless otherwise specified)* | |
| baked potato with skin (1 large) | 4.0 |
| acorn squash | 3.8 |
| peas | 3.0 |
| creamed, canned corn | 2.7 |
| Brussels sprouts | 2.3 |
| asparagus (¾ cup) | 2.3 |
| corn kernels | 2.1 |
| zucchini | 1.4 |
| carrots (cooked) | 1.2 |
| broccoli | 1.1 |

## *Drink Water with Fiber*

How many people do you know who say "But I *do* eat tons of fiber and I'm *still* constipated!"? Probably quite a few. Well, the reason they remain constipated in spite of their high-fiber diet is because they are not drinking water with fiber. Water means water. Milk, coffee, tea, juice, or soft drinks are not a substitute for water. Unless you drink water with your fiber, the fiber will not bulk up in your colon to create the nice, soft bowel movements you so desire. Think of fiber as a sponge. Obviously, a dry sponge won't work. You must soak it with water in order for it to be useful. Same thing here. Fiber without water is as useful as a dry sponge. You gotta soak your fiber! So here is the fiber-water recipe:

- Drink two glasses of water with your fiber. This means having a glass of water with whatever you're eating. (Even if what you're eating does not contain much fiber, drinking water with your meal is a good habit to get into!)
- Drink another glass of water after you eat.

It's also important to eat probiotic foods to keep levels of healthy, or "good," bacteria in your colon, particularly if you are having regular enemas or douching your rectal/anal area. See Chapter 6 for more on probiotic foods.

# Flower Power

Tea-tree oil is a natural antiseptic. Use it to supplement sterilization of all objects and body parts that need to be sterilized. Bathe daily in a sitz bath of tea-tree oil and lavender, especially after high-risk anal acts. You can also rinse with tea-tree oil after rimming or use as a gargle after vigorous oral sex.

# How to Move

If you're engaging in anal sex, anal dilation and relaxation exercises can assist in a better experience. You should do the following by yourself, until you are confident you can accommodate a penis:

1. Make yourself comfortable in bed lying on a towel or lying on your back in a warm bath.
2. Raise your knees toward your chest.
3. Explore the anal area with a finger covered in lubrication. Use a water-based lubricant only.

4. Use gentle pressure with a finger moving in a circle around the anus; this will relax the sphincter enough so you will be able to insert one digit.

5. Once the finger can be comfortably inserted, begin to stretch the sphincter with circling motions inside the anus.

6. Further dilation by relaxation, not stretching, can be done with the aid of a dilator, known as a butt plug, which you leave inside. Butt plugs can be purchased at quality sex shops.

# PART III

# When There's a Problem

# 10

# When You Have a Sexually Transmitted Disease (STD)

EVEN THOUGH SAFER sex practices have been taught for more than fifteen years, sexually transmitted diseases continue to spread. Today, more than twenty million North Americans are infected with STDs each year, and women and teenagers carry the burden of STD infection. STD refers to any disease that can be transmitted through sexual contact: viruses, bacteria, lice, and other parasites. Each era has always had a name for STDs. In the early twentieth century, STDs were known as the clap, which was slang for gonorrhea, and bad blood, for syphilis; in the 1960s and 1970s, STDs were known as VD, short for venereal disease. VD originally encompassed five traditional infections: gonorrhea, syphilis, herpes (cancroid), lymphogranuloma venereum, and granuloma inguinale. The term *sexually transmitted disease* has come to replace these terms. More than twenty organisms and syndromes, including HIV, are considered STDs.

It's important to note that STDs can also be transmitted from mother to baby during pregnancy or childbirth and breast-feeding. It's also important to note that you can get some STDs, such as herpes, by kissing and caressing or by having casual contact (sharing the same glass) with infected areas.

The most common STDs are chlamydia, herpes, gonorrhea, genital warts, syphilis, hepatitis B, and crabs.

In early 1996 Canadian researchers discovered that common bacterial infections, many of which are STDs, can actually play a role in causing hardening of the arteries, which leads to heart disease. Bacteria can trigger the buildup of fatty plaque in your arteries. These preliminary findings were reported in the *Journal of Clinical Microbiology*. Chlamydia was particularly implicated as a chief agent in heart disease because people in the study with atherosclerosis (hardened arteries) all tested positive for chlamydia—just another reason to wear condoms.

# Asymptomatic STDs

The trouble with many STDs is that there are often no symptoms in the early stages. By the time you have symptoms, a lot of damage (e.g., pelvic inflammatory disease [PID]) may already have been done (see further on).

## *Chlamydia*

Chlamydia is a very common STD and is cited as the most common cause of female-factor infertility. In 2000 some three million new cases were diagnosed. As many as 85 percent of infections in women and 40 percent of infections in men are asymptomatic. When it is not treated, chlamydia can lead to PID.

Chlamydia was discovered in the late 1970s and is neither a typical bacteria nor a virus. It is very small in size, like a virus, and has some characteristics of bacteria but can't manufacture its own energy the way bacteria or viruses can. Instead, it acts like a parasite, entering cells and using their energy. It is caused by an organism known as *Chlamydia trachomatis*, but it is not always easy to detect. Ten percent of the time, people who have chlamydia will test negative for it.

Some experts estimate that chlamydia causes 50 percent of all pelvic infections and 25 percent of all tubal pregnancies due to scarring of the fallopian tubes. It can also cause urethral infections, cervicitis (inflammation of the cervix), and PID, which can lead to infertility or complications during pregnancy or childbirth.

In men, chlamydia can cause nongonococcal urethritis (NGU). Nongonococcal means the infection is not caused by gonorrhea; urethritis means inflammation of the urethra. If a man with NGU has sex with a healthy woman, she will probably get chlamydia. Finally, chlamydia can also cause proctitis, which is inflammation of the rectum.

The symptoms of early-stage chlamydia are usually nonexistent for four out of five women afflicted with the disease. The most common symptom, if any, is increased or abnormal vaginal discharge, which usually develops about fourteen days after infection. Sometimes a strong, rather foul vaginal odor develops as well. Painful urination, unusual vaginal bleeding, bleeding after sex, and low abdominal pain may also be signs, and the cervix may become inflamed (noticeable when you are examined by a doctor). If your cervix bleeds easily after a Pap smear, this is also a major clue. If chlamydia spreads to your uterus and fallopian tubes, it will have progressed to PID, and you may develop some of the symptoms discussed further on.

One way to find out whether you have chlamydia is to ask your partner whether he has symptoms of NGU. Painful urination or urethral discharge that appears one to three weeks after infection are telltale signs. About 10 percent of the time, men show no symptoms of chlamydia either. Chlamydia can now be detected in men through a simple urine test. The best thing you can do if you're sexually active is to be regularly screened for chlamydia by your family doctor. The test is 90 percent accurate. The screening is simple: your doctor takes a culture swab of cervical mucus. It can be done in conjunction with a Pap test. How regularly should you be swabbed? Every time you have a new partner. If you test negative but still suspect it, request antibiotic treatment anyway. Even if you are treated for nonexistent chlamydia, the treatment is relatively harmless to you, other than the mild side effects of antibiotics discussed further on.

NGU can also be caused by *Ureaplasma urealyticum* (T-Mycoplasma), another STD. Some practitioners feel that this can also cause PID in women. However, culturing for ureaplasma is very difficult. If it is suspected, your doctor will find it easier to just treat you for ureaplasma and not bother culturing.

The good news about chlamydia is that it is extremely easy to treat: tetracycline will cure both chlamydia and ureaplasma infections. The drug usually prescribed is called doxycycline, a derivative of tetracycline. Two doxycycline capsules per day for ten days will do the trick. Tetracycline is cheaper and must be taken four times a day for seven days, but many people forget to take that many pills, which is why the doxycycline is better. If you are pregnant or cannot be on tetracycline, you'll be given erythromycin. Penicillin, on the other hand, is not effective here.

As many as 10 percent of all pregnant women are believed to be infected with chlamydia. This can lead to all kinds of complications during pregnancy or at birth, including miscarriage, infant pneumonia, infant conjunctivitis (severe eye infection), and even infant blindness. If you're pregnant, request a screening for chlamydia as soon as you can. If you have chlamydia, you can be treated with erythromycin. The antibiotics should be taken as prescribed, or the infection could resurface. After you've finished your antibiotics, you will need to be rescreened to make sure that the infection is gone. Abstain from all sexual activity until you're sure that you are cured.

A final note on chlamydia: the best way to avoid chlamydia is to practice safer sex, discussed in Chapter 7. It is also believed that hormonal contraceptives increase your risks of exposure because the cervical mucus changes and is therefore a better host for chlamydia. The most disturbing fact about chlamydia is that it is a leading cause of infertility. Physicians believe that if more attention were paid to preventing chlamydia, infertility clinics would lose revenue, and the infertility "epidemic" going on today in North America would dramatically decrease.

## *Gonorrhea*

Rates for gonorrhea have gone up rather than down in the last twenty years. Between 1997 and 1999 in the United States, the rate of gonorrhea climbed roughly 10 percent. Gonorrhea is caused by the bacterium gonococcus. This bacterium makes a home for itself in the genitals and urinary organs and affects the cervix, urethra, and anus. You can transmit the virus through oral sex, anal sex, and regular intercourse. If an infected person has gonorrhea discharge on his or her fingers and then touches your eyes, you can also get gonorrhea and develop conjunctivitis.

Gonorrhea is fairly common and does more damage to women than to men. However, it is less common than chlamydia. If you're diagnosed with gonorrhea, you'll also be treated for chlamydia. The reasoning is that if you managed to contract gonorrhea, there's an enormous chance that you already have chlamydia. In fact, women can often be simultaneously infected with both chlamydia and gonorrhea if the partner is a carrier of both infections. Women are thought to have a 30 percent chance of contracting gonorrhea after one sexual contact with an infected partner and almost a 100 percent chance if they are on hormonal contraception. Like chlamydia, early-stage gonorrhea is asymptomatic about 80 percent of the time. Symptoms depend on where the gonococcal bacteria are living.

Gonococci (plural for gonococcus) love the cervix most of all, so cervical infection is the most common. About three days after infection, a discharge develops, caused by an irritant released when the gonococci die. You may notice it yourself, or your doctor may be able to see redness on the cervix. If your urethra was infected, you'll experience painful and more frequent urination. Conjunctivitis, menstrual irregularities, spotting after intercourse, and swelling of the vulva (vulvitis) are also symptoms. If gonorrhea spreads to your fallopian tubes, it will have progressed to PID, and you may have PID symptoms, discussed further on. Most PID is caused by gonorrhea or chlamydia.

If you contracted gonorrhea in your throat through oral sex, you may have a sore throat and swollen glands. When gonorrhea progresses into something called disseminated gonococcal infection, symptoms can get really nasty: rashes, chills, fever, painful joints and tendons in the wrists and fingers, and sores on the hands, fingers, feet, and toes. During your annual pelvic exam, your doctor will check your cervix for any unusual discharge and may take a culture as a routine screening. Usually, gonorrhea tests are 90 percent accurate if a culture test is done; if only a gram stain (in which the discharge is smeared onto a slide and stained) is performed, the test is only 50 percent accurate for women but very accurate for men with symptoms. The best thing to do if you suspect gonorrhea is to request two culture tests one week apart.

If you do have gonorrhea, you will either be screened for chlamydia or automatically treated for it. Gonorrhea is easily treated with antibiotics: one dose of ceftriaxone (Rocephin) and a follow-up prescription of doxycycline to cure the probable chlamydia. The Centers for Disease Control may revise recommended treatment to include certain oral antibiotics. If you're pregnant, you should be routinely screened for gonorrhea, but double-check! All hospitals now treat the eyes of newborns with silver nitrate or antibiotic drops to prevent gonococcal infection, just in case.

A crucial point is that many women self-diagnose gonorrhea discharge as a yeast infection. They then self-treat with over-the-counter yeast infection medication (see Chapter 6). Vaginal discharge can mean anything, including the presence of tumors. Whenever you notice unusual discharge, always get it checked by a qualified primary care physician or gynecologist.

## Human Papillomavirus (Genital Warts)

Discussed more in Chapter 3 (on cervical health), human papillomavirus (HPV) is the most common sexually transmitted infection in North America and is now considered to be the cause of cervical dysplasia and cervical cancer. Fortunately, a vaccine for HPV will soon be available.

This virus is very similar to the one that causes skin warts, but there are several types of HPV floating around. Warts are painless and can appear on the vulva, cervix, or penis. Unless the warts are on the cervix, your doctor can usually spot them and treat them with a solution that will burn the wart off. HPV on the cervix can take the form of raised or flat lesions. Both types of lesions will be picked up by a Pap smear. If left untreated, HPV can cause the cells on the lining of your cervix to change, which can lead to cervical cancer. Detection of HPV by a Pap smear, colposcopy, and treatment is discussed in Chapter 3. HPV is rampant in sexually active women ages eighteen to thirty-five. Practicing safer sex (as discussed in Chapter 7) can prevent HPV.

HPV can be treated but never technically cured. Once the warts are removed, the virus may not cause any further problems. However, recurrences are common. It's also possible to be infected with another strain of the virus, since infection with one strain doesn't protect you from another. There are more than seventy strains of HPV. Follow-up Pap smears for the first couple of years after HPV diagnosis and annual Pap smears after that will enable you to nip HPV in the bud should it decide to erupt again. See Chapter 3 for more information on treating cervical dysplasia and HPV.

## Hepatitis B

Hepatitis B is a virus that causes inflammation of the liver. It is a serious STD that is on the rise, and it is a hundred times more infectious than HIV. It is transmitted through contaminated needles or blood and also through mucus-sharing activities that involve saliva, semen, or vaginal fluid, which enter the bloodstream of an uninfected person. Like HIV, hepatitis B can flourish in an anal-sex environment and among drug users. Tattooing and ear piercing are other common routes of infection. Mothers can also pass on this virus to newborns during childbirth. Those at highest risk for hepatitis B are intravenous (IV) drug users, gay men, health care workers, and prostitutes.

For hepatitis B it can take up to 180 days after infection for any hepatitis symptoms to develop. In an extreme case of hepatitis B, symptoms are nasty and include skin lesions, arthritis, fever, fatigue, nausea, diarrhea, vomiting, and so on. The second phase of the illness is characterized by jaundice, dark urine, pale stools, and a tender, enlarged liver.

Most people who get hepatitis B remain well, have no symptoms, and completely recover. However, even if you're asymptomatic, the virus can cause damage to the liver, which can lead to serious illness and even death. Those who do get sick generally experience flulike symptoms, jaundice, darker urine, and lighter stools. Generally, you will recover from hepatitis, but if you're unlucky, the illness can overwhelm you for several months; you don't want to get hepatitis if you can avoid it. Some people will always carry the hepatitis B virus and will remain infectious to others.

There is no cure for hepatitis B, but there is a vaccine. In fact, safer sex is not considered adequate protection from hepatitis B; only a hepatitis B vaccine will protect you. The vaccine is given by injection, three doses over a six-month period. The second shot is given one month after the first shot; the third shot is given five months after the second. Side effects from the vaccine are rare, other than a sore arm for a day or two. If you do suffer from any side effects, you'll experience general feelings of unwellness and fatigue. Contact the physician or clinic that administered the vaccine.

# Symptomatic STDs

The STDs discussed in the following sections can be asymptomatic and can be transmitted without the person knowing she or he has the virus. But unlike the STDs just discussed under "Asymptomatic STDs," symptoms often do make an appearance in early stages.

## *Herpes*

Since the 1970s herpes rates have only increased. In white teens, genital herpes has quintupled; in African Americans older than eleven, 45.9 percent tested positive for genital herpes. The nature of herpes sores (see further on) makes it easier to be infected with HIV. Surveys show that roughly 80 percent of Americans are unaware of how widespread genital herpes has become, while 65 percent say they are not concerned. This is perhaps the most alarming statistic of all. Recent data, however, suggest that only 37 percent of patients who acquire herpes simplex virus type II have symptoms, although overt disease may follow.

Herpes is caused by the herpes simplex virus. The virus enters the body through the skin and mucous membranes of the mouth and genitals and then permanently sets up shop at the base of the spine. Herpes was the "AIDS" of the 1960s and 1970s—it was the STD everyone feared most because it was permanent. There are two types of herpes: herpes simplex virus type I (HSV I), which is characterized by cold sores and fever blisters on the mouth and face, and herpes simplex virus type II (HSV II), which is the dreaded genital herpes. HSV I can be transmitted through kissing. You can also contract both HSV I and HSV II if you have oral sex or intercourse with an infected partner or HSV I if you receive oral sex from an HSV I–infected partner. Herpes is contagious whether the sores are active or not; it is most contagious, however, when the sores are active, although most infection takes place when the sores are inactive. This is when herpes is known to be asymptomatic. When the sores are active, they're visible and stand as a warning to the other partner "not to touch." Indeed, touching the sores with your fingers and then touching the skin of a healthy person may transmit the virus. That's how potent the sores are. However, when there are no visible sores, the virus can still be transmitted.

The herpes sores are called vesicles; they are painful, watery blisters that occur anywhere from two to twenty days after infection. Just before the vesicles appear, a herpes outbreak can be preceded by a tingling or itching sensation on the skin surrounding the outbreak. This is known as the prodromal period. More than 50 percent of herpes is transmitted from people who don't even know they carry the herpes virus. People with herpes often have no symptoms of herpes or have such mild, vague symptoms, such as swollen glands, fever, or fatigue, that they dismiss it. Experts refer to this type of transmission as asymptomatic shedding, which frequently occurs within the first hundred days of initial infection. Women will often shed herpes from the cervix, passing it on to a partner. One study found that in 150 mutually monogamous heterosexual couples, 10 percent transmitted herpes to each other within a one-year time span. Like HIV, women are more likely to get it from men than vice versa, and in half of those cases, the virus will be transmitted through shedding. It's also common to live with a herpes carrier for years and never become infected.

Stress can trigger the first herpes episode. The vesicles that women get in HSV II are most commonly found on the labia, clitoris, vaginal opening, and perineum and sometimes on the vaginal walls, buttocks, thighs, anus, and navel. Women can also have sores on the cervix, but these are not painful. Within a few days, the vesicles rupture, leaving behind shallow blisters that may ooze or bleed. After three or four days, scabs form and the vesicles fall off, healing by themselves without treatment.

The initial herpes outbreaks are by far the worst. You may find it painful to urinate. Filling an empty shampoo bottle or squeeze-top bottle with warm water and simultaneously pouring it on the sores as you urinate will help. (The urine burns the sores, which is very painful.) You can also urinate in the shower or bath if the pain gets really bad. You may experience dull aches or burning sensations on your vulva, or you might develop vulvitis, which is inflammation of your vulva. Fever, headaches, and swollen lymph nodes around the groin are also common with the first outbreaks. The initial outbreaks also take longer to heal, lasting about two to three weeks. Then the virus will start to taper off, and you may go from monthly initial outbreaks to just annual outbreaks. The usual pattern is nasty initial outbreaks, followed by milder recurrent episodes within three to twelve months after the first herpes outbreak. Then recurrences become milder and far more sporadic, perhaps once every two years. Factors such as poor diet, caffeine, and hormonal elements trigger herpes outbreaks. The presence of other infections, such as vaginitis, genital warts, or yeast, can also trigger a recurrence.

## New Facts About Herpes

Apparently, the older you are, the more at risk you are for herpes. The incidence of this disease increases with age. Roughly 17 percent of those between the ages of fifteen and twenty-nine years are infected with HSV II, while 20 percent of those between the ages of thirty and forty-four have HSV II.

Like many viruses, there is still no cure for herpes; but there is treatment available to both control the symptoms of outbreaks and prevent future outbreaks. The standard treatment for a primary infection or first outbreak episode is oral antiviral medication, in the form of oral acyclovir, valacyclovir, or famcyclovir. Other therapies, such as sitz baths, and natural treatments can help as well (see under "What to Eat" and "Flower Power").

## How Oral Sex Has Changed Herpes Forever

While 70 percent of the people on this planet have cold sores, which sounds much better than herpes simplex virus I (HSV I), the popularity of oral sex has now transferred HSV I (once only seen above the belt) to below the belt. In short, HSV I can be transmitted to the genital area, and HSV II (once seen only below the belt) can be transmitted to the mouth. Basically, the labeling of HSV I and HSV II is starting to blur to the point where doctors don't even bother to distinguish I from II. They simply call herpes sores in the genital area "genital herpes," regardless of whether it's HSV I or HSV II. What doctors can tell you is that HSV I below the waist is always much milder than HSV II and tends to occur far less frequently. Similarly, HSV II above the waist is much milder than HSV I and occurs far less frequently as well.

Previous infection with HSV I may provide some resistance to HSV II or make HSV II less severe. About 25 percent of people with HSV II may also never experience a recurrence. To obtain a definite diagnosis, a culture is recommended. A blood test can also detect whether you have herpes antibodies present. The problem with this test is that it can only tell you that there has been an infection at some point. It doesn't tell you when the initial infection occurred. When you have only subtle symptoms of herpes, there's a 30 percent chance that you can have a false negative test result, but you can test positive for herpes after one bout of mouth cold sores. Standard blood tests cannot accurately distinguish between HSV I and HSV II. Another problem is that just because you have a lesion on your mouth or genitals doesn't mean it's always herpes. In fact, 50 percent of the time it's not. That also means that about 30 percent of the time a doctor will mistake nonherpes lesions for herpes.

The only blood test that can distinguish between HSV I and HSV II is the Western Blot test, which is not performed at most labs. But if you want to catch a plane, train, or bus and head over to the Department of Virology at the University of Washington in Seattle, you can get the test done without a problem.

For more information on natural therapies, contact the Herpes Resource Center, which operates a hotline, 919-361-8488, or the Herpes Hotline and Advice Center, at 212-213-6150. Also refer to Appendixes A and B for sources of additional information. More than thirty million North Americans are currently infected with herpes, but only about 25 percent of them know they have it. Preventing herpes is easily done by practicing safer sex, discussed in Chapter 7.

If you have herpes:

1. Don't have sex when you have active sores, and insist your partner wears a condom, even when there are no sores present. (Or you can wear the female condom.) If you're in a monogamous relationship and wish to conceive, ask your primary care physician for advice. The risk of passing on herpes to your spouse or partner years after an initial outbreak may be quite low if you don't suffer from recurrent herpes.

2. Don't donate blood during an initial outbreak. (Men should not donate sperm.)

3. Take care of yourself. Exercise, get enough sleep, and eat well. Cut down on the bad habits (smoking, drinking, etc.). This will help prevent outbreaks.

4. If you're not receiving the care you need from your doctor, go someplace else. A doctor who cannot provide you with good information about herpes, or who is insensitive to herpes, doesn't deserve your loyalty. Request a referral to a dermatologist or infectious disease specialist if you feel you're being mismanaged.

5. Consider a herpes support program. This will help you find other women who can lend companionship and support and will help you realize you're not alone. Support groups can also help you find a good herpes practitioner.

The language of herpes is broken down into the following:

- *Primary genital herpes:* This means a genital herpes infection in an individual not previously infected with either HSV I or HSV II.
- *First episode genital herpes:* This refers to the first recognized attack of genital herpes in an individual previously infected by either HSV I or HSV II.
- *Asymptomatic shedding:* This refers to the shedding of the virus from the skin's surface, in the absence of symptoms.
- *Recurrent genital herpes:* This refers to recurring attacks of herpes, where there are visible sores on the anus or genitals.

### Herpes Vaccines

Herpes vaccines are currently under development and in testing stages. The most successful vaccine showed effectiveness only in women, not men, and only in women who had not been previously infected with HSV I, the strain responsible for most cases of oral herpes.

## Syphilis

In the past, syphilis was a very serious, incurable disease that often resulted in madness. Today, it's easily treated with antibiotics. Syphilis is caused by a bacterium known as spirochete. There are four stages of syphilis: primary, secondary, tertiary (late stage), and neurosyphilis. It's transmitted through sexual or skin contact with someone who is already infected. A pregnant woman can also transmit the disease to her unborn child. Syphilis spreads through open sores called chancres or rashes that pass through the mucous membrane lining the mouth, genitals, anus, or broken skin.

During the 1970s syphilis was virtually eliminated as an STD because it had been treated so aggressively in previous decades. In 1985, however, the incidence of syphilis began skyrocketing in the United States and has continued to rise ever since.

Diagnosing syphilis is tricky. Known as the Great Masquerader, syphilis has symptoms that imitate other symptoms and can be misdiagnosed. Syphilis is diagnosed through a blood test that checks for antibodies to spirochetes in the bloodstream. Syphilis is a miserable, damaging disease. The first two stages of syphilis can be completely cured, leaving no permanent damage. Tertiary syphilis and subsequent neurosyphilis (when the disease spreads to the brain) can also be cured, preventing any further damage. Once damage is done, however, that damage can't be repaired. Amazingly, syphilis is treated with simple antibiotics, either penicillin or tetracycline. After you've been treated for syphilis at any stage, you'll need to have a follow-up test to make sure you've been cured.

## Primary Syphilis

In primary syphilis a chancre will develop. Chancres can look like pimples, open sores, or blisters and are generally painless. It can take between nine and ninety days for a chancre to develop after infection. Chancres usually appear on the genitals, but they can also show up on the fingertips, lips, breasts, anus, or mouth. Ninety percent of the people with chancres don't notice them. This is unfortunate, since it is at the primary stage that syphilis is most infectious. If left untreated, syphilis progresses to the secondary stage within six weeks to three months after infection.

## Secondary Syphilis

Secondary syphilis can last for months, even years. Symptoms include hair loss, sore joints, widespread rashes including on the palms or soles, swollen lymph nodes, and weight loss. (It can possibly be misdiagnosed as HIV or a severely complicated HIV infection.) Flulike symptoms are common as well. There may also be a raised area around the genitals and anus. At this point syphilis can be transmitted through mucus and contact with the raised patches. If it's still not treated by this time, syphilis will go into a type of remission known as a latent stage. Here, someone with syphilis will feel fine and experience no symptoms at all. When syphilis goes into a latent stage, it can last for up to twenty years. The disease is also no longer infectious by this stage, but it can do a lot of damage to men or women and attack the body at full force at the late, or tertiary, stage.

## Tertiary Syphilis (Late Stage)

If the syphilis remains untreated, it will move to the tertiary stage, where it can attack the heart, eyes, nervous system, or brain. It's extremely rare for anyone to get to this stage, but HIV-positive persons are less likely to be successfully treated for primary syphilis and may in fact wind up with tertiary syphilis. Request a syphilis screening if you suspect it or have been having unprotected sex with numerous partners. Tertiary syphilis is not contagious.

## Neurosyphilis

If tertiary syphilis is not treated, it can move into the final, most advanced stage of syphilis, neurosyphilis, which can cause serious problems in the brain and nervous system. It is diagnosed through a spinal tap. Symptoms are headaches, stiffness in the neck, confusion, blurred vision, blindness, abnormal eye movements, facial weakness, hearing loss, or loss of balance. This stage is not contagious.

# Infestations

Human beings regularly have things crawling around on their skin. Some microscopic beings, such as dust mites, are always there. Other beings live in our genital areas and can be passed on to other people through sexual activity or even sharing clothing or bedding that has been infested.

## Crabs (or Pubic Lice)

The name of this particular kind of louse (singular of lice) is *Phthirus pubis*. These round, pinhead-size bugs look like crabs. If you look hard enough, you can actually see them. They live in pubic hair, chest hair, armpit hair, and even eyelashes and eyebrows. You generally get crabs by having pubic-hair-to-pubic-hair contact with someone else who has them. But you can also get them from sleeping on infested bedding, using infested towels, or borrowing clothing from someone (like a roommate) who has them. Crabs are also bloodsuckers, and the main health danger to you is that they can give you other diseases such as typhus. You can't have crabs and not know it: you'll have an intolerable itching in the infested area, and you can see the crabs yourself without a microscope. Unfortunately, scratching the itch makes it worse and can transfer the lice to other parts of your body.

Treatment involves pesticide lotions: permethrin 5 percent (Elimite) and lindane 1 percent (Kwell), both of which should be used very carefully. If you're pregnant, you shouldn't use these. There are safer, nonprescription drugs you can ask your pharmacist about. None of these drugs can be used around the eyes, however. If you do have crabs in this area, petroleum jelly is recommended; it will smother the crabs. You can also see an ophthalmologist (eye specialist), who can prescribe a pesticide lotion that is safe for this area.

Once you're treated, you'll need to wash all your clothing, bedding, and towels in hot water, or just dry-clean them. The reason for this is because the eggs can live up to six days, and you can reinfest yourself or someone else.

## Scabies

Scabies are mites that live under the skin. They're trickier than crabs because they cause skin irritations that resemble eczema, allergies, or even poison ivy. The eggs and feces of the scabies will cause tremendous irritation and itching as well. You may find raised bumps or ridges on the skin between fingers, under the breasts, or around the waist, wrists, genitals, or buttocks. You can get scabies through both sexual contact and contact with infested clothing, bedding, towels, or even furniture. Lindane 1 percent is about the only treatment there is. For pregnant women, crotamiton (Eurax) is prescribed.

For both crabs and scabies, see a dermatologist in addition to your primary care physician. Because both the infestations and the treatments irritate the skin, it's wise to have soothing lotions on hand to apply after treatment.

# Rare STDS

The STDs discussed in this section are extremely rare but are still seen.

## *Chancroid*

Chancroid is very similar to herpes and is caused by the bacterium *Haemophilus ducreyi*. It begins as a dark spot on the genitals, called a macule. The macule enlarges, fills with pus, and develops into a painful ulcerlike sore. Unlike herpes, chancroid can be cured with antibiotics. Chancroid is rare and definitely not on the top-ten list of common STDs. Like herpes, you can get chancroid through intimate contact with an infected person, or by touching the pus and then touching your mucous membrane. This is usually a "just for men" STD. Chancroid is also known as soft chancre or mixed chancre. It's normally treated with azithromycin in a single dose.

## *Lymphogranuloma Venereum (or Frei's Disease)*

Lymphogranuloma venereum, also known as fifth venereal disease in medical-speak, is actually a strain of chlamydia. It is characterized by three stages: the first stage manifests with open sores or ulcers around the genitals; in the second stage, enlarged lymph nodes develop around the genital area; the third stage is a kind of genital elephantiasis, where the lymph nodes fill with lymph fluid and become noticeably large and obstructed. The rectal opening can also narrow due to scarring, which makes bowel movements painful. This disease is quite rare, transmitted sexually, and cured with antibiotics.

## *Granuloma Inguinale (or Donovanosis)*

Again very rare, granuloma inguinale is an STD that is similar to chancroid but attacks only women. It is characterized by deep ulcers on the vulva; they're found mainly on the mons, pubis, and labia. It is caused by the bacterium *Calymmatobacterium granulomatis* and tends to affect persons with darker pigmentation. It is also known as fourth venereal disease in medical-speak. It is transmitted through direct contact with an infected person. This STD is usually treated with the antibiotic azithromycin.

# Pelvic Inflammatory Disease (PID)

*Pelvic inflammatory disease* is a general term that refers to infection and inflammation of one or more of your pelvic organs: your cervix, uterus, fallopian tubes, or ovaries (known as your upper genital tract). These infections can also spread to other parts of your body, infecting your abdominal cavity, kidneys, liver, lungs, and so on. PID is a serious condition that affects more than one million women each year in North America. It's been more easily diagnosed since the availability of laparoscopy in the 1970s. Prior to laparoscopy, women with chronic pelvic pain were hard to diagnose. As a result, women with chronic PID were often misdiagnosed or were branded hypochondriacs when they complained of chronic pelvic pain or other PID symptoms, outlined further on.

## *What Causes PID?*

Bacteria. Normally, the cervix acts as a barrier and prevents bacteria from getting inside the upper pelvic region. But when the uterus is invaded by an STD or dilated for any reason, bacteria can enter the uterus and do a lot of damage. For example, when certain bacterial STDs—primarily gonorrhea and chlamydia—remain untreated, the infection can spread higher inside your pelvis and cause PID.

Bacteria can also get inside your pelvis through IUD insertion, the second major cause of PID in countries that use IUDs; douching; certain pelvic surgical procedures such as abortions, D & Cs, and amniocentesis; and natural phenomena such as miscarriages and childbirth. Smoking has also been linked to PID. Both current and past smokers were found to be twice as likely as nonsmokers to develop PID. The reasons why are not known, however.

In many cases, PID can be avoided by an accurate diagnosis of the initial STD that caused PID in the first place. In the majority of cases, PID is actually preventable.

## *Symptoms of PID*

Because PID is a general label that doesn't tell you where the infection is, the symptoms can vary depending on what's infected. Although there are several symptoms associated with PID, the common pattern is to experience only one or two of them. Some women have only mild symptoms, some women have symptoms so severe they can't function, and some women experience no symptoms at all and may discover they have PID only when they investigate infertility.

The most common symptom is lower abdominal pain. This pain may be sporadic or chronic and may occur only during or after intercourse, menstruation, or ovulation. Often the pain is on one side of the abdomen and increases with movement: walking, climbing, and so forth. This pain is always present during a pelvic examination, when your doctor feels your pelvic region manually to check for enlargements or abnormalities. Sometimes the pain is present when you urinate or have a bowel movement.

Other symptoms include lower back pain, nausea and dizziness, a low fever, chills, bleeding between periods, bleeding after intercourse, heavier menstrual cramps and flows, frequent urination, burning during urination or an inability to empty the bladder, unusual vaginal discharge with a foul odor, feeling like you have to constantly move your bowels, a general feeling of ill health, and abdominal bloating.

PID most commonly localizes in the fallopian tubes, causing salpingitis, or inflammation of the fallopian tubes. The tubes close up or scar as a result, leading to infertility (this is often reversible, however). Ectopic pregnancy can also result from PID for the same reasons. PID is divided into three categories of infection: acute, meaning severe; subacute, meaning less severe; and chronic, meaning that you have a fresh acute infection or that scarring has developed as a result of a previous infection.

## *Diagnosing PID*

First, during the speculum examination, your doctor will look for pus that might be coming out of the cervix, a symptom of cervicitis. If there is pus, a sample will be taken and sent to a lab. During a normal pelvic exam, your doctor should always perform what's known as a bimanual examination. Here, two fingers are inserted into your vagina, while your abdomen is felt on the outside simultaneously with the other hand. This procedure is comparable to fitting a comforter inside its cover: one hand on the inside, the other on the outside to adjust and feel for contours and abnormalities. Pain and swelling are classic signs of PID that an experienced gynecologist or primary care physician will immediately notice.

Upon diagnosis, your doctor will prescribe the appropriate antibiotic medication. You could conceivably be cured at this point. Your partner will also need to be treated for infection to prevent reinfecting you or someone else. (Treatment is discussed further on.) After treatment a follow-up exam and repeat cultures are necessary.

A blood test can indicate whether you're fighting an infection of some sort. If you are, you'll have increased levels of white blood cells.

An ultrasound test may also be helpful. It is most useful in determining whether an abscess has formed on the organs. Frequently, however, the ultrasound will be normal. In women with chronic PID and extensive tubal damage, there may be abnormal findings on the ultrasound.

Finally, if all else fails, a laparoscopy can be performed, which will definitely confirm a PID diagnosis. A laparoscopy might also be done if it's suspected you have abscesses (resulting from severe inflammation) that have burst—a potentially life-threatening situation. Laparoscopy is discussed in Chapter 13.

## *Antibiotic Therapy*

Once your PID is diagnosed, you'll be given what's known as broad-spectrum antibiotic therapy, which can eradicate chlamydia, gonorrhea, and other STDs and bacteria.

By far the best treatment approach is very high-dose intravenous antibiotic therapy followed by bed rest. To receive intravenous antibiotics, you'll need to be admitted into the hospital; in some cases, you can go home with a portable IV unit, but it depends on the hospital. Oral antibiotics for ten to fourteen days, in conjunction with rest, may follow. There are many different kinds of antibiotic regimens that work.

Yeast infections are one of the most common side effects of antibiotic therapy. (Review Chapter 6 for more information on managing yeast.) Antibiotics can also suppress your immune system, predisposing you to other health problems. Each antibiotic has its own side-effect profile available in the *Physicians' Desk Reference*. It's important to discuss what side effects to expect with your doctor.

Bed rest may need to accompany your treatment, and you should refrain from sexual activity while you're healing. Intercourse can spread pus around your pelvic cavity.

## *Surgical Treatment for PID*

Inflammation is one thing, abscesses are another. An abscess is when the inflamed tissue forms a collection of pus. The abscess can then rupture and spread the bacterial infection elsewhere, causing your PID to move to other parts of your pelvic region. Even though severe PID often involves inflammation with no abscesses, when there are abscesses, surgically removing them may be necessary, and surgically removing the badly abscessed organ may be an option. In either case, surgery is an emergency decision, made on the spot by your doctor as a necessary life-preserving step, or an elective decision, in which you choose surgery as a treatment option in advance and have time to prepare for it. If your abscesses have ruptured or are about to rupture, your doctor will schedule emergency surgery. Some patients may need more extensive surgery, which requires about a four-inch incision (laparotomy) in the abdomen. At this point, the surgical procedure performed will depend on the severity of PID and your desire for future fertility. It's crucial that you discuss exactly what kind of surgery to expect and take every precaution to preserve your reproductive organs if possible.

Both laparoscopy and laparotomy procedures are considered major surgery and are performed under a general anesthetic. A laparotomy is also performed if a salpingectomy, surgical removal of the fallopian tubes, is necessary. Depending on the severity of your PID and the location of the infection, this might actually be the best option for you. As mentioned before, it's most common for PID to localize in the fallopian tubes, which can cause a host of uncomfortable and painful symptoms for you. If the tubes are badly infected and have abscessed, removing them may just be the answer. This is often done to preserve your ovaries and uterus and prevent the PID from spreading further.

If abscesses have formed in the uterus or on the ovaries, more drastic surgery may be necessary, in the form of either a hysterectomy (surgical removal of the uterus) or an oophorectomy (surgical removal of the ovaries) or both. Both procedures are discussed in Chapter 20.

If surgery is being recommended to relieve your pain but there are no active infections, abscesses, or inflammations present, a procedure known as a presacral neurectomy is an option. In this operation, the sensory messages from the organs of the pelvis, carried along the presacral nerve, are eliminated by removing the nerve itself. Hence, the pain is also eliminated. This is also major surgery and requires a very skilled surgeon, since the nerve is close to large blood vessels. A presacral neurectomy is a more difficult operation to perform than a hysterectomy, but the surgery is about 75 percent effective in eliminating pelvic pain (a very promising statistic), and it does not affect fertility.

## *Prevention of PID*

The good news is that in almost all cases, PID is completely preventable. The number-one cause of PID in North America is an untreated STD; chlamydia and gonorrhea are the two STDs that are considered principally implicated in causing PID. If you're not practicing safer sex, request a screening for chlamydia and gonorrhea every time you have sex with a new partner. (Safer sex is discussed in Part II of this book.)

Partners of women with PID have infection rates as high as 53 percent with chlamydia and as high as 41 percent for gonorrhea. A large percentage of these infections are asymptomatic; the partners need to be treated for their STDs or women can be reinfected, which can develop into a second bout of PID.

Avoiding IUDs is another prevention factor; women who use IUDs are three to nine times as likely to develop PID. First, bacteria normally screened by your cervix can enter your uterus during IUD insertion. Second, even if no bacteria enter during insertion, the IUD can irritate your uterus later on, causing a local infection. (IUD advocates counter that an antibiotic can be prescribed at the time of insertion.)

If you're an IUD wearer in a mutually monogamous relationship, your risk of an IUD-related infection is small. However, if you're exposed to gonorrhea or chlamydia, you're more likely to develop PID.

There is also evidence that hormonal contraceptives affecting your cervical mucus may increase your chances of contracting an STD during unprotected sex. Apparently, the mucus is not as effective in screening out harmful bacteria as is "untampered," or natural, mucus.

Douching is also a factor in primary prevention. Douching may alter the vaginal environment and make it less protective against harmful bacteria, and douching may flush vaginal and cervical bacteria into the upper pelvic region, causing infections, which may lead to PID.

# What to Eat

When you're doing battle with an STD of any kind, it's important to keep your immune system strong. Follow the dietary guidelines for immune boosters given in Chapter 3.

It's also important to eat probiotic foods, which will populate your body with good bacteria and prevent fungal infections such as yeast. This is especially vital if you're taking antibiotics. (See Chapter 6 for information on probiotic foods.)

## Diet for Herpes

Women suffering from herpes can control initial and future outbreaks with diet and herbs (see under "Flower Power"). Foods high in caffeine (such as coffee, chocolate, and colas), sugar, or alcohol can trigger outbreaks. Avoid these foods during outbreaks. The following foods can help boost immunity and shorten outbreaks:

- red or purple grapes
- brewer's yeast
- vitamins C, A, and E (see Chapter 1)

## Lysine

Lysine, one of ten essential amino acids, has been shown to reduce herpes outbreaks and lessen their severity and frequency. Foods high in lysine include meat, cheese, yogurt, brewer's yeast, legumes, and wheat germ. Studies have proven that it works.

## Water

If you suffer from herpes, urinating during outbreaks can be painful. By drinking three eight-ounce glasses of water daily and by avoiding coffee and alcohol, you can help to dilute the concentration of your urine, which will make it more comfortable to urinate during outbreaks.

# Flower Power

Whichever STD you're battling, bathing in one or a combination of the following essential oils can dramatically improve symptoms such as burning or itching; these aromatherapy baths are especially helpful when you're suffering from a herpes outbreak. All of these oils can be added pure to a bath (see Chapter 1).

- basil
- cajeput
- calendula
- cedarwood
- cinnamon (this is strong—just two drops)
- citronella
- cloves
- eucalyptus
- geranium
- ginger
- lavender
- lemon
- lemon balm
- myrrh
- niaouli
- oregano
- patchouli
- peppermint
- rosemary
- sage
- tea tree
- thyme (strong—just two drops; excellent for scabies!)

The following herbs can help during herpes outbreaks:

- olive leaf extract
- *Prunella vulgaris*
- *Opuntia streptacantha*
- Chinese herbs of gentian, rhubarb, water plantain seed, and plantain (these are common treatments for herpes in traditional Chinese medicine)

The following herbs can help with any STD infection:

- burdock
- feverfew
- gentian
- goldenseal
- hyssop
- lemon
- pennyroyal
- red clover
- sarsaparilla
- Saint-John's-wort
- wintergreen
- wormwood

# How to Move

Stress can dramatically affect your immune system and predispose you to more frequent herpes outbreaks as well as leaving you vulnerable to other STDs and infections. By practicing breathing, yoga, or qi gong exercises, you can decrease your stress. The following yoga postures are considered helpful to boost immunity:

- The Tree
- Pose of Tranquility
- The Crocodile
- The Plough
- Angle Posture
- Spinal Twist
- Half or Full Shoulder Stand
- Sun Salutations

# 11

# HIV and Her

FIRST REPORTED IN women in 1981, AIDS became by 1990 the sixth leading cause of death in North American women aged twenty-five to forty-four. By 1998 AIDS was the fifth leading cause of death for women aged twenty-five to forty-four years and the third leading cause of death for black women in this age group. By 1999 women accounted for 23 percent of new AIDS diagnoses and 32 percent of newly reported HIV diagnoses. Information gathered through the AIDS Public Information Data Set and HIV/AIDS Surveillance Reports estimates that at least 54 percent of all AIDS cases in women came through heterosexual contact with a person not known to be infected or of high risk. Because of socioeconomic factors, women of color account for almost three-fourths of HIV infections reported among women between the ages of thirteen and twenty-four years. We also know that roughly 40 percent of all women who contract AIDS are exposed as teenagers or in their early twenties. Ten percent of new AIDS cases are in adults older than fifty, while rural populations are seeing a steady increase in AIDS. In older women, symptoms of HIV or AIDS are often masked by signs of aging and menopause. Women in this group often feel immune to HIV because of their age but forget that they could still have been infected through the blood supply, unprotected sex with a new partner, or an unfaithful partner. The thinning of vaginal tissues, combined with possible internal lesions, can make older women an extremely vulnerable target for HIV. Women primarily contract HIV from unprotected sex with infected partners or from high-risk partners (IV drug users or bisexuals). More high-risk practices, such as anal sex or sex during menstruation, both of which many women do as a way to avoid pregnancy, also put women at risk.

When it affects women, AIDS is a gynecological disease. Early signs of HIV in women include vaginal infections, abnormal Pap smears, or STDs that are unusually severe, recurrent, and resistant to treatment. As a result, HIV-positive women will need to undergo more pelvic exams, Pap smears, and gynecological treatments or procedures than will healthy women.

Women who are HIV positive will also need to practice meticulous birth control and abstain from any mucus-sharing sexual activity. Finally, women with AIDS need to practice stricter gynecological hygiene. This book does not cover the issues concerning pregnancy and HIV and pediatric AIDS.

There are a number of psychosocial circumstances that make women more vulnerable to HIV through heterosexual contact. Despite AIDS awareness and education efforts, many women still do not ask enough questions about their partner's history, and even when they do, many men will simply lie. This results in a classic scenario of women remaining in stable, long-term monogamous relationships with HIV-positive partners, who may not even know that they are HIV positive until they exhibit symptoms. Sex educators also report that bisexual men often consider themselves at low risk for HIV simply because they have heterosexual relationships. Bisexual men often have sex with men without disclosing this to their female partners.

Former IV drug users espouse similar fantasies. Many are convinced that since they only abused drugs once or twice in the past, they are not truly at risk. The irony is that women who are infected by these kinds of partners often exhibit symptoms of HIV-related illnesses long before their partners, creating a "which came first?" scenario.

Women are also being infected through partners who have hemophilia, a sex-linked genetic disease almost exclusively affecting males. Hemophilia is a blood-clotting disorder, which, until the late 1970s, was often fatal. However, a miracle drug called Factor VIII was developed to control the disease. This is administered in a similar way as is insulin and was considered a godsend to thousands of families affected by hemophilia—until 1985. As dramatized in the film *And the Band Played On* (based on the book by Randy Shilts), Factor VIII was produced from unscreened blood products well beyond what was considered ethical by many experts. Roughly 90 percent of all hemophiliacs treated with Factor VIII between 1978 and 1985 were infected with HIV.

Apparently, having unprotected sex with an infected, uncircumcised male partner can double the risk of contracting HIV. This is because not only do uncircumcised males tend to have infections or small breaks in the skin of the penis, but their foreskins make better hosts for a number of viruses, including HIV.

# What Is AIDS?

AIDS is short for acquired immune deficiency syndrome. It is a disease that slowly destroys the body's immune system; without our immune systems, we cannot fight off germs or cancers. HIV is the virus that causes AIDS; it destroys a type of white blood cell known as the CD4 T lymphocyte, or T cell. Referred to as the quarterback of the immune system, the CD4 cells are crucial in warding off germs; as the CD4 cells dwindle in supply, common germs invade the body, leading to opportunistic infections. When you begin to develop opportunistic infections, you officially have full-blown AIDS. If you are HIV positive but have not succumbed to opportunistic infections, your status is HIV positive, and you do not yet have AIDS. It can take years before HIV weakens the body's immune system to the point of AIDS. There appear to be two types of HIV: HIV-1 and HIV-2. HIV-2 is rare outside Africa.

## *Managing HIV or AIDS*

Thanks to a group of drugs called protease inhibitors (also known as antiretroviral drugs, or anti-HIV drugs in lay terms), introduced in 1996, AIDS has actually graduated to a chronic disease, such as diabetes. Taken with older AIDS drugs, protease inhibitors can actually reduce the level of HIV in the blood to undetectable levels in many HIV-positive persons. However, there is a hefty price tag attached to these drug therapies, which can be cost-prohibitive for many without adequate drug coverage. Various programs such as the Ryan White CARE Act facilitate coverage for drugs. Your local AIDS organization can direct you to the appropriate agencies to apply for coverage. Drug companies also have funding available.

In spite of the amazing feats of antiretroviral therapy as an AIDS management strategy, they don't work well for everyone. Their success depends on interactions with other medications, status of liver and kidneys, and overall health (for example, are there opportunistic infections that affect absorption of the drugs?). The body can quickly become resistant to these drugs, too. Blood tests that look at one's genotype and phenotype assays can help to detect whether the body is resisting a particular drug.

There is no single drug in antiretroviral therapy; instead, a cocktail of various drugs is used. That's because HIV mutates so quickly, it soon is able to resist any single treatment. So when HIV becomes resistant to one drug, it gets killed by another. Over time, HIV may become resistant to multiple drugs, and antiretroviral therapy can fail to prevent AIDS. Most people can be switched around on various combination therapies for years, which obviously can buy a lot of time for new and better treatments to be developed.

Cocktail therapy can involve taking twenty to fifty pills per day—at exactly the same time each day—to keep the doctor away. Taking so many pills every day is problematic because people are only human, and it's impossible to expect that everyone is going to stick to the rigid schedule of taking the drugs at exactly the times specified each day. This is worrying many AIDS researchers and health care providers because not taking the drugs on time, or properly, can lead to drug-resistant strains of HIV. Problems with human compliance also leads to drug resistance.

Antiretroviral therapy is designed to target HIV at different stages in its life cycle. There are drugs that can kill HIV during entry (killing HIV before it latches on to the T cell), during early replication (HIV can replicate itself by making an enzyme called reverse transcriptase, which translates its RNA into DNA), during late replication (killing HIV once it has inserted its own DNA into the normal cell), or during assembly (the stage at which HIV "hijacks" the normal cell, using it to create new HIV).

Hormonal factors and pregnancy may affect the choice of antiretrovirals for women. Some drugs may decrease the effectiveness of hormonal contraceptives, for example.

What most doctors recommend to newly diagnosed HIV-positive persons is to wait until the immune system starts to fail before administering the drug. That's because there are numerous, harsh side effects to these drugs (see further on). Your doctor can observe the status of your immune system by doing a blood test that counts how many CD4 lymphocytes are present (a CD4 lymptocyte count), which is currently the best indicator of how far HIV has progressed. A normal CD4 cell count ranges from 700 to 1,300. Symptoms begin to show up once the count dips below 500, and at full-blown AIDS, the count dips below 100.

Your doctor can also measure your "viral load," which looks at how much HIV is in the blood, expressed as an HIV RNA viral load of X copies per milliliter. The viral load can also be measured through cervical and vaginal secretions obtained through cervical discharge.

An undetectable viral load means that HIV in the plasma is too low to be detected by laboratory testing, but HIV can still be present in the body and be transmitted. A low level is 50 copies per milliliter. That's about as good as it gets. The current tests are not able to detect it as low as zero yet; instead, it will just come back as undetectable if it's much lower than 50.

## Side Effects

The side effects of antiretroviral therapy can be nasty. The most commonly reported side effects within beginning therapy include:

- nausea and vomiting, which can last for a few months and will subside once your body gets used to the drugs
- diarrhea, though if this lasts for more than three days, call your doctor
- rash, often a sign that you are allergic and may need to be switched to another drug cocktail
- insomnia or sleep disturbances
- fatigue

- pain, numbness, tingling, and/or burning in the hands and/or feet
- kidney stones (only with one drug)
- lipodystrophy syndrome, a condition where there are changes in the way your body distributes fat—you can develop a roll of fat between the shoulders ("buffalo hump") or in the abdomen, enlarged breasts, and loss of fat in the face, arms, and legs
- insulin resistance, which can predispose women to type 2 diabetes, weight gain, and heart disease

Very little research has investigated the effects of hormone replacement therapy (HRT) on the natural history of HIV disease in women. Nobody knows how these drugs will affect HRT, or how HRT affects HIV in general.

### Under Investigation

AIDS drug research is ever changing. As of this writing, drugs that help the body fight HIV, such as interleukin-2 (IL-2), are in testing with humans, while a host of immune stimulators are in development. Another class of drugs, called antisense drugs, interferes with HIV's ability to replicate itself. One drug from this class is also in human testing.

# Getting Tested

Most people order home HIV kits and test at home. Anonymous testing is available at any lab or through your doctor. All HIV testing assigns you a number, and then the results are based on a number rather than a personal identity. The stigma of HIV has made it unwise to do anything but anonymous testing. If you have a positive result, you need to follow up immediately with your doctor.

### *False Negatives and Positives*

The standard HIV test is the ELISA (enzyme-linked immunosorbent assay) blood test, which detects HIV antibodies. After you've been initially exposed to HIV, it takes four to twenty-four weeks to make enough antibodies to show up on the ELISA, which would mean a positive test, hence the term *HIV positive*. Roughly 50 percent of people exposed to HIV will make antibodies within two months, but 95 percent will make antibodies by six months. That is why it is advised that you get another HIV test at the six-month mark following a negative HIV test.

There are also false positive tests. Other conditions that cause the ELISA test to show a positive result are when people have other autoimmune diseases, such as rheumatoid arthritis. Positive HIV tests are always confirmed with another blood test called a Western Blot test. This is a test for antibodies to specific parts of the HIV virus.

## The PCR Test

PCR stands for polymerase chain reaction. This test looks for DNA of the AIDS virus. This test is not yet FDA approved, but it is performed by Quest Laboratories using a kit prepared by Roche Laboratories. As of this writing, the HIV PCR kit is commercially available, and its distributors claim that it is 95 percent accurate in detecting the presence of HIV virus after twenty-eight days. There are higher false positive results with this test, but a second test with ELISA will confirm a positive result, which the lab will do at no extra charge.

## If You Test Positive

Contact all sexual partners you might have exposed or who could have infected you. Suggest that they, too, be tested. See your primary care physician and/or gynecologist immediately for a full physical and pelvic examination. Inform the doctor about your HIV status. As an HIV-positive woman, you're prone not only to more general infections but also to more gynecological infections, so the person doing your pelvic exams will need to be alerted. Anyone who comes in contact with your blood—a dentist, a health care worker, and so on—needs to know that you're HIV positive. It is your moral and ethical duty to inform them.

If you're pregnant, there are a number of options and special concerns. You should request a referral to a pediatric AIDS specialist or an obstetrician who is experienced with managing HIV-positive pregnancies. (This book does not cover issues related to pregnancy.)

## HIV Hygiene

If you are HIV infected, you must practice the following health and hygiene guidelines:

- Don't go near any cat litter boxes. Cat feces carry the parasitic protozoan *Toxoplasma gondii*, which causes toxoplasmosis, a possibly very dangerous disease. Once you're infected, the parasite enters the bloodstream and lymphatic system and the central nervous system. Toxoplasmosis causes encephalitis (swelling of the brain) and blindness. Cats are wonderful pets, however, which can have a calming and positive effect on your health. If you want to keep your cat, you do have a couple options. You can easily train the cat to go outside in the yard. Or find yourself a litter helper to handle all litter box duties. If neither of these options will work, find another home for your cat. Using rubber gloves to change the litter will not protect you from infection because the infectious material may get into the air and be inhaled when the litter is disturbed. Be sure to wash your hands each time after you touch your cat. Finally, try to avoid places that have cats—the litter may not be clean!

- Don't accept any kind of vaccination unless your doctor knows that you're HIV positive. Killed viruses in the vaccine are fine, but avoid viruses that are altered.

- Don't donate blood, plasma, body organs, or other tissue (change your driver's license donor card as well). Men should not donate sperm!

- Don't engage in high-risk behavior (see Chapter 9).

- Don't breast-feed your child if you've just delivered.

- Cover any cuts or grazes with a waterproof bandage.

- Avoid sharing toothbrushes (gums bleed) or razors to reduce transferring contaminated blood to someone else.

- Clean up any spilled blood, vomit, or other bodily fluids immediately. Wash the surface down with one part bleach, ten parts water.

- Wash dirty clothes, linen, towels, and so forth in the hot wash cycle in an ordinary washing machine.

- Burn used sanitary napkins and tampons, or put them into a sealed plastic bag and dispose of safely.

- Use two condoms for sexual intercourse and latex gloves or dental dams for other activities where your partner could be exposed. (See Chapters 7 and 9.)

- Do not share sex toys or any of your personal hygiene or makeup items, such as mascara or dental floss.

## *What to Expect When You're Expecting AIDS*

It's natural to expect to develop some life-threatening illness after testing positive for HIV, but it just doesn't work that way. The pattern of HIV progression from initial exposure until AIDS is very slow, and as I stress again and again in this chapter, HIV can often be halted before you even experience an AIDS-defining illness. Nevertheless, here's what happens immediately after HIV exposure, assuming no drug therapy intervention:

1. *Acute infection:* HIV-positive people will experience a flulike illness roughly six to eight weeks after initial exposure to HIV. This stage is known as acute infection and includes symptoms such as fever, sweats, malaise, fatigue, achiness, joint pain, headaches, a sore throat, trouble swallowing, and enlarged lymph glands. These symptoms are so general and often mild that very few people would even consider seeing a doctor. This initial episode tends to dissipate after a couple of weeks.

2. *Seroconversion:* After acute infection, the body tries to make antibodies to HIV to fight off this infection. This is what blood tests detect when you test positive for HIV: HIV antibodies. In most cases, it takes your body six to twelve weeks to make HIV antibodies, sometimes up to a year. This stage is known as seroconversion.

3. *Asymptomatic stage:* You can be infected with the HIV virus but not show any symptoms whatsoever of immune suppression. Outwardly, you will appear to be as healthy as anyone else, but you will be capable of infecting someone else with the virus, who, in turn, can either show symptoms or be asymptomatic for a time.

4. *HIV disease:* You can be infected with HIV and display common symptoms seen in HIV-infected persons (such as fatigue, weight loss, persistent swollen lymph nodes, yeast infections, and so on) but still have enough CD4 cells left to ward off opportunistic infections categorized as AIDS-defining illnesses. In other words, you may get sick a lot and take longer to get well, but you'll respond to treatment for the specific illness. Over the years, people in this category were defined as having AIDS-related complex. This terminology has been upgraded to HIV disease. Most of the health problems during this stage are experienced by the healthy population, too. But with HIV, these health problems are chronic and persistent. Research suggests that your immune system's initial response to HIV infection can predict the rate of disease progression. In other words, if you remained asymptomatic for a long time, you may have a much longer life span without drug therapy than someone who progressed to this stage sooner.

5. *Full-blown AIDS:* Your immune system has deteriorated to the point where your CD4 cells are rapidly declining (known as a low cell count). As a result, you frequently fall prey to opportunistic infections. Many people don't find out that they have been exposed to HIV until they develop an AIDS-defining illness.

### When You're Diagnosed with AIDS (but Never Knew You Were HIV Positive)

The classic female AIDS experience is to learn you have AIDS after suffering for months from what you think are purely gynecological health problems, perhaps chronic yeast infections, changes in your periods, or cervical dysplasia that may be progressing to invasive cervical cancer (see Chapters 3 and 18). These symptoms may also be combined with flulike symptoms and swollen glands, which may be diagnosed as chronic fatigue. Women do not develop the same AIDS-defining illnesses as men (e.g., Kaposi's sarcoma, the purple splotches that men typically develop in early AIDS, does not generally develop in women). Many female AIDS patients wander from doctor to doctor with numerous complaints of malaise and gynecological ailments but are never tested for HIV until they sprout something truly AIDS-defining, such as pneumonia or one of the opportunistic infections discussed further on. Many doctors are still using "male" guidelines to diagnose AIDS—guidelines based on gay men with AIDS in the 1980s.

In men, Kaposi's sarcoma is usually one of the first AIDS-defining illnesses they exhibit. In women, cervical cancer is often the first AIDS-defining illness. In fact, cervical cancer was the first truly female AIDS-defining illness. Nobody knows how many undiagnosed women who have died of cervical cancer were in fact HIV positive or in the late stages of AIDS.

Similar to men, women in early stages of immunosuppression will also develop *Pneumocystis carinii* pneumonia, esophageal candidiasis, mycobacterial infections, bacterial pneumonias, and non-Hodgkin lymphomas.

## Gynecological Health and HIV

In 1982 the Centers for Disease Control defined AIDS by pulling together a list of life-threatening disorders indicating severe immune deficiency from HIV disease. Since then, the definition of AIDS has been revised twice. Unfortunately, this list continues to exclude many HIV-related conditions common in women, which means that doctors may not recognize conditions that indicate HIV disease in women. Seventy-five percent of all HIV-positive women will experience some or all of the gynecological problems discussed in this section.

Most gynecological disorders are not considered opportunistic infections, but they can badly aggravate and complicate HIV infection. This section covers what has been researched so far on HIV infection and gynecological problems.

## Menstrual Problems

Overall, HIV does not appear to have a clinically relevant effect on menstruation or other vaginal bleeding, although some of the drugs in antiretroviral therapy can cause menstrual problems.

## Candidiasis: Yeast

A recent study showed that 37 percent of patients who initially had recurrent vaginal yeast infections eventually sought care for HIV. Candidiasis is the medical term used to describe the overproduction of the yeast *Candida albicans*. It is said to be the most common initial symptom of HIV infection in women. The symptoms, diagnosis, and treatment of vaginal yeast or candidiasis is the same for all women, regardless of their serostatus. However, both vaginal candidiasis and oral candidiasis (called thrush) tend to be chronic in HIV-positive women, while only vaginal candidiasis is common in HIV-negative women. One study found that 50 percent of all HIV-infected women with previous episodes of vaginal yeast infections experienced more frequent and severe vaginal yeast infections six months to three years prior to their HIV test. When thrush develops, the tongue and skin lining the inside of the mouth are coated in a milky white goop. It's very unsettling, but it is not life threatening. You may also experience burning or stinging. Thrush sometimes occurs in HIV-negative people who are on antibiotics or cortisone. Women with diabetes may also develop thrush. Oral thrush, however, never develops unless there is some kind of medical problem. Roughly 80 percent of HIV-positive people whose HIV has progressed will have thrush at some point.

Thrush is treated with topical or oral antifungal agents. Also see information on diet and herbal therapies under "What to Eat" and "Flower Power." Many women who are not HIV positive suffer from chronic vaginal yeast infections as well, and it is notorious in diabetic women. HIV-positive women are generally found to have nutritional deficiencies, which can complicate the yeast scenario.

## Premature Menopause

Many HIV-positive women seem to suffer from premature menopause, which is more common in immune-suppressed women. The symptoms and effects of premature menopause are no worse or different from general menopausal symptoms, discussed in Chapter 19.

However, HIV-positive women who experience hot flashes at night may be misdiagnosed as having night sweats, common to other HIV-related diseases such as TB or diseases that cause "wasting" (an involuntary loss of 10 percent or more of a person's usual body weight). Vaginitis (irritation or inflammation of the vagina caused by dryness) is also a common menopausal complaint that can be mistaken for a yeast infection. Furthermore, menstrual irregularities could be caused by this early menopause. It's important to keep track of your cycles and report your suspicions to your doctor to avoid misdiagnosis or hormonal treatments that may not be necessary.

## *Other STDs and HIV*

Chapter 10 discusses the symptoms, diagnosis, and treatment of STDs other than HIV, as well as other infections. Additionally, there are a number of considerations regarding "traditional" STDs of which HIV-positive women need to be aware.

First, there already is an epidemic of traditional STDs in HIV-negative women. For HIV-positive women, an STD can do a lot of damage: it is more difficult to treat and can cause HIV disease to progress more quickly. It's crucial that HIV-positive women do everything they can to prevent contracting an STD. Abstinence or the female condom is probably the best course of prevention at this stage, since some STDs can be transmitted from the base of the penis, not covered by the male condom. And, of course, condoms can break.

Second, when you have an STD coexisting with HIV, you are more infectious. Not only are you more likely to pass on your STD to a partner during unprotected sex, but you're more likely to pass on HIV as well. If STDs are present, and your CD4 count is below 500, you should talk to your doctor about using prophylaxis medications to prevent pneumonia, TB, and MAC (*Mycobacterium avium* intracellular complex), discussed further on. Finally, HIV-positive women tend to suffer more frequently from genital herpes than men.

## *HPV, Cervical Cancer, and Pap Tests*

As discussed in Chapter 3, HPV + HIV = invasive cervical cancer. Again, if you are HIV positive, you're thirty times more likely to develop cervical cancer when you have HPV than is an HIV-negative woman. You're also more likely to develop cervical dysplasia and genital warts. Furthermore, you may be more likely to develop cancers of the vulva and perianal region when you have the HPV-HIV viral combination. Because of this, HIV-positive women must get a Pap test done at least every six months for the rest of their lives.

If you have a CD4 cell count less than 500, you should be going for a colposcopy exam every six months. If your count is less than 200, you should be having both a Pap smear and a colposcopy every three months. In general, smoking can put women more at risk for cervical cancer, so if you're HIV positive, avoid smoking. Pap smears detect whether the cells on the cervical lining are abnormal. The test is about 70 percent accurate, and false positives do occur more frequently in HIV-positive women. To get the most out of your Pap test, refrain from intercourse, douching, vaginal medications, or tampons for at least two days before the Pap test. Since HPV treatment is less successful in HIV-positive women, a Pap smear and a follow-up colposcopy should be done every three months for life. Treatments for cervical cancer are discussed in Chapter 3.

# Common AIDS-Defining Illnesses

AIDS-defining illnesses are what we refer to as opportunistic infections, as discussed at the beginning of this chapter. When you have an AIDS-defining illness, it means that your HIV infection has progressed to AIDS. Many women are not even diagnosed as being HIV positive until they develop an AIDS-defining illness. However, many of these illnesses can be prevented, treated, and controlled, to prolong life for several years. The following is just a brief overview; in most cases, specific drug treatments for individual conditions are not discussed because they are updated too frequently to have meaning in a traditional book.

## Pneumocystis Carinii *Pneumonia (PCP)*

PCP (a.k.a. AIDS pneumonia) is an infection of the lungs that is caused by an organism known as *Pneumocystis carinii*. Symptoms include shortness of breath, dry cough without sputum, and fever. At first, you may only notice shortness of breath when you exercise. As your condition worsens, you'll start to notice it more frequently during various activities until you're short of breath when you're at rest. As for your fever, it will climb to only about 100°F and will come on later in the day or night. PCP seems to occur very frequently in women as a first or second AIDS-defining illness, but diagnosis is often delayed until the PCP becomes severe. In other words, PCP is often the first sign that a woman has developed AIDS. All HIV-positive women with a CD4 cell count less than 200 should take specific PCP prophylaxis to help prevent it. PCP is an opportunistic infection that can be prevented in 90 percent of the people who take appropriate prophylaxis. There are a variety of drugs used to prevent and treat PCP.

## *Esophageal Candidiasis*

Also an opportunistic infection, esophageal candidiasis is the same yeast infection that occurs vaginally or orally, but it develops in the esophagus. This is another AIDS-defining illness that can be controlled in the same way as are vaginal yeast infections, through diet, exercise, antifungals, and so forth. Symptoms include painful swallowing, weight loss, and vomiting.

## Mycobacterium Avium *Intracellular Complex (MAC)*

MAC is really an atypical form of tuberculosis. In this case, the cough is less severe, but you will suffer from severe gastrointestinal symptoms. Other symptoms of MAC include weight loss, chronic high fever, severe anemia, chills and night sweats, abdominal pain, chronic diarrhea, swollen lymph nodes, reduction in white blood cells (neutropenia), and the enlargement of the liver and spleen.

MAC is a serious AIDS-defining infection that tends to occur later on in the disease and is more common in women. Usually MAC doesn't occur unless you have a CD4 cell count less than 50.

## *Tuberculosis (TB)*

There are two kinds of TB: pulmonary TB (in the lungs) is an HIV-related disease, whereas widespread, or disseminated, TB is an AIDS-defining illness that affects the liver, central nervous system, adrenal glands, lymph nodes, skin, reproductive organs, and heart. Both forms of TB develop while the immune system is still intact with a CD4 cell count between 300 and 500. TB is aggravated by urban smog and pollution and places with poor ventilation. It may result from a new infection or the reactivation of an old infection. Make sure you're living in a properly ventilated area, and if you have the opportunity to move into a more rural community with less pollution, you should consider it. Find out if any of your close friends or family have had TB or have ever been exposed to it. If they have, you can be tested for TB before symptoms develop. Symptoms include fever, cough, bloody sputum, chest pain, sweats, and weight loss. TB in HIV-infected people can be cured, but it may take a while. There is a simple test that diagnoses it. If you have TB, you'll need to be on multiple medications for more than a year. Obviously, the sooner it's discovered, the greater the chance of recovery. Like PCP, TB often develops gradually over a period of weeks or months. Daily vitamin $B_6$ (50 mg), taken over the course of a year, is added to your drug therapy. Recent advances in TB therapy have shown that the drug thalidomide (banned in the 1960s because it caused horrendous birth defects) is actually helpful.

## *Kaposi's Sarcoma (KS)*

Kaposi's sarcoma is the classic AIDS-defining illness in men but develops far less frequently in women. KS was once thought of as a rare form of skin cancer. It is now described as a collection of abnormal blood vessels caused by a variety of body chemicals interacting with immune suppression. KS symptoms are hard, not-very-painful purplish splotches found on the skin and also on internal organs. A recent study in London of KS in bisexual and homosexual men with AIDS indicated that men who came into contact with each other's feces (via anal sex) were more at risk for KS. Currently, only about 3 percent of women with AIDS develop KS.

## *Wasting*

Wasting is an involuntary weight loss of 10 percent or more of a person's usual body weight. Wasting often occurs as a symptom of other diseases but can occur in the absence of major infection as well. In women, wasting can be misdiagnosed as anorexia nervosa, bulimia, or crash dieting, but it is a serious AIDS-defining illness that leads to severe malnutrition. Diarrhea is the major symptom. Specific infections such as parasites should be ruled out first before any of the weight-gain strategies are investigated. Any doctor or nutritionist can prescribe a weight-gain diet. If nausea and vomiting are the cause, small, frequent, bland meals may be the route to take, along with nausea-control medications. In more severe cases, intravenous feeding may be necessary. See more information under "What to Eat."

# Late-Stage Illnesses

The following illnesses occur in end-stage AIDS only:

- *AIDS dementia complex:* This occurs in 30 to 50 percent of HIV-positive people and is seen in the late stages of AIDS. Experts believe this is caused when HIV invades the brain. Symptoms are dementia (changes in a person's mental faculties) and loss of muscle control.

- *Bacterial pneumonia:* This is different than PCP in that symptoms appear suddenly. Shortness of breath, fever, and a cough that often produces thick yellow or green sputum are telltale signs, along with painful breathing. Treatment is similar to that for PCP.

- *Cryptococcal meningitis:* This is a yeast infection that causes inflammation of the brain, but it can also infect the lungs, heart, and skin. Symptoms include high fevers and severe headaches.

- *Cryptosporidiosis:* Cryptosporidium is a contagious parasite that causes a severe form of watery diarrhea ten to twenty times a day. Cryptosporidiosis can be diagnosed through a stool exam, and treatment depends on its severity and whether fever and abdominal pains accompany it. It is the most common cause of chronic diarrhea in HIV-positive people.

- *Cytomegalovirus (CMV) infection:* This is one of those viruses that half the population carries but never worries about. However, with HIV infection, CMV can cause a host of problems, including abnormal vision (CMV retinitis), pneumonia (CMV pneumonitis), hepatitis (CMV hepatitis), colitis (CMV colitis), fever, fatigue, and brain inflammation (CMV cerebritis). CMV doesn't usually affect you until the late stages of AIDS.

- *Herpes zoster (a.k.a. shingles):* This is not the same thing as the STD herpes, even though it's characterized by the same painful blisters. Herpes zoster causes a number of non-STD infections, including shingles and chicken pox. Most of us have this virus, but our intact immune systems do not allow the virus to develop. In HIV-positive persons, shingles (which is an infection of the sensory nerve) can develop, accompanied by small, painful blisters on the skin along the path of the nerve, usually on one side of the chest or stomach.

- *Lymphoma of the brain:* This means "brain tumor." Approximately 1 to 3 percent of people with HIV infection will develop this problem. Treatment varies depending on the size, but you will need to be evaluated by an oncology team. Lymphoma of the brain is usually diagnosed when treatment for encephalitis or meningitis is unsuccessful (meaning that you didn't have an infection to begin with, but an actual tumor). Neither encephalitis nor meningitis cause brain tumors, however.

- *Oral hairy leukoplakia (OHL):* This is an oral infection characterized by white patches on the tongue and/or in adjacent areas in the mouth; also, microscopic "hair" forms on the tongue's surface. These white patches can be as thick as an inch and can coat most of the tongue. A sore mouth and sometimes changes in voice can also develop. OHL is often misdiagnosed as thrush but will not respond to thrush treatment. The treatment for OHL is high doses of acyclovir taken in pill or capsule form.

- *Sinusitis:* This is an inflammation of the sinuses, which are behind the forehead just above the eyes and also behind the cheekbones. You will feel stuffed up and headachy and have lots of green nasal discharge. The only difference between this form of sinusitis and non-HIV-related sinusitis is that with HIV, sinusitis is chronic. Decongestants, anti-inflammatories, and antibiotics can often keep sinusitis under control.

- *Skin problems:* Common skin rashes such as a red rash all over the body are not uncommon with HIV. This is often a reaction to medications. Other causes of red rashes could be allergies to soap, cosmetics, sun, and so on, or they could be caused by a fever.

  Small, colorless bumps may also appear around the face, mouth, or genitals and are caused by a virus. A dermatologist can remove the bumps by surgery or freezing.

  Seborrhea (flaking, scaling, patches of rash) are also common and occur on the scalp (a.k.a. dandruff), face, ears, chest, and genital area. Seborrhea is very common with HIV—roughly 80 percent of all HIV-positive persons develop it at some point. Psoriasis, another type of flaking rash, is also common with HIV.

  Thick, discolored fingernails and toenails are also common and are caused by a fungus. This is different than patches of red, flaking skin on the feet, which is either athlete's foot or ringworm—also caused by a fungus.

  To treat a variety of rashes, 1 percent hydrocortisone cream (used sparingly), Aveeno oatmeal bath, and antihistamines can all work. Antifungals will treat fungus-related problems. Nizoral shampoo may help the fungal causes of scalp itch, while Lotrisone and Nizoral cream can help with skin fungus.

# Serious HIV-Related Illnesses

There are a number of HIV-related conditions that are not considered AIDS-defining, but rather complications of HIV or AIDS.

## *Endocarditis*

Endocarditis is a bacterial infection that causes inflammation of the heart valves. If left untreated, it could lead to heart failure and death. This occurs most often in IV drug users. The most common symptoms are fever, heart murmurs, irregular heartbeat, chills, headache, back and chest pain, stomachache, nausea, and vomiting. It can be treated successfully with antibiotics. Keep a health chart and record all of your symptoms.

## *Blood Disorders*

There are several blood disorders to which HIV-positive women are prone. They include anemia (low red-blood-cell count), common in all HIV-positive women, and a garden variety of disorders that interfere with blood clotting, to which drug users and persons with hemophilia are prone. Anemia can seriously complicate HIV infection but can be easily controlled with proper nutrition and vitamin supplements.

Thrombocytopenia is another serious blood condition, occurring in 40 percent of people with AIDS. Steroid treatment is available and usually is successful. Finally, there is a condition known as neutropenia, caused by a low number of a certain white blood cell. Drugs that damage the bone marrow can trigger it, but it is rarely life threatening. Good nutrition and vitamin supplements help prevent it.

## *A Word to Caregivers*

It's a good idea to wear disposable surgical gloves when you're handling bodily fluids of someone with HIV, since the virus can be transmitted through cuts and abrasions on your hands or arms, urine, vomit, diarrhea, or blood. Each time you touch your loved one or handle his or her bodily fluids, wash your hands in warm soapy water. You may also want to wear a disposable medical gown when handling bodily fluids.

If your loved one has an active cough, he or she should wear a mask to prevent the spread of TB (even if you're not sure whether it is TB). And if you yourself have a cold or cough, you should wear a mask to protect your loved one. All used tissues, soiled bandages, dressings, gloves, pads, and tampons should be disposed of immediately in sealed plastic bags. They should then be tossed into a trash can with a secure lid. All washable surfaces should be cleaned with a solution of one-fourth cup bleach to one gallon water and then rinsed well with plain water.

You probably know this already, but remember that it's completely safe to share the same bathroom (toilet, sink, and tub), food, bed, linens, and swimming pool with your HIV-infected loved one. As long as you wash eating utensils and dishes in hot, soapy water and dry them thoroughly, these are also perfectly safe. Hugging and closed-mouth kissing is perfectly safe, too.

# What to Eat

If you are HIV positive but not showing signs of disease, the general diet to adopt is a healthy, balanced diet (see Chapter 1). At the same time, taking immune-boosting supplements (see Chapter 3) is also key, as well as making sure your diet is high in probiotics (see Chapter 6), to fight off fungal infections.

## *Combating Eating Problems*

If you are on antiretroviral therapy, or showing signs of illness, you may be suffering from any of a number of specific problems that can interfere with eating and drinking. Such problems include:

- *Pain or difficulty when swallowing:* In addition to a liquid supplement such as Ensure Plus, try such soft foods as mashed potatoes, scrambled eggs with cheese, yogurt, cottage cheese, custards, flaked fish, ground meat, and tuna, egg, or chicken salad. If problems are severe, food may be put through a blender or baby food may be eaten. Avoid salty, spicy, and "rough" foods such as raw vegetables and all citrus fruits. To prevent the irritation of ultrasensitive tissue in the mouth, the temperature of foods should not be too hot.

- *Diarrhea:* The BRAT diet is key—bananas, rice, applesauce, and tea, as well as plenty of other liquids to replace lost fluids. Gatorade or Pedialyte (sold in the infant department of pharmacies) will help replace electrolytes depleted by diarrhea. Avoid seeds, bran, nuts, whole wheat bread, the skins of fruits and vegetables, dairy products, and caffeine.

- *Nausea:* Eat crackers, dry toast, pretzels, or bland cookies (arrowroot biscuits or vanilla wafers, for example). Also try cold foods like chicken or tuna salad and cottage cheese with fruit. Avoid spicy, greasy foods as well as those with a strong odor. If vomiting occurs, maintain a liquids-only diet consisting of clear broth, apple juice, tea, and ginger ale. Jell-O and popsicles are usually well tolerated. Ask your doctor to prescribe an antinausea medication (a.k.a. antiemetic).

- *Loss of appetite:* Some prescription appetite stimulants (such as Megace or Marinol) are effective under such circumstances, so speak to your doctor about prescribing one for you. In addition, make your meals small, frequent, and calorie/protein dense, and try doing some form of relaxation exercise (qi gong and yoga are especially effective) twenty to thirty minutes before eating (see Chapter 1).

## Foods to Avoid
- raw or undercooked meat (especially pork)
- raw seafood (sushi, oysters, etc.)
- raw eggs (in homemade mayonnaise, for example), as well as eggs—poached, boiled, scrambled, or fried—that are not thoroughly cooked
- luncheon meats made from a variety of unspecified meats and fillers
- unwashed or broken-skinned fruits and vegetables
- unpasteurized milk and milk products
- leftovers after two days (due to an increase in bacterial growth)
- foods with an excessive fat content (although often suggested as a remedy for AIDS-wasting syndrome, high fat content aggravates diarrhea)

- foods that have been left unrefrigerated for long periods of time or have been prepared under unsanitary or questionable conditions (such as items sold by street vendors)

## Flower Power

All of the immune-boosting herbs discussed in Chapter 3 can be taken as a supplement, but it is crucial to check with your pharmacist, an herbal expert, or your doctor about drug interactions—particularly since you may be taking many drugs.

Essential oils, such as lavender, geranium, and the others listed in Chapter 1, will help keep gynecological infections at bay. Bathing each night in one or more of these oils will help.

## How to Move

It's very important to keep your stress levels down. Practice the exercises discussed in Chapter 1 on a daily basis. In addition, reflexology and acupuncture (see Chapter 16) can be very restorative.

# 12

# Unwanted Pregnancy

IF YOU WANT to terminate a pregnancy for any reason, this is the chapter to read. Roughly 43 percent of North American women have had at least one induced abortion by age forty-five. One of the most famous studies on abortion involved the work of psychologist Carol Gilligan, author of *A Different Voice*, which demonstrated that women make moral decisions based on how that decision will affect the other relationships in their lives. When Gilligan interviewed women about how they made their decision to terminate a pregnancy, the decision to abort or not to abort was made to preserve the relationship with the father. In some cases, aborting would threaten the relationship, while in other cases, continuing the pregnancy would threaten the relationship. If other children were involved, similar considerations were often made; if continuing the pregnancy would interfere with the well-being of existing children, for example, the decision to terminate could be made.

Access to safe abortion is considered a public health triumph. The horrible image of Geraldine Santoro, a woman who hemorrhaged to death in her cheap motel room after an unsafe abortion, haunted millions when her picture was run on an early cover of *Ms. Magazine*, in the 1970s, and later, in *Our Bodies, Ourselves*. The story of Geraldine's life is depicted in the documentary film *Leona's Sister Gerri* (1995). Gerri, a normal housewife, who got tangled up in an affair, sought out an illegal abortion in desperation and died from complications. Prior to safe and legal abortion, it's estimated that roughly 100,000 women died each year worldwide from complications following abortion.

Prior to the late 1990s, only surgical abortion was available in North America. But abortion has become much safer with the introduction of medical abortion, also known as chemical abortion, which allows women to take abortion pills, aborting in privacy at home rather than having to go to a clinic. All studies that looked at women's preferences between medical or surgical abortion concluded that women will trade the shorter, surgical procedure for aborting at home with induced uterine contractions to have the privacy.

Two popular drugs, mifepristone (a.k.a. RU 486) and methotrexate, followed by misoprostol, are now considered the gold standard approach to first-trimester abortions. And because performing medical abortion with drugs does not require surgical training, many more health care providers can offer abortion services.

Indeed, the volume of literature surrounding abortion is enormous; most of it is literature concerning the ethical debate over abortion, the various moral dilemmas faced by women seeking abortion, and the wider social, ethical, and legal implications of abortion. But the no-nonsense health literature on abortion is fairly straightforward. Abortion is a relatively simple, low-risk procedure. This chapter focuses on the health information. As a feminist sociologist and bioethicist, I am indeed tempted to provide a chapter that covers a more social perspective on this issue. But the act of merely providing you with all the right health information speaks volumes about my own views.

Since abortion laws vary from state to state, and each month new laws are banned while others are passed, no meaningful legal information on what is currently the abortion law can be provided in a paper book such as this. Instead, check the Internet links in Appendix B, and search out your legal rights at the appropriate website. Abortion laws do not distinguish between medical and surgical abortion, and as of this writing, a slew of newly proposed legislation will seek to get the distinctions clear; this will have an enormous impact on abortion law all over the world.

# First-Trimester Abortion

Technically, the word *abortion* simply refers to pregnancy loss before the twentieth week. This may be either a spontaneous abortion, also known as miscarriage (which includes complete, missed, or incomplete abortion), or a therapeutic abortion, a deliberate termination of pregnancy for medical or social reasons. Most people think that a therapeutic abortion refers only to the kind of procedure sought out, for instance, by a couple who discovers they are carrying a defective fetus. This just isn't so. A teenager who hasn't the financial means to support a child or the support structures to take care of the child will also be a therapeutic abortion candidate. A woman who was impregnated during a rape will be a therapeutic abortion candidate. Finally, a woman who simply does not desire a child, for any combination of reasons, is also a candidate for a therapeutic abortion. The abortion is "therapeutic" because it enhances the quality of life for the mother and prevents the inevitability of a life of poverty, unreasonable struggle, or unreasonable trauma for both the mother and the unborn, unwanted fetus.

Whether you have a medical or surgical abortion procedure will depend on whether you're in your first or second trimester of pregnancy. After the pregnancy has progressed beyond a certain number of weeks in the second trimester (usually twenty-four weeks, but the limit may vary depending on your state), you will not be able to elect to terminate the pregnancy legally. But all women in North America can expect to have a legal abortion up until at least their twentieth week of pregnancy.

## *Medical Abortion (a.k.a. Chemical Abortion)*

Today, any doctor who can follow a recipe can provide abortion services; your doctor can prescribe two medications that, when taken together, induce abortion through uterine contractions. Abortion is possible in the privacy of the home, making it difficult to know who is aborting chemically and who is having a natural miscarriage.

Depending on what you read, the failure rates of medical abortion range from roughly 2 to 15 percent, much higher than the failure rates of surgical abortion (0 to 4 percent). But surveys reveal that out of the women who have had medical abortions, 95.7 percent stated they would recommend the method to others, and 91.2 percent would choose it again.

Medical abortion requires two drugs taken at two stages. One drug, a progesterone antagonist (antiprogestin), blocks the action of progesterone, which is crucial in order to sustain a pregnancy. In fact, many women miscarry because they have insufficient amounts of progesterone in their system. Without progesterone, the lining of the uterus breaks down and menstruation begins, expelling any fertilized egg. This simulates what happens in a natural miscarriage (a.k.a. spontaneous abortion). The second drug helps the uterus to contract enough to expel the lining. The first drug used will be either mifepristone (RU 486) or methotrexate. The second drug used is misoprostol, which is a prostaglandin that causes the uterus to contract.

Medical abortion can be done as soon as you confirm the pregnancy, but it is generally not recommended beyond nine weeks. In the natural setting, however, women frequently miscarry up to twelve weeks. The medical abortion is usually followed up with an ultrasound, just to make sure that it worked. As in any natural miscarriage, sometimes not all the contents of the uterus have been expelled, requiring surgical intervention with a D & C or a vacuum extraction. An advantage of a medical abortion is that it can be done at the earliest stages of pregnancy; surgical abortion (discussed further on) cannot be done until at least seven weeks along in a pregnancy. Other advantages of medical abortion are that it is less expensive than surgical abortion, does not require as much surgical expertise, allows for greater privacy for women, and offers less risk from anesthesia and surgical complications.

## What to Expect

The first drug (mifepristone or methotrexate) will be administered thirty-six to forty-eight hours before the second drug, misoprostol. Most women are prescribed both drugs at the same time and given specific instructions about when to take the second drug. Medical abortion requires at least two visits to your doctor. The first visit involves timing the pregnancy to ensure that medical abortion can be done rather than surgical abortion. (The cutoff for medical abortion is at nine weeks; otherwise, you'll be too uncomfortable.) Ultrasound can date the pregnancy. If you're within the right time frame, you'll be given a consent form to sign (see "What Is Informed Consent?" in the Introduction), along with the pills or a prescription for the pills. In some cases, you'll only be given the first drug and be asked to return for the second drug; in most cases, this is unnecessary, and you can take the second drug on your own at home. Two weeks after you've aborted, you'll need to return to the doctor to make sure you are no longer pregnant. Another ultrasound will confirm this.

At the first visit, you'll need to find out:

- how and when to self-administer the second drug (misoprostol) at home, or when to return to the office for that drug (in about 2 percent of cases, women will abort without the second drug—ask about this before you go home)
- what activities and medications to avoid
- how to manage symptoms and side effects
- who to call in case of a problem or question
- when to return to confirm that the abortion worked

## Who Should Not Have a Medical Abortion

Women in certain circumstances cannot have a medical abortion. This would include women who have any of the following:

- a confirmed or suspected ectopic pregnancy
- an IUD still in place
- an adrenal gland disorder
- a disease being treated with corticosteroid therapy
- allergies to mifepristone, misoprostol, or other prostaglandins
- bleeding disorders or a condition being treated with anticoagulant therapy

## Side Effects

A medical abortion is indistinguishable from a natural or spontaneous miscarriage. You should expect cramping and heavy bleeding. The drugs may cause nausea, vomiting, diarrhea, and warmth or chills, but women who naturally miscarry report these symptoms, too. Some women report headache, dizziness, back pain, and fatigue. The blood loss itself and the cramping can cause all of these symptoms. If you've never had a miscarriage before, this will be bleeding that is heavier than you've ever experienced. The bleeding is a good thing and means you're expelling the contents of the uterus and pregnancy. Don't be alarmed if you pass clots in varying sizes and amounts. What is visible to the naked eye at nine weeks is simply the placenta and the uterine lining. Bleeding or spotting typically lasts nine to sixteen days, but for up to 8 percent of women it may last thirty days or more. The longer you've been pregnant, the more blood there is; that's why the cutoff of nine weeks for medical abortion exists. If the bleeding is too heavy, a D & C can finish off the job (see further on). Some women continue to bleed lightly for a couple of months after the medical abortion. If the bleeding is light and getting progressively lighter and spottier as the days wear on, there is no need to intervene with a surgical procedure. If the bleeding is heavy and stays heavy beyond two weeks, you should have that evaluated. Infection, which can occur after surgical abortion, is rare in medical abortions since no one is using any instruments that can introduce bacteria into the uterus. Medical abortion works 90 to 98 percent of the time, meaning that approximately 2 to 10 percent of women who have a medical abortion will not completely expel the pregnancy and will need surgical abortion.

## *Surgical Abortion*

If you require an abortion beyond nine weeks, you will probably require a surgical abortion, although some doctors may allow you to still have a medical abortion, depending on the circumstances. A surgical abortion procedure in the first trimester basically involves variations of the D & C procedure described in Chapter 17.

In North America, about 90 percent of all surgical abortions are performed during the first trimester; 95 percent are done before sixteen weeks. First-trimester abortions are less traumatic and safer, resulting in fewer complications. To find a qualified abortion practitioner, call the National Abortion Federation at 800-772-9100.

The first-trimester procedure revolves around what's called a vacuum aspiration procedure. A wide tube is inserted into the cervical opening to dilate it, and an electronic pump is used to suck out the uterine contents. This procedure is used for all first-trimester surgical abortions, including emergency care for women who naturally miscarried but did not expel the entire pregnancy, and women who did not completely expel the pregnancy as a result of a medical abortion procedure. Your cervix is typically dilated prior to the procedure. This procedure has many names and in the past was called suction curettage, aspiration abortion, preemptive abortion, endometrial aspiration, menstrual extraction (not an accurate label but used anyway), and menstrual regulation.

This procedure takes about fifteen minutes. You'll probably be given a local anesthetic, but many clinics may tell you that you don't need it. (A local anesthetic is a good idea.) A long, thin tube will be inserted into the cervical canal that leads to the uterus. The doctor will then place a long, flexible plastic syringe through the tube into the uterus and manually suck out the contents. As the tissue is removed, your uterus will start to contract in an effort to shrink back to its normal size and push out the rest of the contents. Most women will feel cramping comparable to a miserable period. It's rare not to feel cramping. Once the tube is removed, the cramps will start to subside, but you'll experience cramping for the next several hours and possibly for a few days. (This is discussed under "What Happens Afterward.")

Some women may need to have a curettage done after the suction. A long, sharp spoon-like instrument, called a curette, is used to scrape out the lining of the uterus. This usually isn't necessary, but it depends on the circumstances and whether the doctor is confident that he or she has removed everything. It's important that no tissue is left behind. If you do need a curettage, your cervix may be dilated further and the curette will be inserted through the cervix while the doctor scrapes out the lining. If you're in the second trimester, it is considered a late abortion, discussed further on.

## What Are the Risks Involved?

Right now, a first-trimester abortion (up to twelve weeks) is considered one of the safest surgical procedures. The risk of major complications is low. In fact, there's only a 0.2 to 0.6 percent chance of something going dramatically wrong during the procedure. The risk of death is also very low, about less than 1.1 per 100,000 abortions. Meanwhile, 10 out of every 100,000 women die during routine childbirth.

There are several minor, correctable complications involved that affect about 3 percent of all procedures. Hemorrhaging is one of the more common, correctable complications that can take place. This can happen during the procedure or later on when you're at home. The causes of hemorrhaging during the procedure can be due to accidentally tearing (lacerating) the cervix during the procedure or accidentally puncturing the uterine wall. If tearing is the problem, this usually heals on its own; a larger tear may need stitches. If the uterine wall is perforated accidentally, the problem may just correct itself, depending on where the puncture is. Otherwise, stitches may be necessary, and you may need to be transferred to a hospital for further observation until you heal.

More common reasons for hemorrhaging are caused by leftover, or retained, tissue in the uterus. Usually, the uterus will contract on its own to get rid of this. But if your uterus doesn't contract enough or at all, drugs can be administered to help the contractions along. If this fails, you may need a second D & C.

Another complication is infection. Any time your cervix is dilated, bacteria can enter the uterus and cause an infection of some sort. Infections are usually aggravated by a pre-existing, untreated sexually transmitted disease like chlamydia or gonorrhea, or preexisting pelvic inflammatory disease, which would be caught in your initial exam. If you do develop an infection, this is easily treated with antibiotics.

Another rare but potential problem revolves around a missed abortion, or continued pregnancy. Again, this is not likely to happen since your doctor will carefully inspect you to make sure nothing was left over. But in some cases, a woman may be aborting a multiple pregnancy or one that involves a double uterus, where one pregnancy is aborted while the other continues uninterrupted. If this is the case, you'll need to repeat the procedure about a week later.

Postabortal syndrome can also develop. It happens if the uterus doesn't contract properly or if a blood clot blocks the cervical opening and prevents blood from leaving the uterus. As blood accumulates in the uterus, you may feel abdominal pain, cramping, or nausea, and your uterus will be tender and enlarged. These symptoms usually occur about one to two hours after the procedure. You'll need to have the uterus suctioned again or have a D & C procedure to get rid of the blood. You may also be given synthetic oxytocin hormone to help stimulate uterine contractions.

Finally, you may have an ectopic pregnancy and not know it. In this case, your pregnancy will be in its very early stages, a test will be positive, and you'll undergo an abortion, only to experience ectopic pregnancy symptoms later on, after the procedure.

## What Happens Afterward

Most women will experience some irregular bleeding, cramping, or spotting. This will go on for about two weeks. Some women will continue to feel menstrual-like cramping and bleeding for as long as six weeks. Taking anti-inflammatory medication is helpful. You should refrain from sexual intercourse until your cervix has resumed its normal size, which you can confirm with your family doctor.

You might also experience feelings of depression. These feelings will stem from normal grief following the abortion and are not abnormal. It's important to seek postabortion counseling.

Your period will return about four to six weeks after the procedure, but this varies depending on how far along you were in your pregnancy at the time of the abortion. Because your lining has been removed and your body is rebalancing its hormones, it will take that long for your menstrual cycle to get back on track. However, you can get pregnant immediately after an abortion, so make sure you review Chapters 7 and 8 to prevent another pregnancy.

# Late Abortion

Late abortion is any abortion beyond twenty-one weeks. It is uncommon among women whose pregnancies are unwanted at the time of conception and who are informed about their options (including abortion). Sometimes, because of genetic information revealed about the fetus in planned pregnancies, the pregnancy becomes unwanted at later stages; it is usually this scenario that warrants late abortion. Uneducated women or women who are very young and do not realize they are pregnant due to irregular "youthful" menstrual cycles will seek out late abortion upon discovering the pregnancy. These are usually women who are coming from disadvantaged backgrounds or small towns without sufficient contraceptive education or awareness of sex education.

## D & E

Late abortion usually involves a D & E (dilation and evacuation) procedure, similar to a D & C. In a very late stage, where abortion is a medical emergency, another procedure, called amnioinduction, or labor induction, is involved, where a woman would birth the fetus after it was injected with a solution that killed it. It is this procedure that particularly fuels the pro-life movement, but it is performed very rarely and not in usual circumstances.

The D & E procedure can be performed at any point in the second trimester and is almost identical to the first-trimester procedure, with just a few variations. First, because you'll be further along in your pregnancy, you'll need to have your cervix dilated several hours prior to the procedure. This means that after your preoperative assessment, screening or exam, and counseling session are complete, you'll have a seaweed root (called laminaria) inserted into your cervical opening twenty-four hours before the procedure. Laminaria is used as a natural dilator of the cervix, thought to cause less irritation because it's organic. After the tube is inserted, you'll be sent home, where you'll experience cramping. You'll report back to the hospital the next day for the procedure. You'll have a fresh dilator (plastic tube or laminaria) inserted into your cervical opening, and the doctor will administer a local anesthetic. You'll have the contents of the uterus suctioned out with the vacuum pump described earlier. Forceps may also be used to help retrieve larger pieces of fetal tissue. You will feel cramping as the uterus contracts. Then a standard D & C is done. The risks and complications experienced after the procedure are virtually identical to those of the first-trimester procedure, and the cramping and bleeding following the procedure are also similar. This entire procedure takes about twenty minutes. (Some sources estimate as little as ten minutes and as long as forty-five minutes.)

Most hemorrhaging after a D & E is caused by retained placental tissue in the uterus. Treatment for complications at this stage is exactly the same as that for first-trimester complications.

If you've had a second D & C to control bleeding caused by retained tissue or to extract blood from the uterus, you might start to notice abnormal bleeding a few weeks later. If this happens, you may need to be put on a progesterone supplement to induce a "withdrawal" bleeding and have your lining shed again. This should take care of the problem. You'll also need to follow the same aftercare guidelines discussed earlier.

If the pregnancy is quite advanced, another procedure, known as intact dilation and extraction (intact D & E), involves dilating the cervix even more and pulling out the fetus feet first (a breech extraction). Here, the fetal skull is collapsed (cephalocentesis) to allow it to pass through the cervix. It is almost impossible, however, to find a doctor who knows how to do this; but there are a handful who specialize in late abortion and have perfected this technique so that it is safe.

Labor induction is an alternative, inferior procedure for late abortion that mirrors labor and delivery. In this case, after the fetus is injected with an agent that kills it, you are given a drug that induces contractions and labor, and you birth the dead fetus. This is the scenario that anyone wants to avoid and is the reason why early prenatal testing is available, as well as safer, medical abortion. But sometimes an illness (e.g., cancer) isn't discovered until the later stages of pregnancy, thereby warranting this procedure. Women who have been molested and conceal pregnancies out of shame may also seek out later abortions.

# Making the Decision

There are numerous different reasons for a woman to choose a therapeutic abortion. Five of the most common reasons are listed here:

1. *Contraceptive failure:* Obviously, any woman who practices some form of contraception does not intend to get pregnant. In circumstances where the condom failed, the emergency contraception pill is available. (See Chapter 8 for more details.)

2. *Socioeconomic concerns:* This would include the inability to support a child financially due to sudden unemployment or separation from a partner. You may have indeed planned or not prevented pregnancy only to find that your personal circumstances may have suddenly changed drastically.

3. *The mother's medical condition:* There are situations where continuing the pregnancy endangers the mother's life. You may have developed a heart condition or a severe illness during the pregnancy, or discovered that you are HIV positive and now have to choose between your life or that of the unborn child.

4. *The nature of the conception:* The pregnancy is the result of rape or incest.

5. *Problems identified with the fetus:* The fetus is malformed or will be born with an inevitable genetic/chromosomal deformity.

### *Finding Abortion Clinics*

Any primary care physician or gynecologist has a legal and moral responsibility to discuss abortion options with you and refer you to a qualified counselor as well.

You can also call the National Abortion Federation in Washington, DC, at 202-667-5881. The federation has a toll-free hotline that gives out referrals for abortion services; the number is 800-772-9100. This organization operates a massive database that contains the names of abortion clinics throughout the United States. You can call anonymously and just tell the operator where you're calling from. You'll then be provided with a list of clinics in your area.

## Alternatives to Abortion

Abortion is not the definitive solution for every unwanted pregnancy. That's why it's important to explore options to abortions first, to make sure that an abortion is what you really want. In general, these are the groups who may not benefit from an abortion:

- *Women who are morally or ethically opposed to abortion:* For example, even though you know you're carrying a child that is malformed, you may not be able to go through with terminating the pregnancy. The psychological trauma to you may be lessened by giving birth to the child and letting fate decide the outcome.

- *Women who don't feel informed enough about their options:* Have you considered adoption or looked into social programs that might support you until you get back on your feet? Have you researched your decision to abort? Are you familiar with what the procedure entails? Have you explored all other solutions?

There are viable options to an abortion, depending on who you are. In white, middle-class North America, there is currently an infertility epidemic (mostly due to age), which is creating a great demand from childless couples for white, healthy newborns. (Some couples may sponsor you through the pregnancy, paying your medical bills, buying you the necessary groceries, and so forth; others may be willing to pay you a lump sum.) If the child isn't healthy or is a visible minority, it will be far more difficult to find a home for that child.

If you are concerned that you may not have the support networks in place to take care of the child, have you exhausted supportive networks in your family? How about the father's family, or the father himself? Have you looked into social programs available to you that are provided by your government or community?

If the concern is financial, have you looked into programs that will support you while you retrain, upgrade your education, or finish school? Government programs are now in place that enforce child support by deducting money from the father's wages.

You could also visit a pro-life organization that can tell you what options it recommends. Typically, pro-life organizations have hefty funding made available to them through private benefactors. That money could be passed on to you in the form of financial support, while you get your life together enough to take care of a child.

## What to Eat

It's important to be on an iron-rich diet to prevent anemia from blood loss. See Chapter 20 for more details. In the event of nausea, diarrhea, or vomiting, drink lots of water and other fluids; Gatorade will replenish electrolytes and prevent dehydration, while a BRAT diet—bananas, rice, applesauce, and tea—can help with diarrhea. Dry crackers can help to alleviate the nausea.

## Flower Power

For centuries, women have used what's called emmenagogues—herbs that can induce menstrual flow. Before legal abortion existed, abortion recipes using emmenagogues were shared by women and included herbs such as parsley, motherwort, mugwort, goldenseal root, blue cohosh root, fresh ginger root, pennyroyal leaves, and dried tansy leaves and flowers. Today, in light of legal and safe medical or surgical abortion, attempting to induce one's period using any of these herbs is considered by all health practitioners to be dangerous to a woman's health and is not endorsed by any feminist health or women's health organization.

If you're looking for "flower power" to support your health following an abortion, aromatherapy is the best complementary approach. You can bathe in the essential oils discussed in Chapter 1 daily to restore balance to your reproductive system. Or, you can diffuse these oils while you recover at home.

## How to Move

The exercises described in Chapter 1 will help you recover from cramping and restore your sense of well-being.

# 13

# Endometriosis

THE MAJORITY OF chronic pelvic pain is caused by endometriosis. Endometriosis is a disease affecting women in their reproductive years. It was widely undiagnosed until the 1980s. The name, as you've probably guessed, comes from the word *endometrium*. The clinical definition of endometriosis is an "abnormal growth of endometrial cells." Between 2 and 22 percent of women with endometriosis don't have any symptoms and may not know they have it; 40 to 60 percent of women with painful periods have endometriosis, while 20 to 30 percent of women who are having difficulty conceiving have endometriosis.

Roughly 5.5 million women throughout North America have endometriosis. Endometriosis was at one time coined "husbanditis" because the pain that characterizes endometriosis was seen as a woman's excuse to get out of her marital duties. In the past, treating women who complained of pelvic pain ranged from tranquilizers to hysterectomies. Unfortunately, many women today are still being told that their symptoms are "in their heads" when, in fact, endometriosis is a physical disease causing real physical symptoms. What happens is that endometrial tissue forms outside the uterus in other areas of the body. This tissue then develops into small growths, or tumors. (Doctors may also refer to these growths as nodules, lesions, or implants.) These growths are usually benign (noncancerous) and are simply a normal type of tissue in an abnormal location. Cancers that arise in conjunction with endometriosis appear to be very rare. Endometriosis is sometimes referred to in the medical literature as a pseudocyst endometrioma.

The most common location of these endometrial growths is in the pelvic region, which affects the ovaries, the fallopian tubes, the ligaments supporting the uterus, the outer surface of the uterus, and the lining of the pelvic cavity. Some 40 to 50 percent of the growths are in the ovaries and fallopian tubes. Sometimes the growths are found in abdominal surgery scars, on the intestines, in the rectum, and on the bladder, vagina, cervix, and vulva. Other locations include the lung, arm, thigh, and other places outside the abdomen, but these are rare.

Since these growths are in fact pieces of uterine lining, they behave like uterine lining, responding to the hormonal cycle and trying to shed every month. These growths are blind—they can't see where they are and think they're in the uterus. This is a huge problem during menstruation; when the growths start shedding, there's no vagina for them to pass through, so they have nowhere to go. The result is internal bleeding, degeneration of the blood and tissue shed from the growths, inflammation of the surrounding areas, and formation of scar tissue. Depending on where these growths are located, they can rupture and spread to new areas, cause intestinal bleeding or obstruction (if they're in or near the intestines), or interfere with bladder function (if they're on or near the bladder). Infertility affects about 30 to 40 percent of endometriosis sufferers, and as the disease progresses, infertility is often inevitable.

The most common symptoms of endometriosis are pain before and during periods (much worse than normal menstrual cramps), pain during or after intercourse, and heavy or irregular bleeding. Other symptoms may include fatigue, painful bowel movements with periods, lower back pain with periods, diarrhea and/or constipation with periods, and intestinal upset with periods. If the bladder is involved, there may be painful urination and blood in the urine with periods. Irregular menstrual cycles and heavier flows are also associated with endometriosis, but women with severe endometriosis usually continue to have regular, albeit painful, periods. Some women with endometriosis may have no symptoms at all.

It's important to note that the amount of pain is not necessarily related to the extent or size of the growths. Tiny growths, called petechiae, have been found to be more active in producing prostaglandins, which may explain the significant symptoms that seem to occur with smaller growths.

Endometriosis can vary in terms of severity. Like other diseases, it is categorized into four stages—the higher the number, the more severe the endometriosis. Stage I is when your endometriosis is minimal and still very thin and "filmy," hence easier to treat. Stage II is mild endometriosis; the endometriosis is still on the thin side but is situated more deeply into your surrounding tissues. Stage III is moderate endometriosis; here, your endometriosis is denser, mixed with some stage I or stage II symptoms. Stage IV means severe endometriosis. In this case, the endometriosis is dense and deep, a bad combination.

# Signs and Symptoms

Since endometriosis includes so many seemingly unrelated symptoms, it's often missed or simply misdiagnosed. The following is a list of symptoms to watch for. If you have at least two of these symptoms during your period or experience them chronically, you may want to get checked out for endometriosis.

- pelvic pain and/or painful intercourse
- infertility (often the only symptom women experience, even with stage IV)
- abnormal cycles or periods
- nausea and/or vomiting
- exhaustion
- bladder problems (there is something called bladder endometriosis, discussed in the next section)
- frequent infections
- dizziness
- painful defecation
- lower backaches
- irritable bowels (loose, watery, and often bloody diarrhea often mistaken for irritable bowel syndrome)
- other stomach problems
- low-grade fever

## *Bladder Endometriosis*

Women who have endometriosis around the bladder can suffer from the urge to urinate, frequent urination, vulvar pain, urge incontinence, and painful urination. In fact, the symptoms of bladder endometriosis mirror interstitial cystitis (IC; see Chapter 16). Many women with IC probably have bladder endometriosis instead.

## *Painful Statistics*

A questionnaire distributed by the Endometriosis Association revealed that 100 percent of respondents experienced pain one to two days prior to their periods. In addition, 71 percent reported pain midcycle, 40 percent reported pain other times, and 20 percent reported pain throughout their cycles, while 7 percent reported intermittent pain with no particular pattern. The pain reported in this questionnaire was mostly abdominal, but the pain of endometriosis can manifest in emotional symptoms such as mood swings, depression, irritability, anxiety, anger, and feelings of helplessness, fear, powerlessness, and insecurity. Plus the financial consequences of endometriosis can be painful, too. Women in the United States aren't always covered for the various diagnostic tests or treatments.

# What Causes Endometriosis?

Environmental estrogens are probably the most logical cause. Environmental scientists have begun to notice that several wildlife species are experiencing hermaphroditic traits. In the Florida swamplands, alligators are simply not breeding. A concerned research team from the University of Florida went into the swamps to find out why. These researchers pulled male alligators out of the water to examine their genitals. The majority of male alligators found were sterile as a result of having either nondeveloped or abnormally shaped penises. A chemical spill in nearby waters was found to be the culprit—it was having an estrogenic effect on the alligators' natural habitat.

Meanwhile, some 1,400 miles north, in a Canadian creek on Lake Superior, scientists found that fish living in waters close to a pulp mill, which contained certain chemicals with estrogenic effects, were now complete hermaphrodites. The male fish in these waters had developed ovaries and were sterile; the female fish had exaggerated ovaries. In other contaminated waters, fish had actually exploded from thyroid hormone overactivity.

Researchers in Sweden and the United Kingdom have been concerned since the late 1980s over a dramatic increase in male infertility in their countries, while there is an increased incidence of male infants being born with cryptorchidism, a condition in which the testicles do not descend into the scrotum, but remain undescended inside the abdomen. One study found that there has indeed been a huge decrease over the last fifty years in the quality of human semen. (A recent study measuring sperm quality in New York City contradicted these findings.) There has also been a huge increase in the incidence of testicular and prostate cancers. In Britain testicular cancer incidence has tripled over the last fifty years; it is now the most common cancer in young men under thirty. In Denmark there has been a 400 percent increase in testicular cancer. As for prostate cancer, its incidence has doubled over the last decade. These male reproductive problems have been linked to environmental estrogens, too.

The scientific literature is slowly becoming saturated with findings linking one organic chemical after another to reproductive cancers and "endocrine disruption" in both wildlife and humans. Every study, from all corners of the world, is reaching the same conclusion: organic chemicals are transforming into environmental estrogens. And they're everywhere. Organic chemicals are found in the air we breathe from numerous air pollutants, in the food preservatives used in numerous canned and packaged goods, and in the pesticides used on fresh produce. These chemicals then contaminate the water and soil, which contaminate the entire human food chain.

Some suggest that environmental estrogens are "feminizing" the planet. Others suggest that women are being overloaded with estrogen, which may be associated with the rise of estrogen-dependent cancers, such as ovarian and breast cancer, as well as estrogen-related conditions, such as endometriosis and fibroids. Estrogen pollutants are also thought to accumulate in fatty tissues (meaning they are stored in fat). Since women generally carry more body fat than men, women may be accumulating more of these toxins. Some studies have already found that women with breast cancer tended to have higher concentrations of the organochlorines DDT and DDE or of PCBs in their fat tissue. In fact, elevated levels of DDE in the blood have been directly linked to a fourfold increase of breast cancer in the United States. We already know that dioxins, also organochlorines, are associated with endometriosis.

Some suggest that the picture is equally dismal for men, many of whom are not only becoming slowly sterilized by this phenomenon, but are also developing reproductive cancers. Several prominent scientists have gone on record to say that this problem is *the* environmental priority of the twenty-first century!

On the flip side, many doctors point out that in the Western world, there has been a huge increase in the "fatness" of the population. This also increases the level of estrogen produced by our bodies. Estrogen dominance can trigger more estrogen-dependent conditions, such as fibroids, endometriosis, and various estrogen-dependent cancers (see Chapter 21 for a detailed discussion).

## *Other Theories*

There are a few other worthwhile theories on the causes of endometriosis. One is the theory of retrograde menstruation, also known as the transtubal migration theory. During menstruation, some of the menstrual tissue backs up into the fallopian tubes, is implanted in the abdomen, and grows. Some researchers believe that all women experience some menstrual tissue backup, which is normally taken care of by their immune systems. An immune system problem or hormonal problem allows this tissue to take root and develop into endometriosis.

Another theory suggests that the endometrial tissue is distributed from the uterus to other parts of the body through the lymphatic system or blood system. A genetic theory suggests that it may be carried in the genes of certain families or that certain families may be predisposed to the disease.

The most interesting theory proposes that remnants of the woman's embryonic tissue (from when she herself was an embryo) may later develop into endometriosis or that some adult tissues retain the ability they had in the embryo stage to transform into reproductive tissue under certain circumstances.

Surgical transplantation of endometrial tissue has been cited as the cause in cases where endometriosis is found in abdominal surgery scars. This latter theory is certainly not possible if endometriosis occurs when surgery doesn't!

# Diagnosis and Treatment

The only way to diagnose endometriosis is with an instrument called a laparoscope (a tube-like telescope with a light in it), used in a procedure known as laparoscopy. The procedure is a form of minor surgery. After a general anesthetic is administered, your abdomen is distended (expanded) with carbon dioxide gas to make the organs easier to see. A tiny incision is made, and a laparoscope is inserted into it. By moving the laparoscope around, your surgeon can check for any signs of endometrial tissue outside the uterus.

Although your doctor can often feel the endometrial growths during a pelvic exam, and your symptoms may be telltale signs of endometriosis, no competent physician would confirm the diagnosis without performing a laparoscopic procedure. The bottom line is that if you've been told you have endometriosis, but you haven't had a laparoscopic procedure done, insist that your doctor perform one, or get a second opinion. Often the symptoms of ovarian cancer (discussed in Chapter 4) are identical to those of endometriosis. If you've been misdiagnosed with endometriosis due to your doctor's failure to confirm it through a laparoscopy, he or she may miss an early diagnosis of ovarian cancer, which is crucial for successful treatment.

A laparoscopic procedure also indicates the location, extent, and size of the endometrial growths and will help your doctor better guide you in treatment decisions and family planning.

Laparoscopy is the only way to absolutely diagnosis the condition. Unfortunately, doctors commonly misdiagnose women with endometriosis and treat them for conditions they really don't have. Again, this occurs because of the confusing group of symptoms that characterize endometriosis. Symptoms sometimes mimic pelvic inflammatory disease (PID; discussed in Chapter 10), irritable bowel syndrome, or a host of other ailments.

If you suspect you have endometriosis, experts recommend requesting a pelvic exam during your period, when endometriosis is in full flare. This may help your doctor find certain clues that will send you in the right diagnostic direction. For example, transvaginal ultrasound is very useful in finding many of the physical clues that endometriosis leaves behind, such as cysts or masses. You may want to request a transvaginal ultrasound even when your doctor doesn't order it.

Treatment for endometriosis has varied over the years, and there is still no absolute cure. If you don't have any symptoms and you're not planning to have any (more) children, then no treatment is necessary—you should just get regular checkups. If you have only mild symptoms and infertility is not a factor, simple painkillers, like acetaminophen (Tylenol) or ibuprofen (Advil or Motrin), may be all that's needed.

## The Goals of Treatment

If you have symptoms and pain, the most obvious goal of treatment is to prevent the pain and progression of endometriosis, either through alternative approaches (discussed under "Flower Power") or with conventional approaches such as hormonal therapy or surgical removal of the endometrial "pieces." Since endometriosis typically improves during pregnancy and after menopause, creating either a pseudopregnancy with oral contraceptives or a pseudomenopause with danazol are standard treatments.

Many women find that oral contraceptives can stop the progression of endometriosis and can treat it. Harsher hormonal therapies include danazol (a derivative of testosterone), which induces menopause and also causes what's known as androgenic side effects, such as acne, weight gain, unwanted hair, hot flashes, reduced libido, oily hair and skin, nausea, and lowering of the voice. Danazol has also been linked to immune suppression, which can trigger autoimmune diseases.

Gonadotropin-releasing hormone (GnRH) is another standard therapy, which is a "copy" of your natural GnRH and shuts it down. The three analogs used to treat endometriosis are leuprolide acetate (an injection), nafarelin acetate (a nasal spray), and goserelin acetate (a subdermal implant). GnRH therapy works in 75 to 92 percent of women with endometriosis.

Treatment with a progestin drug is commonly done as well; the progestin that is most commonly used for endometriosis is medroxyprogesterone. In the United States, the dosage is usually 20 to 30 mg per day for up to six months.

Sometimes just taking pain relievers with nonsteroidal anti-inflammatory drugs (NSAIDs) such as ibuprofen can manage the symptoms without necessitating hormone therapy.

## Surgical Treatment

The definitive treatment of endometriosis is removing the growths surgically via laparoscopy or laparotomy (there is no difference in effectiveness between the two types of surgery). There is also a surgery that interrupts the neural pathways for the conduction of pain, known as ablation, or resection, of the uterosacral nerve. This can, however, interfere with other sensations in the pelvic area; it's imperative that you discuss all the risks of this procedure before you consent.

Conservative surgery involves removing the growths themselves, rather than any reproductive organs. Through a laparoscope, surgery is done with a laser, a cautery, or small surgical instruments. Conservative surgery is the treatment of choice for women under thirty-five who are diagnosed with endometriosis in the early stages and who want to have children. About 40 percent of these women will go on to conceive. After conservative surgery, between 20 and 50 percent of endometriosis patients will need more radical surgery.

No one should be recommending hysterectomy for endometriosis in this day and age. If your doctor recommends this procedure, find another doctor. Recommending hysterectomy is a sign that the doctor's stuck in the 1980s.

## What's the Best Therapy?

The best therapy for endometriosis depends on your symptoms and your own reproductive goals. If you have no symptoms but are infertile and want to get pregnant, conservative surgery is best in this case. If you have no symptoms and don't wish to get pregnant, doing nothing is fine. There is no reason to treat endometriosis unless you're in pain or it is affecting your quality of life; it is a perfectly benign, harmless condition. Within naturopathic circles, natural progesterone therapy (discussed in Chapter 21) is a mainstay therapy for endometriosis.

If you have pain and don't want to get pregnant, try an oral contraceptive before anything else; this usually does the trick. Failing that, you'll need to weigh the side effects of danazol and GnRH therapy against surgery.

## Pregnancy as a Cure

Believe it or not, pregnancy does cause endometriosis to go into temporary remission, because you don't ovulate when you're pregnant. Furthermore, permanent remission of endometriosis has been known to occur after childbirth; the growths in this case shrink, and the pain associated with the disease stops. The problem is, the longer you have endometriosis, the greater your chance of becoming infertile. If you have been diagnosed with endometriosis, are planning to have children, and are in a position to have a family (that is, you have a supportive partner and are financially stable), then getting pregnant is a good idea. In other words, why wait? In addition, the disease may also worsen with time.

Pregnancy as a prescription is not feasible in many cases. For some, infertility may have already set in; also, many women don't have the means in place to have a child. Even under the best of circumstances, women with endometriosis have a higher risk of ectopic pregnancy and miscarriage. One study found that full-term pregnancies and labor are more difficult when the mother has endometriosis.

## *Menopause as a Cure*

In general, menopause does cure endometriosis, which is why a hysterectomy used to be recommended. But a severe case of endometriosis can be reactivated if you begin hormone replacement therapy or continue producing hormones after menopause, which is common. Menopause is discussed in more detail in Part IV.

# Adenomyosis: Internal Endometriosis

There is a related condition to endometriosis known as adenomyosis, in which the endometrial tissue (the uterine lining, glands, and connective tissue) invades the deeper muscle layers of the uterus. Usually there's a barrier between the endometrium and the deeper layers of the uterine wall that acts as a defense against invasion from endometrial tissue. Women who develop adenomyosis don't seem to have this defense.

Unlike endometriosis, some researchers believe that adenomyosis may set in after pregnancy and delivery; women in their forties and fifties who have given birth to at least one child are more likely to develop adenomyosis. Other researchers believe that, like endometriosis, genetics plays a role, and still others believe it may have to do with some sort of hormonal imbalance. The bottom line is that no one knows exactly what causes it, but treatments are available.

## *Looking at the Symptoms*

About 40 percent of the time in cases of adenomyosis, women have no symptoms, but when they do, the symptoms are similar to endometriosis: painful and heavy periods and sometimes chronic pelvic pain. The more involved the uterine glands are, the heavier the flow; the deeper the penetration into the uterine wall, the greater the discomfort. An enlarged, soft, or tender uterus is a classic sign of adenomyosis.

## *Diagnosing and Treating Adenomyosis*

In the past, adenomyosis was diagnosed only by a pathologist, often after a hysterectomy was performed for another uterine problem. Adenomyosis is often present in conjunction with other uterine conditions, such as fibroids (discussed in Chapter 14). The diagnosis is difficult. Therefore, to diagnose this condition accurately, your doctor must play detective.

It may be possible to detect adenomyosis with a magnetic resonance imaging (MRI) scan or a hysteroscopy (a telescope, similar to the laparoscope, placed through the cervix). However, an MRI is expensive, while a hysteroscope will at least rule out fibroids under the uterine lining.

Until recently, a hysterectomy was the suggested course of treatment for adenomyosis, but this is no longer an appropriate approach. Women have responded well to oral contraceptives or a progestin for this condition, too, which is preferable to danazol. Ablation may be an option as well. Refer to Chapter 14 for more information.

# What to Eat

A low-estrogen/low-saturated fat diet is recommended for endometriosis. Limiting your exposure to environmental estrogens starts in your kitchen. Your weekly groceries probably contain residues from pesticides and other organochlorines (on store-bought fruits and vegetables), hormones in meat products, as well as a number of extras you may not have bargained for, such as feed additives, antibiotics, and tranquilizers, which were fed to the animals your meat came from. Meanwhile, anything packaged will most likely contain dyes and flavors from a variety of chemical concoctions.

Airborne contaminants, waste, and spills affect the water and soil, which affect everything we ingest. When one species becomes unable to reproduce, we could lose not just that species but all those that depend on it, thus disrupting the food chain. Cleaning up the food chain is all part of creating a healthy, contaminant-free diet for ourselves. To be sure you will purchase contaminant-free foods on your next shopping trip, first do the following:

- You can find out what the animal source of your meat has eaten and whether it was injected with anything by contacting the USDA information line: 202-720-2791.
- You can find out what waters your fish has swum in by contacting the aforementioned organization.
- You can find out what your produce was sprayed with by contacting the aforementioned organization.
- You can find "safe food" that is organically grown or raised through a number of natural produce supermarkets or by getting in touch with the Organic Trade Association at ota.com.

- You can find out more about your supermarket's buying habits when it comes to produce by contacting your supermarket's head office.

# Flower Power

Natural progesterone therapy is the gold standard alternative treatment for endometriosis. This is thoroughly discussed in Part IV.

In traditional Chinese medicine, the standard herbal therapy for endometriosis is Jin Hi Chongji. This contains an infusion of Cherokee rose and spatholobus stem; it is also used to treat pelvic inflammatory disease (see Chapter 10).

The essential oils discussed in Chapter 1 are also helpful in balancing hormone levels and maintaining the reproductive organs.

## *Mistletoe Therapy*

Studies have shown mistletoe to be an excellent therapy to relieve endometriosis pain. So far, it is just as effective as harsher hormonal therapies. It has been suggested that mistletoe therapy can be the new medical therapeutic agent in endometriosis patients with intractable pain despite the conventional medical or surgical treatment.

# How to Move

Progesterone receptors, according to Dr. Katherina Dalton (see Chapter 8), stop functioning in the presence of adrenaline, the stress hormone. When that happens, you may have an imbalance of estrogen. The calming exercises discussed in Chapter 1 can help you to relieve stress and will facilitate more balanced hormones. (This won't make any difference, however, if you're on hormonal therapy.) The following yoga postures are recommended to help with the symptoms of endometriosis:

- The Butterfly
- Squatting Posture
- Knee and Thigh Stretch
- Chest Expander
- Stick Posture

- Knee Squeeze
- Legs Up
- Pose of Tranquility
- The Crocodile
- Star Posture
- Spread Leg Stretch
- Child's Pose
- Pelvic Stretch
- Lying Twist
- Side Leg Raise
- Half Moon
- Spinal Twist

# 14

# Fibroids

FIBROIDS ARE BENIGN (noncancerous) tumors that grow inside your uterus. They can be miserable to have, but they usually don't pose any danger to your gynecological health and are quite harmless. It is not the fibroids themselves that are questionable and controversial—instead, it is the method used to treat them. A hysterectomy is still the treatment recommended for most women with fibroids (discussed more in Chapter 20). In fact, fibroid tumors are the most common reason for hysterectomies in North America, accounting for 30 percent of all hysterectomies performed in the country, about 200,000 hysterectomies per year.

Fibroid tumors are one of the most common gynecological complaints. For the majority of women, fibroid symptoms are minor or nonexistent, but 40 percent of women who have fibroids experience such symptoms as an enlargement of the uterus, abnormal uterine bleeding, pelvic pain, and infertility. The size of uterine fibroids can vary from that of a pinhead to larger than a melon. In fact, fibroid weights of more than twenty pounds have been reported.

Most fibroids occur in women of reproductive age; they are diagnosed in African American women two to three times more frequently than in Caucasian women. It is currently believed that obesity has a lot to do with fibroid development. Because fat cells make estrogen, women who are obese are more prone to estrogen-dependent conditions, which include fibroids. It has also been observed that women who have never been pregnant are at higher risk for fibroids than women who have had children; this has to do with the fact that women who have not had children have not had a break from ovulation and, hence, estrogen production.

Although there are some fibroid cases that do warrant a hysterectomy, with current technology most women with fibroids can avoid radical surgery and their reproductive organs can be left intact.

# What Are Fibroids?

The term *fibroid* is actually medical slang. The correct medical term for what we've come to know as a fibroid is *leiomyoma uteri*. The word *fibroid* is really just an adjective that refers to anything fibrouslike or resembling a fibroma, a benign tumor made of connective tissue, like muscle. So, describing a tumor as "fibroid" is like describing a sweater as "cotton"—it's simply referring to the fabric of which the tumor is made. This means that a fibroid tumor can exist anywhere in the body, not just in the uterus.

Leiomyoma uteri is a benign tumor made of smooth uterine muscle. *Leio* means "smooth," *my* means "muscle," and *oma* means "benign growth." In general, muscle tumors called leiomyoma can also be found in the stomach and other parts of the body, but the uterus is the most common site. In fact, the uterus consists mainly of muscle. A tumor is essentially a clump of abnormal cells that form a lump, cyst, or mass. It usually starts with one cell that reproduces again and again. Why these cells develop in the first place is still a mystery. When these cells are benign, they are harmless. When these cells go awry, however, they develop into a clump within the myometrium, the smooth muscle coat of the uterus, which forms the main part of the organ. Fibroid tumors are therefore a collection of innocent uterine muscle cells that form a noticeable hard lump.

Fibroids develop most commonly in women who are in their thirties and forties, but they can also develop earlier or later than this. In fact, about 30 percent of all women will develop fibroids by the time they reach thirty-five. An estimated 20 percent of white women and 50 percent of black women over thirty years old have fibroids.

Fibroids are grayish white, firm, round, and ring shaped. They come in all sizes, and it's common to have several fibroids growing at once. The main problem is that once fibroids develop, they may continue to grow, and even if they're surgically removed, there's a 10 percent chance they'll grow back. This is the main reason why so many doctors recommend hysterectomies for women with fibroids.

Fibroids are classified by location:

- *Intramural or interstitial:* fibroids in the outer or innermost layer of the uterus.
- *Subserous/serosal:* fibroids that protrude into the abdominal cavity and can be pedunculated (they grow on a stalk, like broccoli).
- *Submucosal:* fibroids that invade the endometrium.

- *Parasitic:* fibroids that migrate out of the uterus and invade the cervix or other pelvic organs, developing their own blood supply.

# What Causes Fibroids?

Nobody knows why fibroids develop. What we do know is that estrogen can trigger fibroids and may make the fibroids grow more quickly. Just as estrogen triggers the uterine lining, or endometrium, to grow and thicken during the estrogen peak in the menstrual cycle, it also triggers the myometrium to grow and thicken, which is where the fibroids are located. So it's not surprising that the fibroids will grow, too, since they consist of uterine muscle tissue.

After menopause, the fibroids will usually shrink. So if you're only a few years away from menopause and you've just developed fibroids, they may shrink on their own without treatment. If you're taking estrogen synthetically as a hormonal contraceptive, going off the contraceptive will often shrink your fibroids as well. A fibroid may not shrink after menopause (or may first develop after menopause) if you are on hormone replacement therapy (HRT), discussed in Chapter 21. Some evidence currently suggests that estrogenic chemicals are responsible for an increase in estrogenic conditions such as fibroids, endometriosis, as well as reproductive cancers. Estrogenic chemicals are man-made chemicals in our environment that break down into by-products that mimic the female hormone estrogen. A good resource on this subject is *Our Stolen Future*, coauthored by Dr. Theo Colborne, a senior scientist with the World Wildlife Fund.

# Are Fibroids Dangerous?

Not at all. Basically, a fibroid is to your uterus what a callus is to the heel of your foot. The callus will keep growing and getting thicker until you cut it off. Even after you cut it off, the callus sometimes grows back.

Imagine, though, what would happen if the callus grew so large that it interfered with your balance and walking. If this were the case, you would need treatment so that you could walk properly again. Depending on their location within the myometrium, fibroids can grow so large that they can press against other reproductive organs and interfere with your pelvic functions. You might experience lower abdominal or back pain or even urinary problems. Menstruation can become heavier, with a gushing flow or clots that could predispose you to anemia. Sometimes these heavier periods are accompanied by more painful cramps, but cramps are often not a symptom. In some cases, the cause of the heavier bleeding is not completely understood. Although fibroids may cause abnormal bleeding between periods, this may be a symptom of another problem and should be evaluated before the bleeding is blamed on the fibroid. In other words, if you have fibroids and are bleeding between periods, you should be checked for other causes of abnormal bleeding. An extremely large fibroid may interfere with a pregnancy simply because it takes up too much space. In fact, fibroids have been known to grow so large that they can make a woman appear to be in her twentieth week of pregnancy. But for the most part, fibroids that large are rare. The average large fibroid usually will not interfere with either conception or pregnancy.

Other symptoms of fibroids include a tender or achy feeling in your uterus or laborlike pains (sometimes the fibroid dies when its blood supply is cut off and the uterus tries to expel it). Pressure in the back of your legs or lower abdomen, backaches, painful intercourse, frequent urination, incontinence, and repeated urinary tract infections are other symptoms.

Just as you can have several calluses on your foot, you can also have several fibroids in your uterus. Keep in mind, though, that fibroids generally are of small to medium size and are symptomless. Women with symptomless fibroids can coexist peacefully with them and are not in any danger. Currently, about 40 percent of all reproductive-age women have one or more fibroid tumors, but only about half of these women experience any symptoms.

# Diagnosing and Treating Fibroids

If you do notice any of the symptoms described earlier, you have symptomatic fibroids. See your doctor and request a full pelvic exam that includes a rectal exam. Unless a rectal exam is done, your doctor can miss the fibroid. Large fibroids can usually be felt in a pelvic exam. Depending on where they're located, smaller fibroids can also cause symptoms, particularly if you have numerous small fibroids. Generally, an ultrasound test or a laparoscopy will confirm whether or not you have smaller fibroids. If you have abnormal bleeding, then an endometrial biopsy should be done to rule out a hormonal deficiency. Hysteroscopy (in which a telescope is passed through the cervix) can determine whether there are more fibroids on or under the uterine lining. Sometimes these fibroids can be removed through the hysteroscope. Treatment for symptomatic fibroids is discussed further on.

What if you suspect you have fibroids but have no symptoms? If this is the case, you don't need to do anything until the fibroids start to bother you. If the fibroids grow larger and you develop symptoms later on, then you can see your doctor and confirm whether you have them.

Often, symptomless fibroids are discovered by your doctor accidentally during a routine pelvic exam. If this happens, just ask him or her to keep an eye on the fibroid(s). Then see your doctor every six months instead of annually for a thorough pelvic exam. The bottom line is that if the fibroid isn't bothering *you*, then you don't need to bother *it*.

## The Symptomless Fibroid Controversy

In the past, if you had symptomless fibroids, once the uterus reached a certain size your doctor would have recommended either a myomectomy (surgical removal of the fibroids only) or, more likely, a hysterectomy. This was done because an enlarged uterus would prevent the doctor from feeling your ovaries and detecting potential problems. In addition, it was difficult to be certain that what he or she was feeling was in fact a fibroid. Back then, fibroid treatment was more radical because there really wasn't any way of absolutely diagnosing fibroids; there was no easy, inexpensive method of proving that the patient truly had only fibroids and not a more serious condition. The philosophy was "Don't take chances."

Today, ultrasound is an accurate and relatively inexpensive method of confirming a fibroid diagnosis that can rule out ovarian abnormalities. In the United States many gynecologists have ultrasound available in their offices. If there is still any doubt after the ultrasound, gynecologists today will continue on with a laparoscopy. Now, when a fibroid is confirmed and the patient doesn't have any symptoms, she has more options available to her. If you're told you have fibroids but you don't have any symptoms, and the diagnosis has been confirmed, seek a second opinion if any surgery, such as a myomectomy or hysterectomy, is recommended. In this situation, these procedures are very likely unnecessary.

Again, for fibroids of any size that are symptomless, leave them be. Removing them because of what they *may* do isn't a good enough reason to subject yourself to the expense (which includes lost time and income from your job), trauma, and consequences of major pelvic surgery. The fibroids may do nothing and may even naturally shrink after menopause anyway.

## The Myths Behind Hysterectomies and Symptomless Fibroids

Medical opinion regarding treatment of symptomless fibroids once went like this: fibroids grow larger with time and become symptomatic as they enlarge, so performing a hysterectomy when the tumors are small will prevent future problems and result in fewer postoperative complications.

But a mid-1990s study conducted by the Iowa College of Medicine and the UCLA School of Medicine, published in *Obstetrics and Gynecology*, yielded startling results. Researchers checked the medical records of ninety-three women who underwent hysterectomy procedures for fibroids. They found that women who had a uterus enlarged by fibroids to the size of a twelve- to twenty-week pregnancy suffered no more surgical complications than did women who had smaller fibroids. The study also revealed that the so-called conventional reasoning behind performing a hysterectomy for symptomless fibroids was rooted in mythology rather than in fact.

Here's the myth-by-myth breakdown:

**Myth:** *Surgery will prevent the development of symptoms, which are inevitable as the fibroid grows larger.*

**Fact:** This is illogical. Not all large fibroids cause symptoms. Surgery can and should be avoided until symptoms develop. Women whose fibroids would never have caused problems would be spared the risk and expense of major surgery.

**Myth:** *Large, symptomless fibroids will interfere with early detection of ovarian cancer. Removing the fibroid can prevent a missed diagnosis of early ovarian cancer.*

**Fact:** As discussed earlier, ultrasound and laparoscopy are used to monitor the ovaries in the presence of an enlarged uterus. But it's important to be aware that even ultrasound may not detect early ovarian cancer, which is why more sophisticated screening methods are currently being developed.

**Myth:** *If irregular or excessive bleeding is being caused by a fibroid, a hysterectomy will take care of the problem.*

**Fact:** Women with symptomless fibroids and irregular bleeding need to have their doctors rule out other causes for the bleeding first, before the fibroid is held responsible. When irregular bleeding is the only symptom present in women with fibroids, there may be another problem that's causing the bleeding, and it usually has nothing to do with the fibroid. An endometrial biopsy can rule out a hormonal cause, and for some patients, hysteroscopy might be useful.

**Myth:** *There is a small but real possibility that a fibroid may develop into a cancerous tumor called a leiomyosarcoma.*

**Fact:** A woman's odds of dying of a hysterectomy (one in one thousand) are much higher than her odds of developing a leiomyosarcoma. Therefore, it's not necessary to do a hysterectomy to prevent leiomyosarcoma. However, if a fibroid suddenly begins growing rapidly, then surgery would be indicated because the fibroid would have become suspicious. In addition, leiomyosarcomas, rare as they are (occurring in less than 0.2 to 0.1 percent of all women), can be treated.

## *Treating Symptomatic Fibroids*

The only reason why symptomatic fibroids need to be treated is to make you more comfortable and alleviate the symptoms. Many of the symptoms experienced are related to the size, location, and number of fibroids. Symptoms may include heavy or prolonged menstrual periods, which can result in anemia; pelvic pain or pressure; pain during sexual intercourse; bladder pressure, causing the urge to urinate frequently; constipation due to pressure on the colon; and pain in the back, flank, or legs due to pressure on nerves. Fibroids can also affect fertility and pregnancies, causing infertility or miscarriage.

Technically, if you can live with the symptoms, the fibroids would not present any danger to your health. Symptomatic fibroids can make you extremely uncomfortable, however, and most women who have them will want to get rid of them. Unless you have enough information to make an informed decision about treatment, you might be railroaded into undergoing a hysterectomy, when in fact this procedure may not be necessary.

The first thing to do when you're diagnosed with symptomatic fibroids is to recheck the diagnosis. Just because you have fibroids doesn't mean you don't have another condition at the same time: endometriosis, PID, STDs, other tumors, and so on. Large fibroids will be felt in a pelvic exam; smaller fibroids are not that easy to diagnose. Before you undergo any kind of surgical diagnostic procedure (such as a laparoscopy to confirm small fibroids) or consent to any kind of treatment for larger, obvious fibroids, it's a good idea to get a second opinion.

Before you consent to either a laparoscopy (see Chapter 13) or a D & C (dilation and curettage) procedure (see Chapter 17), request an ultrasound first. Often, the fibroids are visible with ultrasound. Transvaginal ultrasound may be a better option for you since a full bladder is not necessary. In this test, a lubricated plastic probe is placed inside your vagina, producing a higher-quality image. Submucosal fibroids are often missed with abdominal ultrasound. If the transvaginal ultrasound fails to confirm a diagnosis, ask about a procedure called hysteroscopy. Here, your doctor places a fiber-optic scope into the uterus, but the procedure can be done in the doctor's office. This is considered an advanced diagnostic tool for confirming fibroids. However, it can only identify those that impinge on the uterine cavity. A laparoscopy allows the surgeon to take a peek at the outer surface of the uterus. Sometimes both procedures are combined and done under anesthesia. Ultrasound, hysteroscopy, or laparoscopy may tell you how many fibroids there are, their sizes, where they're located, and how fast they're growing. A hysteroscopy or laparoscopy will always confirm a fibroid diagnosis.

Hysteroscopy is considered to be far more sensitive and accurate than a D & C when it comes to finding and removing small uterine fibroids. In one study, large numbers of polyps and fibroids were missed by a D & C because less than 50 percent of the uterus was scraped in 60 percent of the patients.

If your fibroids are smaller than a quarter-inch, have a stalk, or are protruding into the uterine cavity, hysteroscopy can remove them quite easily. In this case, normal periods return in 50 to 87 percent of women undergoing this procedure.

Larger fibroids (between one and two inches or larger) can also be removed with hysteroscopy but should be shrunk with hormonal therapy first.

If your uterus is larger than the size of a fourteen-week pregnancy, hysteroscopy is not appropriate, and you need to seek out other treatment options.

Hysteroscopy can, incidentally, be used to detect, treat, or monitor other uterine conditions, such as endometrial hyperplasia (discussed in Chapter 17). In fact, hysteroscopy is now considered the gold standard in diagnosing or monitoring conditions that used to warrant a D & C.

## Uterine Artery Embolization (UAE)

First introduced in 1990, this is a new approach in the treatment of uterine fibroids. Here, the blood vessels that supply nutrients and oxygen to fibroids are blocked off. This blockage causes the fibroid muscle cells to degenerate and form scar tissue, which shrinks the fibroid and eliminates the symptoms. UAE is considered a minimally invasive procedure; it involves an overnight hospital stay. In many hospitals UAE can be done as an outpatient procedure. Most women notice the greatest improvement in their fibroid symptoms within the first eight weeks.

### Risks

There are some risks to this procedure: the procedure will probably leave you infertile, and there is a possibility of premature ovarian failure and/or earlier menopause. An immediate risk of the procedure is that following UAE, women tend to experience severe pelvic pain as viable uterine tissue becomes scarred. This is known as postembolization syndrome, which in addition to pelvic pain may include fever, malaise, nausea, and vomiting. For this reason, staying overnight in the hospital might be the best route. Narcotic drugs, nonsteroidal anti-inflammatory agents, and an antinausea drug can be prescribed if you want to recover at home.

You need to weigh these risks against more dramatic surgeries such as hysterectomy (which used to be the only remedy offered to women with symptomatic fibroids), discussed more in Chapter 20. Health care providers are also concerned that they may miss diagnoses of various gynecological cancers after UAE.

## Other Treatment Options

How old are you? Do you have that much further to go until menopause? Can you live with the symptoms until then? For example, you could treat your fibroid symptoms with palliative measures, taking painkillers until the fibroids shrink naturally in menopause. Are you already past menopause and taking synthetic hormones (see Chapter 21)? If so, tell your doctor that you want to go off any kind of synthetic estrogen product you might be taking. Then wait and see if your symptoms subside on their own. Are you taking oral contraceptives with estrogen? If you are, go off them for a while and see if the symptoms subside. (Other methods of contraception are discussed in Chapter 8.)

## Hormone Therapy

If you are not taking synthetic estrogen and are more than a decade away from menopause, request a short trial period of estrogen-blocking drugs, such as danazol, also used to treat endometriosis. There's a good chance that these drugs may shrink your fibroids and your symptoms might improve. Although these drugs do have side effects, they are far less invasive than major surgery and may work fine for a short period of time. Hormonal therapy with GnRH antagonists can dramatically reduce the size of your fibroids and therefore treat the symptoms. Once you stop therapy, however, the fibroids will grow again if you're not past menopause.

## Endometrial Ablation

Endometrial ablation is another treatment option that involves laser surgery through hysteroscopy. During this procedure, fibroids under the uterine lining can be removed and the remaining uterine lining tissue destroyed. This will prevent bleeding, leaving you infertile, but will not interfere with your ovarian functions. Some women continue to have some bleeding, but it's usually much lighter. Because the endometrium may regrow, a tubal ligation at the same time may be necessary, since it's not known how damaging a pregnancy could be. There's also concern that the procedure could cause scarring of the uterine cavity that might complicate an endometrial cancer diagnosis. If your doctor considers you a high risk for endometrial cancer, then a hysterectomy may be more appropriate therapy after all. Essentially, endometrial ablation is a high-tech, irreversible D & C, except that a laser or electric cautery is used to manually scrape the lining of the uterus instead of the curettage instrument. Your surgeon uses a hysteroscope and minicamera, which bounces a visual image off a television screen to guide the surgery. Overall, endometrial ablation eliminates bleeding in 40 to 50 percent of the women undergoing the procedure and significantly reduces bleeding in another 40 to 50 percent. There is, therefore, a 20 percent chance that the procedure will resolve nothing at all.

Endometrial ablation has become increasingly popular because it preserves the uterus and ovaries completely. It is now considered the definitive treatment for submucosal fibroids, adenomyosis, endometriosis, and abnormal heavy uterine bleeding.

## Myomectomy

Myomectomies are effective surgical procedures for removing fibroids. In this procedure, an incision is made through your abdomen and the fibroid is removed while leaving your uterus and reproductive organs intact. Myomectomy has been around for years and was used to treat fibroids on younger women who still wanted children. But because it's a more time-consuming procedure than a hysterectomy, older women with fibroids are often not offered myomectomies as an option. A gynecologist experienced in reconstructive surgery is an appropriate myomectomy surgeon. Some fibroids can also be removed at the time of laparoscopy.

Your doctor might tell you that a myomectomy is more complicated than a hysterectomy and, if you're past menopause, may question your reasons for wanting one. But studies show that when a surgeon is skilled in myomectomies, there are no more complications involved than in a hysterectomy, and it has none of the postoperative consequences of a hysterectomy either. In addition, a myomectomy can be performed with laser surgery, which involves far less bleeding.

If your doctor tells you that neither a myomectomy nor microsurgery is as effective as a hysterectomy, get another opinion. This response indicates that your doctor is unfamiliar with the procedures and prefers to rely on what he or she is comfortable doing rather than on what's in your best interest.

Fertility surgeons are often skilled in both myomectomies and microsurgery. You can ask your gynecologist or primary care physician to refer you to a reproductive or fertility surgeon, who is usually a reproductive endocrinologist.

You can call the Hysterectomy Educational Resources and Services (HERS) Foundation. This is a nationwide referral service that will provide you with lists of doctors who specialize in myomectomies and other alternatives to hysterectomies. The HERS Foundation can be reached at 422 Bryn Mawr Avenue, Bala Cynwyd, PA 19004 or 610-667-7757. Information can be found online at hersfoundation.com. The foundation also offers phone counseling.

### Hysterectomy

Hysterectomy should be your last resort for the treatment of fibroids. There are very few cases that warrant hysterectomy. For more information, see Chapter 20.

# What to Eat

Because fat cells make estrogen, losing weight through conventional means is considered a good strategy to help shrink fibroids. But that may not be enough, given how much estrogen all of us are exposed to through diet. Managing fibroids through diet means that you follow a low-estrogen diet. Extra estrogen can come from many sources, including:

- animal fat (meat and dairy)
- pesticides and other chemicals that mimic the action of estrogen in the body (called environmental estrogens)

You can also make extra estrogen when your liver is not functioning well or you have other nutritional deficiencies or bowel problems.

Taking all the B vitamins in doses of 50 to 100 mg a day as well as an additional 200 mg of B$_6$ a day can help improve liver function. Choline, methionine, and inositol also improve the breakdown of estrogen in the liver. Bitter greens such as endive, escarole, dandelion greens, and radicchio also stimulate liver function. Swedish bitters are another very helpful tonic to stimulate liver action and improve digestion. Supplements such as evening primrose oil, vitamin E, vitamin C, and bioflavonoids may also help.

Applying hot castor oil packs to the abdomen three to five times a week can improve regularity and also help to draw out the toxins from the body.

# Flower Power

Bathing in any of the essential oils discussed in Chapter 1 may help with symptoms, such as heavier and crampier periods. Clary sage, which is particularly helpful when you have heavier periods, can be added to any of those oils. Essential oils specifically recommended for stress relief (see further on) are ylang-ylang, neroli, jasmine, cedarwood, lavender, chamomile, geranium, patchouli, rose, sage, clary sage, sandalwood, bergamot, myrrh, and tangerine.

## *Herbs for the Liver*

A combination of liver herbs (such as milk thistle, dandelion root, artichoke, burdock root, and wild ginger root) taken twice daily can strengthen the liver, which can reduce excess estrogen.

## *Natural Progesterone*

Discussed in detail in Chapter 21, one-fourth to one-half teaspoon twice daily from day 12 to day 26 of your menstrual cycle can help to balance excess estrogen in the body and can help to shrink fibroids.

## *Bach Flower Remedies*

Many experts in fibroids observe that they develop in women who suffer from stress-related anger and resentment. Progesterone receptors do not function in the presence of adrenaline, the main stress hormone, which we also make when our blood sugar is low; this can cause an imbalance of estrogen.

One of the most popular natural emotional rescues people are turning to in droves is what's known as the Bach flower remedies. The Bach flower remedies comprise thirty-eight homeopathically prepared plant and flower liquid extracts. Each flower remedy is designed to treat a different emotion. Dr. Edward Bach invented this healing tradition in the 1930s (during a time of extreme economic and social misery). Bach classified emotions into seven major groups (e.g., fear, uncertainty, or loneliness), creating thirty-eight different emotional states and corresponding flower remedies. These remedies work through homeopathic principles, stimulating the body's own capacity to heal itself. The flower remedies are made available as a liquid, which is preserved in brandy. Taking the remedy involves diluting two drops of the pure liquid into 30 ml of mineral water. You then take four drops of the dilution orally four times a day. You can also put two drops of the pure remedy into a glass of water and just sip it throughout the day.

The following is a complete list of the Bach flower remedies and the corresponding emotional states they help to calm or quell:

*Agrimony:* mental torture behind a cheerful face
*Aspen:* fear of unknown things
*Beech:* intolerance
*Centaury:* the inability to say "no"
*Cerato:* lack of trust in one's own decisions
*Cherry Plum:* fear of the mind giving way
*Chestnut Bud:* failure to learn from mistakes
*Chicory:* selfish, possessive love
*Clematis:* dreaming of the future without working in the present
*Crab Apple:* the cleansing remedy, also for self-hatred
*Elm:* overwhelmed by responsibility
*Gentian:* discouragement after a setback
*Gorse:* hopelessness and despair
*Heather:* self-centeredness and self-concern
*Holly:* hatred, envy, and jealousy
*Honeysuckle:* living in the past
*Hornbeam:* procrastination, tiredness at the thought of doing something
*Impatiens:* impatience
*Larch:* lack of confidence
*Mimulus:* fear of known things
*Mustard:* deep gloom for no reason
*Oak:* the plodder who keeps going past the point of exhaustion
*Olive:* exhaustion following mental or physical effort

*Pine:* guilt

*Red Chestnut:* overconcern for the welfare of loved ones

*Rock Rose:* terror and fright

*Rock Water:* self-denial, rigidity, and self-repression

*Scleranthus:* inability to choose between alternatives

*Star of Bethlehem:* shock

*Sweet Chestnut:* extreme mental anguish, when everything has been tried and there is no light left

*Vervain:* overenthusiasm

*Vine:* dominance and inflexibility

*Walnut:* protection from change and unwanted influences

*Water Violet:* pride and aloofness

*White Chestnut:* unwanted thoughts and mental arguments

*Wild Oat:* uncertainty over one's direction in life

*Wild Rose:* drifting, resignation, apathy

*Willow:* self-pity and resentment

# How to Move

Stress-reducing exercises involve deep-breathing exercises and movements that work with the life force energy, or *qi* (see Chapter 1). In the presence of stress, progesterone receptors don't work properly. The yoga postures recommended for endometriosis in Chapter 13 work well for fibroids, too.

Dr. Christiane Northrup, who writes about the emotional aspects of women's illnesses, observes that fibroids often represent a block in creative energy for women. Creativity, referring to art in all its forms (words, fine arts, visual arts, healing arts, performing arts, hobbies, or sport), can dramatically lower stress levels. In particular, writing—in the form of journaling or writing poetry or letters—can be healing. A new study published in the *Journal of the American Medical Association* found that people suffering from chronic ailments actually felt better when they wrote about their ailments.

# 15

# Pelvic Prolapse

*PELVIC PROLAPSE* IS a general term referring to any combination of vaginal or uterine prolapse, which can also involve the bowel. This problem only affects women who still have a uterus. Basically, the problem has to do with the uterus sagging or sinking and literally falling down as the woman ages. When you experience a uterine prolapse, you may feel as though something is falling out. You may also experience a heaviness in your lower abdomen, constant lower back pain and pressure, menstrual-like cramps that seem to worsen after long intervals of standing, difficulty with penetration during intercourse, constipation combined with the urge to bear down, and urinary incontinence. Uterine prolapse is classified by degree. In first-degree uterine prolapse, the cervix is visible when you press on the perineum area. In second-degree prolapse, the cervix is visible outside of the vaginal opening, while the uterine fundus remains inside. In third-degree prolapse, the entire uterus is outside of the vaginal opening. Complications of uterine prolapse can be incontinence (see Chapter 5), vaginitis (see Chapter 6), cystitis (see Chapter 5), and a higher risk of uterine cancer (see Chapter 18).

The uterus can fall down a little, called a straight line prolapse, or the entire length of the vagina can fall. In more severe cases, the cervix protrudes between the labia, which could interfere with intercourse. This is dangerous because the cervix can get infected through contact with urine or feces.

The first symptom of prolapse is usually urinary incontinence. Women initially see a urologist with complaints of stress urinary incontinence.

Because the uterus supports or rests on a variety of other organs, a uterine prolapse can be associated with prolapse of other pelvic organs, such as:

- *Cystocele:* This is a falling bladder. You may feel as though you can't empty your bladder completely and may have a UTI or stress incontinence.
- *Urethrocele:* In this case, the muscles supporting the urethra separate, and the urethra sags into the vagina.
- *Rectocele:* Here, the rectum falls into the vagina, causing constipation. Your stools may also pack into a sort of pouch, forming a bulging rectum.
- *Enterocele:* This is when the small intestine falls into the back of the vagina.

In 1995 the International Continence Society adopted the Pelvic Organ Prolapse Staging System. This system measures the extent of the prolapse in centimeters, measuring from the hymen (the opening of the vagina) upward. If the prolapse has fallen to the hymen, that is considered the final prolapse stage. Most women notice symptoms at stage 0 or stage 1, which are early prolapse stages. Stage 4 would be when the prolapse has reached the hymen.

# Causes of Prolapse

Pregnancy and childbirth are major contributors. The uterus and tissue expand to such an extent that they lose their elasticity and ability to retain normal positions. During labor the muscles in the vagina and perineum can be torn. Nonmuscle tissue, ligaments, and fascia may not have the resiliency to retain their normal position and shape. Women who have had ten kids or more (not seen as much today as in the past) often have internal tearing that destroys their pelvic configuration.

Obesity and poor nutrition are other causes. Poor nutrition prevents tissues from getting enough blood and nutrients. In obese women, fat hangs inside the abdomen like an extra organ pushing directly on the pelvis, uterus, and bowels or pushing the intestines into the pelvis, ruining normal bowel function. The constant pressure from this extra fat tears the tissue and damages elasticity.

Estrogen loss after menopause causes the mucosal tissue of the ligaments and fascia to thin and weaken (just like the vagina). In this case, taking supplemental estrogen from natural sources can help; taking HRT in the short term may prove beneficial, but see Chapter 21 for the new rules concerning HRT in light of studies suggesting risks for long-term use.

Occasionally, a large fibroid can push down on the uterus and vaginal wall, causing a prolapse. The fibroid may also put pressure on the bladder and stretch tissues. See Chapter 14 for more information on the treatment of fibroids. Finally, simple aging—heredity and gravity—may be the culprit.

Hysterectomy or other pelvic surgery can cause prolapse as well. Activities that entail repetitive bearing down, such as chronic constipation, chronic coughing, or frequent heavy lifting, are known causes, too.

# Preventing (Further) Prolapse

One of the best ways to prevent prolapse is to keep the uterine muscles toned. This can be done through Kegel exercises and through exercises using a pelvic floor trainer, such as Epi-No. (Chapter 5 offers more information on both forms of exercise.) An excellent and increasingly popular way to tone uterine muscles is—don't laugh—belly dancing. See under "How to Move" for more details.

## *Weight Loss*

Women who are carrying too much weight are far more at risk for prolapse than women who are trim. See Chapter 17 "What to Eat" and "How to Move" for nutrition and exercise tips. All of the diet and exercise information in Chapter 1 is relevant here, too.

## *Quit Smoking*

Studies reveal that more than half of all women who experience pelvic prolapse smoke. See Chapter 3 for some smoking-cessation tips.

# Using a Pessary

A device similar to the outer ring of a diaphragm, a pessary is placed in the vagina to help reposition and support the uterus or bladder. Pessaries are usually made of silicone and, like diaphragms (see Chapter 8), must be fitted by your doctor. Since women come in all shapes and sizes, so do pessaries. Frequently, you can manage minor prolapse through the use of a pessary and pelvic floor exercises, which can tone the muscles. Pessaries are also called pelvic support devices and can help with stress urinary incontinence (see Chapter 5).

You may find that over time, you'll need to switch pessaries to accommodate changing shapes due to a worsening or an improvement in prolapse.

## *Side Effects of Pessaries*

Some women notice more vaginal discharge and may also develop vaginitis. If you notice discharge with an odor, you should be screened for bacterial vaginosis. Douching should be avoided as well, as this can drive bacteria higher up in the pelvic tract.

If the pessary isn't fitted properly, or if you are straining to lift something, your pessary may fall out. Resizing the pessary may be necessary. The following are other signs that your pessary needs to be refitted:

- Your pessary is falling out during intercourse.
- You are noticing chronic constipation since you began wearing the pessary.
- You have been getting urinary and vaginal infections since you began wearing the pessary.

### *Caring for Pessaries*

Most pessaries can be worn for several days in a row, but keeping the pessary clean is key to avoid garden-variety infections (see Chapter 6). Pessaries can be cleaned with ordinary soap and water. Avoid anything that is heavily perfumed or products that have a lot of commercial chemicals because this can predispose you to irritation.

# Repair Surgery

Prolapse can often be surgically repaired without the need for a hysterectomy. Urologists frequently become involved with the surgical correction of pelvic prolapse. Most doctors will recommend a hysterectomy (usually the vaginal procedure). Studies show that about 16 percent of hysterectomies are performed to correct prolapse; many of these hysterectomies can be avoided with alternatives.

To find out about alternatives to hysterectomy in this case, refer to Chapter 20 or contact the Hysterectomy Educational Resources and Services (HERS) Foundation at 610-667-7757 or hersfoundation.com. In some instances, HRT or ERT (estrogen replacement therapy) may help with urinary incontinence but cannot repair prolapse. Before you decide on treatment, find out why your uterus is falling. Weight loss may improve the situation as well.

# What to Eat

Most women dealing with pelvic prolapse can benefit from losing some weight and adopting a high-fiber diet to help prevent the straining involved with constipation or harder stools. In addition to the tips that follow, review Chapter 1 on a balanced diet, Chapter 9 on a high-fiber diet, and Chapter 17 on a low-estrogen/low-saturated fat diet.

### *Reading Food Labels*

When women need to lose weight, they often gravitate to low-fat products to supplement cravings. Since 1993 food labels have been adhering to strict guidelines set out by the Food and Drug Administration and the U.S. Department of Agriculture's Food Safety and Inspection Service. All packages will include labels on the side or back listing "Nutrition Facts." The "% Daily Values" column tells you how high or low that food is in various nutrients, such as fat, saturated fat, and cholesterol. A number of 5 or less is "low"—*good* news if the product shows <5 for fat, saturated fat, and cholesterol, but *bad* news if the product is <5 for fiber. Serving sizes are also confusing. Foods that are similar are given the same *type* of serving size defined by the FDA. That means that five cereals that all weigh X grams per cup will share the same serving sizes.

Calories (how much energy) and calories from fat (how much fat) are also listed per serving of food. Total carbohydrate, dietary fiber, sugars, other carbohydrates (which means starches), total fat, saturated fat, cholesterol, sodium, potassium, vitamins, and minerals are given in "% Daily Values," based on the 2,000-calorie diet recommended by the U.S. government.

But that's not where the confusion ends—*or even begins*! You have to wade through the various claims and understand what they mean. For example, anything that is "X-free" (as in sugar-free, saturated fat–free, cholesterol-free, sodium-free, calorie-free, and so on) means that the product indeed has no "X" or that "X" is so tiny, it is dietarily insignificant. This is not the same thing as a label that says "95% fat-free." In this case, the product contains relatively small amounts of fat but still has fat. This claim is based on 100 gm of the product. For example, if a snack food contains 2.5 gm of fat per 50 gm, it can be said to be "95% fat-free."

A label that screams "low in saturated fat" or "low in calories" does *not* mean that the food is fat-free or calorie-free. It means that you can eat a large amount of that food without exceeding the Daily Value for that food. In potato-chip country, that might mean you can eat twelve potato chips instead of six. So if you eat the whole bag of "low-fat" chips, you're still eating a lot of fat. Be sure to check serving sizes.

"Cholesterol-free" or "low cholesterol" means that the product doesn't have any or much, respectively, animal fat (hence, cholesterol). This doesn't mean "low fat." Pure vegetable oil doesn't come from animals but *is* pure fat!

### *"Less and More"*

And then there are the comparison claims, such as "fewer," "reduced," "less," "more," or, my favorite, "light" (or worse, "lite"!). These words appear on labels of foods that have been nutritionally altered from a previous "version" or a competitor's version. For example, Brand X Potato Chips Regular may have much more fat than Brand X Potato Chips Lite "with less fat than Regular Brand X," but that doesn't mean that Brand X Lite is fat-free, or even low in fat. It just means it's B% *lower* in fat than Brand X Regular.

On the flip side, Brand X may have a trace amount of calcium, while Brand Y "now with more calcium" may still have only a small amount of calcium, but 10 percent more than Brand X. (In other words, you may still need to eat one hundred bowls of Brand Y before you get the daily requirement for calcium!)

To be light (or "lite"!) a product has to contain either one-third fewer calories or half the fat of the regular product. Or a low-calorie or low-fat food contains 50 percent less sodium. Something that is "light in sodium" means it has at least 50 percent less sodium than the regular product, such as canned soup.

# Flower Power

Review the herbs listed in Part IV as well as the essential oils listed in Chapter 1. These are designed to strengthen and tone the uterus and pelvic floor.

# How to Move

The best exercise to prevent or manage prolapse is belly dancing, also known as Middle Eastern Dance, or Raks Sharki. Originally, belly dancing was a ceremonial dance that worshiped women as mothers. This ancient form of dance is becoming popular in the West because of its amazing gynecological health benefits. Not only does it keep you fit and improve posture, but it beautifully tones the pelvic floor muscles. It is particularly good for toning pelvic floor muscles after childbirth. Women of all shapes and sizes can belly dance. It does not tax your body in the same way as traditional exercise. For this reason, it's considered low-impact exercise.

In order to learn how to belly dance, you have to go to a class. Beginner, intermediate, and advanced classes are available in almost every urban center.

The movement of belly dancing involves graceful hip drops, rolls, and pivots that use muscle groups in the abdomen, trunk, spine, neck, and, most especially, the pelvic area. Belly dancing firms and tones your entire body, including legs, arms, shoulders, and abdominal area. It is also helpful for lower back pain, which many women are plagued with around their periods.

In addition, small muscle groups deep in the back that are normally underexercised are used and strengthened, which helps to realign the posture and pelvic floor. Another benefit is improved hip flexibility. Belly dancing is also a weight-bearing exercise, which can help prevent osteoporosis.

Other exercises that can help tone the pelvic floor are yoga and qi gong (see Chapter 1), as well as the exercises discussed in Chapter 5 on urinary health.

# 16

# Interstitial Cystitis (IC)

As DISCUSSED IN Chapter 5, many women with chronic cystitis are found to have interstitial cystitis (IC). This is an inflammation of the interstitium, the space between the bladder lining and bladder muscle. This can cause chronic pelvic pain, frequent urination, and a shrunken, ulcerated bladder. The bladder itself is lined with a protective layer that is secreted, like mucus, by the cells that line the bladder. This layer protects the inside of the bladder from acids and toxins in the urine and prevents bacteria from sticking to the bladder wall. If this layer is damaged, infection can result.

IC symptoms are the same as those of cystitis, but you may also feel bruised around your clitoral area. If your urine cultures continue to be negative after a few bouts of what seems to be normal bacterial cystitis, you probably have IC. IC is difficult to diagnose and therefore is frequently missed or misdiagnosed. It is almost exclusively a woman's disease; roughly half a million North American women currently suffer from IC.

There is no consensus in the medical community about the exact cause of IC, but stress seems to play a huge role in triggering symptoms (see further on). Stress is particularly suspect since many IC sufferers also suffer from other stress-related ailments, such as increased incidence of irritable bowel syndrome, allergies, and rheumatological disorders. Some urologists believe IC could be an autoimmune disorder, which can be brought on by stress; there has also been research into infectious causes. It's more likely that IC has multiple causes, which could include sensitivities to toxic agents. What women need to know about IC is that it is a real, organic problem and not a psychological disorder—something that many women with IC used to hear in the days of yesteryear.

What distinguishes IC from other bladder problems is the absence of any apparent cause (such as a bacterial infection, a fibroid, etc.) with the symptoms of extreme urinary frequency, pain, urgency, as well as nighttime frequency (known as nocturia). Nighttime frequency also causes sleep deprivation. Sometimes interstitial cystitis is called bladder hypersensory disorder.

What most health care providers classify as IC is a collection of frequency, urgency, and bladder pain symptoms that persist in the absence of cystitis.

IC was first described in 1936 by Joseph Parrish in a medical textbook about urinary disorders. Parrish wrote about "an extremely painful nervous condition characterized by great suffering in the urinary organs with violent attacks." Nothing much has changed; IC is so debilitating for women who suffer from it that it affects quality of life and can trigger depression. Stress appears to be the main trigger for IC, and many women may exhibit symptoms of IC without even realizing how much stress is in their lives.

## Signs and Symptoms

In various questionnaires, the symptom breakdown appears to be as follows: urge and frequency, nighttime frequency, and pain. Ninety percent of patients with IC are women, and the condition is most common in women forty to sixty years of age; 25 percent of patients with IC are under the age of twenty-five. Women who have IC report having to urinate up to sixty times per day and every twenty to thirty minutes during the night. The typical scenario is to suffer from these symptoms for about four to seven years before obtaining the correct diagnosis. Symptoms tend to worsen over time—urge and frequency are usually the beginning stages of IC; pain and nighttime frequency represent later stages of IC.

There are a host of nonbladder-related symptoms IC sufferers report, but they have to do with signs of sleep deprivation, depression, and stress-related ailments. For example, 56 percent of IC sufferers report that they suffer from "low mood," 63 percent report suffering from fatigue, 49 percent report that they have difficulty concentrating, while 49 percent report insomnia or hypersomnia (oversleeping).

A delay in diagnosing IC can lead women into an array of therapies for bacterial cystitis (see Chapter 5), endometriosis (see Chapter 13), and other gynecological ailments. In fact, the symptoms of bladder endometriosis mirror interstitial cystitis, and women diagnosed with bladder endometriosis may have IC instead. It's important for women who have urge and frequency symptoms to realize that early interstitial cystitis often has no pain associated with it; the pain is a sign of more advanced IC that tends to worsen over the years.

## Managing IC

Managing IC tends to be concentrated on pain relief. In addition to the classic medications used to treat IC, such as narcotics (a.k.a. opioid analgesics), muscle relaxants, antianxiety medications, bladder antispasmodics, analgesics, and anticholinergics, various clinical trials are experimenting with a wide assortment of medications for IC that include:

- *Mucosal surface protectants:* These work by helping to restore the bladder surface, which can ease pain.
- *Tricyclic antidepressants:* These have a sedative effect and can also block certain neurotransmitters that cause pain.
- *Antihistamines:* These can affect the mast cells, which are thought to play a role in IC symptoms.
- *H2 blockers:* Normally used to treat heartburn, ulcers, and acid indigestion, these have been found to have some effect on IC symptoms.
- *Leukotriene inhibitors:* These are asthma medications that can help reduce inflammation.

Most IC sufferers practice self-care; many share information on the Internet about what works best. (By searching on the phrase "interstitial cystitis," you'll connect to a host of sites.) The remedies range from over-the-counter medications and herbal therapies to diet changes and physical comfort measures.

The medical community has researched other therapies, including hydrodistension, which involves "stretching" the bladder, as well as pelvic floor exercises aimed at decreasing the symptoms of urgency and frequency. Some believe that dysfunctional pelvic floor muscles may be responsible for the urgency-frequency symptoms. Laser therapy is another experimental therapy that has had some success, while a repair surgery, known as enterocystoplasty, is also being done.

The bottom line is that there are no standard therapies for IC. The best management strategies come from self-help groups, which use diet, over-the-counter pain medications, and lifestyle modification strategies aimed mainly at lowering stress levels. Some of these stress-lowering techniques are discussed under "How to Move," further on.

## *Smoking*

Smoking can badly aggravate bladder problems. See Chapter 3 for smoking-cessation tips.

## *The Role of Stress*

More than 60 percent of IC sufferers report that their symptoms worsen while they're under stress. It is well known that stress can dramatically affect the immune system, and stress is considered the major trigger for conditions ranging from irritable bowel syndrome to rheumatoid arthritis. Thus looking at meditative, more relaxed activities is an important management strategy.

While telling you that it's stress may sound trite, it's important to understand that stress causes real, physical, and biological changes in your body.

Generally, stress is defined as a negative emotional experience associated with biological changes that allow you to adapt to it. In response to stress, your adrenal glands pump out stress hormones that speed up your body: your heart rate increases and your blood sugar levels increase so that glucose can be diverted to your muscles in case you have to "run." This is known as the fight-or-flight response. These hormones are technically called the catecholamines, which are broken down into epinephrine (adrenaline) and norepinephrine.

The problem with stress hormones in the twenty-first century is that the fight-or-flight response isn't usually necessary, since most of our stress stems from interpersonal situations rather than being chased by a predator. Occasionally, we may want to flee from a bank robber or mugger, but most of us just want to flee from our jobs or our kids! In other words, our stress hormones actually put a physical strain on our bodies and can lower our resistance to disease. Initially, stress hormones stimulate our immune systems. But after the stressful event has passed, stress can suppress the immune system, leaving us open to a wide variety of illnesses and physical symptoms.

Hans Selye, considered the father of stress management, defined stress as the "wear and tear" on the body. Once we are in a state of stress, the body adapts to the stress by depleting its resources until it becomes exhausted. The wear and tear on our bodies is mounting; we can suffer from stress-related:

- allergies and asthma
- back pain
- cardiovascular problems
- dental and periodontal problems
- depression
- emotional outbursts (rage, anger, crying, irritation—seen in recent reports on "air rage" and "desk rage")
- fatigue
- gastrointestinal problems (digestive disorders, bowel problems, and so on)
- headaches
- herpes recurrences (especially in women)
- high blood pressure
- high cholesterol
- immune suppression (predisposing us to viruses, such as colds and flu; infections; autoimmune disorders; and cancer)

- insomnia
- loss of appetite and weight loss
- muscular aches and pains
- premature aging
- sexual problems
- skin problems and rashes

As you can see from this lengthy list, stress greatly contributes to ill health and disease. For more on reducing stress, consult my books *Women Managing Stress* or *50 Ways to Prevent and Manage Stress.*

# What to Eat

Managing IC through diet involves avoiding foods that may irritate the bladder. These include:

- aged cheeses, sour cream, yogurt, and chocolate (white chocolate, nonaged cheeses such as cottage cheese, frozen yogurt, and milk are fine)

- fava beans, lima beans, onions, tofu, soybeans, and tomatoes (homegrown tomatoes may be less acidic)

- apples, apricots, avocados, bananas, cantaloupes, citrus fruits, cranberries, grapes, nectarines, peaches, pineapples, plums, pomegranates, rhubarb, strawberries (melons, blueberries, and pears are fine)

- rye and sourdough breads (other breads, pasta, potatoes, and rice are fine)

- aged, canned, cured, processed, or smoked meats and fish, as well as anchovies, caviar, chicken livers, corned beef, and meats that contain nitrates or nitrites (fresh meats and fish are fine)

- nuts, with the exception of almonds, cashews, and pine nuts

- alcoholic beverages (including beer and wine), carbonated drinks such as sodas, coffee or tea, and fruit juices, especially citrus or cranberry juice (noncarbonated bottled water; decaffeinated, acid-free coffee and tea; and some herbal teas are fine)

- mayonnaise, ketchup, mustard, salsa, spicy foods (especially seasonings used in Chinese, Indian, Mexican, and Thai cuisines), soy sauce, miso, salad dressing, and vinegar, including balsamic and flavored vinegars (garlic is fine)

## Preservatives

The following preservatives should be avoided: benzyl alcohol, citric acid, monosodium glutamate (MSG), artificial sweeteners such as aspartame and saccharine, and foods containing preservatives and artificial ingredients and colors.

## Caffeine

Caffeine is one of the worst IC aggravators. Following is a list of how much caffeine certain beverages and foods contain, with the number of milligrams of caffeine in parentheses.

**Coffee (5-ounce cup)**
brewed, drip method (60–180)
brewed, percolator (40–170)
instant (30–120)
decaffeinated, brewed (2–5)
decaffeinated, instant (1–5)

**Tea (5-ounce cup)**
brewed, imported brands (25–110)
brewed, major brands (20–90)
instant (25–50)
iced, 12-ounce glass (67–76)

**Other**
6-ounce glass of caffeine-containing soft drink (15–30)
single-ounce serving of dark chocolate, semisweet (5–35)
single square of baker's chocolate (26)
5-ounce cup of cocoa beverage (2–20)
single-ounce serving of milk chocolate (1–15)
8-ounce glass of chocolate milk (2–7)
serving of chocolate-flavored syrup (4)

## *Fiber*

Constipation can aggravate IC symptoms. See Chapter 9 for tips on a high-fiber diet.

## *Quercetin*

This is a bioflavonoid that has been shown to have potential in the treatment of IC. Quercetin can be derived from grape skin, onion skin, grapefruit rind, and green algae.

# Flower Power

Studies have looked at traditional Chinese herbal formulas in teas and pill form to treat IC. A Chinese herbal tea for IC has been developed, containing Shanyurou (Cornus), Zhizi (gardenia), Xianmao (Curculigo), Dahuang (rhubarb), Buguzhi (Psoralea), Shutihang (Rehmannia, cooked).

Natural polysaccharides, which include glucosamine, chondroitin, and aloe vera, have been shown to be helpful. Marshmallow root and spirulina are also recommended.

## *Stress Relief*

Since stress is indicated as one of the chief triggers of IC in women, the following substances can help:

- *Gamma-aminobutyric acid (GABA):* This is an amino acid that is supposedly an antianxiety agent, which may also help you to fall asleep if you suffer from sleeplessness or insomnia.

- *Inositol:* This is a naturally occurring antidepressant that is present in many foods, such as vegetables, whole grains, milk, and meat, and is available over the counter.

- *Dehydroepiandrosterone (DHEA):* This is a hormone produced by the adrenal glands; production declines as we age. It has been shown to improve moods and memory in certain studies.

- *Melatonin:* This is a hormone that improves sleep and helps reset the body's natural clock.

- *Phosphatidylserine (PS):* This is a phospholipid, a substance that feeds brain-cell membranes. Some studies show that it has natural antidepressant qualities.

- *Tetrahydrobiopterin (BH4):* This substance activates enzymes that control serotonin, noradrenaline, and dopamine levels, which are all important for stable moods. Some studies show that BH4 is an effective natural treatment for depression.

- *Phenylethylamine (PEA):* This is a nitrogen-containing compound found in small quantities in the brain. Studies show that it works as a natural antidepressant.

- *Rubidium:* This is a natural chemical in our bodies, belonging to the same family as lithium, potassium, and sodium. Studies show that it can work as an antidepressant.

# How to Move

Pressure point therapies involve using the fingertips to apply pressure to pressure points on the body, believed to help reduce stress, pain, and other physical symptoms associated with IC. There are different kinds of pressure point therapies, all outlined in the following.

## *Acupuncture*

Acupuncture is an ancient Chinese healing art that aims to restore the smooth flow of life energy, or *qi*, in your body. Acupuncturists believe that your *qi* can be accessed from various points on your body, such as your ear, for example. And each point is also associated with a specific organ. So depending on your physical health, an acupuncturist will use a fine needle on a very specific point to restore *qi* to various organs. Each of the roughly two thousand points on your body has a specific therapeutic effect when stimulated. Acupuncture can relieve many of the physical symptoms and ailments caused by stress; it's now believed that acupuncture stimulates the release of endorphins, which is why it's effective at reducing stress, anxiety, pain, and so forth.

## *Reflexology*

Western reflexology was developed by Dr. William Fitzgerald, an American ear, nose, and throat specialist who talked about reflexology as "zone therapy." But in fact, reflexology is practiced in several cultures, including Egypt, India, Africa, China, and Japan. In the same way as the ears are a map to the organs, with valuable pressure points that stimulate the life force, here the feet play the same role. By applying pressure to certain parts of the feet, hands, and even ears, reflexologists can ease pain and tension and restore the body's life force energy.

Like most Eastern healing arts, reflexology aims to release the flow of energy through the body along its various pathways. When this energy is trapped for some reason, illness can result. When the energy is released, the body can begin to heal itself. A reflexologist views the foot as a microcosm of the entire body. Individual reference points or reflex areas on the foot correspond to all major organs, glands, and other parts of the body. Applying pressure to a specific area of the foot stimulates the movement of energy to the corresponding body part.

## Shiatsu

Shiatsu massage also involves using pressure points. A healer using shiatsu will travel the length of each energy pathway (also called meridian), applying thumb pressure to successive points along the way. The aim is to stimulate acupressure points while giving you some of the healer's own life energy. Barefoot shiatsu involves the healer using his or her foot instead of hand to apply pressure. Jin shin jyutsu and jin shin do are other pressure point therapies similar to acupuncture.

## Working Your Own Pressure Points

You can relieve stress with your own hands, too. Here are some simple pressure point exercises you can try:

- With the thumb of one hand, slowly work your way across the palm of the other hand, from the base of the baby finger to the base of the index finger. Then rub the center of your palm with your thumb. Push on this point. This will calm your nervous system. Repeat this using the other hand.

- To relieve a headache, grasp the flesh at the base of one thumb with the opposite index finger and thumb. Squeeze gently and massage the tissue in a circular motion. Then pinch each fingertip. Switch to the other hand.

- For general stress relief, find sore pressure points on your feet and ankles. Gently press your thumb into them, and work each sore point. The tender areas are signs of stress in particular parts of your body. By working them, you're relieving the stress and tension in various organs, glands, and tissues. You can also apply pressure with bunched and extended fingers, the knuckles, the heel of the hand, or a gripping motion.

- Use the technique for general stress relief also for self-massage on the hands, looking for tender points on the palms and wrists.

- Use the technique for general stress relief also to self-massage the ears. Feel for tender spots on the flesh of the ears and work them with vigorous massage. Within about four minutes the ears will get very hot.

## Bladder Exercises

All the bladder exercises, such as Kegel, and the pelvic floor trainer, Epi-No, discussed in Chapter 5 can also be used to manage IC.

# 17

# Abnormal Bleeding

EXPERIENCING ABNORMAL BLEEDING from the uterus, vagina, or cervix is the pelvic equivalent of finding a lump in the breast. Many women panic and jump to conclusions, fearing they have some horrible kind of cancer. Usually, abnormal bleeding is caused by a benign condition, which is often hormonal. In fact, it is the pelvic cancers that *don't* cause bleeding, such as ovarian cancer, that are far more destructive. Abnormal bleeding usually indicates either a benign or treatable condition. Other signs of pelvic problems are less obvious: unusual discharge (of which we're often not aware), abdominal pain, lower back pain and cramping, bowel problems, and bladder problems.

## A Look at the Suspicious Symptoms

Abnormal bleeding means that you're bleeding or cramping when you're not having your period or when you're beyond menopause; these symptoms are considered abnormal. Any change in your normal menstrual flow (heavier or lighter flow or variances in consistency, duration, or timing) is also abnormal. Unless you are expecting these symptoms as either postoperative side effects (following a D & C procedure or cryotherapy, for example) or as a side effect to a particular hormone or therapy (as in hormone replacement therapy or oral contraceptives), you need to report these symptoms. There are usually noncancerous reasons why you may be experiencing suspicious symptoms. Other suspicious symptoms include:

- *Any unusual growths or sores on or near your vulva:* Cervical cancer is now believed to be the result of human papillomavirus infection. This virus can cause the cells that line the cervix to change, which, if left untreated, can lead to cancer. It can spread beyond your cervix toward the uterus or vagina. Cauliflower-type, flesh-toned lesions near your vagina and vulva, known as condyloma, meaning "raised wart," are often found early during a Pap smear and treated long before the virus triggers precancerous cell changes. Vulvar cancers are basically pelvic skin cancer. Therefore, any raised sores or ulcers that are painful, ooze pus, or bleed, or that won't heal, are suspicious. (Herpes sores always heal, however.)

- *Unusual vaginal discharge:* Watery, bloody discharge after menopause is especially suspect; unusual vaginal discharge is usually a sign of a vaginal infection (see Chapter 6) but may indicate something is up elsewhere. Always report this symptom. When it's fishy smelling, it's likely a bacterial infection or an STD; herpes sores sometimes wind up on your cervix and can ooze pus that imitates vaginal discharge as well. If the discharge has a sweeter odor, like baking bread or even beer, and is cottage-cheesy and white, you've most likely got a yeast infection. However, unusual discharge could also be a sign of cervical or endometrial cancer. See your doctor if you notice unusual discharge.

- *Pelvic pain:* Pelvic pain could indicate endometriosis (see Chapter 13), PID (see Chapter 10), or symptomatic fibroids (see Chapter 14) or may be a symptom of a gynecological cancer.

- *Spotting after intercourse:* Unless you are a virgin and are bleeding as a result of a ruptured hymen, spotting after intercourse indicates that you may be bleeding in your upper pelvic region. This is not normal; get this looked at.

- *Any lumps that you can feel in your abdomen, or a noticeable bloating or increase in abdominal width:* Bloating is a common PMS symptom, so you'll have to decide what constitutes "abnormal" bloating. If you're still bloated right after your period and you have noticed that belts or pants don't seem to fit when you haven't put on weight elsewhere, this is generally a sign that something's up. It is often a symptom of PID, fibroids, or hyperplasia, but it could also mean uterine or ovarian cancer.

- *Swollen glands in the groin area:* These are lymph glands that may show signs of metastasis (a cancerous "invasion"). These glands will be enlarged for the same reasons but will not be affected by the menstrual cycle the way glands around the breasts are. These should be treated as swollen lymph nodes in the neck and investigated immediately.

- *Abdominal pain, nausea, vomiting, gas, constipation, weight loss, or loss of appetite:* This is a long list of miscellaneous ill-health symptoms. If any of these symptoms continues, it's a sign that you're not well. Abdominal pain is also a classic symptom of endometriosis or PID. Although these symptoms could be linked to almost anything, they can also be signs of ovarian, fallopian tube, or uterine cancers.

- *Painful, frequent, or difficult urination:* Most often, this is a sign of urinary tract infection, interstitial cystitis (see Chapter 16), or a fibroid pressing against the bladder (see Chapter 14). But it could also mean other problems such as metastasis. Check it out.

# Investigating Abnormal Bleeding

The first steps in investigating abnormal bleeding are a thorough physical exam, a pelvic exam, and a Pap smear to rule out various commonplace sources: bladder infections, STDs, hemorrhoids, and so on. If the bleeding is an isolated event, your doctor may choose to do nothing and see if the episode recurs. Depending on other symptoms accompanying your bleeding, you may be required to undergo a transvaginal ultrasound procedure, a laparoscopy (discussed in Chapter 13), or a D & C (dilation and curettage). Another important procedure is an endometrial biopsy. This is an in-office procedure that involves placing a small plastic cylinder inside the cervix. The cylinder contains a suction device that sucks up only a small portion of the endometrial lining. The lining is then sent to a lab and analyzed. The procedure is an excellent diagnostic tool, takes only about thirty seconds to do, and is far less invasive than either a D & C (which removes the entire lining) or a laparoscopic procedure. An endometrial biopsy would be done after a transvaginal ultrasound in the event of abnormal uterine bleeding. However, since it biopsies only one area, some doctors may still prefer to do a D & C. (Neither a transvaginal ultrasound nor an endometrial biopsy is recommended as a routine procedure. They should be done only when there's a problem.)

D & C is one of the most common operations performed on women of all ages. It is a short surgical procedure that can be done under a general or local anesthetic. The cervix is dilated to the size of a thumb, and the lining of your uterus is then scooped out with a spoonlike instrument called a curette. A D & C is most commonly done to find the cause of irregular uterine bleeding. A D & C might be recommended when an endometrial biopsy cannot be performed. This would be the case if the cervical opening is too small. This procedure can pinpoint a whole batch of problems: fibroids, uterine cancer, cervical polyps, and so on. D & Cs are also done to "clean out" the uterus. (D & C, for this reason, has also been dubbed "dusting and cleaning.") Women who have had miscarriages or have not delivered the placenta in childbirth are classic D & C candidates. D & Cs are also used to terminate first-trimester pregnancies (see Chapter 12).

A D & C is usually an outpatient hospital procedure. Here, a metal speculum is placed into your vagina, and the vagina and cervix are washed with an antiseptic solution. The doctor puts a clamp on the cervix and passes an instrument through the cervix that measures the depth of the uterus. This will tell the doctor how large your uterus is. Your cervix is gradually opened up using a series of metal rods or dilators, starting with straw-size rods and ending with thumb-size rods. The lining of your uterus is then carefully removed using curettes. A curette has a long handle and sharp edges that can scrape the inner walls of the uterus. These scrapings are then sent to the lab for analysis. Finally, the doctor removes the speculum and puts a sanitary napkin in place to soak up the blood. The whole procedure takes about fifteen minutes, and you can usually go home the same day (unless there were complications indicating an infection). You'll feel cramping and soreness for about a day, and you'll continue to spot for a few weeks. If you continue to bleed heavily for more than a week, see your doctor. Since your cervix is dilated, make sure you avoid getting bacteria into your uterus, which can cause PID. Review the precautions mentioned in Chapter 10. Your periods will also be interrupted (since the lining was removed) but will return to normal after about six weeks.

# Endometrial Hyperplasia

Abnormal uterine bleeding is often a hormonal problem that has to do with anovulatory bleeding. This is responsible for abnormal bleeding about 70 percent of the time and is particularly common in women approaching menopause. For some reason, ovulation does not occur properly, and the lining of the uterus thickens without shedding. When this happens, a condition known as endometrial hyperplasia can develop. Hyperplasia means "overgrowth," so endometrial hyperplasia means "overgrowth of, or too much, endometrium." Unless the lining of the uterus sheds regularly, tissues and glands will build up and may later become a breeding ground for abnormal cells. In essence, hyperplasia can lead to uterine cancer, but it is not yet cancer. It is, instead, a precancerous condition, meaning it is potentially cancerous.

Remember in Chapter 2, where I discussed the "need to bleed"? The chapter recommended that any woman of childbearing age who has missed more than two consecutive periods—but is not pregnant—should investigate possibly having her period induced. Preventing the development of hyperplasia is the reason. (Preventing hyperplasia is also a concern for postmenopausal women on unopposed estrogen therapy, discussed in Chapter 21.)

Depending on how long your lining has been growing, some stages of hyperplasia are more advanced than others. Cystic glandular hyperplasia (also called cystic endometrial hyperplasia, or mild hyperplasia) means that you have too much lining but your endometrial cells are still normal, which is good news. This kind of hyperplasia is always caused by too much estrogen (see further on) and rarely develops into cancer.

Adenomatous hyperplasia without atypical cells is a mouthful to say but is still good news. *Adenomatous* is an adjective that refers to harmless glandular cells. (An adenoma, therefore, is a benign tumor made up of harmless glandular cells.) When mild hyperplasia isn't treated, you get adenomatous hyperplasia, which means that the glandular endometrial cells are growing but are still benign. Again, this kind of hyperplasia rarely develops into cancer. If left untreated, 15 to 30 percent of all women with this condition would go on to develop endometrial cancer within five years.

Atypical adenomatous hyperplasia (also called severe hyperplasia, or even carcinoma in situ [CIS]) is not great news but isn't necessarily bad news either. This means that either a small area on your endometrium or sometimes the entire lining consists of cells that are abnormal and not necessarily benign. The cells seem to be more aggressive but may still be harmless. What you can say about this condition is that it's suspicious. More women with severe hyperplasia go on to develop uterine cancer.

If you've been diagnosed with any kind of hyperplasia, the next crucial step is getting rid of that lining. Potent progesterone supplements are often the route; if these don't work, a D & C might be the next logical step. Another route is discussing an in-office procedure called hysteroscopy, where a lighted tube is introduced through the cervix. This is considered to be a more sensitive and accurate procedure than a D & C, for both diagnosis and treatment of abnormal bleeding.

A relatively new procedure, endometrial ablation, offers an alternative to hysterectomy for severe situations. This permanently removes the lining of the uterus but leaves the rest of the uterus intact. The procedure eliminates heavy bleeding in about half of the cases and reduces it for another 40 to 50 percent. There are risks to this procedure, and in about 10 percent of cases, it does not help at all.

For any kind of hyperplasia, many doctors still suggest a hysterectomy, which is totally unnecessary for both mild hyperplasia and hyperplasia without atypical cells. Although you might be more inclined to accept a recommendation of a hysterectomy for severe hyperplasia, this procedure is not necessary unless the hyperplasia persists after the lining is removed via progesterone supplements, D & C, or hysteroscopy or after the failure of endometrial ablation. In younger women particularly, severe hyperplasia can be reversed with hormonal therapy. The bottom line is that if your doctor suggests an immediate hysterectomy for any stage of hyperplasia, see another doctor! Even severe hyperplasia is still a precancerous, often treatable, condition. (Make sure you ask what kind of hyperplasia it is.)

Once the lining is shed, you'll need to get your hormones checked via a simple blood test. In fact, hyperplasia almost always develops because of a hormonal imbalance (too much or not enough progesterone). When this is the case, hormone therapy is the cure. For an estrogen surplus, progesterone will counteract it; for a progesterone deficiency, progesterone supplements are also the therapy. The menstrual cycle will often correct itself after several assisted cycles.

After your lining has been shedding more regularly, you'll need a second endometrial biopsy or even a D & C to see if the lining is normal again.

If you're premenopausal, you might produce too much estrogen because of excess body fat. Women who are twenty-five to fifty pounds overweight are three times as likely to develop hyperplasia as women who are at normal weights. Women who are more than fifty pounds overweight are nine times as likely to develop hyperplasia.

Your ovaries may be the culprit and simply produce too much estrogen for a variety of reasons. Sometimes excess estrogen production is a genetic trait, seen in women who have long family histories of estrogen-dependent cancers.

If you've always had irregular periods, you're a classic hyperplasia candidate. Diabetic women, for unknown reasons, seem to be more at risk for hyperplasia.

There is also a long list of external factors responsible for excess estrogen in the body. This includes environmental toxins, certain herbs such as ginseng, hormone-fed meats and poultry, certain cosmetics made from estrogen, and hormonal contraceptives that contain estrogen. If you've been given estrogen therapy for another reason, discuss alternative therapies with your doctor and see if going off the therapy helps put your menstrual cycles back on track.

If you're postmenopausal and you still have your uterus, unopposed estrogen replacement therapy (ERT) can predispose you to hyperplasia, too. Balancing the therapy with the right amount of progesterone is all you need to do (this is known as HRT). An estrogen-progesterone combination therapy can reverse as much as 96.8 percent of all postmenopausal hyperplasia cases.

If severe hyperplasia persists and keeps redeveloping despite HRT and a repeat D & C, then a hysterectomy is the next logical step. This means that you've continued to bleed despite therapy and that a repeat endometrial biopsy or D & C after the lining has shed still shows suspicious cells. If you're an older woman, you are also at a higher risk of progressing to uterine cancer and should be particularly open to a hysterectomy at this point.

# Should I Worry About Endometrial Cancer?

Although a large portion of women are diagnosed with hyperplasia and not endometrial cancer, it's important to be aware of the risk factors for both. About 99 percent of all uterine cancer is really endometrial cancer and might be prevented through better nutrition and the early balancing of irregular menstrual cycles. The following characteristics are more prevalent in women who have had or are more at risk for endometrial cancer, but they are not definitive causes of this kind of cancer.

- They are at least twenty-five pounds overweight.
- They have diabetes or high blood pressure (which may be related to weight).
- They have a history of irregular menstrual cycles and irregular bleeding.
- They experienced menopause after fifty (late menopause).
- They have a family history of endometrial cancer.
- They eat a high-fat, high-cholesterol diet (this may be the same as being overweight).

## Should I Worry About a Pelvic Tumor?

Millions of women will be diagnosed each year with either a benign pelvic tumor, such as a fibroid (see Chapter 14) or ovarian cyst (see Chapter 4), or a benign but possibly precancerous condition known as hyperplasia (discussed earlier). PID (see Chapter 10) and endometriosis (see Chapter 13) are extremely common causes of abnormal bleeding and are often the culprits behind all kinds of symptoms, but they may be suspected as cancer until they are diagnosed.

When cancer of the reproductive organs does strike, it most often involves the uterus, which is usually treatable. Uterine cancer—or endometrial cancer, as it's called—has an 85 to 92 percent survival rate, and about thirty-five thousand North American women develop uterine cancer each year. Ovarian cancer is rarer (about twenty thousand North American women develop this each year). Although ovarian cancer is dangerous and difficult to detect, the majority of women are not in a high-risk group for this kind of cancer. Ovarian cancer has an average survival rate of roughly under 40 percent, but when it's detected in its early stages, it has an 80 percent survival rate.

Cancer almost never originates from the fallopian tubes or vagina (fewer than one thousand U.S. women each year develop cancer of the vagina or fallopian tubes; only five in one million women develop vaginal cancer). Fewer than three thousand women develop cancer of the vulva. The only exception to the vaginal and vulvar cancer statistics is among DES daughters, who do tend to develop these kinds of cancers more frequently at young ages (at about age nineteen). The only reason a woman dies from vaginal or vulvar cancer is usually because she is not having routine pelvic exams. As discussed in Chapter 18, the signs of these kinds of cancers are obvious and treatable and are now known to be almost 100 percent preventable through safer sex and good hygiene. For the most part, however, when the vagina, vulva, and fallopian tubes are involved, the cancer originates from the uterus, cervix, or ovaries. Vaginal cancer nevertheless has a survival rate of 50 percent; cancer of the vulva has a survival rate of 80 percent. Cancer of the fallopian tubes has an even lower survival rate than does ovarian cancer—only 30 percent.

Cervical cancer is more common than uterine cancer. But thanks to the Pap test (discussed in Chapter 3), detecting early, or "embryonic," cervical cancer is so advanced it's often treated before it has a chance to progress to a life-threatening stage. Because Pap tests are so routine now, cases of advanced cervical cancer have dropped dramatically. Still, about 13,500 women in the United States develop cervical cancer each year. If it does advance, it will spread to the uterus and is curable via hysterectomy. But unlike uterine cancer or ovarian cancer, cervical cancer can be prevented through safer sex.

Pelvic cancers can be divided into two categories: estrogen-dependent cancers and disease-dependent cancers. Cervical, vaginal, and vulvar cancers tend to be associated with the presence of an STD. That's why hesitating to report symptoms of obvious STDs is particularly dangerous. Curing the diseases early may prevent them from developing into certain cancers.

Estrogen-dependent cancers are stimulated by estrogen. One theory about how these cancers begin is that estrogen flourishes in women who have large amounts of fat stores. The fat cells turn into estrogen factories, increasing the amount of estrogen produced by the body. Breast cancer, endometrial cancer, and ovarian cancer all fall into these categories and are more common in women who are more than twenty-five pounds overweight. This is why high-fiber and low-fat diets are encouraged; they seem to help prevent estrogen-dependent cancers from developing. There are also numerous other reasons, as well as external factors, for estrogen surplus in the body. Oral contraceptives may protect against ovarian cancer.

# What to Eat

Following a low-estrogen diet that is also low in saturated fats can help to combat abnormal bleeding caused by excess estrogen. Foods high in saturated fat include processed meat, fatty meat, lard, butter, margarine, solid vegetable shortening, chocolate, and tropical oils (coconut oil is more than 90 percent saturated). Saturated fat should be consumed only in very low amounts.

## Quick Tips to Trim the Fat

You can cut down on fat by following these simple tips:

- Whenever you refrigerate animal fat (as in soups, stews, or curry dishes), skim the fat from the top before reheating and re-serving. A gravy skimmer will also help skim fats; the spout pours from the bottom, which helps the oils and fats to coagulate on top.

- Substitute something else for butter, perhaps yogurt (great on potatoes) or low-fat cottage cheese, or, at dinner, just dip your bread in olive oil with some garlic, Italian style. For sandwiches, any condiment without butter, margarine, or mayonnaise is fine (e.g., mustards, yogurt, etc.).

- Powdered nonfat milk is in vogue again; it is high in calcium and low in fat. Substitute it for any recipe calling for milk or cream.

- Dig out fruit recipes for dessert. Things like sorbet with a low-fat yogurt topping can be elegant. Remember that fruit must be planned for in a diabetes meal plan.

- Season low-fat foods well. That way, you won't miss the flavor that fat adds.

- Lower-fat proteins come from vegetable sources (whole grains and bean products), and higher-fat proteins come from animal sources.

If you're preparing meat:

- Broil, grill, or boil meat instead of frying, baking, or roasting it. (If you cook in water and drain the fat before eating, baking or roasting should be fine.)

- Trim off all visible fat from meat before and after cooking.

- Adding flour, bread crumbs, or other coatings to lean meat adds calories, and hence fat.

- Try substituting low-fat turkey meat for red meat.

Learning to read the fat content in milk is also a very good way to cut down on saturated fat:

- Whole milk is made up of 48 percent calories from fat.

- Two percent milk gets 37 percent of its calories from fat.

- One percent milk gets 26 percent of its calories from fat.

- Skim milk is completely fat-free.

- Cheese gets 50 percent of its calories from fat, unless it's skim milk cheese.

- Butter gets 95 percent of its calories from fat.

- Yogurt gets 15 percent of its calories from fat.

In addition, an iron-rich diet, discussed in Chapter 19, is important if you have been bleeding heavily. Heavy bleeding is the most common cause of anemia in women.

## Flower Power

Supplementing your diet with iron-rich herbs (see Chapter 19), as well as herbs that help to balance the reproductive system and hormones (see Chapter 2), can help with both heavy bleeding or blood loss and reducing the bleeding if it is hormone related.

## How to Move

Aerobic exercise is the best way to burn fat if you are trying to lose weight, which can dramatically reduce your risk of developing endometrial and ovarian cancer. The following are all aerobic activities:

- running
- jogging
- stair stepping or stair climbing
- trampoline
- jumping rope
- fitness walking
- race walking
- aerobic classes
- roller-blading

- ice-skating
- biking
- tennis
- swimming

### Variations on Jogging

- After warming up with a fifteen-minute walk, simply walk quickly with maximum exertion for two minutes, then slow down for one minute. Keep your heart rate up on the downhill portion of a walk or a hike by adding lunges or squats.

- Vary the way you walk for coordination and balance. Try lifting the knees as high as you can, as if marching. Alternate with a shuffle, letting the tips of your fingers touch the ground as you walk. Do a sideways "crab" walk. To strengthen the rarely used muscles of the ankles and feet, walk first on the outsides, then on the insides, of your feet. Or practice walking backward.

- Use a curb for a step workout. Or climb stairs two at a time.

### Water Workouts

- Start by walking in water that's relatively shallow (waist- or chest-deep). Your breathing and heartbeat will determine how hard you are working. Since you'll be moving fairly slowly, pay attention to your body.

- For all-over leg toning, take fifty steps forward, fifty steps sideways, in crablike fashion, then fifty steps backward, and fifty steps to the other side.

- To tone your arms, submerge yourself from the neck down, bringing the arms in and out as if clapping. The water will provide natural resistance here.

- Deep-water workouts are the most difficult, because every move you make is met with resistance. Wear a flotation vest and run without touching the bottom for optimum exertion and little or no impact. You may also want to try buoyant ankle cuffs and Styrofoam dumbbells or kickboards.

# 18

# When They Tell You It's Cancer

CONTRARY TO WHAT women are programmed to think, gynecological (GYN) cancer is not a death sentence—it is usually treatable. For example, cervical and endometrial cancers are almost always successfully treated, even if they are caught in a later stage. And thanks to the Pap test, advanced cervical cancer is often preventable.

Ovarian cancer does not carry very high survival rates (under 40 percent) because it is rarely caught in an early stage. It is treatable 80 percent of the time when it is caught early. Baseline ultrasounds, followed by regular ultrasound screenings, may become valuable diagnostic tools in finding early ovarian cancer (see Chapter 4). To date, ovarian cancer is still considered rare and only accounts for about 4 percent of all GYN cancers.

Cancer of the fallopian tubes has even more dismal statistics, carrying a survival rate of only 30 percent. Again, this is because it's rarely caught early. However, fewer than three thousand women each year develop it, and ultrasound screening may also assist in finding abnormalities around or on the fallopian tubes. Vaginal cancer and vulvar cancer are quite rare, too. Vaginal cancer accounts for 1 to 2 percent of female cancers. Vulvar cancer accounts for 3 to 5 percent of all female cancers, it is very curable, and it carries an overall 80 percent survival rate; vaginal cancer is considerably lower, at 50 percent, but this is because it is not often caught early enough. It's crucial to note, though, that these cancers are associated with a preexisting STD and are preventable with regular health maintenance and good hygiene.

Whether you're diagnosed with pelvic cancer or breast cancer, there are many aspects to the diagnostic and treatment route. In addition, cancers share similar patterns of behavior regardless of where they are growing. The purpose of this chapter is to provide you with a general understanding of GYN cancer, the treatments you'll experience, the side

271

effects of each treatment, and the posttreatment follow-up process. I'll also discuss coping with cancer and suggest some techniques that work. Finally, for those of you facing a life-threatening situation, this chapter includes a discussion of palliative care, which refers to treatment of symptoms rather than the disease itself.

Each cancer scenario is unique. Treatment and survival rates depend on all kinds of factors: age, overall health, genetics, history, weight, what stage the cancer is in (metastasis), what kind of cancer cell is involved (see further on), and so on. Think of this chapter, then, as providing everything you need to know to get acquainted with your cancer. For those of you simply concerned with the possibility of GYN cancer, this chapter will give you the fundamentals you'll need to know, should you face it down the road. This chapter does not discuss breast cancer; instead, consult another of my books, *The Breast Sourcebook*, for information.

# Cancer 101: An Introduction

*Cancer* is the general term for abnormal growth of cells—a cluster of cells that go out of control and multiply. When the abnormal cell reproduces, it has the ability to invade, or metastasize, to other parts of the body. The actual word *cancer* means "crab." The characteristics of the crab—slow moving, persistent, roundish, with multiple legs that can reach out—represent the "spirit" of a cancer cell but really don't give an accurate description of what a malignant cell looks or acts like.

Unlike bacteria or viruses, the cancer cell itself is not dangerous, but its impact on the rest of your organs is. As it spreads into various parts of your body, it interferes with regular cells, confuses other organs, and can wreak havoc on your body. It's basically a "terrorist" cell that hijacks organs and other cells. Cancer cells use the lymph system to get into the bloodstream and travel throughout the body. These cells love organs that have multiple blood vessels and nutrients, such as the bones, lungs, and brain.

Cancer cells are classified into two groups: carcinoma and sarcoma. A carcinoma refers to cancerous cells made of epithelial cells, which line various tissues. You'll find carcinomas in organs that secrete milk, mucus, digestive juices, and so on. Common sites for carcinomas are the breasts, lungs, skin, and colon; common gynecological sites are the breasts, ovaries, cervix, and endometrium. Carcinomas account for 80 to 90 percent of all human cancers, are generally slow growing, and tend to spread through the nerve endings.

The word *carcinoma* means the cells are malignant. A prefix attached to the word *carcinoma* will tell you where the carcinoma is growing and the kinds of cells that are involved. An adenocarcinoma, for example, is a carcinoma made of glandular cells. When you see the word *oma* by itself, it means "benign." An adenoma refers to a clump of benign glandular cells, a fibroma refers to a clump of benign fibrous cells, and so on.

Sarcomas are cancerous cells made up of supporting connective tissue, such as the uterus. Sarcomas are rare and account for only 2 percent of all human cancers, but they tend to be more aggressive than carcinomas. Again, the prefixes before the word tell you where the sarcoma is located, what it's made of, what shape it is, and so forth.

The difference between a carcinoma and a sarcoma is similar to the difference between a sweater and a boot—both are different but related. They have different physical properties and are made of different material. (You can also have a carcinosarcoma—a carcinoma and sarcoma all in one.)

The words *in situ* and *invasive* are used in conjunction with a carcinoma or a sarcoma. In situ means "in one place." A carcinoma in situ is cancer that is confined to a specific area and has not spread. This is good news and means your cancer is not invasive. Invasive carcinoma is cancer that has spread to surrounding tissue, the lymph nodes, or other organs. This is not good news and means your cancer can spread.

GYN cancers can involve a lymphoma, which refers to malignant cells that originate in the lymph nodes, seen in Hodgkin's disease, for example. Here, malignant cells spread to other parts of your body, such as the breast or reproductive organs, through the lymph nodes. Lymphomas involve white blood cells that go astray and attack functioning organs. Although lymphomas may involve the reproductive organs and breasts, this kind of cancer rarely originates in these areas.

Cancer cells fall into two behavioral categories: differentiated and undifferentiated. These terms refer to the sophistication of the cancer cells. Differentiated cancer cells resemble the cells of their origin. A differentiated cancer cell that originates in the breast ducts looks more like a normal ductal cell than does an undifferentiated cancer cell in the breast ducts. For this reason, differentiated cancer is more treatable and carries higher survival rates. Often you won't find a purely differentiated cell. It may look just moderately abnormal. Because of this, there are subclassifications: mildly differentiated, moderately differentiated, well differentiated, or poorly differentiated. These classifications refer to the cell's grading. A high grade means that the cell is immature, poorly differentiated, and fast growing; a low-grade cancer cell is mature, well differentiated, slow growing, and less aggressive.

Undifferentiated cancer is made up of very primitive cells that look "wild" and untamed, bearing little or no resemblance to the cells of origin. They don't assist the body at all and are therefore able to spend all of their time reproducing. This is more dangerous because the cells may then spread faster. There are times, though, where undifferentiated cancer is not very aggressive, despite the fact that it's a more primitive cell. This is often the case in breast cancers.

There are also mixes of these different cells, which affect the aggressiveness of the disease. For example, you can have mostly differentiated cells mixed in with a few undifferentiated cells, or vice versa. Whatever you have the most of will affect the behavior of the cancer; differentiated cells will slow down whatever undifferentiated cells exist, while undifferentiated cells will speed up whatever differentiated cells exist.

Dozens of other cancer cell traits have a direct bearing on how well the cells respond to treatment. In breast cancer, many cells respond to either estrogen or progesterone and hence can be treated with hormone therapy in addition to other traditional treatments. Pathologists can pinpoint where your cancer cells have invaded surrounding tissue and then break down the metastasis into vascular invasion (cancer within a blood vessel) or lymphatic invasion (cancer within a lymph node). Pathologists can also determine how fast the cell is reproducing and whether any dead cancer cells are present, which means the cells are growing so fast they have cut off their own blood supply and are leaving a dead cell trail (called necrosis). All of these factors are important and will affect your treatment and prognosis. Where the cancer is growing determines the kind of cancer cell you have.

## *What Causes Cancer?*

When it comes to determining the causes of cancer, it's now known that genetics plays a huge role. Breast cancer and ovarian cancer run in families. Researchers have isolated various oncogenes within our genetic makeup. The word *onco* means "tumor"; the field of oncology, therefore, means "tumorology." One theory is that every individual has certain oncogenes that remain dormant in the body until an external agent turns them on like a switch. Once turned on, the oncogene is responsible for transforming normal cells into abnormal cells. The oncogene responsible for colon cancer was recently isolated. People carrying these oncogenes would find that once activated, their colon cells would begin to transform into abnormal cells. In other cases, women carrying ovarian oncogenes (not yet isolated) would find that their ovary cells would transform when their oncogenes were activated. However, it's believed that external or environmental factors are responsible for turning on these oncogenes. These outside forces include tobacco, x-rays, excess estrogen, sunlight, radioactive fallout, and industrial agents. While one cigarette may irritate your lung cells, twenty years of smoking may provide multiple "hits" to these cells that trip the lung cancer switch. One sunburn probably won't give you skin cancer, but ten years of sun worshiping could trip the skin cancer switch.

Therefore, understanding your family history is a crucial factor in cancer prevention. This is particularly apparent when it comes to ovarian cancer: women who do not have a family history of ovarian cancer are not considered at high risk for the disease. Uterine or endometrial cancer and ovarian cancer are all estrogen dependent in that an increased amount of estrogen is linked to them. Is the capacity to overproduce estrogen a genetic trait? Researchers currently believe this is a strong possibility. However, since women also ingest estrogen either for contraceptive purposes or for various hormone therapies, the estrogen question is more difficult to define.

All of these factors make the future of cancer detection very promising. Blood tests that detect various oncogenes are already being developed, and by the year 2010, screenings for a variety of oncogenes may be possible. This would mean that women can be treated or monitored long before their cancers become life threatening.

Certain blood tests already detect cancer "trails" (sheddings from cancer cells) in the bloodstream. The CA-125 blood test may detect ovarian cancer cell sheddings; the CA-15-3 blood test detects breast cancer cell sheddings. These tests are currently being used to detect recurrences of these cancers in women who have already been treated.

STDs (see Chapter 7) are also identified as a probable precursor to certain GYN cancers, such as cervical, vulvar, and vaginal cancer. Strains of the human papillomavirus (HPV) were found in more than 90 percent of all cervical cancers. Vaginal and vulvar cancers will not develop without the presence of certain strains of HPV.

Another "cause" of cancer is aging. Women are living longer and therefore working their reproductive organs harder. All this takes its toll and exposes the organs to more factors that can cause malignant cells to sprout. Are more women developing cancer today than fifty years ago? Yes, but women are living twice as long as they did fifty years ago. Breast cancer and ovarian cancer are classic "over fifty" cancers.

A toxic environment can also be cited as a major cause of cancer. Increased levels of radiation in the air, countless pollutants, chemicals in our food, and decreased ozone layer protection all play a role in tripping the oncogene switch.

Stress, now known to trigger autoimmune diseases, is a major contributor to cancer as well. In the same way that stress can "give" you an ulcer, it may also turn on our oncogenes.

Finally, a high-fat diet in women can cause increased levels of estrogen in the body that are stored in fat cells. This can make you a more desirable host for estrogen-dependent cancer cells, which is why high-fiber and low-fat diets are encouraged.

We now know that smoking is a cofactor for vulvar and cervical cancer. We also know that GYN cancers are on the rise due to the increase in STDs such as HPV as well as the increase of HIV-positive women. Invasive cervical cancer is an AIDS-defining diagnosis in women. Women with GYN cancers face these and other issues, which other cancer survivors do not, even breast cancer survivors. Since this is information that is still extremely difficult to find, and often ignored, the remainder of this chapter will focus on GYN cancers. If you know of someone going through GYN cancer, please try to get the following pages to her or her caregiver.

# Cancer Below the Belt

Gynecological oncology is a subspecialty comprising surgery, chemotherapy, and radiation therapy for women with cancer of the vulva, vagina, cervix, endometrium, ovaries, and the fallopian tubes. This subspecialty is open only to certified obstetricians and gynecologists, who must train for an additional two to four years.

The good news is that cancer of the vulva, vagina, and cervix are all detected and treated much earlier than they were thirty years ago. And because of the advancements made in surgical technique, survivors are far less disfigured than they were even ten years ago. Nevertheless, because many GYN cancer treatments involve radical hysterectomy, or removing parts of the vagina, GYN cancer can create a physically painful sex life and extremely negative feelings about body image, self-esteem, and sexual identity. Some women may also feel devalued as sexual partners or fear losing their sexual partners.

Experts in this field observe that women who are comfortable discussing sexual issues surrounding treatment tend to find their way back to sexual health faster than do women who are afraid to ask questions. In fact, healing from GYN cancer surgery involves healing your sexual health, not just your physical health. For instance, if you have pain in a specific area during sexual intercourse or have problems with arousal (particularly if your clitoris has been removed), it's crucial to voice these problems aloud to your oncologist prior to having intercourse. If you have trouble speaking about these issues, write down your concerns and discreetly pass your notes on to one of your practitioners; this is another way of voicing your problem. Almost 90 percent of the sexual concerns of GYN cancer patients can be solved through frank discussions about basic anatomy.

The psychological effects of a GYN cancer often depend on your age, lifestyle, and ability to cope. However, a recent U.S. study revealed some astonishing facts. The study compared three groups of women: one group comprised gynecological cancer patients, the second comprised breast cancer patients, and the third comprised healthy women. Eighty-two percent of GYN cancer patients reported a poor body image, 38 percent of the healthy women reported a poor body image, while just 31 percent of the breast cancer patients reported poor body image.

Other common issues GYN cancers bring up are fears of dying or recurrence (common to all cancer patients), infertility (common to many who undergo chemotherapy), and treatment-related body changes. These are all addressed later in this chapter.

## The Isolation Factor

Women who have a GYN cancer are dealing with cancers of essential female organs that have a powerful emotional and sexual significance. Like breast cancer patients, women treated for GYN cancer have surgery or chemotherapy, which triggers menopause as well as infertility. But unlike women with breast cancer, GYN cancer patients have great difficulty finding comrades or support within their communities.

Consequently, feelings of stigma and isolation result. Worse, women with GYN cancer have their cancer at the exact site where sex takes place. This is an enormous issue. It's common to feel as though your sex life is the enemy because sex is a constant reminder of your cancer. As one psycho-oncologist aptly put it: "That's a real double whammy for the woman with GYN cancer."

Unlike breast cancer, GYN cancer is "hidden" from the public eye, creating a very private pain. This makes the issue of disclosure far more painful as well. For instance, it's very normal for GYN cancer patients to experience shame and embarrassment, as well as baser feelings of being damaged, dirty, soiled, contaminated, defective, and broken. Cervical cancer, because it is actually caused by an STD, brings these feelings to the surface more dramatically, as cervical cancer patients often feel that they are being punished for promiscuity.

## Cervical Precancer

Many women who would have developed invasive cervical cancer will now be treated at the precancerous stage. The classification of Pap smears is discussed in Chapter 3. It's now thought that HPV is responsible for cervical, vaginal, and vulvar cancer. Ninety-five percent of all squamous cell cervical carcinomas (which represent 90 percent of all cervical cancers) contain the DNA of HPV. There are more than fifty types of HPV: among them, types 6 and 11, responsible for raised cauliflower-type genital warts (known as condyloma), are commonly seen as precursors to cervical, vaginal, and vulvar cancers, while types 16, 18, 31, and 33 are responsible for dysplasia, flat lesions associated with cervical, vaginal, and vulvar cancers. This is why the news of an HPV vaccine is so welcome (see Chapter 3). A Pap test will detect genital warts or dysplasia before your cervical cells become cancerous. Most women who might have gone on to develop in situ or invasive cervical cancer thirty years ago will today be treated for cervical precancer, identified by their Pap smear. A technique known as speculoscopy, when it is used in conjunction with a Pap smear, is also helpful in detecting early signs of cervical cancer. Here, a speculum with special lighting and magnification helps your doctor view the cervix more thoroughly.

A Pap test can also detect carcinoma in situ, a cancerous tumor limited to the cervix. This is very easily treated, with survival rates at almost 100 percent. Finally, a Pap test can detect invasive cervical cancer, in which the cancer has spread beyond the cervix. Although the Pap test can't tell you how extensive the cancer is in this case, invasive cervical cancer can mean several things. It can mean that the cancer has spread only as far as the uterus, which can be successfully treated with a hysterectomy, or it can mean your entire pelvic and abdominal cavity is involved. Usually, invasive cervical cancer means that the cancer is confined to the uterus and is therefore removable. Survival rates are pretty high for invasive cervical cancer, ranging from 67 to 88 percent. In fact, out of the sheer millions of women who will develop cervical precancer, fewer than seven thousand will die from it. This is a very low statistic considering the high diagnosis rate. In short, most of you will be fine and go on to live a normal life span.

## *The Stages of Invasive Cervical Cancer*

If you are diagnosed with invasive cervical cancer, your cancer will then be broken down into stages, with perhaps some crossover into the class system discussed in Chapter 3. Stage 0 is the same as a class 4 Pap smear, carcinoma in situ, which carries a five-year survival rate of 100 percent. Thanks to the Pap smear, invasive cervical cancer is found so early that its staging system is extremely advanced. Stage 1a means that the cancer is confined to the cervix with just minimal invasion. The five-year survival rate is close to 100 percent. In stage 1a2 there is slightly more invasion on the cervix, and the survival rates dip to 80 to 90 percent. Stage 1b is a slightly more advanced version of stage 1a2, also with survival rates of 80 to 90 percent.

In stage 2 the cancer extends beyond the cervix or into the vagina, but not yet into the pelvic wall. Survival rates are still 80 to 90 percent. Stage 2b indicates that the cancer extends more into the parametrium, and survival rates dip to 65 percent. Stage 3 means the cancer involves other pelvic organs and the vagina; survival rates drop to 40 percent. Stage 4a indicates that the bladder or rectum is involved, and stage 4b denotes distant invasion into other organs. Survival rates for 4a are about 10 percent, while fewer than 10 percent of women with stage 4b survive. Because cervical cancer is caused by the STD human papillomavirus, cervical cancer carries a social stigma, and self-punishment often accompanies this kind of diagnosis. However, HPV is so pervasive as an STD, with so many strains, that even having just one sexual partner can lead to HPV.

As is the case with HIV, monogamous women are often overlooked as being at high risk for cervical cancer. If you're in a long-term, stable monogamous relationship, your doctor may say, "You don't need an annual Pap test; come back in three years." During that time, your monogamous partner can bring home HPV from a hidden sexual encounter and literally give you cervical cancer because you're not being screened for it. For this reason, cervical cancer is often called the relationship destroyer.

Another common scenario is to be told that you have cervical cancer (wham!), then be told you are HIV positive (bam!), and after that be told that your invasive cervical cancer means your HIV has progressed to AIDS (wham-bam!). This is a most unfortunate reality in our times. As discussed in Chapters 3 and 11, HPV + HIV = invasive cervical cancer. If you are exposed to either HIV or HPV and then exposed to a second STD, invasive cervical cancer is almost certain to follow unless you're religiously having Pap smears. In 1993 invasive cervical cancer was the only female disease to be put on the Centers for Disease Control's list of AIDS-defining illnesses. If, for some reason, your doctor does not screen you for HIV and AIDS after a cervical cancer diagnosis, please request it so that you can get yourself on the AIDS drugs, which can prolong your life indefinitely.

## The Stages of Endometrial Cancer

There's a big difference between endometrial cancer and uterine cancer. Endometrial cancer is always a carcinoma; uterine cancer means uterine sarcoma, which is discussed separately further on. Seventy-five percent of endometrial cancer is discovered in stage 1, but endometrial cancer can also be diagnosed at stage 0, when the cancer is found only inside the uterus and is only in the surface layer of the endometrium. Stage 1a means that the cancer is limited to the uterine lining, but the depth of invasion, cell type, and grade of cells are also important. Treatment will involve a hysterectomy, an oophorectomy, and/or a salpingectomy to remove the possibility of cancer developing beyond the uterus. Survival rates are generally 90 to 95 percent. In stage 1b the cancer has invaded the uterine wall; survival rates range from 70 to 80 percent. Stage 2 may involve the lymph nodes in the groin area; they'll be examined individually during a hysterectomy procedure to determine the extent of metastasis. Stage 2a means that the glands lining the cervix are involved; stage 2b indicates that the cervix itself is involved. Both stages 2a and 2b have survival rates of 60 percent. In stage 3 the cancer has spread into the lymph nodes and beyond the uterus into the greater pelvic area. Stage 3a involves the uterine surface, tubes, and ovaries; stage 3b involves the vagina; and stage 3c involves the pelvic lymph nodes. Survival rates drop in all three cases to 30 percent. Stage 4 is rarely seen and means that the cancer is involving other organs: bowels, the abdominal cavity, the bladder, whatever. Stage 4a means the bladder and rectum are affected, while stage 4b indicates distant invasion. Survival rates in either case hover around 5 percent. Treatment varies and depends on what organs are involved. Few women ever experience stage 4 endometrial cancer.

## The Stages of Uterine Cancer

Uterine sarcomas are fairly rare, accounting for only 1 to 5 percent of all uterine cancers. But these cancers are very aggressive. In stage 1a the sarcoma is limited to the endometrium, with a survival rate of 75 percent. Stages 1b and 1c indicate that the sarcoma has invaded the uterine wall, with survival rates of 50 percent. Stage 2a means the lymph glands or the endocervical canal is involved, while stage 2b involves the cervix. Survival rates for both these stages remain at 50 percent. In stage 3a the sarcoma has gone beyond the uterus to the tubes and ovaries. Survival rates here dip to between 0 and 20 percent. Stages 3b and 3c are worse; stage 3b means that the vagina is involved, while stage 3c indicates that the pelvis and lymph nodes are involved. Survival rates range between 0 and 10 percent. Stage 4a means that the bladder and rectum are affected, while stage 4b shows that there is distant invasion. Survival rates here only range from 0 to 5 percent.

## *The Stages of Ovarian Cancer*

Ovarian cancer is usually discovered beyond stage 1. About one in seventy women will develop ovarian cancer, and most will be over age forty. Most ovarian cancer originates in the epithelial cells lining the ovaries. About 10 percent of ovarian cancer originates in the eggs and is known as ovarian germ cell cancer. In fact, two-thirds of all ovarian cancers are detected after the cancer has already spread. In stage 1 the cancerous tumor is limited to the ovaries. This is treatable and has a survival rate of 60 to 100 percent. Nobody knows if age plays a role in the survival rates.

Stage 2 means the cancer involves one or both ovaries and has spread into other areas of your pelvis. Evidence suggests the survival rate for stage 2 ovarian cancer is now about as high as it is for stage 1. Current statistics put it at about 60 percent. Prior to this study, stage 2 ovarian cancer survival rates were believed to be significantly lower.

In stage 3 the cancer involves one or both ovaries but has spread beyond the pelvis into the bowel and abdominal cavity. Survival rates drop to only about 20 percent.

Stage 4 ovarian cancer means that the cancer has spread to the lungs or other major organs far beyond the bowels and abdominal cavity. The statistics are dismal: 10 percent survival rate. Ovarian cancer is not more dangerous or insidious than other kinds of cancers; it is simply more difficult to find and therefore has more opportunity to spread.

Ovarian germ cell cancer paints a brighter picture. Stage 1 carries statistics as high as 95 percent, and stage 2 is as high as 80 percent, while both stage 3 and stage 4 have survival rates of about 75 percent. As discussed in Chapter 4, ovarian cancer is far more lethal because it is so difficult to detect early on. By the time women see their doctors about symptoms, the cancer is often quite advanced. In fact, 70 percent of women first see their doctors after the tumor has spread into their upper abdominal area. So use this rule: if you are reading this section out of interest, are forty years old or older, and experience any of the symptoms listed in Chapter 4—especially those of a gastrointestinal nature—insist on being investigated for ovarian tumors. If your doctor doesn't feel you're at risk, go elsewhere to rule out this type of cancer.

## The Stages of Vulvar Cancer

Vulvar cancer accounts for about 3 to 5 percent of all GYN cancers. Eighty percent of all vulvar cancers develop as a result of exposure to HPV. Other vulvar cancers develop after exposure to the following STDs: syphilis, lymphogranuloma venereum, and herpes (all discussed in Chapter 10). Smokers are also more vulnerable.

Eighty-six percent of all vulvar cancer is squamous cell carcinoma. Melanoma, a very aggressive type of skin cancer, represents about 6 percent of all vulvar cancers. Four percent of vulvar cancers originate in Bartholin's glands, 2 percent are sarcomas, and 0.5 percent are Paget's disease (the same Paget's disease as seen in breast cancer). However, no matter what kind of vulvar cancer you have, it's usually confined to the skin anywhere from one to ten years before it spreads. Symptoms include lumps, open sores, itching, discoloration, roughness, pain, burning, bleeding, and discharge. Statistics reveal that whenever vulvar cancer is diagnosed, two-thirds of the women have had symptoms for more than six months, while the remaining third have had symptoms for more than a year. In the past, vulvar cancer was normally seen only in postmenopausal women. Today, 40 percent of all vulvar cancers are seen in women under forty, particularly in women with multiple partners.

Stage 0 is vulvar carcinoma in situ, and survival rates are 100 percent. In stage 1 the cancer is confined to the vulva, with survival rates at 90 percent. Stage 2 is similar to stage 1, but the cancer is slightly more advanced, with survival rates of 80 to 90 percent. Stage 3 indicates that the vagina, anus, urethra, or lymph nodes are involved, with survival rates at 50 percent. Stage 4a means the upper urethra, bladder, rectum, or pelvic bone is involved, and survival rates plummet to about 15 percent. In stage 4b there is a distant spread, and depending on where the cancer has spread to, survival rates range from 5 to 25 percent. If melanoma is the cause, survival rates range from 40 to 80 percent.

## The Stages of Vaginal Cancer

Vaginal cancer is a cousin to cervical cancer but accounts for less than 2 percent of all GYN cancers. Like cervical cancer, the most common vaginal cancer develops on the surface of the cells that line the vagina. Called vaginal intraepithelial neoplasia (VAIN), it is caused by HPV; that is, the cells begin to grow abnormally after exposure to HPV. A Pap smear that collects cells lining the vagina will find early abnormal cell changes in the vagina, just as it finds them on the cervix. The symptoms of vaginal cancer are vaginal bleeding and a foul-smelling discharge often attributed to an infection. Women who develop advanced vaginal cancer are clearly ignoring their symptoms.

Another kind of vaginal cancer is seen in DES daughters, where the cancer originates in glands within the vaginal wall. It is possible to develop melanoma in the vagina, but this accounts for a tiny portion of all vaginal cancers.

Stage 0 means vaginal carcinoma in situ and has a survival rate of 100 percent. In stage 1 the cancer is limited to the vaginal wall, with survival rates of 70 to 80 percent. Stage 2 involves the adjacent vaginal tissue, excluding the pelvis; survival rates are about 50 percent. Stage 3 means that the cancer has penetrated the pelvic wall, and survival rates dip to 30 percent. Stage 4a indicates that the cancer involves the bladder or rectum; stage 4b shows that there is distant metastasis. Survival rates in both cases plunge to about 10 percent. Even if you have had a hysterectomy, you still have a chance of developing vaginal cancer.

## Who Will Manage Your GYN Cancer Treatment?

Doctors work in teams to manage cancer therapy. This means that your primary care physician, gynecological oncologist (surgeon for GYN cancers), radiation oncologist (in charge of radiation therapy), and medical oncologist (in charge of chemotherapy) will all be involved together with your treatment.

If your regular gynecologist also does gynecological oncology, you may not need to see anyone else. He or she will be qualified to do colposcopies and biopsy procedures and perform the necessary scans, laser surgery, cryosurgery, or major surgery. For chemotherapy and/or radiation, you'll be referred to a medical oncologist, a radiation oncologist, or both. If your cancer was diagnosed by either a primary care physician or a gynecologist who does not do gynecological oncology (please ask!), you'll need to be referred to a gynecological oncologist. Surgery, chemotherapy, and radiation are usually necessary only for ovarian cancer and cancer of the fallopian tubes. Invasive cervical cancer and stage 3 endometrial cancer generally involve surgery and radiation. With the exception of ovarian cancer, chemotherapy for GYN cancers is necessary only when other organs have been invaded. Your gynecological oncologist will serve as the project manager in charge of your treatment.

The first thing you'll need to do after your cancer has been diagnosed is to get some answers directly from your gynecological oncologist. Schedule a separate appointment with him or her, and use the entire appointment time for a question-and-answer period. Write down all of your questions ahead of time, and tape-record the answers so that you can review them later by yourself or with a supportive spouse, partner, or friend. When we're anxious, we often don't hear correctly, and we misconstrue facts and block out what we don't want to hear. Questions will vary depending on the person and the conditions, but here are some general areas to get you started:

1. Have the doctor draw you a diagram of the cancerous organ or part and shade in where the cancer is situated or has spread. Visualizing the cancer makes it easier to understand.

2. Ask whether the cancer is differentiated or undifferentiated. Reproductive organs can be invaded by either kind of cancer cell.

3. Find out how long the cancer has been growing, where it can spread (or continue to spread), and what stage it's in now.

4. Find out what treatment is being recommended and why, and what kind of diagnostic procedures (tests, scans, and so forth) you'll need to have.

5. Find out how the treatment will help, the risks and side effects associated with it (including how all this affects your menstrual cycle), and the survival rates associated with successful treatment.

6. Find out what will happen to you if you choose not to undergo treatment. Say, for example, that you have an advanced stage of a particular cancer. If you are told that you will most likely not survive and that chemotherapy treatment is not considered to be significantly useful, you may choose to fight the cancer with less toxic and unpleasant therapies. That way, you can more fully enjoy the time you do have left. Many women do not regret this choice.

7. Find out where and when the treatments will take place and how long they'll last. This will help you plan your life.

8. What if you miss one treatment? Can you make it up?

9. What other health problems should you be on the lookout for during treatment?

10. How can you contact your managing doctor between visits?

11. Can you take other medications during treatments? How will the treatments affect other medications you're taking?

12. What about alcohol? Considering what you're going through, you might want a glass of wine or a shot of hard liquor occasionally. Is this OK?

13. If you're not given a very good prognosis, find out if you can participate in new studies or clinical trials using new drugs or therapies.

14. Find out where you can go for more information, and ask to be referred to a support group or a therapist or social worker who specializes in working with patients who have your particular kind of cancer.

15. Find out about your hormonal function and whether you can have hormone replacement therapy (HRT) after your cancer treatment.

16. Find out exactly what kind of hysterectomy may be indicated.

17. Find out exactly how much of your reproductive and genital organs will be affected. For example, will you still be able to have an orgasm? (Some women lose their ability to reach orgasm without a cervix.)

18. Find out if your vagina is going to be left the same length. (Vaginas can shrink from radiation or may be shortened from a radical hysterectomy.)

# Treatment for GYN Cancer

Once you're diagnosed, you will need to undergo various scans, blood tests, and possibly more biopsies throughout the treatment process. Depending on where your cancer is located, scans will vary, and you may need to undergo pelvic procedures such as endometrial biopsies, examinations via hysteroscope and colposcope, and possibly D & Cs. All of these diagnostic tests and procedures may seem exhausting and time consuming but are necessary to determine the extent of your cancer, determine appropriate treatment, gauge how well you're responding to treatment, and determine whether the cancer has gone into remission. Treatment usually starts with surgery and, depending on the stage and the kind of cancer you have, is followed by chemotherapy, hormone therapy, drugs to boost your immune system, and finally radiation therapy.

## *Cervical Carcinoma in Situ*

If you haven't yet read Chapter 3, go back and read the section on positive Pap smears, which covers treatment for precancerous Pap test results. Cervical carcinoma in situ is treated with a minor surgical procedure known as conization, or cone biopsy. This can now be done using a laser or a wire loop (such as LEEP, also discussed in Chapter 3). If your gynecological oncologist even suspects carcinoma in situ, he or she will remove a cone-shaped chunk of tissue from your cervix. Your doctor will then remove all the abnormal tissue as well as some of the healthy surrounding tissue. This procedure can completely cure cervical carcinoma in situ. You'll then need to be closely monitored and go for follow-up colposcopies and Pap tests religiously.

A procedure known as endocervical curettage may also need to be done. This is exactly the same procedure as a D & C (see Chapter 17), except instead of cleaning out the uterine lining, the cervical canal leading to the uterus is scraped. This helps the gynecologist see the condition of your cervical cells. You may also need a D & C so that your gynecologist can check the condition of the uterine lining and make sure that the cervical cancer was indeed in situ. If a hysterectomy is recommended for cervical carcinoma in situ, you may want to get a second opinion. What you decide depends on your age, your childbearing status, whether the cancer is a recurrence, or whether it is likely to recur in the future.

## *Invasive Cervical Cancer and Endometrial Cancer*

You will need a radical hysterectomy for invasive cervical cancer and a radical hysterectomy and oophorectomy (with possible salpingectomy) for endometrial cancer. In either situation, the cervix, uterus, and tissue around the cervix and surrounding lymph nodes are all removed, as well as the ovaries and fallopian tubes for endometrial cancer. To date, removing cancer-free ovaries for invasive cervical cancer is considered premature, but many surgeons will remove them as a preventive measure. This is one circumstance where a prophylactic oophorectomy (see Chapter 4) may be a good idea.

You may be required to undergo either pre- or postoperative radiation treatment, discussed further on. For extremely advanced endometrial or cervical cancer, you may also need chemotherapy. Chapter 20 discusses hysterectomy surgery in detail. You may need to have an abdominal procedure done in the case of cancer. Review the postoperative complications of hysterectomy in Chapter 20; you will not suffer all of these, but you will go into surgical menopause after an oophorectomy. Chapter 19 discusses both natural and surgical menopause in detail. If you were diagnosed with stage 0 endometrial cancer, you may escape with just a D & C followed by hormone therapy, and you may have to go off any estrogen-containing drugs such as HRT if you're postmenopausal.

## Ovarian Cancer

A radical hysterectomy, bilateral oophorectomy (removing both ovaries), and bilateral salpingectomy (removing both fallopian tubes) should be done if you have ovarian cancer in any stage. Anything beyond stage 1 will need to be treated with chemotherapy and radiation therapy. When your treatment is completed, you may need to undergo follow-up laparoscopies and/or laparotomies. In certain select cases of stage 1 ovarian cancer, removing one ovary and one tube may be done if you wish to preserve your fertility.

In theory, advanced ovarian cancer usually remains in the abdominal cavity and should be a very curable kind of cancer. But this isn't the case because the tumor itself advances to the point where it actually becomes resistant to drug therapy.

Researchers have found that advanced ovarian cancer patients who receive tamoxifen (Taxol), which is derived from the bark of the Pacific yew tree, with cisplatin, the platinum-based cancer-killing agent, live twice as long as their counterparts who are receiving conventional cisplatin-based therapy. The new cancer drug topotecan hydrochloride (Hycamtin) is the latest drug used to treat ovarian cancer. Clinical trials showed this drug was much better tolerated than older chemo drugs.

One of two types of radiation therapy is usually offered to ovarian cancer patients after surgery. One method, called intraperitoneal radiotherapy, involves using a liquid form of radioactive phosphorus. Studies are now under way to see if intraperitoneal radiotherapy is more effective than the current method of injecting the anticancer drugs into the bloodstream. Another, more traditional form of radiation involves external radiation, where a beam is directed at the abdomen and pelvis. There is no convincing evidence that radiotherapy can improve survival in patients who are still not cancer-free after platinum chemotherapy. Right now, the five-year survival rate for all stages of ovarian cancer combined is 42 percent; it's low because only 23 percent of ovarian cancer cases are detected at a localized stage, as most women are diagnosed at stages 3 and 4.

Second-look surgery is common as well; this is usually done through laparoscopy, which is a less invasive method for second-look evaluations. The purpose of second-look surgery is to evaluate the effect of the various treatments you may be undergoing. Most women with ovarian cancer will have a recurrence at some time after initial surgery and chemotherapy, and it is still unclear whether another course of chemotherapy is beneficial over repeat surgery.

## Vulvar Cancer

In the past, a disfiguring surgical procedure known as a vulvectomy (removal of the vulva) was a traditional treatment for this kind of cancer. Today, treatment can include laser surgery, cryosurgery, radiation, or topical chemotherapy drugs. Surgery is usually confined to a local excision of a particular cluster of tumors. Advanced invasive cancer may still require a vulvectomy.

The treatment of vulvar cancer has evolved dramatically since the late 1940s. In the past, the whole vulva—the hair-bearing area between the thighs and buttocks, including the clitoris and the labia—and the lymph nodes were removed. This was the standard surgery for about twenty years. Today, it's standard practice to do minimal surgery, have lymph nodes removed, as well as take skin grafts from the thighs or buttocks to help rebuild the vulva and create an artificial vulva or vagina.

Four kinds of vulvectomy procedures are performed today. Skinning vulvectomy takes out only the skin of the vulva that contains the cancer. Simple vulvectomy takes out the entire vulva but no lymph nodes. Partial vulvectomy takes out less than the entire vulva, while a radical vulvectomy takes out the entire vulva as well as the surrounding lymph nodes. If the cancer has spread outside the vulva, surgery may involve the lower colon, rectum, or bladder (depending on where the cancer has spread), along with the cervix, uterus, and vagina.

Radiation therapy has been used in the past to treat vulvar cancer, but the vulva doesn't respond well to radiation. However, an ointment containing a chemotherapy drug may be used in certain situations.

Today, great effort is made to maintain as much of the clitoris and other genitalia as possible. In many cases, the majority of men wouldn't know the difference. While skin grafting will cause a little contour change, the appearance is far more normal than in the past.

When the clitoris is removed, experts strongly urge sexual counseling to help you achieve the maximum sexual pleasure. For example, some women, with mental imagery and concentration, have been able to achieve sexual pleasure by having their inner thighs stroked.

## *Vaginal Cancer*

For early stages of vaginal cancer, a vaginectomy, laser therapy, intravaginal chemotherapy, and radiation are used. For later stages, treatment can include a vaginectomy, a hysterectomy, and removal of lymph nodes, while late-stage vaginal cancer involves chemotherapy with any combination of these procedures. In stage 0, laser surgery may be all that's necessary. Here, cancer cells are killed with a narrow beam of light. If any vaginal tissue is removed or damaged, skin grafts may be necessary.

If the cancer has spread outside the vagina and the other reproductive organs, your doctor may take out the lower colon, rectum, or bladder (depending on where the cancer has spread), along with the cervix, uterus, and vagina (called exenteration). You may also need skin grafts and plastic surgery to make an artificial vagina after these operations.

If you have stage 4b cancer of the vagina, the most advanced stage, you may be offered radiation treatment to relieve symptoms such as pain, nausea, vomiting, or abnormal bowel function.

### Cancer of the Fallopian Tubes

This cancer is so rare that most gynecologists will never see even one case in their lifetimes. It is as hard to detect as ovarian cancer because of the murky symptoms. There are also no real statistical data on who's at risk, the stages of this kind of cancer, or survival rates for each stage. It's suspected that inflammation of the fallopian tubes may be one precursor. The treatment scenario is identical to that of ovarian cancer.

# Chemotherapy

Whether you're having chemotherapy for ovarian cancer, leukemia, or breast cancer, your experience will be similar to that of other chemotherapy patients. Of all treatments, chemotherapy is by far the most miserable. For many women, it makes the notion of having cancer a reality.

Chemotherapy involves treating a medical condition with drugs. Technically, taking aspirin for a migraine headache, an antifungal suppository for a yeast infection, and an antibiotic for a bacterial infection are all forms of chemotherapy. When it comes to cancer, you are taking anticancer drugs. These drugs are designed to kill cancer cells. They interfere with the process of cell division or reproduction so that the cells can't divide and therefore will die. But the drugs are not very selective and kill healthy cells that are also dividing, including hair cells and bone marrow cells. There is a fine line between a therapeutic dosage and a toxic dosage, and for this reason only a highly experienced medical oncologist is qualified to manage your chemotherapy. (In some cases, certain gynecological oncologists or surgeons are trained in administering chemotherapy.)

Chemotherapy drugs can be administered orally or intravenously. You might be given only one kind of drug or a combination of drugs. Each anticancer drug has the ability to destroy one kind of cancer cell; however, cancer is made up of more than one kind of cell. Because it destroys more cancer cells, combination drug therapy is often used. In the past, chemotherapy was reserved for cases where surgery failed to treat the cancer. Today, even when there is no sign of cancer after surgery, chemotherapy is used as a preventive or prophylactic therapy; this is known as adjuvant chemotherapy and is common for early-stage breast cancer that responds well to surgery.

No matter how balanced your chemotherapy dosage is, your healthy cells will be affected. The side effects to chemo are frightening and unpleasant, but the reactions do vary from person to person. Some of the more common reactions include tiredness, weakness, body aches, bloating and weight gain, night sweats, nausea, and changes in your sense of taste and smell. Chemo can also cause a chemically induced depression and dramatic mood swings. If you're menstruating, your periods may become irregular, or they may just stop altogether. This is because your ovaries begin to fail, which causes you to go into surgical menopause, discussed in Chapter 19. In some cases, periods may return to normal after the treatment is over.

Now for the most disturbing side effect: hair loss. It's important to be prepared for this, although there is a possibility that your hair may not fall out. For most women, the idea of hair loss is worse than the reality of it; it is a stripping away of femininity and an announcement to the world that you have cancer. Talking to a counselor and sharing your feelings with other chemo patients will help put this side effect into perspective. Your hair may thin gradually, or you may lose it all very suddenly. It may come out in clumps; this happens about three or four weeks after your first chemo treatment. Scarves, hats, or turbans and good wigs (do not have someone else pick one out for you) will come in handy.

Other side effects include a decrease in your blood platelets, which are responsible for blood clotting. You might find that you bleed more or suddenly. This will improve after your treatment.

Drugs you may come across in your treatment include cyclophosphamide (Cytoxan), used for ovarian cancer; amethopterin (Methotrexate); mitomycin-C (Mutamycin); and cisplatin (Platinol), a drug with platinum used to treat ovarian, cervical, and uterine cancers. Note: a drug known as 5-fluorouracil (5-FU, or Efudex) is also a chemotherapy drug used for a variety of cancers. There are also a number of antinausea drugs that can be added to your chemotherapy, as well as a drug (epoetin alpha) that helps you manufacture red blood cells to combat fatigue and anemia.

Chemotherapy often induces chemical menopause, which means that you will suffer from menopause symptoms, discussed in Chapter 19. Many younger women with GYN cancer are not informed about the possibility of chemical menopause and are rudely awakened to discover that they are in menopause after treatment. If you go into chemical menopause, you will need to manage the symptoms of estrogen loss. (See the discussion on HRT in Chapter 21.)

# Radiation Therapy

In some instances, radiation therapy may be recommended. Radiation therapy involves using high-dose x-rays or other high-energy rays to kill cancer cells. It is not chemotherapy. Therefore, your hair will not fall out unless your scalp is being radiated. Radiation treatment is very exact and directs radiation only at the areas where the cancer has spread. For ovarian and endometrial cancers, you'll be given internal radiation, where small amounts of radioactive materials are placed high inside the pelvic cavity (discussed further on).

The concept of radiation is very simple. Radiation destroys the DNA (the molecules that carry genetic information) in the cancer cell's nucleus (center) in the body cells it targets, arresting the reproduction of cancer cells. The actual process, however, is a little more complex. You'll be referred to a radiation oncologist, one who specializes in radiation therapy (not to be confused with a radiologist, a doctor who specializes in reading x-rays and diagnostic test results).

Radiation therapy is given over a long period of time because it involves, again, a fine balance: enough radiation to destroy cancer cells, but not enough to destroy your healthy tissue. Certain cancer cells are also more sensitive to radiation than are others, in the same way that some cockroaches are killed by poison while others aren't. The dose of radiation you receive is determined by a number of factors, including the radiosensitivity of the tumor, the normal tissue tolerance, and the volume of the tissue being irradiated. The "gray" has now replaced the "rad" (radiation absorbed dose) as the accepted unit of measurement for radiation dosage: 1 gray (Gy) = 100 rads.

## External Radiation Therapy

If you're having external radiation (meaning a beam aimed at the outside flesh), the radiation oncologist will "tattoo you" by injecting tiny dots of special dye in precise areas he or she has marked off in red ink (these will wash off). The therapist will use the tattoo as the bull's-eye of a squared-off section predetermined by the radiation oncologist.

The amount of external radiation treatment varies for each individual, depending on the severity of your cancer. For example, you might need only thirty seconds of radiation every weekday for a month, while another woman may require four minutes of radiation every day for six weeks. The average dose is about two to four minutes of radiation for five consecutive days each week for a period ranging from two to eight weeks. You'll receive a total dose of radiation, which is then referred to in terms of daily doses. This is called fractionation. The radiation clinic will have a number of radiation therapists on staff who will operate the actual machinery and administer your treatment. You'll go into a dark room and lie down on something that looks like an examination table with a device overhead. The overhead device activates the beam. Then you'll be covered in lead blankets, and only your targeted area will be exposed. The beam will then be turned on.

Although the procedure itself is painless, the aftereffects are not. If you're fair skinned, you'll have a worse reaction than do people with darker pigments. A small raw area might develop in places where your skin rubs together, such as the folds between your thighs and buttocks. Not all patients will experience skin changes because equipment is more refined now than it was even a few years ago. But if you do have a problem, you'll need to treat your skin as though it were sunburned: avoid sun, cover up exposed skin, don't use any deodorants or perfumes, and use lotions safe for sunburned skin. To help with the sunburn symptoms, either use over-the-counter sunburn creams or ask the radiation oncologist or radiation therapist on staff to recommend something. If a small area of skin actually peels and is raw, a 1 percent hydrocortisone cream helps. For itchiness, cornstarch in a bath or applied topically with a towel and covered with a bandage will help.

You may also experience a dry cough or sputum if the radiation is in your lung region. Cough suppressants shouldn't be used because you need to cough up the sputum. A humidifier will help to loosen the sputum so that you can get rid of it.

You'll also feel tired by the third or fourth week of treatment; the procedure is mentally as well as physically draining. You may experience some nausea or just loss of appetite. As soon as the treatments are finished, you'll start to feel much better and begin to regain your strength. You'll then need to undergo an imaging scan to see how well the treatment worked.

For certain stages of endometrial or uterine cancer, you may have external radiation directed at the abdominal-pelvic region. Skin reactions will be the same as just discussed; you'll also experience tenderness in the abdominal area, nausea, and usually diarrhea. In a standard, five-to-six-week regimen for the abdominal-pelvic area, the beam begins to affect the bowels after about two weeks. There are medications available to control your diarrhea, such as atropine and diphenoxylate (Lomotil) and Imodium A-D. If your rectal area is being radiated, your anal opening will be irritated. This can be soothed with hydrocortisone cream. Finally, if your bladder area is being targeted, you'll experience bladder problems such as urinary stress or urge incontinence and bladder infections (see Chapter 5). Phenazopyridine (Pyridium), oxybutynin (Ditropan), or terazosin (Hytrin) may help with urinary incontinence or frequency. Many women also experience urinary stricture from radiation, which causes their urinary tract to close up as a result of scar tissue. A good urologist can reopen your urinary tract.

For most women, radiation is the toughest and the longest part of GYN cancer treatment. Radiation can cause not only severe gastric symptoms and vaginal shrinkage but painful sex. See the sexuality section further on in this chapter for more information.

## *"Internal" Radiation Therapy: Intercavity Radiation*

For pelvic cancers, radiation therapy in the pelvic-abdominal area is usually administered by placing a radioactive solution into the pelvis and abdomen through a thin tube, coating the organs and total abdominal contents. Specially designed hollow applicators are placed in the uterus while you are under a general anesthetic. After you wake up, a small plastic tube containing the appropriate radioactive isotope (an unstable element) is inserted into the applicators. The isotope is left in place for forty-eight to seventy-two hours—you'll be required to stay in bed during this time. You'll also be required to stay in isolation because some radioactivity leaks out. Some hospitals developed a way to do this on an outpatient basis, giving a more potent dose of radioactivity with a shorter half-life. Sometimes the applicator is placed in the vagina. This can cause scarring of the vaginal walls, redness, and vaginal dryness. If the applicator is placed in the abdomen, you'll also experience skin irritations in the treated areas and sometimes bowel and bladder problems (which can be corrected via surgery). Loss of energy and appetite, nausea, and vomiting may also occur, but again, you'll begin to feel better after treatment.

## Preventing Surgical Menopause: The Oophoropexy

Any woman receiving radiation to the pelvic region will lose ovarian function either temporarily or permanently after about two weeks of treatment. This will cause surgical menopause. There is a surgical procedure called an oophoropexy that literally moves the ovaries out of the way of the radiation beam.

After your treatment is over, the ovaries are repositioned correctly. This procedure will preserve ovarian function. Request the procedure if it's possible. Unfortunately, if you're receiving chemotherapy either alone or in conjunction with radiation therapy, this procedure will do you no good.

## Everything You Need to Know About Sex but Are Afraid to Ask

Your sex life will change after GYN cancer treatment. In many cases, the time needed for emotional and physical adjustments heals these sexual wounds. About 5 percent of women seek out sexual therapy with a sex therapist or counselor after GYN cancer treatment.

If you've had a radical hysterectomy, numbness is one of the first things you'll notice about intercourse. Gradually, some feeling will start to come back, but it will never feel quite the same. Numbness around the hysterectomy scar as well as nerve damage after an incision are common and almost to be expected. Having lost your uterus will also mean that you will not experience as intense an orgasm as you once may have, resulting in a sort of muted experience. Incisions that are horizontal or transverse tend to damage more nerves than those occurring lengthwise or vertically. Most incisions will be a bikini-line cut.

## The "No Painful Sex" Rule

One of the first rules of resuming your sex life is to make sure that you're not having painful sex. Pain will turn off all sexual desire, and experiencing repeated painful sex will cause you to avoid sex. And the more you avoid sex, the less desirous of sex you become.

There are a number of ways to treat painful sex, but before you attempt treatment, have a good gynecological evaluation done so that you know what physical barriers actually exist. For example, if you have scarring from radiation, you may benefit from using a dilator. If your vagina mucosa is thin as a result of estrogen loss, estrogen replacement therapy or estrogen cream can do wonders to restore vaginal luster.

After your exam, one of the first things you should consider when resuming your sex life is a good lubricant, such as Astroglide, as well as a good vaginal moisturizer, such as Replens. The vaginal moisturizer also helps the vaginal lining stay smoother and more plumped up, even in the presence of scar tissue.

During your sex act, immediately communicate any discomfort to your partner so that you can change positions or activities. After GYN cancer treatment, many women find that being on top is the best position, because they feel more in control and, therefore, more relaxed. Being able to control when penetration occurs, how fast it occurs, and how deep it is can do wonders to get things back on track.

Apparently testosterone replacement for some women helps restore libido. Testosterone is produced by the ovaries in small amounts, which helps drive the female libido. Some women have had pharmacists prepare special testosterone cream, which they use topically like an estrogen cream. It's reported to be helpful.

## Coping with Vaginal Shrinkage

Radiotherapy as well as some surgeries can shrink the vagina, making sex very painful or even impossible. To avoid shrinkage, experts advise estrogen therapy immediately (unless you had an estrogen-dependent cancer, and even then, estrogen cream is usually fine). After that, it's also crucial to begin using a vaginal dilator continuously for several months. This will definitely help preserve the length of your vagina. Because the vagina has an incredible Lycra-like quality to it, dilators will help the vagina resume its full length again even if part of the upper vagina was removed, which is done in a radical hysterectomy.

Candles make excellent dilators. They are very convenient, easily washed, and can slip in your purse without looking odd. And since they come in all different sizes, you can comfortably pick the size that's just a little too tight for you—the one you'll want to use as a dilator. Of course, you can buy candles anywhere with complete comfort. Dildos may also be used as dilators; you may purchase these in sex toy shops, on the Internet, or via mail-order catalogs. The general rule is to keep your dilator in place for some short period of time every day or even every few days to help reopen the vagina. Dilators will also prevent scar tissue (which make your vagina much smaller) from forming. Some women may also experience more fibrosis (scarring) than others, which will mean that having comfortable sex could take more time and effort.

If you're a lesbian, resuming sexual activity may be even more frustrating if your physician is ignorant about your sexual practices. If these issues are not being addressed, it's important that you find your voice and ask whatever you need to. Dilators can easily become part of your sexual routine and can be inserted by your partner, too. (Not a bad idea for heterosexual couples, either!) In addition, you'll need lubricants, vaginal moisturizers, and estrogen cream.

## Sexual Healing

As a result of cancer treatment, couples often need to change their sexual repertoire. For example, oral sex or a different kind of stimulation of the clitoris (if it's still intact), instead of vaginal intercourse, may be more pleasurable and healing.

Sexual fantasy is also a key component after GYN cancer treatment. Frequent fantasizing will help your mind become sexual once again. As one doctor puts it, femininity is between the ears, not the legs. If you're not in the habit of fantasizing, try recalling movies or images that arouse you. (Mel Gibson, anyone?) Remembering an evening of great sex with your own partner, a past one, or an unrequited one is another way of getting your mind in the mood.

Comfortable sex also means feeling emotionally comfortable. Don't be afraid to change the rules a little bit either. Saying things like "I'm going to try being on top" or "let me just do you, and let me pass for now" are important ways of letting your partner know that you are willing and ready—and in control.

## Men!

Let's face it: traditional cultures may not furnish many women with very accepting partners. It happens. One physician described a cervical cancer patient whose husband left her because she was "not a woman anymore" in his eyes. In fact, her husband feared that his friends would think of him as a homosexual if he continued to have sex with her. He ended the relationship, and she was devastated. Some men are afraid to have sex because they say they are afraid of either hurting their partner or, believe it or not, catching cancer.

Similar issues arise between lovers after breast cancer as well. What's most important to remember is that cancer exposes the real relationship between you and your partner—it does not create it. A man who leaves you in sickness signifies that the relationship was not healthy to begin with. On the flip side, many male partners are wonderful, loving, and flexible, and just as many relationships are strengthened in the face of GYN cancer.

## Losing Your Fertility

This issue isn't immediate for most GYN cancer patients. It's common to only begin thinking about the loss of fertility a few years after your treatment. Experts note that the hardest thing for many women is the idea of losing their choice to reproduce. In other words, whether you have no children or four doesn't seem to make a difference in grieving. Consult my book *The Fertility Sourcebook* for the latest information on new reproductive technologies.

## Waking Up in Menopause

Surgical menopause is like going to bed with your period and waking up in menopause. Symptoms are often more severe, and biological depression is often triggered, all compounded by the stressful event of actually having cancer. See Part IV of this book for all the issues surrounding menopause and hormone replacement therapy.

## Self-Educating About Sexual Issues and Cancer

Several studies that have surveyed the quality of information women with GYN cancers receive about sexual issues have found that most women are not being given adequate or correct information. Studies find that doctors are generally uncomfortable discussing sex and were also not knowledgeable about the sexual problems that cancer can cause. If you can't find the information you need, CancerBACUP (cancerbacup.org.uk) is a good place to start. This cancer support and information service gives explicit answers to sexual questions (cancerbacup.org.uk/info/sex/sex-9.htm). It also offers "solutions to sexual problems caused by cancer and its treatment" (cancerbacup.org.uk/info/sex/sex-5.htm), covering pain during intercourse, loss of libido, changes in body image, and erectile dysfunction for men.

Women generally report that there is almost no information provided to them about sexual issues after GYN cancer. Many women suffer greatly from the absence of this information because they don't understand the causes of their sexual problems or realize that they are not alone. You have the right to know:

- which sexual problems may occur
- why sexual problems may occur
- that sexual activity will not cause a recurrence
- that sexual problems are normal
- that advice or help is available

Health care providers have listed the following reasons for neglecting to discuss sexual issues:

- They feel it is not their responsibility.
- They feel embarrassed or not knowledgeable enough.
- They don't feel there is anywhere private to discuss the issues.
- They don't have enough time.

## Hormone Therapy and Immunotherapy

After your surgery, if your lymph nodes are positive, your doctor may recommend this treatment. It is an estrogen-blocking drug that inhibits the growth of hormonally sensitive tumors.

The most common drug used is called tamoxifen, but there are many other estrogen-blocking drugs available. Tamoxifen interferes with protein synthesis and prevents an estrogen-responsive cancer cell from extracting estrogen from the body. The drug blocks the estrogen from the cancer cell. This will stop the estrogen cancer cell from growing. In immunotherapy you may be given interferons and interleukins to boost your immune system.

## Follow-Up Treatment

Follow-up treatment involves regular visits to all your cancer doctors: medical and radiation oncologists, breast surgeon, and gynecological oncologist. Each specialist will see you about every three months for the first two years, then every six months for the next four or five years, and annually thereafter. Each visit will entail various diagnostic tests: blood tests, chest x-rays, bone scans, CAT scans, mammograms (for breast cancer follow-up), full pelvic exams and Pap tests for pelvic cancers (especially cervical cancer), a second-look laparoscopy or laparotomy for endometrial or ovarian cancers, and endometrial biopsies and ultrasound. The ultimate question is, are you cured after all these treatments? The answer depends on the stage your cancer was in to begin with (see the sections earlier in this chapter on the stages of various cancers). Statistically, the answer is "usually."

Cancer goes into remission, meaning that the cells stop growing and what was there has been removed or effectively killed. But cancer cells can start up again and begin to grow at some future point. Endometrial cancer and cervical cancer rarely come back. Ovarian cancer may recur but can be detected with the CA-125 blood test for ovarian cancer.

# Recurrent Disease

Recurrent disease means your cancer has come back (recurred) after being treated. It can recur in the same place as the original cancer or elsewhere in your body. If your cancer recurs, you will need to repeat your therapy or have more extensive treatment, which can involve more surgery, chemotherapy (often for the first time), radiotherapy, hormonal therapy, immunotherapy, or a combination of all five.

The longer you go cancer-free, the greater your chances are of being permanently cured.

# Palliative Care

Palliative care refers to symptom relief and is a component of all medical care, whether the intent is to cure a disease or to eliminate its symptoms. People at all stages of an illness will want to be free of spiritual, psychological, and physical symptoms from the earliest stage of diagnosis until they are cured or die. But what does it mean to treat the symptoms of a disease rather than the disease itself? What it sometimes boils down to is different goals.

Whenever anyone needs medicine or therapies to relieve the pain or symptoms of any given illness, it's known as palliative care. Palliative care generally enters into the cancer picture in a situation where metastatic disease has developed and there are no therapies available that can cure the disease. In this case, the goals of therapy change from what doctors call a curative approach, meaning that therapies and medications are designed to cure the cancer, to a palliative approach, where medications and therapies are designed not to cure but to make you comfortable and alert so you can carry on as normally as possible.

Your cancer specialist can refer you to a palliative care team—which may consist of several consulting doctors, nurses, a physiotherapist, a pharmacist, a psychologist, a social worker, a member of the clergy, a dietitian, and volunteers—at your medical center. Palliative care can also be "portable." Although you may be hospitalized for treatment, depending on your health, you may instead receive treatment as an outpatient through regular visits to the hospital or your palliative care specialist.

You have the right to expect the following from your palliative care team:

1. An open-ended approach to therapy. In other words, your care should be flexible to meet your changing needs rather than rigid and finite.

2. No blanket reassurances that everything will be fine. Your team should be frank about your prognosis but sensitive to your feelings.

3. As much information as you want, whenever you want it.

4. Jargon-free explanations. This means nontechnical descriptions of what's happening in your body and nontechnical descriptions of the therapy recommended to relieve symptoms.

5. Ongoing assessment. You should be regularly assessed by your doctor and informed about your illness's progression and symptoms to expect. It is possible that your health may be changing daily.

6. Participation in your treatment.

7. The goals of your treatment defined in black and white. For example, if you're having radiation therapy to your chest area to shrink a tumor, the goal is to shrink the tumor so you can breathe more easily—not to cure the cancer.

8. Techniques for coping with family and friends. You should be able to count on your team for supportive advice in dealing with family or friends who are in conflict or denial about your situation.

## The Symptoms You're Palliating

One of the most common symptoms of metastatic disease is shortness of breath. This has a number of causes ranging from fluid accumulation, which can be removed; pneumonia, which can be treated with antibiotics; hyperventilation due to anxiety, relieved through breathing techniques or antianxiety medications; or a tumor pressing down on the lungs, which may require you to be on oxygen at home or in the hospital. As a final step, if there is no way to remove the cause of shortness of breath, narcotics such as morphine or hydromorphine will decrease the *sensation* of breathlessness.

Loss of appetite (called anorexia) is another common symptom associated with advanced cancer. Sometimes this has to do with the location of your cancer; other times it's a response to pain medication. The most upsetting aspect of appetite loss is what it does to the people around you. You should have your palliative team reassure your family and friends that food is not a guarantee of a longer life span. Generally, dietitians recommend that you have your food prepared in very small portions. You'll find food much more appetizing this way. You might also choose meal replacement drinks. Drinking a can or two throughout the day will provide you with some calories and vitamins.

Mild to severe nausea is also a symptom in advanced cancer and is caused either by where your cancer has spread or by various medications. The solutions vary from antinausea medications to adjusting diet or medications accordingly.

Constipation is a classic symptom of narcotic pain relief and can be alleviated with laxatives and stool softeners.

Another symptom can be bladder incontinence, which can be alleviated with either a catheter or by wearing bladder control undergarments.

Fatigue strikes again with advanced cancer. Fatigue in this case is often a sign that you're not sleeping well at night because your pain is waking you up. This means that you need a stronger pain control medication, discussed in the next section. Fatigue can, of course, be a side effect of treatments such as radiation or narcotic medications like codeine or morphine.

# Pain Management

You can be seriously ill without having severe physical pain and may require nothing more than some over-the-counter drugs. However, when advanced cancer causes severe pain, you're going to need some strong stuff to control it. Your doctor will usually start with a nonnarcotic and work up to a narcotic painkiller, known as an opioid (the root word comes from opium, one of the oldest narcotics). Narcotic medication for severe pain control is generally not addictive in the sense that you would wait for your next fix and become strung out on drugs. What happens instead is that when the drug wears off, you'll feel the pain again, so you'll want another dose just to feel *normal*. And that's fine. That's what a narcotic is designed to do.

Many narcotics now come in pain patches (worn on the skin like nicotine patches), thereby eliminating much of the dosage administering of days gone by.

So while narcotics may be a godsend, they're still, of course, powerful drugs that you can't just take by yourself when you feel like it. You're going to need someone who is an expert at administering the lowest possible dose of a narcotic, based on a number of factors: where your pain is located, the cause of your pain, how much pain you have, and your overall health. But patients and their families are being encouraged by specialists to become their own gauge in managing and administering their narcotic dosages.

Pain is a sign that something's wrong. *You* already know that now, but your *body* doesn't know you know. In the same way that your smoke detector will continue to ring until the smoke clears, your body will continue to send pain signals until you remove the cause of the pain. Until that day comes (which is probably unlikely in advanced cancer), you have to deaden the pain. Your nerve endings act as the smoke detectors in your body. Every part of your body has free nerve endings, while the spinal cord has pain receptors, which tell your brain to tell those nerve endings to send the pain.

Sometimes it's the nerves themselves that are damaged, due to nerve compression or compression of the spinal cord. This will cause that intermittent, stabbing pain, often accompanied by a burning or numbness. Other times pain is caused by tumors that infiltrate bone or press down on other organs. This will lead to more continuous, aching pain.

Pain has many shapes and forms, which will help tell your palliative care team what's going on. For example, you can have acute pain, which means that the pain has a clear beginning, middle, and end. Acute pain also has physical signs, such as sweating, pupil dilation, and a pounding heart.

Chronic pain is harder to describe because it goes on and on in a continuous aching. It's difficult for your doctors to tell sometimes when you have chronic pain because people may describe it as "discomfort" or "unwellness." In others, chronic pain triggers depression, irritability, or sleeplessness.

Or as your illness advances and you become more debilitated, depressed, or anxious about your circumstance, your awareness of pain increases, which will make the pain feel worse (even though it may actually be the same pain you've been dealing with for a while).

There's another condition, known as total pain. This is when you're just maxed out from a variety of pains related to your illness: pain from the disease itself, side effects of your treatment or medications, emotional pain, and so on. It's the equivalent of pain burnout.

The number-one goal of pain management in cancer is to either prevent or completely control pain. Period. No exceptions. So the first thing your doctor will do is try to figure out what's causing your pain. For example, if a tumor is pressing down on an organ, it can often be shrunk with radiation or surgically removed, which will then eliminate the pain without your having to resort to narcotic drugs.

Your doctor will also try to get you to assess your pain on a number system from 0 to 5, where 0 = no pain, 1 = mild, 2 = discomforting, 3 = distressing, 4 = horrible, and

5 = excruciating. This will tell your doctor what type of medications you need for pain control. Obviously, a 5 will require the "hard stuff," while you may be able to manage a 2 or 3 with a nonnarcotic medication.

## Drugs That Control Pain

There are classes of drugs used to control pain, which doctors prescribe in a stepped care approach. That means they start with the least powerful drug and work their way up as the pain increases.

On the bottom step is a class of drugs known as nonopioids (a.k.a. nonnarcotics). These are basic painkillers (analgesics) such as acetylsalicylic acid (aspirin), acetaminophen (Tylenol), and nonsteroidal anti-inflammatory drugs such as ibuprofen (Advil) or naproxen (Naprosyn). These drugs work by interfering with body chemicals called prostaglandins, which normally cause inflammation and increase your body's pain receptor "firing." Non-narcotics are used not just for mild pain, but also for bone pain and other forms of severe pain.

The second step up the pain ladder is what's called a weak opioid, which is often mixed with a nonopioid. A weak opioid is codeine, and it's often mixed with acetaminophen in a drug such as Tylenol #3. The third and final step up is a strong opioid. This is when morphine or hydromorphone is used. Both weak and strong opioids are known as narcotics. These work in the central nervous system (the brain and spinal cord) and inhibit the transmission of pain. Most narcotics used in advanced cancer treatment are morphine preparations and hydromorphone (Dilaudid). Less common are propoxyphene (Darvon), oxycodone (Percodan), and oxymorphone (Numorphan).

## Coanalgesics

On every "step" in the pain management ladder, your doctor may decide to combine your analgesic with a drug that will relieve other symptoms of your illness or that will prevent the side effects of your painkiller. For example, anticonvulsants, antidepressants, steroids, membrane-stabilizing drugs, or antianxiety drugs may all be added to nonopioids or to weak or strong opioids.

## Taking Drugs "as Needed" Versus Round the Clock

As discussed, depending on the kind of pain you have, your doctor will want to prevent it or control it. To prevent pain, you'll be on what's called a regular dosing schedule, whether you have pain or not. This is better than waiting for the pain to build up, and it is also much less stressful for you. However, you must take the dose as prescribed—no more drug, no less drug, and taken no more or less frequently than prescribed. Otherwise, either the pain will not be managed properly or else too much of the drug will build up in your system so that it becomes toxic to your general health.

Taking medications "as needed" (known as p.r.n. in pharmacy-speak) is a little trickier. You must take the drug as soon as you start to feel the least bit uncomfortable. If you wait until the pain increases (in an effort to tough it out until it gets really bad), the drug just won't work as well, and you'll have to take higher doses. Of course, it may well be that you don't need to be on as high a dose of the drug as you are or that another drug may work better. So be on the lookout for "postdose" symptoms such as agitation or extreme drowsiness. This may mean that your doctor needs to adjust the dosage or switch the drug.

So long as your doctor knows what's causing your pain, you should be able to have as much analgesia as you need to control the pain. In fact, nurses on palliative care wards in hospitals should have standing orders to increase your pain medication if it's not strong enough.

Dosing is another issue around narcotics. There is no standard or maximum dose for these medications. Dosing varies on the individual situation—and the individual. It's important for you or your family (if you're not able) to keep a diary of when you're experiencing pain so you and your doctor can develop a regular dosing schedule that prevents what's called breakthrough pain.

Balancing your medications is another issue, particularly when coanalgesics (see earlier discussion) are added to your pain medications. Ask your doctor or pharmacist to draw up a chart that you can follow, listing all the medications you need to take and when you need to take them. It's usually fine to take all your various medications as a group (i.e., analgesic, antidepressant, and narcotic) in the morning, for example, and then at other times in the day as prescribed.

## If You're Not Finding Relief

Most people do best with a combination of prescription and over-the-counter painkillers. Specialists usually encourage their patients to manage painkillers on their own as much as possible. Since you are, after all, the one experiencing your pain, it's presumed that you should be more expert on your pain than anyone else. If you're not finding relief, however, it may be a case of inappropriate administration rather than an ineffective narcotic. Is the doctor prescribing the drug regularly, around the clock? Is the drug's duration of action matched to its dosing schedule? In other words, if the drug lasts for two hours but is only being prescribed every four, you'll be in pain for two hours in between! That's *not* a proper way for a painkiller to be administered. In addition, you may simply need a stronger dose of a drug that is not effectively treating your pain.

Ironically, the longer you're made to wait for another dosage of the drug, the more pain you'll feel, out of anticipation and stress. Worse, you're more likely to feel dependent on the drug and watch the clock when you're forced to wait for relief.

## Issues Surrounding End of Life

If you're in poor health, at some point you'll need to decide whether you want to be treated at home or in a hospital or somewhere in between, such as a hospice. What factors into this decision is the availability of home care or a caregiver as well as equipment or devices such as an adjustable bed, special mattresses, bedpans, IV lines, handrails, mechanical aids for bath or shower, oxygen and suction equipment, walkers, chairs, wheelchairs, and so on. If you're currently hospitalized, you can request an overnight pass and try going home for a night to see whether your family is able to give you the kind of care you require. This is one way to experiment with different arrangements.

Sometimes the solution is to go for respite care, meaning temporary hospital stays, to give your family some time off from providing ongoing caregiving or to give a paid caregiver some time off. Temporary hospital stays can last from one to two weeks.

When it comes to palliative care, more and more hospitals are encouraging patients to receive their care at home. In some cases, this is a response to escalating costs; in other cases, it's a response to a decrease in the number of beds available. At any rate, it's important to make sure that you're in an environment with the following:

- proper equipment and resources
- access to ongoing assessment
- access to proper symptom and pain control
- access to caregiver "substitutes" to relieve caregiver exhaustion
- access to emergency care in case of a problem

## What to Eat

There is no single "cancer therapy" diet. Different chemo cocktails and individual treatment plans will dramatically affect diet and eating problems. The general rule is to maintain a balanced, healthy diet that is high in protein. Milk products, eggs, meats, poultry and fish, beans (or legumes), nuts, and seeds are all high in protein. Review Chapter 1 for the elements of a good, balanced diet. A balanced diet will help you get your energy back, especially if you're suffering from fatigue.

What most women find while undergoing cancer therapy is that they suffer from loss of appetite (anorexia). Sometimes this has to do with where your cancer is located; other times it's a response to pain medication. Generally, dietitians recommend that you have people prepare foods in very small portions—"single-wrapped" or "finger food" formats. On good days you can also prefreeze your own meals, so on bad days you don't have to worry about preparing food. Meal replacement drinks, packed with a fair number of calories and vitamins, can also solve some problems. You can sip on a can or two throughout the day.

If you've had a hysterectomy, you may find that you feel full after only a few bites of food (called early satiety). You may also suffer from bloating and gas. The antibloat diet is one that is high in fiber (see Chapter 9) as well as rich in fluids. Drinking lots of water with fiber can greatly reduce gas. Eight to ten cups of liquids such as prune juice, warm juices, teas, and hot lemonade daily can also help. Limit carbonated drinks, broccoli, cabbage, cauliflower, cucumbers, dried beans, peas, and onions. To lessen the amount of swallowed air, do not use straws or chew gum.

Constipation, a classic symptom of narcotic pain relief, can also be alleviated with more fiber, which can be accompanied by laxatives and stool softeners.

Mild to severe nausea, which is either a result of your cancer or a response to various medications, is also a symptom in advanced cancer. The solutions here vary from taking antinausea medications to adjusting diet or medications accordingly.

If you have diarrhea, try the BRAT diet (see Chapter 11).

## Combating Funny-Tasting Food

Chemotherapy can alter your taste buds, and foods may not taste quite right. Here are a few tips:

- Season foods with lemon, vinegar, or other tart flavors.
- Season foods with strong flavors, such as garlic, onion, chili powder, and so on.
- Rinse your mouth with tea, ginger ale, salted water, or water with baking soda before eating to help clear your taste buds.
- Have more cold foods. Hot foods can produce more smells.
- Keep melon, grapes, or oranges in the freezer and eat them frozen.
- Try to have more fresh, and less canned or processed, foods.

### *Hygiene Rules*

Because you're usually immune suppressed while undergoing cancer therapy, it's important to reduce your exposure to certain raw or uncooked foods that can predispose you to infections. See Chapter 11, under "What to Eat," for more information.

# Flower Power

As just mentioned, you're generally immune suppressed while undergoing cancer therapy. This can predispose you to common infections, flu, and pneumonia. Immune boosters stimulate your immune system or strengthen it to help fight diseases, including cancer. See "Flower Power" in Chapter 3 for an overview of some of the well-known immune boosters.

# How to Move

One of the best forms of movement during cancer therapy is deep breathing (see Chapter 1). Massage therapy is one of the best forms of complementary healing available for cancer therapy.

Massage therapy can be beneficial whether you're receiving the massage from your spouse or a massage therapist trained in any one of dozens of techniques, from shiatsu to Swedish massage. In the East, massage was extensively written about in *The Yellow Emperor's Classic of Internal Medicine* (the text that frames the entire Chinese medicine tradition), published in 2700 B.C. In Chinese medicine, massage is recommended as a treatment for a variety of illnesses.

Swedish massage, the method Westerners are used to experiencing, was developed in the nineteenth century by a Swedish doctor and poet, Per Henrik, who borrowed techniques from ancient Egypt, China, and Rome.

It is out of shiatsu in the East and Swedish massage in the West that all the many forms of massage were developed. While the philosophies and styles differ in each tradition, the common element is the same: to mobilize the natural healing properties of the body, which will help it maintain or restore optimal health. Shiatsu-inspired massage focuses on balancing the life force energy. Swedish-inspired massage works on more physiological principles: relaxing muscles to improve blood flow throughout connective tissues, which ultimately strengthens the cardiovascular system.

But no matter what kind of massage you have, there are numerous gliding and kneading techniques used along with deep circular movements and vibrations that relax muscles, improve circulation, and increase mobility. This is known to help relieve stress and often muscle and joint pain. In fact, a number of employers cover massage therapy on their health plans. Massage is becoming so popular, in fact, that the number of licensed massage therapists enrolled in the American Massage Therapy Association has grown from twelve hundred in 1983 to more than thirty-eight thousand today. Massage is more technically referred to as soft-tissue manipulation.

**Benefits of Massage**
- improved circulation
- improved lymphatic system
- soothed aches and pains
- reduced edema (water retention)
- reduced anxiety

**Types of Massage**
- deep-tissue massage
- manual lymph drainage
- neuromuscular massage
- sports massage
- Swedish massage

# PART IV

# Issues Surrounding Natural and Surgical Menopause

# 19

# Menopause Naturally

CONSIDERING HOW MANY women are just beginning to *really* live by the time they hit their midforties and early fifties, it almost seems absurd to read about menopause, doesn't it? How could *you* possibly relate to books about "enjoying your grandchildren" or "preparing for midlife" or "your golden years" or the dozens of other euphemisms for "hey—you're getting old!" Many of you probably have young children at home—or young lovers, perhaps. Many of you are in the peak of your careers. Many of you are just re-singled, coming out of long-term marriages or relationships. Somebody tell them to turn back the clock! You're just gettin' rollin'!

In 2001 almost twenty million women in the United States were between the ages of forty-five and fifty-four—the largest number of women in that age group in all of history. Your generation is already demedicalizing and demystifying menopause, repositioning it not as a disease but as a natural stage in life. It is up to you to take back your body and make your own choices about how you want to live, as well as about the quality of life you want to maintain or enjoy. And this "social work" won't stop at fifty, sixty, seventy, or even eighty. We need to seriously question how our culture treats its aging and more vulnerable population. As you begin to watch your parents age, ail, and die, you will begin to rise up and demand that the current "warehousing" and dismissal of our aging, vulnerable population *stop*. How the Western world treats its older population is unacceptable. And you're the generation that will effect the most significant social policy changes in senior health care than ever before. Why? *Because there are so many of you.* Today, more than one hundred million North Americans are over sixty-five. And by 2010, the growth rate of the older population will be *three and a half times* as high as that of the total population.

Native American folklore records that we are in the midst of massive earth changes that will climax around 2013. It's been said that these earth changes will bring heat, floods, and incredible upheaval to the world's population. By then, more than fifty million women will have achieved menopause and will have gone through their own heat (via hot flashes), floods (via heavy bleeding), and upheaval. Some question whether we are entering a "mass menopause" or "collective menopause." Earth changes notwithstanding, the mass menopause that will take place in the next few years will be felt. Your menopause, in many ways, is a social menopause—a time for our culture to stop and change the way we think about aging.

This chapter gives you the facts about perimenopause (a term that literally means "around menopause"—the time where the physical signs and changes of menopause make their appearance) and both the short-term and long-term consequences of estrogen loss. The "Flower Power" section provides you with an extensive body of information about herbal remedies, therapies, and alternatives to pharmaceutical drugs typically prescribed to women approaching menopause. And "How to Move" offers a range of activities, postures, and exercises that can help to offset the general discomforts of perimenopause and estrogen loss.

# How Menopause Became a Disease

If menopause is a natural stage in your life, why is it treated by the medical profession as a "disease"? Why are words like *symptoms* used to describe the natural changes associated with estrogen loss? Why are you led to believe that you now have a "hormone deficiency syndrome" resulting from estrogen loss, and why are you treated as though you are in a "diseased state" when you are perfectly well? The answer is simple: you live in a Western culture where *everything* is medicalized and pathologized—from womb to tomb. It's not just menopause that is being medicalized. This trend can be seen with pregnancy and prenatal care, pediatric care (e.g., millions of children are being "diagnosed" with "behavior disorders" that in the past were considered normal), mental health (where people are put on medication for social causes of angst, anxiety, and depression), and so on. In short, *all* the normal physical processes of the human body have been pathologized by medicine. But more frequently, it is women's normal physical processes that are subject to the mass marketing of prevention drugs or not well-tested therapies. In our twenties and thirties, we are sold drugs to prevent pregnancy (see Chapter 8) and "regulate" our cycles. In our thirties and forties (and now, fifties), we are put on fertility drugs to "regulate" our cycles so we *can* get pregnant. And in our fifties and beyond, we are put on estrogen replacement drugs to "regulate" our cycles, too, and prevent health problems associated with estrogen loss. But to date, the number-one bestseller for pharmaceutical companies is hormone replacement therapy, which is now being seriously questioned in light of the most recent studies. Chapter 21 discusses HRT in detail.

## The Lost Hormone

It wasn't until the 1960s that the idea of giving estrogen to menopausal women took hold (which coincided with the introduction of the Pill). A 1963 article by Dr. Robert Wilson entitled "The Fate of the Nontreated Menopausal Woman: A Plea for the Maintenance of Adequate Estrogen from Puberty to the Grave," in the *Journal of the American Geriatrics Society*, was the breakthrough article that promoted HRT. This article outlined the "serious consequences" of estrogen loss: heart disease, hypertension, osteoporosis, "tough, dry, scaly and inelastic skin, flabby atrophic breasts, and shrinking labia." The final blow came when Wilson stated that menopause was a "mutilation of the whole body [and that] no woman can be sure of escaping the horror of this living decay." Thus a new disease was coined, and the menopause "industry" was born. To Wilson, estrogen loss was just like any other hormone deficiency, such as insulin in diabetes. If the lost hormone could be replaced, it *should* be replaced. This is the attitude that has prevailed.

Since Wilson, menopause "apologists" have surfaced in abundance; these are researchers who explain menopause as an accident of nature. The "apology" is an apology to women for nature's failings. You see, a woman's ovaries were supposed to work until she died; but because of a huge increase in human longevity within a short time span, there is now a gap in the natural life of a woman and the natural life of her ovaries. The message of this apology is "It's all a big mistake; you weren't supposed to live to see menopause. It's not your fault; medicine can fix this." (In recent years the phenomenon of "andropause"—a deficiency of testosterone—is being sold to men as the answer to their fatigue and loss of pep in their midlife.)

## Natural Menopause Versus "Discomfort Control"

Today, there are at least twenty million women in North America who are older than fifty. It seems absurd to suggest that this enormous number of women are all sick and need to take medication. Yet this is the reality of our times. In essence, we are medicating huge numbers of well, healthy women with powerful drugs. Should doctors be doing this? Or should doctors sit back and allow unnecessary discomfort and suffering when that suffering can be prevented?

Only *you* have the answer. If you feel physical discomfort and want your discomfort to be treated, you have that right. If you want to do everything you can to prevent long-term complications of estrogen loss (such as osteoporosis), you have that right, too. And you have the right *not* to be judged by your peers for choosing to be relieved of your discomfort or for choosing preventive therapies for serious diseases associated with estrogen loss. Would your grandmother have chosen estrogen if it had been offered to her? Would your grandmother have chosen to be uncomfortable when comfort was an option? Would your grandmother have chosen to experience a hip fracture or opt for information on preventing such a fate?

On the other hand, if you want to embrace the changes of your body as something nature intended and experience your menopause as a rite of passage, so to speak, you ought not be coerced into viewing these natural changes as a disease or coerced into treating the natural rhythms and flows of your body. In many non-Western cultures, menopause is considered a powerful time for women, where they are perceived as vessels for powerful energies that flow through them. Why should you be forced to deny yourself this powerful experience? You have the right not to be judged by your doctors or peers for choosing natural menopause (just as you would not be judged for choosing natural childbirth).

Many of you will fall between these two viewpoints. You may decide to investigate diet, herbs, and simple lifestyle changes to offset your discomforts. Within this chapter are a number of solutions for you to choose from. Mix 'n' match. There are no rules.

# Natural Menopause

Your first period (menarche) and your last (menopause) have a lot in common: they are both *gradual* processes that women ease into. A woman doesn't suddenly wake up to find herself in menopause any more than a young girl wakes up to find herself in puberty. However, when menopause occurs *surgically*—the by-product of an oophorectomy or of ovarian failure following a hysterectomy (see Chapter 20) or certain cancer therapies (see Chapter 18)—it can be an extremely jarring process. *One out of every three women in North America will not make it to the age of sixty with her uterus intact.* These women may indeed wake up one morning to find themselves in menopause, and as a result, they will suffer far more noticeable and severe signs of menopause than their natural menopause counterparts. It is because of *surgical* menopause that hormone replacement therapy (HRT) and estrogen replacement therapy (ERT; or unopposed estrogen) have become such hotly debated issues in women's health. The loss of estrogen, in particular, leads to drastic changes in the body's chemistry that trigger a more aggressive aging process (discussed further on). Menopause is a recent phenomenon in our society. A hundred years ago, most women simply died prior to, or not long after, menopause. Outliving the ovaries is a fairly recent event in history, thanks to higher standards of living and quality health care throughout the life span.

When menopause occurs naturally, it tends to take place when you are anywhere between the ages of forty-eight and fifty-two, but it can occur as early as your late thirties or as late as your midfifties. When menopause occurs *before* you are forty-five, it is technically considered early menopause, but just as menarche is genetically predetermined, so is menopause. For an average woman with an unremarkable medical history, what she eats or does in terms of activity will *not* influence the timing of her menopause. However, women who have had chemotherapy or have been exposed to high levels of radiation (such as radiation therapy in their pelvic area for cancer treatment) may go into earlier menopause. In any event, the average age of menopause is fifty to fifty-one.

Other causes that have been cited to trigger an early menopause include mumps (in small groups of women, the infection causing the mumps has been known to spread to the ovaries, prematurely shutting them down) and women with specific autoimmune diseases, such as lupus or rheumatoid arthritis (in some of these women, their bodies develop antibodies to their own ovaries and attack the ovaries).

## The Stages of Natural Menopause

Socially, the word *menopause* refers to a process, not a precise moment in the life your menstrual cycle. But medically, the word *menopause* does *indeed* refer to one precise moment: the date of your last period. However, the events preceding and following menopause amount to a huge change for women both physically and socially. Physically, this process is divided into four stages:

1. *Premenopause:* Although some doctors may refer to a thirty-two-year-old woman in her childbearing years as premenopausal, this is not really an appropriate label. The term *premenopause* ideally refers to women on the cusp of menopause. Their periods have just *started* to get irregular, but they do not yet experience any classic signs of menopause, such as hot flashes or vaginal dryness. A woman in premenopause is usually in her mid- to late forties. If your doctor tells you that you're premenopausal, you might want to ask how he or she is using this term.

2. *Perimenopause:* This term refers to women who are in the thick of the process of menopause—their cycles are wildly erratic, they are experiencing hot flashes and vagi-

nal dryness. This label is applicable for about four years, covering the first two years prior to the official "last" period to the next two years following the last menstrual period. Women who are perimenopausal will be in the age groups discussed earlier, averaging to about fifty or fifty-one.

3. *Menopause:* This refers to your final menstrual period. You will not be able to pinpoint your final period until you've been completely free from periods for one year. Then you count back to the last period you charted, and *that* date is the date of your menopause. *Important: after more than one year of no menstrual periods, any vaginal bleeding is now considered abnormal.*

4. *Postmenopause:* This term refers to the last third of most women's lives, ranging from women who have been free of menstrual periods for at least four years to women celebrating their one-hundredth birthday and beyond. In other words, once you're past menopause, you'll be referred to as postmenopausal for the rest of your life. Sometimes the terms *postmenopausal* and *perimenopausal* are used interchangeably, but this is technically inaccurate.

Used in a social context, however, nobody really bothers to break down menopause as precisely. When you see the word *menopausal* in a magazine article, you are seeing what's become acceptable medical slang, referring to women who are premenopausal and perimenopausal—a time frame that *includes* the actual menopause. When you see the word *postmenopausal* in a magazine article, you are seeing another accepted medical slang word, which includes women who are in perimenopause and "official" postmenopause.

### Determining Premenopause or Perimenopause

When you begin to notice the signs of menopause, discussed next, either you'll suspect the approach of menopause on your own or your doctor will put two and two together when you report your "bizarre symptoms." There are two simple tests that will accurately determine what's going on and what stage of menopause you're in. Your follicle-stimulating hormone (FSH) levels will dramatically rise as your ovaries begin to shut down; these levels are easily checked from one blood test. In addition, your vaginal walls will thin and the cells lining the vagina will not contain as much estrogen. Your doctor will simply do a Pap-like smear on your vaginal walls—simple and painless—and then just analyze the smear to check for vaginal atrophy—the thinning and drying out of your vagina. In addition, as I'll discuss further on, you need to keep track of your periods and chart them as they become irregular. Your menstrual pattern will be an additional clue to your doctor about whether you're pre- or perimenopausal.

## *Signs of Natural Menopause*

There are really just three classic short-term signs of menopause: erratic periods, hot flashes, and vaginal dryness. All three of these signs are caused by a decrease in estrogen. As for the emotional signs of menopause—such as irritability, mood swings, melancholy, and so on—they are actually caused by a rise in FSH. As the cycle changes and the ovaries' egg supply dwindles, FSH is secreted in very high amounts and reaches a lifetime peak—as much as fifteen times higher; it's the body's way of trying to jump-start the ovarian engine. This is why the urine of menopausal women is used to produce human menopausal gonadotropin (HMG), the potent fertility drug that consists of pure FSH.

Every woman entering menopause will experience a change in her menstrual cycle. However, not all women will experience hot flashes or even notice vaginal changes. This is particularly true if a woman is overweight. Estrogen is stored in fat cells, which is why overweight women also tend to be more at risk for estrogen-dependent cancers. What happens is that the fat cells convert fat into estrogen, creating a type of estrogen reserve that the body will use during menopause, which can reduce the severity of estrogen loss.

### Erratic Periods

Every woman will begin to experience an irregular cycle before her last period. Cycles may become longer or shorter with long bouts of amenorrhea. There will also be flow changes, where periods may suddenly become light and scanty or very heavy and crampy. The heavy bleeding occurs because of a sudden drop in progesterone levels (this is why *all* women get their periods). But when progesterone levels are higher than normal for premenopausal women, the uterine lining just keeps growing thicker. Then when you do bleed, it just floods and gushes (and clots—oh, boy!). It's not unusual to bleed heavily for as long as ten to fourteen days. You will lose iron when you bleed this heavily. See the "What to Eat" and "Flower Power" sections for iron-rich herbs and foods.

### Hot Flashes

Roughly 85 percent of all pre- and perimenopausal women experience what's known as hot flashes. Eastern cultures view a hot flash as a release of cosmic electricity (known as kundalini energies), which not only rewires your individual nervous system but gives you healing energies for your entire community. The intensity of your hot flash can be compared to the intensity felt during anger, orgasm, or even enlightenment, which all involve kundalini energies, too.

*Keeping Your Cool About Hot Flashes.* Hot flashes can begin when periods are either still regular or have just started to become irregular. The hot flashes usually stop one to two years after your final menstrual period. A hot flash can feel different for each woman. Some women experience a feeling of warmth in their face and upper body; others experience hot flashes as a simultaneous sweating with chills. Some women feel anxious, tense, dizzy, or nauseous just before the hot flash; others feel tingling in their fingers or heart palpitations just before. Some women will experience their hot flashes during the day; others will experience them at night and may wake up so wet from perspiration that they need to change their bed sheets and/or night clothes.

Nobody really understands what causes a hot flash, but researchers believe that it has to do with mixed signals from the hypothalamus, which controls both body temperature and sex hormones. Normally, when the body is too warm, the hypothalamus sends a chemical message to the heart to cool off the body by pumping more blood, causing the blood vessels under the skin to dilate, which makes you perspire. During menopause, however, it's believed that the hypothalamus gets confused and sends this "cooling off" signal at the wrong times. A hot flash is not the same as being overheated. Although the skin temperature often rises between four and eight degrees Fahrenheit, the internal body temperature drops, creating this odd sensation. Why does the hypothalamus get so confused? Decreasing levels of estrogen. We know this because when synthetic estrogen is given to replace natural estrogen in the body, hot flashes disappear. Some researchers believe that a decrease in luteinizing hormone (LH) is also a key factor, and a variety of other hormones that influence body temperature are being looked at as well. Although hot flashes are harmless in terms of health risks, they are disquieting and stressful. Yet certain groups of women will experience more severe hot flashes than others:

- Women who are in surgical menopause (discussed further on).
- Women who are thin. When there's less fat on the body to store estrogen reserves, physical changes associated with estrogen loss are more severe.
- Women who don't sweat easily. An ability to sweat makes extreme temperatures easier to tolerate. Women who have trouble sweating may experience more severe hot flashes.

Just as you must chart your periods when your cycles become irregular, it's also important to chart your hot flashes. Keep track of when the flashes occur and how long they last, numbering their intensity from 1 to 10. This will help you determine a pattern for the flashes and allow you to prepare for them in advance, which will reduce the stress involved in the flashes to begin with. It's also crucial to report your hot flashes to your doctor, just as you would any changes in your cycle. Hot flashes can also indicate other health problems, such as circulatory problems and so on.

***What You Can Do About Hot Flashes.*** Short of replacing estrogen (there are several natural estrogen herbs that are not factory-made) or looking into natural progesterone therapy (see Chapter 21), the only thing you can do about your hot flashes is to lessen your discomfort by adjusting your lifestyle to cope with them. The more comfortable you are, the less intense your flashes will feel. Once you establish a pattern by charting the flashes, you can do a few things around the time of day your flashes occur. Some suggestions:

- Avoid synthetic clothing, such as polyester, because it traps perspiration.
- Use only 100 percent cotton bedding if you have night sweats.
- Avoid clothing with high necks and long sleeves.
- Dress in layers.
- Keep cold drinks handy.
- If you smoke, cut down or quit. Smoking constricts blood vessels and can intensify and prolong a flash.
- Avoid trigger foods such as caffeine, alcohol, spicy foods, sugars, and large meals. Substitute herbal teas for coffee or regular tea.
- Discuss the benefits of taking vitamin E supplements with your doctor. Evidence suggests that it's essential for proper circulation and the production of sex hormones.
- Exercise to improve your circulation.
- Reduce your exposure to the sun; sunburn will aggravate your hot flashes because burnt skin cannot regulate heat as effectively. (The sun is discussed further on.)

## Vaginal Changes

Estrogen loss will also cause vaginal changes. Since it is the production of estrogen that causes the vagina to continuously stay moist and elastic through its natural secretions, the loss of estrogen will cause the vagina to become drier, thinner, and less elastic. This may also cause the vagina to shrink slightly in terms of width and length. In addition, the reduction in vaginal secretions causes the vagina to be less acidic. This can put you at risk for more vaginal infections. As a result of these vaginal changes, you'll notice a change in your sexual activity. Your vagina may take longer to become lubricated, or you may have to depend on lubricants to have comfortable intercourse.

Estrogen loss can affect other parts of your sex life as well. Your sexual libido may actually increase because testosterone levels can rise when estrogen levels drop. (The general rule is that your levels of testosterone will either stay the same or increase.) However, women who *do* experience an increase in sexual desire will also be frustrated that their vaginas are not accommodating their needs. First, there is the lubrication problem: more stimulation is required to lubricate the vagina naturally. Second, a decrease in estrogen means that less blood flows to the vagina and clitoris, which means that orgasm may be more difficult to achieve or may not last as long as it normally has in the past. Other changes involve the breasts. Normally, estrogen causes blood to flow into the breasts during arousal, which makes the nipples more erect, sensitive, and responsive. Estrogen loss causes less blood to flow to the breasts, which makes them less sensitive. And finally, since the vagina shrinks as estrogen decreases, it doesn't expand as much during intercourse, which may make intercourse less comfortable, particularly since it is less lubricated.

# Surgical Menopause

Surgical menopause is the result of a bilateral oophorectomy—the removal of both ovaries before natural menopause. Surgical menopause can also be the result of ovarian failure following a hysterectomy (see Chapter 20) or following cancer therapy, such as chemotherapy or radiation treatments. A bilateral oophorectomy is often done in conjunction with a hysterectomy or sometimes as a single procedure, when ovarian cancer is suspected, for example. In this section, I refer to menopause symptoms instead of signs or changes, because menopause, in this case, is medically induced, rather than a natural occurrence.

## *Bilateral Oophorectomy Symptoms*

If you've had your ovaries removed after menopause, you won't be in surgical menopause. You won't feel any hormonal differences in your body, although you may experience some structural problems. If you've had your ovaries removed before you've reached natural menopause, you'll wake up from your surgery in *post*menopause. Once the ovaries are removed, your body immediately stops producing estrogen and progesterone. Your FSH will skyrocket in an attempt to "make contact" with ovaries that no longer exist. Unlike women who go through menopause naturally, women wake up after a bilateral oophorectomy in immediate estrogen withdrawal. It's that sudden: one day you have a normal menstrual cycle, the next, you have none whatsoever. This can cause you to become understandably more depressed, but you'll also *feel* the physical symptoms of estrogen loss far more intensely than a woman in natural menopause. That means that your vagina will be extremely dry, your hot flashes will feel like sudden violent heat waves that will be very disturbing to your system, and, of course, your periods will cease altogether, instead of tapering off naturally. The period that you had prior to your surgery will have been your last, so you won't even experience pre- or perimenopause—just postmenopause. That means you'll need to discuss your options regarding ERT immediately following surgery to prevent these sudden symptoms of menopause.

### If You've Had Just One Ovary Removed

If the blood supply leading to your ovary was not damaged during your surgery, then you should still be able to produce enough estrogen for your body. If you begin to go into ovarian failure, the symptoms will depend on how fast the ovary is failing; you may experience symptoms more akin to natural menopause, or you may experience sudden symptoms, mirroring the surgical menopause experience.

## Ovarian Failure Resulting from Cancer Therapy

Chemotherapy and radiation treatments that involve the pelvic area may throw your ovaries into menopause. As just described, you may experience a more gradual menopausal process, or you may be overwhelmed by sudden symptoms of menopause. This depends on what kind of therapy you've received and the speed at which your ovaries are failing. Before you undergo your cancer treatment, discuss how the treatments will affect your ovaries and what menopausal symptoms you can expect. Gynecological cancer is discussed in Chapter 18.

# Long-Term Effects of Estrogen Loss: Postmenopausal Changes

The long-term effects of estrogen loss have to do with traditional signs of aging. One of the key reasons why women will choose HRT or ERT is to slow down or even reverse these changes. Yet it's important to keep in mind that the long-term effects of estrogen loss will not immediately set in after menopause. These changes are subtle and happen over several years. Even women who experience severe menopausal changes will not wake up to find that they've suddenly aged overnight; these changes occur gradually whether you experience surgical or natural menopause.

## Skin Changes

As estrogen decreases, skin, like the vagina, tends to lose its elasticity; it too becomes thinner because it is no longer able to retain as much water. Sweat and oil glands also produce less moisture, which is what causes the skin to gradually dry, wrinkle, and sag.

Good moisturizers and skin care will certainly help to keep your skin more elastic, but there is one known factor that aggravates and speeds up your skin's natural aging process, damaging the skin even more: *the sun*. If you cut down your sun exposure, you can dramatically reduce visible aging of your skin. Period. The bad news is that much of the sun's damage on our skin is cumulative from many years of exposure. In fact, many researchers believe that when it comes to visible signs of aging, estrogen loss is only a small factor. For example, it's known that ultraviolet rays break down collagen and elastin fibers in the skin, which cause it in turn to break down and sag. This is also what puts us at risk for skin cancer, the most notorious of which is melanoma, one of the most aggressive and malignant of all cancers.

Other sun-related problems traditionally linked to estrogen loss are what we call liver spots, light brown or tan splotches that develop on the face, neck, and hands as we age. First, these spots have nothing to do with the liver; they are sun spots and are caused by sun exposure. In fact, they are sometimes the result of HRT, known in this case as hyperpigmentation.

Currently, dermatologists are recommending sunblocks with a minimum of SPF 15. In fact, sun damage is so widespread in our population that today sunblock is often part of North American women's daily cosmetic routine; women will put it on as regularly as a daily moisturizer.

# What to Eat

Because estrogen loss puts you at greater risk for cardiovascular disease and osteoporosis, adopting a more heart-smart and calcium-rich diet is key at this time in your life.

For heart health, you already know the drill—a varied diet that is lower in saturated fats and higher in "good fats." For more information, see *50 Ways Women Can Prevent Heart Disease*. In the meantime, following are some more nutrition tips.

## Vitamins and Minerals for Heart Health

The following vitamins and minerals are essential to heart health. Supplements of all the following are widely available:

- B vitamins (B$_{12}$, B$_6$, etc.)
- vitamin C
- vitamin E
- lycopene (a cousin of beta-carotene, it helps protect against heart disease; found in red fruits and veggies, including tomatoes, pink grapefruit, watermelon, guava, and apricots)
- niacin
- magnesium

To nourish or tone the heart, try the following:

- *Wheat germ oil:* Use one tablespoon (15 ml) or more daily.

- *Vitamin E oil:* Use one tablespoon (15 ml) or more daily.

- *Flaxseed* (Linum usitatissimum): Also known as linseed, this is considered the best heart oil—but only if it is absolutely fresh and taken uncooked. One to three teaspoons (5 to 15 ml) of flaxseed oil first thing in the morning is recommended. You can also grind the seeds and sprinkle them on cereals or salads. Or soak flaxseeds in water and drink the whole thing first thing in the morning.

- *Borage seed or black currant seed:* Heart-protective oils can be found in these.

- *Plantain, lamb's-quarter, or amaranth:* Essential fatty acids can be found in these.

- *Hawthorn berry tincture:* Use twenty-five to forty drops of the berry tincture up to four times a day. Expect results no sooner than six to eight weeks.

- *Seaweed:* Seaweed is a rich source of phytoestrogens.

- *Carotene-rich foods:* Look for bright colored fruits and vegetables. The richer the color, the richer they are in carotene.

- *Garlic* (Allium sativum): Greatest heart benefits come from eating it raw, but you can also purchase deodorized caplets.

- *Lemon balm:* Steep a handful of fresh leaves in a glass of white wine for an hour or so and drink it with dinner. Or make lemon balm vinegar to use on your salads.

- *Dandelion root tincture:* Use ten to fifteen drops with meals.

- *Ginseng* (Panax quinquefolium): Chew on the root or use five to forty drops of tincture.

- *Motherwort* (Leonurus cardiaca): Use a tincture of the flowering tops, five to fifteen drops several times a day as needed.

### *Increase Your Calcium*

Calcium will help maintain bones and prevent osteoporosis. A daily intake of 1,500 mg calcium is recommended past menopause. When you're trying to increase calcium in your diet, it also means avoiding foods that cause you to use up or pee out calcium, such as alcohol or coffee. Refer to Chapter 2 under "What to Eat" for a detailed discussion on how to increase your calcium intake.

### *Iron for Heavy Flows*

If you're coping with very heavy menstrual flows (a.k.a. flooding), then it's important to consume roughly 2 mg iron from herbs or foods while the bleeding persists. This will help to prevent anemia. Iron is best in small doses throughout the day, rather than in one big gulp. Coffee, black tea, soy protein, egg yolks, bran, and calcium supplements over 250 mg can also impair iron absorption. Bleeding can be aggravated by aspirin, Midol, and larger doses of ascorbic acid (vitamin C supplements) because they thin the blood. In general, foods rich in bioflavonoids and carotene will help with blood loss.

## Flower Power

This section gives you plenty of ideas if you're wondering about herbal remedies, including herbs that nourish and tone during perimenopause and after menopause. The variety in this section is here to give you choices, not to suggest that you must try *everything*. Have fun! You may wish to start an herbal group, where you and some of your friends or contemporaries compare notes about what works best.

# How to Have "Safe Herbs"

1. Buy herbs that are labeled with the botanical name specific to only one plant. For example, "sage" can refer to at least five plants in five different areas, but *Salvia officinalis* means garden sage only.

2. Introduce yourself to one herb at a time, and try to learn all you can about your new herb. That means experimenting: does it work best at different times of day, or with certain foods or other herbs you know well?

3. Herbs can be tonic (maintenance herbs) or active (sedating or stimulating). Tonic herbs include birch, black cohosh, blackstrap molasses, chaste tree, dandelion, dong quai, echinacea, false unicorn, ginseng, hawthorn, horsetail, lady's mantle, motherwort, peony, sarsaparilla, spikenard, wild yam, and yellow dock. Active herbs include catnip, cinnamon, ginger, hops, licorice, myrrh, passion flower, poplar, primrose, sage, skullcap, uva-ursi, valerian, vervain, willow, and wintergreen.

4. Herbs can also be toxic in high quantities. Toxic herbs include cayenne, cotton root, goldenseal, liferoot, poke root, rue, sweet clover (melilot), and wormseed.

## For Irregular Cycles

If you are suffering from erratic periods during perimenopause, there are herbs that you can take to help regulate your periods. See Chapter 2 under "Flower Power" for a detailed discussion.

## Iron-Rich Herbs

As mentioned earlier, if you're coping with very heavy menstrual flows, it's important to consume roughly 2 mg iron from herbs or foods while the bleeding persists. The following herbs are rich in iron:

- *Dandelion leaves:* This is the best source of usable iron, containing roughly 30 gm iron per ounce.

- *Yellow dock root:* An alcohol or vinegar tincture is best: twenty drops of alcohol tincture or three teaspoons (15 ml) vinegar, taken in tea or water, gives you 1 mg iron to the blood.

- *Lady's mantle* (Alchemilla vulgaris): This alchemical weed controlled menstrual hemorrhage in virtually all of more than three hundred women in a recent study.

- *Wild yam root:* As a tincture, twenty to thirty drops daily for the two weeks before your period can help reduce flow.

## For Hot Flashes

Hot flashes deplete your body of vitamins B and C, magnesium, and potassium. Red clover or oatstraw infusions will replace these lost nutrients. Vitamin B supplements ($B_2$, $B_6$, and $B_{12}$), vitamin C, and vitamin E supplements are also helpful.

### Herbal Remedies

It's suggested that you choose one of the following to help reduce the severity of hot flashes:

1. A "cooling" herb such as chickweed, elderflower, violet, oatstraw, mint, seaweed, all parts of the mallows (*Malva* species), and the flowers and leaves of any hibiscus plant.

2. A liver-nourishing herb, such as dandelion, yellow dock, Lowenzahn (*Taraxacum officinale*) root, Ho Shou Wu (*Polygonum multiflorum*) root (also sold as Fo-ti-tieng), milk thistle (Syllibum), chicory (*Cichorium intybus*), or oatstraw.

3. A plant estrogen, such as black cohosh. (See Chapter 21 for a list of phytoestrogens.)

A big mug of infusion using any of the following herbs is equal to 250 to 300 mg calcium. Add a big pinch of horsetail and increase the calcium by 10 percent:

- nettles
- sage
- chickweed

- red clover
- comfrey leaf
- raspberry leaf
- oatstraw

## Aromatherapy

The following essential oils can help ease hot flashes. Use one or a combination on a cold compress, in a bath, or in a diffuser.

- calamus/sweet flag
- basil
- thyme
- chamomile
- rose
- lavender

## Miscellaneous

You might find doing the following will also help alleviate hot flashes:

- Use a hand-held fan.
- Use cologne, which is mostly alcohol and cooling.
- Bathe using three ounces (80 ml) rubbing alcohol.

# Chinese Herbs

Chinese angelica root, raw and cooked Rehmannia, peony root, and thorowax root are commonly used to treat menopausal symptoms. In addition, traditional Chinese medicine practitioners may be familiar with the following:

- *Ba Zhen Wan (Women's Precious Pills):* These are commonly prescribed in traditional Chinese medicine for menopausal symptoms. These pills reportedly help with *qi*, which is the life force energy.

- *Zhe Bai Di Huang Wan (Six Rehmannia Pills Plus Two):* This is another traditional Chinese medicine remedy, for hot flashes, restlessness, and night sweats.

# How to Move

Acupuncture is helpful in treating a host of menopausal discomforts and can be combined with the herbal remedies already suggested. The following yoga postures are also helpful:

- The Butterfly
- Knee and Thigh Stretch
- Mountain Posture
- Angle Balance
- The Tree
- Balance Posture
- Chess Expander
- Abdominal Lift
- Rock and Roll
- The Fish
- Pose of Tranquility
- Back-Stretching Posture
- Spread Leg Stretch
- The Plough
- Pelvic Stretch
- The Camel
- The Cobra
- The Bow
- Lying Twist
- Side Leg Raise
- Spinal Twist
- Sun Salutations

## Conventional Exercise

Any kind of physical exercise can decrease hot flashes because it increases endorphin levels, which immediately counteract hot flashes. The recommended "dose" is twenty minutes three times a week. In addition, the following exercises can alleviate hot flashes and other gynecological conditions:

### For Hot Flashes
- Sit on the floor with knees bent. Hold the point below your middle toe with your right hand, maintaining steady pressure for one to three minutes.

- Move your right hand to the point behind your ankle bone. Again, hold with steady pressure for one to three minutes and repeat both exercises on the left side.

- With your left hand, hold the point on your right hand just outside of the fourth finger. Repeat on the left side.

**For Hot Flashes, Excessive Menstrual Bleeding, and Other Disturbances of the Reproductive Tract**
- Lie on the floor with your knees bent. Place a knotted towel between the shoulder blades on the spine and hold for one to three minutes.

- With arms crossed across the chest, press your thumbs against the insides of your arms above the elbows. Hold for one to three minutes.

- Move your left hand to the point at the base of the sternum or breastbone. Hold with steady pressure while you move your right hand to the point where the spine meets the back of the skull. Hold for one to three minutes.

- Interlace your fingers and let them rest below your breasts. Press the tips of your fingers into your chest area with steady pressure. Hold for one to three minutes.

- Slide a knotted towel downward until it rests below your waistline. Apply steady pressure to the tailbone with your right hand and to the tip of the pubic bone with your left hand. Hold for one to three minutes.

- Lie on your back. Gently roll one, then the other shoulder inward, shortening the distance between your shoulder blades. Bring your knees to your chest, supporting your hips with your hands. Gently bring your legs up and over your body until they are resting on a chair behind you. Lift the spine by stretching the back muscles as much as possible. Breathe deeply and hold.

- Lie on your back with your knees bent. Gently roll one, then the other shoulder inward, shortening the distance between your shoulder blades. With hands supporting the hips, slowly thrust your pelvis toward the ceiling. Breathe deeply, feeling the stretch all along the front of your body. Release.

# 20

# When a Hysterectomy Is Necessary (and Unnecessary)

THE LATEST STATISTICS show that a hysterectomy (removal of the uterus) is most likely to be performed for endometriosis, fibroids, and uterine prolapse. All three of these conditions can be successfully treated with alternative procedures or therapies as discussed in Chapters 13, 14, and 15, respectively. About 600,000 women have hysterectomies every year. The problem is that only about 10 percent of hysterectomies are performed to treat life-threatening conditions such as cancer of the uterus or invasive cervical cancer. Ninety percent of hysterectomies are therefore elective surgery; of those, 30 to 50 percent are considered clearly unnecessary, while roughly 10 to 20 percent could be avoided using a different or an alternative approach.

Considered the most common major surgery performed in the United States and Canada, it is also estimated that 30 to 50 percent of North American women have their uterus removed before they reach sixty-five; hysterectomy is usually done on women ages twenty to forty-nine. This is alarming, considering the rate of hysterectomies in European countries is only 10 percent, a rate that matches the number of truly necessary hysterectomies.

In the United States, studies found that women who live in the southern or central parts of the country were more likely to have hysterectomies than women living in the Northeast or on the West Coast; the discrepancy is directly related to self-education. Women with higher levels of education are simply more aware of the options and alternatives to hysterectomies for a number of conditions that do not clearly warrant hysterectomies. It was also found that American surgeons on salary at teaching hospitals in academic centers perform fewer hysterectomies than those paid per operation.

The gender of one's physician can also impact hysterectomy rates; a Swiss study found that female gynecologists perform 50 percent fewer hysterectomies than their male counterparts.

Hysterectomy was first performed in the 1800s when life-threatening situations warranted it. In 1930 only fifteen hysterectomies were performed in the United States; by the late 1990s that number had climbed to 500,000 at a cost of $3 billion annually.

Hysterectomies are performed primarily on women in their thirties and forties, and about 40 percent of these women will wind up with their ovaries removed as well.

## When Is a Hysterectomy Necessary?

You will need a hysterectomy if you have invasive cancer of the uterus, ovaries, cervix, vagina, or fallopian tubes (very rare). All of these cancers are discussed in Chapter 18. You may also need a hysterectomy for severe PID, severe, uncontrollable bleeding (rare but associated with childbirth, blood-clotting disorders, and endometriosis), life-threatening blockages of the bladder or bowels by the uterus or growths on the uterus, and rare childbirth complications, such as a uterine rupture. Finally, a fibroid condition that truly interferes with your quality of life will also warrant one. Because so many unnecessary hysterectomies are performed, it's important to investigate alternatives first before you agree to surgery. There are several types of hysterectomies to choose from:

- A total, complete, or simple hysterectomy (often called a partial hysterectomy) removes the entire uterus with the cervix. The fallopian tubes and ovaries can be left intact, however. If they are, you will continue to ovulate, but you will not experience a menstrual period. The egg will just be absorbed by the body. It's important to note that the term *complete hysterectomy* is strictly a lay term. The medical description for this kind of hysterectomy is salpingo-oophorectomy.

- A subtotal or partial hysterectomy removes the uterus above the cervix but leaves the cervix intact. Fewer nerves are severed during this procedure, so the bladder, bowel, and sexual functions aren't as damaged. This procedure does not make you immune to cervical cancer, however. The ovaries and tubes can be left intact as well.

- A radical hysterectomy is done only if there is invasive cancer. It removes the uterus, about one-third of the upper vagina, and lymph nodes around the groin for sampling. It can also mean removing the ovaries and tubes, but they can be left intact.

- A modified or type II radical hysterectomy is the same as a radical hysterectomy but tries to preserve nerve fibers to the bowel and bladder to maintain normal function. Again, the tubes and ovaries can be left intact.

- A laparoscopically assisted vaginal hysterectomy (LAVH) is "hysterectomy by video." With the aid of a laparoscope and a video camera, the surgeon can make a small incision through the abdomen, view everything clearly on the video screen, maneuver various instruments inside the abdomen accordingly, and then complete the surgery through the vagina using traditional vaginal hysterectomy surgical techniques. The value of this procedure is that it may enable some women with fibroids, endometriosis, or PID to avoid the larger abdominal incision required for standard abdominal hysterectomy. In addition, recovery time is reduced.

The hysterectomy can be done either through an incision in the abdomen, where a six-to-eight-inch incision is made just below the pubic hairline (a bikini scar), or through the vagina, where an incision is made. But some conditions, including most cancers, require vertical incisions so that the surgeon can carefully examine the entire abdomen and remove large tumors. The benefit of a vaginal incision is that you'll have no visible scar. It also involves fewer complications and a shorter recovery period. The abdominal hysterectomy is done on women with large fibroids, invasive cancer, severe PID, or a history of abdominal surgery.

When your doctor recommends a hysterectomy, here are five questions you need to ask before you decide:

1. Who is performing the surgery? Make sure your surgeon is qualified.
2. What is being removed? (Many women don't know.) Be clear and comfortable about the fate of your ovaries.
3. When does this procedure need to be done? If it's not an emergency, use the time to get second and third opinions.
4. Will a vaginal or an abdominal incision be made? Why is that particular incision being recommended?
5. Why do I need a hysterectomy? Invasive cancer, for example, is a valid reason (see other reasons discussed earlier).

## When May a Hysterectomy Be Unnecessary?

If your doctor suggests a hysterectomy for any of the following conditions, you should question the procedure and seek a second and even third opinion:

- *Fibroids:* This accounts for about one-third of all hysterectomies. All the alternatives to hysterectomy for fibroids are discussed in Chapter 14.

- *Uterine prolapse (see Chapter 15):* Kegel exercises or a pessary may be used to hold the uterus in place. Small amounts of estrogen used vaginally can strengthen the area; however, if symptoms are severe, a surgical repair and/or reconstruction of the uterus, bladder, rectum, and their supporting structures may be performed. In some cases, a severely prolapsed uterus may have to be removed.

- *Endometriosis (see Chapter 13):* There is no evidence that hysterectomy is useful.

- *Pelvic pain or PID:* For PID, intravenous antibiotics are considered the best conventional therapy. Acupuncture can also be helpful for chronic pelvic pain that does not have a known origin. Many women who have been sexually abused, for example, suffer from chronic pelvic pain.

- *Ovarian cysts:* See Chapter 4.

- *Premenstrual syndrome (PMS):* See Chapter 2.

- *Adenomyosis:* See Chapter 13.

- *Benign ovarian cysts:* See Chapter 4.

- *Hyperplasia:* See Chapter 17. This can be better treated with hormonal therapy using natural or synthetic progesterone. Progesterone causes the excess lining of the uterus to shed itself.

- *Stress incontinence (leaking urine when you cough or sneeze):* See Chapter 5. There is no reason to have a hysterectomy for this problem, and there is no evidence to suggest that a hysterectomy can help; however, there is evidence that a hysterectomy will worsen incontinence.

- *Moderate vaginal bleeding:* This is usually caused by a hormonal imbalance, which can be corrected with hormonal medication rather than surgery.

- *Any type of inflammation: vulvitis, vaginitis, endometritis, and so on:* Hysterectomy is absolutely not indicated for inflammation. In these cases, fungal, bacterial, or viral infections are usually the culprits and can be treated.

# Facts About Hysterectomy

According to Hysterectomy Educational Resources and Services (HERS), 98 percent of women who HERS referred for a second opinion found they did not need a hysterectomy for the condition they were diagnosed with. HERS, a nonprofit organization, works to educate women about alternative treatments for noncancerous health problems. The organization provides lists of board-certified gynecologists for second opinions. HERS can be reached at 888-750-HERS or 610-667-7757 or online at hersfoundation.com or uterinearteryembolization.com.

The following are "Facts About Hysterectomy," according to HERS:

*Fact:* Women experience a loss of physical sexual sensation as a result of hysterectomy.

*Fact:* A woman's vagina is shortened, scarred, and dislocated by hysterectomy.

*Fact:* Hysterectomy's damage is lifelong. Among its most common consequences, in addition to operative injuries, are:

- heart disease
- osteoporosis
- bone, joint, and muscle pain and immobility
- loss of sexual desire, arousal, and sensation
- painful intercourse and vaginal damage
- displacement of bladder, bowel, and other pelvic organs
- urinary tract infections, frequency, and incontinence
- chronic constipation and digestive disorders
- altered body odor
- loss of short-term memory
- blunting of emotions, personality changes, despondency, irritability, anger, reclusiveness, and suicidal thinking

*Fact:* No drugs or other treatments can replace ovarian or uterine hormones or functions. The loss is permanent.

*Fact:* Most women are castrated at hysterectomy. The medical term for the removal of the ovaries is *castration*.

*Fact:* The uterus and ovaries function throughout life in women who have not been hysterectomized or castrated.

*Fact:* Twice as many women in their twenties and thirties are hysterectomized as women in their fifties and sixties.

*Fact:* Ninety-eight percent of women HERS has referred to board-certified gynecologists after being told they needed hysterectomies discovered that, in fact, they did not need hysterectomies.

*Fact:* Gynecologists, hospitals, and drug companies make more than $5 billion a year from the business of hysterectomy and castration.

HERS is the only independent national organization dedicated to the issue of hysterectomy and advocating for fully informed medical choices by women.

Source: The HERS Foundation, hersfoundation.com, 2003. Reprinted with permission.

# Hysterectomy as Treatment for Debilitating Periods

Some women opt to have a hysterectomy for debilitating periods, particularly as they approach perimenopause. The following are alternative ways to manage debilitating periods:

1. Over-the-counter anti-inflammatory and pain reliever drugs for painful periods or some antihistamines can bring the bleeding under control. (Check with your pharmacist, as some antihistamines are not recommended for this.)

2. Correct an underlying iron deficiency. See under "What to Eat."

3. Correct an underlying thyroid problem. Hypothyroidism (an underactive thyroid) typically causes heavy bleeding and crampier periods. Consult *The Thyroid Sourcebook for Women* for more information.

4. Explore the option of using natural progesterone to regulate bleeding and periods. See Chapter 21 for more details.

5. Try losing some excess weight. Fat tissues produce extra estrogen, which can increase bleeding.

6. Consider alternative therapies, such as acupuncture and an herbal approach. See also under "Flower Power" and "How to Move."

For more information on managing abnormal bleeding, see Chapter 17.

# The Prophylactic Hysterectomy

A prophylactic hysterectomy means removing the uterus to prevent other health problems or diseases you may be at risk for, such as ovarian cancer or uterine cancer. Prophylactic hysterectomy to prevent ovarian cancer may be an option if you're at very high risk for this cancer; however, prophylactic hysterectomy should not be considered as a prevention of uterine cancer. Uterine cancer is a very treatable cancer, although at the time of diagnosis, it is possible a hysterectomy may certainly be warranted. But if you are not on unopposed estrogen, and abnormal bleeding is investigated and treated through hormonal means (see Chapter 17), then the risk of uterine cancer is very low.

Ovarian cancer strikes about one in one hundred women; it drops down to one in one thousand after hysterectomy with the ovaries intact, and it is completely prevented with oophorectomy (see further on), which is the removal of the ovaries. Ovarian cancer is a deadly cancer that may well be worth avoiding if you are considered at high risk for this cancer because of family history or a genetic predisposition. However, the preferred route generally is a prophylactic oophorectomy that preserves the uterus, which can prevent some of the complications of hysterectomy such as incontinence, prolapse, and so on. For more information on ovarian health and prophylactic oophorectomy, see Chapter 4.

# Complications of a Hysterectomy

Women need the uterus and its surrounding ligaments to keep the organs separate from intestines and allow the bladder and rectum to maintain their correct position. So removing the uterus can cause other complications aside from surgical menopause, which include constipation, bloating, painful sex, and incontinence. These are the long-term surgical complications of hysterectomy. Short-term complications of hysterectomy include postoperative infections and hemorrhage.

As many as half the women who undergo a hysterectomy will experience some of the following complications in the short or long term:

- *Hemorrhaging:* One in ten women will require a blood transfusion as a result of hemorrhaging (blood loss) after or during the procedure. Often a preexisting condition of anemia is the cause. You may want to consider banking some of your own blood prior to the procedure—or before any elective surgery, for that matter. This is called autologous blood donation. In the event of heavy blood loss during your surgery, you are transfused with your own blood.

- *Eventual ovarian failure:* If your ovaries are left intact, the unfortunate truth is that you may still go into surgical menopause. Women are often told that their hormone levels will not be affected if their ovaries are left intact. This is not necessarily true. Even when your ovaries are not removed, there's a chance they will stop producing hormones. A rich network of blood vessels lies between the uterus and the ovaries and can be disturbed by removal of the uterus. Between 25 and 50 percent of all women who have intact ovaries after a hysterectomy will experience ovarian failure and go into surgical menopause. In addition, premenopausal women who lose their uterus but still have their ovaries go into menopause five years earlier than do women who don't have hysterectomies. The hormonal side effects of hysterectomy are discussed in Chapter 19.

- *Blood clots:* Blood clots can develop up to one week following the operation.

- *Depression:* Postoperative depression after a hysterectomy sets in three times more often than in other major surgical procedures. Whether you're prone to this depends on why your hysterectomy was done, your psychological state before your surgery, and whether you want to bear (more) children. Many women mourn the loss of the uterus, and some women feel as though their femininity has been stripped from them. In addition, surgical menopausal symptoms can aggravate some of these natural emotions. Hormone replacement therapy can help. For more information, consult my book *Women and Depression.*

- *Infections:* Fifty percent of all hysterectomy patients will suffer from various bacterial infections, which can be controlled with antibiotics. These infections include UTIs, discussed in Chapter 5.

- *Urinary incontinence:* The uterus and its surrounding ligaments support the rest of your pelvic contents, allowing the bladder and rectum to maintain their correct positions. After a hysterectomy, you can become constipated and bloated but also find that you can't hold in your urine. A study published in *The Lancet* indicates that women who have undergone a hysterectomy procedure are far more likely to suffer from urinary incontinence. The researchers indicate that they have a 60 percent higher risk of being incontinent by age sixty. Aside from UTIs, sensory nerves may be cut and women can lose both the sensation of having to urinate and control over bladder functions.

- *Bowel problems:* If there is damage to the intestines during surgery, scar tissue can form and complicate your bowel function. This occurs in about 2 percent of all hysterectomy patients.

- *Narrowing of the vagina:* If a vaginal repair was performed in the event of prolapse, scar tissue can form from improper healing, which will narrow your vaginal opening, making intercourse painful.

- *Nerve damage:* Nerves are severed during the surgery, which could cause numbness in your thigh, your leg, or other parts of your body below your pelvic region. However, severed nerves can occur in any surgery and are not exclusive to hysterectomies.

- *Decreased pleasure during orgasm:* Orgasm can result from stimulation of the clitoris, uterus, or both. Pressure on the cervix, the uterus, and its surrounding ligaments and membranes can heighten an orgasm.

- *Residual ovary syndrome:* Following hysterectomy with conservation of the ovaries, scar tissue forms around the ovaries and cysts tend to form, resulting in pain. This condition is difficult to treat medically and may require removal of the ovaries.

- *Fatigue:* According to a study by researchers at UCLA Medical Center, based on telephone surveys with three hundred women who had had hysterectomies over the past two years, 74 percent reported that they experienced moderate to severe fatigue following surgery, compared to 63 percent of women who said that they experienced moderate to severe pain.

- *Diminished sex life:* Some women find that a hysterectomy increases their quality of life, leaving them free from bleeding and pain that can dramatically affect their sex life. Unfortunately, the majority of women report their sex life diminishes after a hysterectomy, largely due to the effects of surgical menopause (see Chapter 19), which can reduce vaginal lubrication, but also because they lose some sensation during intercourse involving the penis's pressure on the cervix, the uterus, and surrounding ligaments and membranes, which for some women can produce an intense and pleasurable orgasm that is different than simple clitoral stimulation. Women who experience primarily clitoral orgasms may not experience a difference in their sex life. Lately, the term *breast orgasm* has surfaced; this refers to an orgasm that is produced through suckling the breast during lovemaking, which stimulates the hormone oxytocin, also responsible for uterine contractions. Oxytocin is the very same hormone active during breast-feeding. Intercourse can also be affected if the vagina has been shortened during surgery; in this case, scar tissue may form in the vagina or pelvis, resulting in pain during sex. This can be corrected by using a candle or an insertion aid to help to stretch the vagina, discussed more in Chapter 18.

# What to Eat

Because of heavy blood loss as a complication of hysterectomy, many women are iron deficient. If you're between the ages of nineteen and fifty, the recommended daily iron intake is 18 mg; if you're past fifty, the recommended daily intake is 8 mg. To give you an idea, three ounces of lean beef provides roughly 3 mg iron, half a cup of beans in tomato sauce provides about 5 mg iron, while one-half cup of Cream of Wheat provides about 8 mg iron because it is fortified. In other words, starting your day with an iron-fortified cereal and incorporating some red meat and legumes in your diet following surgery can help to boost your iron levels. The most absorbable iron, heme iron, comes from animal sources: beef, fish, poultry, pork, and lamb. Plant foods contain less absorbable iron. Iron supplements are usually not necessary; a multivitamin will give you about 10 to 15 mg iron.

If you're only getting iron from plant sources (because you're vegetarian, for example), including vitamin C with each meal can maximize absorption of nonheme iron. You should also avoid drinking tea with your meals.

To combat depression and fatigue, a varied diet is recommended. For more information on depression, consult my books *Women and Depression* or *50 Ways to Fight Depression Without Drugs*.

# Flower Power

The Chinese herb dong quai is known to help reduce bleeding. To combat anemia from blood loss, what is known in Chinese medicine as Return Spleen Tablets (*giupi wan* in Chinese) is used. For depression, thorowax root, Chinese angelica root, white peony root, and licorice are frequently used. For exhaustion, Korean ginseng, royal jelly, and astragalus are used in Chinese medicine.

### *Aromatherapy*

Reportedly aphrodisiacs, the following oils are thought to aid with sexual arousal: rose, neroli, clary sage, patchouli, ylang-ylang, jasmine, black pepper, cardamom, and sandalwood.

# How to Move

If you've had a hysterectomy, strengthening your bladder can help to prevent urinary incontinence. Review Chapter 5 for Kegel exercises and other exercises that strengthen your urinary tract. The movements listed in the following sections can help with other complications of hysterectomy.

## For Anemia

If you have suffered from blood loss or excessive bleeding after a hysterectomy, the following yoga postures are helpful:

- Fish Posture
- Pose of Tranquility
- Back-Stretching Posture
- The Cobra
- Half Locust
- Half or Full Shoulder Stand
- Sun Salutations

The following kinds of yogic breathing are also recommended: complete breathing and cooling breathing.

## For Depression

Activity and exercise will help to create endorphins—"feel good" chemicals that are known to combat depression. The following yoga postures are helpful for combating depression:

- Sun Salutations
- Pose of Tranquility
- Angle Balance
- The Tree
- Balance Posture
- Chest Expander
- The Plough
- The Cobra
- Spinal Twist
- Half or Full Shoulder Stand

Alternate nostril breathing, antianxiety breathing, cleansing breathing, and complete breathing are also recommended daily.

## *Fatigue*

Going for short walks daily is helpful in fighting fatigue. The following yoga postures are also recommended:

- Sun Salutations
- Mountain Posture
- Prayer Pose
- The Tree
- Chest Expander
- Stick Posture
- Legs Up
- Child's Pose
- Half or Full Shoulder Stand
- Candle Concentration
- Pose of Tranquility
- The Crocodile

The following yogic breathing is also recommended: alternate nostril breathing, antianxiety breathing, cleansing breathing, complete breathing, humming breathing, and singing breathing. The eye exercise in yoga called Eye Splashing is also recommended to combat fatigue.

# 21

# What to Do About Hormone Replacement Therapy (HRT)

IN JULY 2001 a study by the U.S. National Heart, Lung, and Blood Institute, part of a huge research program called the Women's Health Initiative, suggested that hormone replacement therapy should not be recommended for long-term use; in fact, the results were so alarming, the study was halted before its completion date. It was found that Prempro, a combination of estrogen and progestin, which was a "standard issue" HRT formulation for postmenopausal women, increased the risk of invasive breast cancer, heart disease, stroke, and pulmonary embolisms (blood clots). However, Prempro *did* reduce the incidence of bone fractures from osteoporosis and colon cancer. Nevertheless, the idea that HRT is a long-term "fountain of youth" is slowly dissolving. The study participants were informed in a letter that they should stop taking their pills. HRT in the short term to relieve menopausal symptoms is still considered a good option, and there was no evidence to suggest that short-term use of HRT was harmful. The study only has implications for women on HRT for long-term use—something that was recommended to millions of women over the past twenty years because of perceived protection against heart disease.

In 1998 an earlier trial, known as the Heart and Estrogen/Progestin Replacement Study, looked at whether HRT was reduced in women who already had heart disease. HRT was not found to have any beneficial effect. Women who were at risk for breast cancer were never advised to go on HRT; similarly, women who had suffered a stroke or who were considered at risk for blood clots were also never considered good candidates for HRT. It had long been known that breast cancer was a risk of long-term HRT, as well as stroke and blood clots. However, many women made the HRT decision based on the fact that it was long believed to protect women from heart disease. Millions of women are now questioning whether they should be on HRT in light of what many experts are calling the "9-11 of HRT." This chapter provides you with the new rules about HRT.

# What Is HRT?

Hormone replacement therapy (HRT) refers to estrogen *and* progestin, which is a factory-made progesterone, given to women after menopause who still have their uterus to prevent the lining from overgrowing and becoming cancerous (known as endometrial hyperplasia, discussed in Chapter 17). Estrogen replacement therapy (ERT) refers to estrogen only, which is given to women who no longer have a uterus after surgical menopause. Both HRT and ERT are designed to replace the estrogen lost after menopause and hence:

1. Prevent or even reverse the long-term consequences of estrogen loss. The only proven long-term benefit of HRT is that it can help to preserve bone loss and reduce the incidence of fractures. Until July 2001 it was believed that HRT protected women from cardiovascular disease, but this is no longer considered true. In women who are at higher risk of breast cancer, HRT was always believed to be risky; now it is believed that it may trigger breast cancer in low-risk women.

2. Treat the short-term discomforts of menopause, such as hot flashes and vaginal dryness. This is all still true, and you can discuss with your doctor how long he or she recommends that you stay on HRT before it becomes risky.

Once you weigh the benefits and risks, if you decide to be treated with conventional HRT or ERT, you have the choice of using it as either a short-term therapy or a long-term therapy.

## *Being a Slave to the Medical System*

An obvious but underreported risk of HRT is that it forces you into another continuous cycle: one of constant doctor visits and tests. And each time you go to your doctor, you risk some sort of invasive procedure or referral for invasive tests. For example, women on HRT are more likely to be prescribed the following tests or medications:

- blood tests for hormone levels
- diuretics for fluid retention
- Ponstan, aspirin, or other analgesics for uterine cramps
- endometrial biopsies to check the endometrium
- D & C for bleeding

- blood pressure tests
- blood tests for cholesterol levels
- baseline mammograms before starting therapy and regular mammograms thereafter
- visits for repeat prescriptions of hormones at least every six months

Women who are not on HRT are not burdened by as many tests, visits, and other procedures. Do these increased doctor visits save lives because they offer early detection of many serious diseases? Critics of HRT argue that women are paying a higher price for their dependency on the medical system and are burdened with too much monitoring and early detection.

## The Forms of HRT and ERT

You can take estrogen in a number of ways. The most common estrogen product uses a synthesis of various estrogens that are derived from the urine of pregnant horses. That way the estrogen mimics nature more accurately. Estrogen replacement comes in either pills, patches (transdermal), or vaginal creams. Other common, synthetic forms of estrogen include micronized estradiol, ethinyl estradiol, esterified estrogen, and quinestrol.

As a short-term therapy, you may only need the vaginal cream to help with vaginal dryness or bladder problems. Estrogen can also be "worn." In this case, it's placed in a small plastic patch about the size of a silver dollar, worn on the abdomen, thighs, or buttocks, and changed twice weekly.

When estrogen is in patch or cream form, it goes directly to the bloodstream, bypassing the liver; this form of estrogen was previously discouraged for some women because it was not considered to have any protection against heart disease. But in light of the recent risk of heart disease with conventional formulations of HRT, the patch may pose no long-term harm, and you may want to discuss whether this is an option for more long-term use. Some women also have an allergic reaction to the skin patch and get a rash. If you're one of them, you can investigate taking the estrogen in other forms.

Finally, you can also have estrogen injected. Each shot lasts between three and six weeks, but this is expensive and inconvenient. Estrogen gel containing estradiol is now being used in some parts of the world, though it is not yet available in North America. The gel is spread over a wide area of the abdomen every second day. The problem women have encountered with this method is a variation in levels of absorption each time the gel is applied.

Even more controversial are the pellets or implants containing estradiol inserted under the skin of the abdomen or buttocks under local anesthetic. Subcutaneous implants are also not yet available in North America, primarily because they are difficult to remove or halt if a woman experiences complications.

## What About Progestin?

This is the synthetic version of progesterone that is found in all combination oral contraceptives and the injectable contraceptive Depo-Provera. Progesterone receptors do not recognize progestin and will not transport it to the cells. This may account for many of the progestin-related side effects that mimic PMS. The most common progestins include Provera, Amen, Curretab, and Cycrin (all brand names of medroxyprogesterone acetate); Duralutin, Gesterol L.A., Hylutin, and Hyprogest 250 (all brand names of hydroxyprogesterone caproate); Norlutate, Norgestrel, and Aygestin (all brand names of norethindrone acetate); Norlutin (norethindrone); and Magace (megestrol acetate). Micronor, Nor-Q.D., and Ovrette are other brand-name progestins on the market.

Progestins are taken in separate tablets along with estrogen. Together, the estrogen and progestin you take is called HRT. HRT can be administered two ways: cyclically or continuously. Taking HRT cyclically is very similar to taking an oral contraceptive because the hormones more closely mirror a natural cycle. The first day you start is considered day 1 of your mock cycle. You take estrogen from day 1 to day 25; you then add the progesterone from day 14 to day 25. Then you stop all pills and bleed for two or three days—just as you would on a combination oral contraceptive. This vaginal bleeding is called withdrawal bleeding, which is lighter and shorter than a normal menstrual period, lasting only two or three days—just like a period on a combination oral contraceptive. In fact, if the bleeding is heavy or prolonged for some reason, this is a warning that something's not right, and you should get it checked.

In addition, you may experience breakthrough bleeding, or spotting, during the first three weeks after you begin HRT. This kind of bleeding is, again, similar to what happens on a combination oral contraceptive. This bleeding usually goes away after a few months, but report it anyway. You may need to switch to a lower dose of estrogen or take a higher dose of your progestin. Once your miniperiod of withdrawal bleeding is finished, you simply start the cycle again. Many women can't tolerate cyclical HRT because they feel as though they should be rid of their periods by now and not have to deal with pads and tampons ever again. However, it is believed that cyclical HRT offers slightly better heart protection.

When HRT is taken continuously, you simply take one estrogen pill and one progestin pill each day. When you do it this way, the progesterone counteracts the estrogen; no uterine lining is built up, so there's no withdrawal bleeding that needs to happen.

## The Appropriate Dosages

Every woman requires a different dosage of estrogen and progestin. But initially you will always be placed on the lowest possible dosage of either one and may have the dosage increased gradually if necessary. If your estrogen dosage is too high, you'll experience side effects similar to those seen with oral contraceptives: headaches, bloating, and so on.

So before you or your doctor determines how much estrogen you'll need, it's crucial to first determine how much your body is still producing; this really depends on your weight, estrogen loss discomforts, and a hundred other things.

## Common Side Effects

If you're taking cyclical progestins with your estrogen because you still have your uterus, bleeding is not a side effect! The whole point of adding progestin to your estrogen is to trigger withdrawal bleeding and get your uterine lining routinely shed. However, if you're taking continuous progestins with your estrogen, bleeding is not the norm and should be checked into.

A common side effect of estrogen is fluid retention, because estrogen will decrease the amount of salt and water excreted by kidneys, which is retained by legs, breasts, and feet, which can swell. Because of the fluid retention, you may weigh more, but you will not necessarily be fatter.

Nausea is another common side effect, also seen with oral contraceptives. This happens during the first two or three months of your therapy and should just disappear on its own. Some women find that taking their dosages at night (for pills) may remedy this. Decreasing the dosage is also an option.

Some other side effects reported include headaches, skin color changes (called melasma) on the face, more cervical mucus secretion, liquid secretion from the breasts, change in curvature of the cornea, jaundice, loss of scalp hair, and itchiness. Again, these side effects vary and depend on the brand you're taking, the dosage, your medical history, and so on.

## Are You an HRT or ERT Candidate?

In light of the recent shadow cast over HRT, clearly it is not for everyone. If you answer yes to any of the following questions, you might consider short-term or long-term use of HRT or ERT:

- Do you suffer from severe hot flashes that don't respond to the natural remedies discussed in Chapter 19 in the section "Flower Power"?

- Are your vaginal changes causing urinary tract infections, vaginitis, or painful intercourse, which does not respond to such remedies as more stimulation of the clitoris during sex or sexual lubricants?

- Are you concerned about developing osteoporosis? Studies still support that using HRT or ERT in the long term may lower your risk of developing osteoporosis. (But so will exercise and a high-calcium diet.) There are now bone-building drugs that are alternatives to HRT and ERT, which you can discuss with your doctor.

## Women Who Shouldn't Be on HRT or ERT

Women who suffer from certain medical conditions should not be on HRT or ERT as discussed in the following list:

- Women with a history of endometrial cancer should not be on unopposed estrogen ERT. Again, if you still have a uterus, you'll be placed on HRT (estrogen and progesterone), which lowers your cancer risk anyway.

- Women with breast cancer or a history of breast cancer or who are considered at high risk for breast cancer should not be on either HRT or ERT.

- Women who have had a stroke should not be on either HRT or ERT.

- Women who have a blood-clotting disorder should not be on either HRT or ERT.

- Women with undiagnosed vaginal bleeding should not be on HRT or ERT.

- Women with liver dysfunction may be on the estrogen patch or use vaginal cream to relieve menopausal discomforts but shouldn't take any pills orally.

## Women Who May Benefit More from HRT or ERT

Discuss with your doctor whether you're a candidate for HRT or ERT, given the protective effects each has against osteoporosis and colon cancer. However, you may need to think twice if you have any of the following other conditions:

- sickle cell disease
- high blood pressure
- migraines
- uterine fibroids
- a history of benign breast conditions such as cysts or fibroadenomas

- endometriosis
- seizures
- gallbladder disease
- a family history of breast cancer
- a past or current history of smoking

# Natural Hormone Replacement Therapy (NHRT)

Many of you may have heard the media hype surrounding natural hormone replacement therapy (NHRT), which includes natural progesterone, versus conventional hormone replacement therapy (HRT). The difference is akin to the difference between breast milk and formula for a baby. NHRT is a combination of human estrogens and natural human progesterone. HRT, on the other hand, is a factory-made estrogen, much of which is derived from horse estrogen, and a factory-made progesterone, called progestin. Now many reports and studies show that the symptoms of menopause are better controlled with NHRT, and with fewer side effects.

## *What NHRT Contains*

When you go on NHRT, you're getting about 60 to 80 percent estriol, 10 to 20 percent estrone, and 10 to 20 percent estradiol, as well as natural human progesterone plus DHEA (dehydroepiandrosterone), a "natural androgen," if you will, that turns into a "natural testosterone" in the body, something all women need to maintain sex drives. On HRT you're getting 75 to 80 percent estrone, 6 to 15 percent equilin (a horse-derived estrogen), and about 5 to 19 percent estradiol, as well as progestin, a factory-made progesterone, and sometimes anabolic steroids, if your libido needs a boost.

The bottom line is that human women do better with human hormones rather than animal-derived hormones, just like human infants do better on human milk than cow's milk. However, as you can see from the range of concentrations of various natural estrogens, it may take a while for you to find just the right dose of each kind of natural estrogen and progesterone, so you have to work with your doctor and experiment until you get it right. There is a perception out there that NHRT is perfect the first time you take it, but many women have to tinker with their "triple estrogens" before they find the right combination: a typical prescription for NHRT is often 10 percent estrone, 10 percent estradiol, and 80 percent estriol, mixed with about 25 to 30 mg natural progesterone after menopause and 10 to 30 mg DHEA, which should, but doesn't always, convert into necessary amounts of testosterone. (If it doesn't, you may need to add a steroid to the mix of natural hormones if your libido is very low, which can be debilitating.)

## *Where Do You Find NHRT?*

All the books and articles about NHRT can mislead you into thinking that NHRT is just available everywhere. This is not so. You can't simply walk into a health food store and buy natural estrogens or progesterones. They need to be prescribed by a doctor (although the doctor need not be an M.D.; several naturopathic doctors are prescribing them, too). A pharmacist, known as a compounding pharmacist, has to prepare a doctor's prescription for NHRT from scratch. Not all pharmacies are compounding pharmacies, so ask your doctor or current pharmacist about where to go to get such a prescription prepared. You can also call the International Academy of Compounding Pharmacists (IACP) or the Professional Compounding Centers of America (PCCA) for the nearest compounding pharmacist in your area. Most compounding pharmacists are members of either or both organizations. You can reach the IACP at 800-927-4227 or go to iacprx.org and the PCCA at 800-331-2498 or pccarx.com.

# Phytoestrogens: The HRT Alternative

If you are uncomfortable with the idea of taking any kind of hormone replacement therapy, you may wish to consider the therapeutic benefits of phytoestrogens, or plant estrogens. Many women treat their discomforts with herbs, as outlined in the "Flower Power" section later in this chapter.

Phytoestrogens contain a multitude of chemicals, including estrogenic substances. Although phytoestrogens have been used in Asian cultures for centuries to treat hot flashes, they're just beginning to catch on in the West. The first controlled trial began in 1996 at Columbia-Presbyterian Medical Center in New York.

Many food sources, such as soy, contain such high concentrations of phytoestrogens that scientists believe it may account for the incredible lack of menopausal discomforts in Japan, which has a soy-heavy diet. Blood levels of phytoestrogens are ten to forty times higher in Japanese women than in their Western counterparts, but Japanese women report hot flashes about one-sixth as often as Western women. Even the average vegetarian would not consume nearly as much soy as the average Japanese woman.

More interesting, plant hormones not only help prevent menopausal discomforts but also may protect you from breast cancer. Breast cancer rates are dramatically lower in Japan than in the United States, but there may be other factors involved, such as childbearing habits and fat intake. After menopause, high-fat diets can increase your risk of heart attack or stroke no matter how much estrogen you take. Meanwhile, bad habits, such as drinking coffee or alcohol or smoking, can all increase your risk of osteoporosis. Right now, most doctors will tell you to go ahead and add as much soy as you want to your diet. It may well help—and it certainly can't hurt! Soy has most recently been declared a "heart-healthy" food.

## *What Are the Drawbacks?*

The problem with phytoestrogens is that they are plant hormones and not human hormones, which means that they will not solve the problem of rising FSH and LH levels (the gonadotropins, which "kick-start" the ovaries). However, some plants do encourage estrogen production, and some do contain flavonoids, which are estrogen-like.

Plant hormones can be converted to human hormones in a laboratory. What plant hormones do is to provide you with hormonal building blocks rather than hormones themselves, which in theory can allow you to create the amounts (and combinations) of hormones you need for your unique menopausal journey.

It is possible to have allergic reactions to a variety of herbs. It's also important to note that because herbal products are not regulated, there is a danger of misuse, overuse, or using poor quality merchandise.

Phytoestrogens can be taken orally or even in creams, which can be applied to your body parts. Creams are "quasi-natural," however, because the plant hormones they contain are modified in a lab. One good question many women are asking is whether phytoestrogens carry the same risks as HRT. The answer is that because plant-based hormones contain chemicals that are similar but not identical to your natural estrogen, the risks of plant hormones are that you may still suffer from discomfort associated with estrogen loss in spite of your dedication to ingesting plant hormones.

# John Lee's Estrogen Dominance Theory

Dr. John Lee is the next big name in the natural progesterone story. In the mid-1990s he began to publish his theory that many women are progesterone deficient due to estrogen dominance, which can be caused by synthetic estrogens in oral contraceptives or other hormone therapies; by obesity, which results in too much estrogen because fat cells make estrogen; by estrogen pollution, caused by the flushed urine of women on all these synthetic estrogens, which gets into our sewage systems and water supply; as well as by another form of pollution known as environmental estrogens, also called xenoestrogens, which are beyond our control. Hormones in meat are other sources of estrogen. Estrogen dominance can cause a myriad of women's health problems. Unless there is an equal ratio of progesterone to estrogen, estrogen dominance can mean a progesterone deficiency. And for some women, that translates into more severe menopausal symptoms as well as more severe PMS symptoms (see Chapter 2).

# Estrogen and Progesterone

**Signs of Estrogen Dominance**
- accelerated aging
- allergies (asthma, rashes, sinus congestion)
- autoimmune disorders
- blood clots and risk of stroke
- breast tenderness
- cervical dysplasia
- decreased libido
- depression, anxiety, and agitation
- difficulty concentrating
- dry eyes
- early menstruation
- fatigue
- fibrocystic breasts
- fibroids
- gallbladder disease
- hair loss
- headaches
- hypoglycemia
- hypothyroidism
- infertility
- insomnia
- irregular cycles
- irritability
- memory loss
- miscarriage
- mood swings
- osteoporosis prior to menopause
- PMS
- slow metabolism
- uterine cancer

- water retention or bloating
- weight gain

## What Estrogen Is Normally Supposed to Do to the Body
- decreases libido
- impairs blood sugar control (counterbalanced by progesterone)
- increases blood clotting (counterbalanced by progesterone)
- increases body fat (counterbalanced by progesterone)
- interferes with thyroid hormone (counterbalanced by progesterone)
- reduces oxygen levels in cells (counterbalanced by progesterone)
- reduces vascular tone
- retains salt and fluids
- slows bone loss (counterbalanced by progesterone)
- stimulates breasts (counterbalanced by progesterone)
- thickens the lining of the uterus (counterbalanced by progesterone)

*Note:* when not counterbalanced by progesterone, many of these normal functions can evolve into diseases, such as breast cancer or uterine cancer.

## What Progesterone Is Normally Supposed to Do to the Body
- maintains the uterine lining with secretions
- counterbalances breast stimulation
- helps convert fat into energy
- acts as a natural diuretic
- acts as a natural antidepressant
- facilitates thyroid hormone (counterbalanced by estrogen)
- normalizes blood sugar levels (counterbalanced by estrogen)
- normalizes blood clotting
- increases libido
- normalizes zinc and copper levels
- restores cell oxygen levels
- stimulates bone-building cells

*Note:* when it's balanced, progesterone helps protect against many diseases, such as breast cancer or uterine cancer.

# Where to Find Natural Progesterone

As discussed earlier, you must go to a compounding pharmacist to find natural progesterone. What you can get over the counter in some health food stores and natural pharmacies are creams containing botanical progesterone, which is progesterone that comes from plants such as wild yam. This is not harmful, but it will not be as pure as the progesterone your doctor prescribes, which often comes from soy and wild yam, too, but is a very pure extraction. The term *natural* does not mean "human"—instead, it means that it is not synthetic. Natural progesterone is recognized by our progesterone receptors as if it were progesterone we made in our bodies.

## *Creams*

Progesterone works very well in cream form. There are a few kinds:

- creams that contain only progesterone in a carrier such as aloe vera or vitamin E
- creams with progesterone and other essential oils or herbs
- creams that contain progesterone and phytoestrogens (plant estrogens)
- creams that contain progesterone and three kinds of natural estrogen

Creams that contain estrogen are not for you; these creams are for menopausal women who are using natural hormone therapy to relieve estrogen loss and other menopausal discomforts.

Natural progesterone can also be found in an oil form (which is taken under the tongue), as tablets, as capsules, as vaginal suppositories, as a vaginal gel, and in an injectable form.

# What to Eat

To try to get phytoestrogens in your diet, eating a high-soy diet may help to reduce the discomforts of perimenopause (see Chapter 19). Some suggested soy foods include:

- *Calcium-fortified soy beverage:* You can substitute this for milk in your cooking, baking, etc.
- *Canned soybeans:* You can add these to soups, chili, stews, etc.
- *Tofu:* Buy this in cubes or squares. You can use tofu as a substitution for meats or add it to most dishes, such as stir-fries, soups, or lasagna (in place of ricotta cheese).
- *Soy flour:* You can replace all-purpose flour with soy flour.
- *Roasted soy nuts:* These are great for snacking.

- *Texturized vegetable protein:* This is a common meat substitute found in most natural food stores.
- *Veggie or tofu burgers and dogs:* You can substitute these veggie alternatives for hamburgers and hot dogs.

# Flower Power

You can find herbal estrogen and progesterone, too.

### *Estrogen Herbs*

The following herbs help promote estrogen production, help stabilize infrequent periods, and may reduce the severity of estrogen-loss discomforts:

- alfalfa and red clover flowers or leaves
- black cohosh roots
- hops (female flowers)
- licorice roots
- sage leaves
- sweetbrier hips or leaf buds
- pomegranate seeds
- any herb containing flavonoids

### *Progesterone Herbs*

The following herbs help promote progesterone production and help stabilize too-frequent periods:

- chaste tree (*Vitex*) berries
- sarsaparilla roots
- wild yam roots
- yarrow flowers and leaves

### *Phytoestrogens*

The following are plant estrogens, which may help with a myriad of menopausal discomforts:

- agave (*Agave americana*; one dose is one-fourth to one teaspoon [1 to 5 ml] of juice of the leaves)
- alfalfa

- black cohosh
- black currant
- black haw
- Bockshornklee
- Casses (*Ribes nigrum*)
- chaste tree (*Vitex agnus castus*)
- cramp bark or guelder rose
- dandelion
- dong quai (*Angelica sinensis*)
- fenugreek (good for hot flashes)
- garden sage (*Salvia officinalis*; good for night sweats)
- Gemeines Kreuzkraut
- ginseng (*Panax quinquefolium*)
- groundsel
- Hopfen
- hops
- Houblon grimpant (*Humulus lupulus*)
- Licorice (note: this can be toxic in high doses, causing high blood pressure and water retention)
- liferoot (*Senecio aureus*)
- Lowenzahn
- Luzerne
- Luzerne cultivee (*Medicago sativa*)
- motherwort (*Leonurus cardiaca*; good for night sweats)
- nettles (*Urtica dioica* or *U. urens*)
- peony (frequently combines with dong quai)
- pomegranate (*Punica granatum*; these seeds pack 1.7 gm estrone for every three ounces—just eat the seeds instead of spitting them out when you consume the fruit, or make them into a smoothie in the blender; you can also grind them and infuse in oil to make your own estrogen cream)
- raspberry
- red clover (*Trifolium praetense*)
- rose "family" (raspberry, strawberry, sweetbrier, and hawthorn; rose hips are an excellent source of flavonoids)
- sarsaparilla (*Smilax officinalis* or *S. regelii*; Jamaican is considered best, with Mexican and Honduran following closely)
- saw palmetto (*Serenoa serrulata*)
- Schlangenwurzel

- Schwarze Johannisbeere
- Senecon Commun (*Senecio vulgaris*) and her sister plant, Jacob's groundsel (Jakobskraut Senecon Jacobee [*Senecio Jacobea*]; these are closely related to liferoot)
- sweetbrier or dog rose, Hagrose, Eglantier (*Rosa canina* or *R. pendulina*)
- Viorne obier (*Viburnum opulus*) or Viburnum (*Viburnum prunifolium*)
- wild yam (*Dioscorea villosa* and all five hundred related species; progesterone cream derived from wild yam has been shown to reverse osteoporosis)
- yarrow (*Achillea millefolium*)

# How to Move

Whether you're on conventional HRT or not, it's important to do three things: maximize bone strength, do a monthly breast self-exam, and strengthen your heart muscle through cardiovascular, aerobic exercises.

## *To Strengthen Bones*

Maintaining bone mass and good bone health is your best defense against bone loss, also known as osteoporosis. Eighty percent of all osteoporosis sufferers are women as a direct result of estrogen loss.

## *Enjoyable Activities That May Help Build Bone Mass*

From this list, choose the one activity that you find to be most enjoyable. If you enjoy your activity, you'll do it more often.

- walking
- running
- jogging
- bicycling
- hiking
- tai chi
- cross-country skiing
- gardening
- weight lifting

- snowshoeing
- climbing stairs
- tennis
- bowling
- rowing
- dancing
- water workouts
- badminton
- basketball
- volleyball
- soccer

The following yoga postures can help to strengthen the bones:

- Squatting Posture
- The Tree
- Balance Posture
- Eagle Posture
- Rock and Roll
- Back-Stretching Posture
- The Plough
- Triangle Posture
- The Cobra
- The Bow
- Lying Twist
- Half Moon
- Angle Posture
- Spinal Twist
- Half or Full Shoulder Stand
- Sun Salutations

## To Strengthen the Heart

The activities that are labeled "more intense" tend to be considered aerobic, meaning that they increase oxygen flow to the heart. Refer to "How to Move" in Chapter 17 for variations on jogging and water workouts.

**More Intense**
- skiing
- running
- jogging
- stair stepping or stair climbing
- trampoline
- jumping rope
- fitness walking
- race walking
- aerobic classes
- roller-blading
- ice-skating
- biking
- weight-bearing exercises
- tennis
- sport swimming
- weight lifting
- wrestling

**Less Intense**
- golf
- bowling
- badminton
- croquet
- sailing
- leisure swimming
- strolling
- stretching

Certain activities, such as wrestling or weight lifting, are usually short but very intense. As a result, people with certain health problems may not be able to partake. For example, if you have heart problems or diabetes or are taking medications that can affect your heart, intense exercise is not recommended.

## Breast Self-Examination (BSE)

This method should be called "get to know your breasts." It involves specific steps of feeling your breasts at the same time each month and distinguishing suspicious lumps from normal lumpy or bumpy breasts. In addition, you can't know if a lump has remained unchanged unless you've been checking your breasts monthly.

Although the steps to BSE are outlined here, make sure your doctor actually *shows* you how to do it as well. In addition, there is a kit available through the National Cancer Institute called the MammaCare Personal Learning System, which consists of a forty-five-minute video and a thirty-page instructional manual. This kit was designed to teach you how to do a breast self-exam using what's known as a vertical grid pattern—currently the most effective pattern. The kit was developed at the University of Florida and was partially funded by the National Cancer Institute.

At any rate, here are the steps to BSE:

1. *Visually inspect your breasts with your arms at your sides.* Stand in front of a mirror and look closely at your breasts. You're looking for dimpling, puckering (like an orange peel in appearance), or noticeable lumps. Do you see any discharge that dribbles out on its own or bleeding from the nipple? Any funny dry patches on the nipple (which may be Paget's disease)?

2. *Visually inspect your breasts with your arms raised.* Still standing in front of the mirror, raise your arms over your head and look for the same things. (Raising your arms smoothes out the breasts a little more so these changes are more obvious.)

3. *Palpate (feel) your breast.* Lie down on your bed with a pillow under your left shoulder and place your left hand under your head. With the flat part of the fingertips of your right hand, examine your left breast for a lump, using a gentle circular motion. Imagine that the breast is a clock, and make sure you feel each "hour," as well as the nipple area and armpit area.

4. *Repeat step 3, but reverse sides* . . . examining your right breast with your left hand.

5. *If you find a lump* . . . note the size, the shape, and how painful it is. A suspicious lump is usually painless, is about one-fourth to one-half inch in size, and remains unchanged from month to month. Get your lump looked at as soon as you can, or if you're comfortable doing so, wait for the next cycle or month. If the lump changes in the next cycle or month by shrinking or becoming painful, it's not cancerous, but it should be looked at anyway. If the suspicious lump stays the same, definitely get it looked at as soon as possible. Keep in mind that breast cysts are common, variable in size, and occasionally tender.

6. *If discharge oozes out of your nipple on its own or if blood comes out* . . . see your doctor immediately. Don't wait.

7. *If your nipple is dry and patchy* . . . see your doctor immediately. Don't wait.

# Appendix A

## *Links to Gynecological Information*

For more information about disease prevention and wellness, visit me online at sarahealth .com, where you will find more than three hundred links—including these—related to your good health and wellness.

### General Gynecological Health
- American Health Care Association: ahca.org
- American Medical Women's Association: amwa-doc.org
- GYN 101—information on how to be an informed health care consumer; especially for younger women: gyn101.com
- Health Oasis—Mayo Clinic: mayohealth.org/mayo/common/htm/index.htm
- National Women's Health Resource Center: healthywomen.org
- Prochoice: prochoiceconnection.com/pro-can/history.html
- Salon.com—sharp, engaging Web magazine for women, with lots of great health information and advice: salon.com
- Women's Health Information Center: ourbodiesourselves.org

### Menstrual Disorders and Endometriosis
- Center for Endometriosis Care—facts on diagnosis, education, and treatment; free newsletter: centerforendo.com
- CyclesPage—Web-based application for tracking your menstrual cycle: cyclespage.com
- Endometriosis Association—information and support: endometriosisassn.org

- Inlet Medical Inc.—information for women experiencing pain during intercourse, pain during menstruation, infertility, endometriosis, difficulty with tampons as a result of a retroverted or tipped uterus, and so on: inletmedical.org
- Institute for the Study and Treatment of Endometriosis: endometriosisinstitute.com
- Melpomene Institute—nonprofit research organization dedicated to women's health and physical activity; good source of information on exercise and menstruation: melpomene.org
- Menstrual Migraine Network—information about hormone-induced headaches: http://members.tripod.com~wbgray/index.html

### Gynecological Cancer–Related Sites
- Alternatives to Hysterectomy—information on alternative treatments: althysterectomy.org/default.htm
- American Cancer Society—information and support: cancer.org
- CancerBACUP—information and support: cancerbacup.org.uk

### Emotional Health
- American Association of Marriage and Family Therapy: amft.org
- American Counseling Association: counseling.org
- American Psychiatric Association: psych.org
- American Psychological Association: apa.org
- Anxiety Disorders Association of America: adaa.org
- Association of Gay and Lesbian Psychologists: psy.uva.nl
- AtHealth.com—mental health links, chat, bulletin board, and so on: athealth.com
- CFS Days—for sufferers of chronic fatigue syndrome and fibromyalgia; information about signs and symptoms, research, diagnosis, treatment, and medications, along with discussion and support group: sunflower.org/~cfsdays/cfsdays.htm
- Depression Knowledge Center—put together by the World Federation for Mental Health, this very comprehensive site offers FAQs, events listings, a list of organizations, an archive, and discussion: depressionnet.org
- International Society for Mental Health: ismh.org
- Internet Mental Health—information on disorders and treatment, with online diagnostic services and psychopharmacology index: mentalhealth.com
- Mental Health at About.com—articles, forums, chat, and a newsletter; updated daily: mentalhealth.about.com
- Mental Health Center—answers to many of the questions you're too scared to ask: mentalhealthcenter.com

- Mental Health Links—Web directory of useful links, associations, news and events, support, self-help, and managed care: mentalhealthlinks.com
- Mental Help—award-winning guide to mental health, psychology, and psychiatry online: mentalhelp.net
- National Alliance for the Mentally Ill: nami.org
- National Association of Social Workers: naswdc.org
- National Center for Post-Traumatic Stress Disorder: ncptsd.org
- National Institute of Mental Health: nimh.nig.gov
- National Mental Health Association: healthtouch.com
- Obsessive Compulsive Foundation: http://pages.prodigy.com/alwillen.ocf.html
- Online Dictionary of Mental Health: shef.as.ulc/~psyc/psychotherapy/index
- Society for Light Treatment and Biological Rhythms (for SAD [seasonal affective disorder] sufferers): websciences.org/sltbr
- Walkers—information, a forum, and chat rooms for depressives and their loved ones: walkers.org

### General Health
- American Health Care Association: ahca.org
- American Medical Association: ama-assn.org
- Center for Medical Consumers and Health Care Information: medicalconsumers.org
- Family Internet—information on diseases, conditions, treatments, prognoses, and so on, with a health and diet file: familyinternet.com
- Food and Drug Administration—regulations and information on drugs and other products: fda.gov
- Health Information Highway—comprehensive health care resource with discussion groups: stayhealthy.com
- Healthy Way at Sympatico.ca—good source of information organized by medical condition; includes self-assessment resources, useful links, and a monthly magazine: healthyway.sympatico.ca
- Intelihealth—home to Johns Hopkins health information, as well as the U.S. Pharmacopoeia database: intelihealth.com
- Mediconsult.com—A–Z medical directory featuring drug, fitness, and nutrition information, news briefs, online events, forums, and chat: mediconsult.com
- Merck Manual—one of the most popular manuals, used by doctors worldwide; detailed information about thousands of conditions: merck.com
- National Institutes of Health—dedicated to providing the public with the latest information about different health issues and ongoing scientific research/special reports: nih.gov

- Pharmaceutical Information Network (Pharm InfoNet)—good resource for drug development information: pharminfo.com

## Green Products
- Gladrags—environmentally friendly menstrual products: gladrags.com
- Lunapads—environmentally friendly menstrual products: lunapads.com
- Many Moons—environmentally friendly menstrual products: pacificcoast.net/~manymoons
- Pandora Pads—environmentally friendly menstrual products: pandorapads.com

## Online Pharmacies and Drug Databases
- cponline.gsm.com
- drugstore.com
- genrx.com
- pharmweb.net
- planetrx.com
- rxlist.com
- soma.com

## Natural and Alternative Medications and Therapies
- EarthMed.com—world's largest website dedicated to natural and alternative practitioners, products, and services: earthmed.com
- Homeopathy Online: homeopathonline.com
- MotherNature.com—information on what natural remedies do and how to take them: mothernature.com

# Appendix B

## *General Websites Related to Women's Health*

Note: THIS IS adapted from a thorough "best women's health on the web" review as of 2000 by the *American Journal of Public Health* vol. 90, no. 9, pp. 1475–76, September 2000.

**Agency for Healthcare Research and Quality Women's Health**
ahcpr.gov/research/womenix.htm

**Alan Guttmacher Institute**
agi-usa.org

**American Medical Women's Association**
amwa-doc.org

**Amnesty International Female Genital Mutilation Information**
amnesty.org/ailib/intcam/femgen/fgm1.htm

**Center for Reproductive Law and Policy**
crlp.org

**Center for Women Policy Studies**
centerwomenpolicy.org

**Centers for Disease Control and Prevention Women's Health**
cdc.gov/health/womensmenu.htm

**Commonwealth Fund Commission on Women's Health**
cmwf.org/programs/women/index.asp

**Department of Health and Human Services, National Centers of Excellence in Women's Health**
4woman.gov/owh/coe/index.htm

**Female Genital Mutilation Education and Networking Project**
fgmnetwork.org

**Forum for Women's Health**
womenshealth.org

**Girl Power Campaign, U.S. Department of Health and Human Services**
health.org/gpower/index.htm

**Harvard Law School Database on Law and Population**
law.harvard.edu/programs/annual_review

**Harvard University Global Reproductive Health Forum**
hsph.harvard.edu/organizations/healthnet

**Health Resources and Services Administration, Bureau of Primary Health Care, Office of Minority and Women's Health**
bphc.hrsa.dhhs.gov/cc/healthywomen.htm

**HRSA Resources for Women**
bphc.hrsa.dhhs.gov/cc/resourceswomen.htm

**HRSA Women's Health Resources**
hrsa.gov/womenshealth/resources.htm
hrsa.gov/womenshealth/wh_orgs.htm

Hysterectomy Educational Resources and Services (HERS) Foundation
hersfoundation.com

JAMA Women's Health Information Center
ama-assn.org/special/womh/womh.htm

Mayo Clinic Women's Health Center
mayo.ivi.com/mayo/common/htm/womenpg.htm

Medscape
medscape.com/px/splash

National Center for Health Statistics, Centers for Disease Control and Prevention
cdc.gov/nchswww

National Institute of Mental Health, Office for Special Populations
nimh.nih.gov/osp

National Institute on Drug Abuse, Women and Gender Research
nida.nih.gov/whgd/whgdhome.html

National Institutes of Health, National Heart, Lung, and Blood Institute, Women's Health Initiative
nhlbi.nih.gov/whi/index.html

National Institutes of Health, Office of Research on Women's Health (ORWH) Links
http://www4.od.nih.gov/orwh/other.html

National Women's Health Information Center
4woman.org/nwhic

New York Times Women's Health Resource Links
nytimes.com/specials/women/whome/resources.html

**North American Menopause Society**
menopause.org

**OBGYN Net Resources for Women**
obgyn.net/women/women.asp

**Planned Parenthood**
plannedparenthood.org

**Public Health Service Coordinating Committee on Women's Health**
hrsa.gov/womenshealth/phs_cc.htm

**Society for Women's Health Research**
womens-health.org

**United Nations Gender and AIDS Links**
unaidsapict.inet.co.th/gend.htm

**University of Illinois at Chicago, Center for Research on Women and Gender**
uic.edu/depts/crwg/outline.htm

**University of Maryland Women's Health Links**
marylandwomenshealth.org/whrg/riderx.html

**University of Wisconsin Women's Health Web**
medsch.wisc.edu/chslib/hw/womens

**U.S. Food and Drug Administration, Non-Government Sources of Women's Health Information**
vm.cfsan.fda.gov/~dms/wh-ngov.html

**U.S. Food and Drug Administration, Office of Women's Health**
fda.gov/womens/default.htm

**Web Sites for Women's Health**
umbc7.umbc.edu/~korenman/wmst/links_hlth.html

**WHO Links: Family and Reproductive Health**
who.org/home/map_ht.html#Family and Reproductive Health

**Women's Health Interactive**
womens-health.com

**World Health Organization**
who.org

**WWWomen Search Directory: Health**
wwwomen.com/category/health1.html

# Bibliography

Abboud, Pascal, et al. "Stronger Campaign Needed to End Female Genital Mutilation." *British Medical Journal* 320 (7242): 1153 (April 22, 2000).

"Abortifacient Drug Approved for Restricted, Physician-Only Distribution." *American Journal of Health-System Pharmacy* 57 (21): 1940 (November 1, 2000).

"About Anal Sex (How to Give and Receive Anal Pleasure)." About Sex: minou.com/aboutsex/analsex.htm. (Retrieved March 5, 2002.)

Adam, Ervin, et al. "Papillomavirus Detection: Demographic and Behavioral Characteristics Influencing the Identification of Cervical Disease." *American Journal of Obstetrics & Gynecology* 182 (2): 257–64 (February 2000).

"Advanced Anal Sex Techniques." Sexuality.org: sexuality.org/l/incoming/aanal.html. (Retrieved March 5, 2002.)

Affara, Fadwa A. "Correspondence from Abroad: When Tradition Maims." *American Journal of Nursing* 100 (8): 52–59 (August 2000).

Agarwal, S. K., et al. "The Association Between Right Lower Quadrant Abdominal Pain and Appendiceal Pathology in Women with Endometriosis." *Fertility & Sterility* 75 (4) Supplement 1: 7S (April 2001).

Alan Guttmacher Institute. "Choice of Female-Controlled Barrier Methods Among Young Women and Their Male Sexual Partners." *Family Planning Perspectives* 33 (1) (January 2001).

Alvarez-Sanchez, Francisco, et al. "Prevalence of Enlarged Ovarian Follicles Among Users of Levonorgestrel Subdermal Contraceptive Implants (Norplant)." *American Journal of Obstetrics & Gynecology* 182 (3): 535–39 (March 2000).

"Anal Sex." Sexual Health InfoCenter: sexhealth.org/bettersex/anal.shtml. (Retrieved March 5, 2002.)

Anawalt, Bradley D., et al. "Desogestrel Plus Testosterone Effectively Suppresses Spermatogenesis But Also Causes Modest Weight Gain and High-Density Lipoprotein Suppression." *Fertility & Sterility* 74 (4): 707–14 (October 2000).

Annas, George J. "Partial-Birth Abortion and the Supreme Court." *New England Journal of Medicine* 344 (2): 152–56 (January 11, 2001).

Appell, Rodney A., et al. "Prospective Randomized Controlled Trial of Extended-Release Oxybutynin Chloride and Tolterodine Tartrate in the Treatment of Overactive Bladder: Results of the OBJECT Study." *Mayo Clinic Proceedings* 76 (4): 358–63 (April 2001).

Arya, Lily A., et al. "Risk of New-Onset Urinary Incontinence After Forceps and Vacuum Delivery in Primiparous Women." *American Journal of Obstetrics & Gynecology* 185 (6): 1318–24 (December 2001).

Aylett, Virginia, and Olwyn Lynch. "Catheterisation in Elderly Women Is No 'Easy' Option." *British Medical Journal* 322 (7292): 997 (April 21, 2001).

Baird, David T., and Anna F. Glasier. "Science, Medicine, and the Future: Contraception." *British Medical Journal* 319 (7215): 969–72 (October 9, 1999).

Bauer, Greta R., and Seth L. Welles. "Beyond Assumptions of Negligible Risk: Sexually Transmitted Diseases and Women Who Have Sex with Women." *American Journal of Public Health* 91 (8): 1282–86 (August 2001).

Bell, Robin. "ABC of Sexual Health: Homosexual Men and Women." *British Medical Journal* 318 (7181): 452–55 (February 13, 1999).

Bent, A. E., et al. "Collagen Implant for Treating Stress Urinary Incontinence in Women with Urethral Hypermobility." *Journal of Urology* 166 (4): 1354–57 (October 2001).

Bland, Deirdre R., et al. "Use of the Pelvic Organ Prolapse Staging System of the International Continence Society, American Urogynecologic Society, and Society of Gynecologic Surgeons in Perimenopausal Women." *American Journal of Obstetrics & Gynecology* 181 (6): 1324–28 (December 1999).

Blonski, Joe. "Is Tolterodine (Detrol) or Oxybutynin (Ditropan) the Best for Treatment of Urge Urinary Incontinence?" *Journal of Family Practice* 50 (12): 1017 (December 2001).

Borgmann, Caitlin E., and Bonnie Scott Jones. "Legal Issues in the Provision of Medical Abortion." *American Journal of Obstetrics & Gynecology* 183 (2) Supplement: S84–S94 (August 2000).

Bowden, Francis J., and Geoffrey P. Garnett. "Why Is Trichomonas Vaginalis Ignored?" *Sexually Transmitted Infections* 75 (6): 372–74 (December 1999).

Brady, C. M., et al. "A Prospective Evaluation of the Efficiency of Early Postoperative Bladder Emptying After the Stamey Procedure or Pubovaginal Sling for Stress Urinary Incontinence." *Journal of Urology* 165 (5): 1601–4 (May 2001).

Breitbart, Vicki. "Counseling for Medical Abortion." *American Journal of Obstetrics & Gynecology* 183 (2) Supplement: S26–S33 (August 2000).

Breitbart, Vicki, et al. "Medical Abortion Service Delivery." *American Journal of Obstetrics & Gynecology* 183 (2) Supplement: S16–S25 (August 2000).

Bumpass, Larry L., Elizabeth Thomson, and Amy L. Godecker. "Women, Men, and Contraceptive Sterilization." *Fertility & Sterility* 73 (5): 937–46 (May 2000).

Burkman, Ronald T., et al. "Current Perspectives on Oral Contraceptive Use." *American Journal of Obstetrics & Gynecology* 185 (2) Supplement: S4–S12 (August 2001).

Butcher, Josie. "ABC of Sexual Health: Female Sexual Problems II: Sexual Pain and Sexual Fears." *British Medical Journal* 318 (7176): 110–12 (January 9, 1999).

"Can I Get HIV from Anal Sex?" Centers for Disease Control & Prevention, National Center for HIV, STD, and TB Prevention, Divisions of HIV/AIDS Prevention: cdc.gov/hiv/pubs/faq/faq22.htm. (Retrieved March 5, 2002.)

Cappellano, Francesco, et al. "Quality of Life Assessment in Patients Who Undergo Sacral Neuromodulation Implantation for Urge Incontinence: An Additional Tool for Evaluating Outcome." *Journal of Urology* 166 (6): 2277–80 (December 2001).

Cerrato, Paul L. "Can 'Healthy' Bacteria Ward Off Disease?" *RN* 63 (4): 71–72, 74 (April 2000).

Charatan, Fred. "Missouri Passes Antiabortion Law." *British Medical Journal* 319 (7214): 874 (October 2, 1999).

———. "U.S. Court Refutes Nebraska's Antiabortion Law." *British Medical Journal* 321 (7253): 70 (July 8, 2000).

———. "U.S. Government Limits Abortion Pill for Poor Women." *British Medical Journal* 322 (7293): 1015 (April 28, 2001).

———. "U.S. Judges Rule in Favour of Abortion 'Hit List.'" *British Medical Journal* 322 (7290): 818 (April 7, 2001).

Chasan-Taber, Lisa, and Meir Stampfer. "Oral Contraceptives and Myocardial Infarction—The Search for the Smoking Gun." *New England Journal of Medicine* 345 (25): 1841–42 (December 20, 2001).

Chez, Ronald A., and Wayne B. Jonas. "Complementary and Alternative Medicine. Part II: Clinical Studies in Gynecology." *Obstetrical & Gynecological Survey* 54 (11) Supplement: 204–11 (November 1999).

Choe, Jong M. "Tension-Free Vaginal Tape: Is It Truly Tension-Free?" *Journal of Urology* 166 (3): 1003 (September 2001).

Christin-Maitre, Sophie, Philippe Bouchard, and Irving M. Spitz. "Drug Therapy: Medical Termination of Pregnancy." *New England Journal of Medicine* 342 (13): 946–56 (March 30, 2000).

Connor, Pamela D., et al. "Determining Risk Between Depo-Provera Use and Increased Uterine Bleeding in Obese and Overweight Women." *Journal of the American Board of Family Practice* 15 (1): 7–10 (January/February 2002).

Costa, Elaine, et al. "Management of Ambiguous Genitalia in Pseudohermaphrodites: New Perspectives on Vaginal Dilation." *Fertility & Sterility* 67 (2): 229–32 (February 1997).

Costa, Pierre, et al. "The Use of an Artificial Urinary Sphincter in Women with Type III Incontinence and a Negative Marshall Test." *Journal of Urology* 165 (4): 1172–76 (April 2001).

Creinin, Mitchell D. "Medical Abortion Regimens: Historical Context and Overview." *American Journal of Obstetrics & Gynecology* 183 (2) Supplement: S3–S9 (August 2000).

Croughan-Minihane, M. S., et al. "The Risk of Ovarian Cancer Associated with Infertility and Infertility Treatments." *Fertility & Sterility* 76 (3) Supplement 1: S69 (September 2001).

Czerwinski, Barbara Shelden. "Variation in Feminine Hygiene Practices as a Function of Age." *Journal of Obstetric, Gynecologic, & Neonatal Nursing* 29 (6): 625–33 (November/December 2000).

Dan, Michael. "Severe Vulvovaginitis Associated with Intravaginal Nystatin Therapy." *American Journal of Obstetrics & Gynecology* 185 (1): 254–55 (July 2001).

Darney, Philip D. "Time to Pardon the IUD?" *New England Journal of Medicine* 345 (8): 608–10 (August 23, 2001).

Davila, G. W., C. A. Daugherty, and S. W. Sanders. "A Short-Term, Multicenter, Randomized Double-Blind Dose Titration Study of the Efficacy and Anticholinergic Side Effects of Transdermal Compared to Immediate Release Oral Oxybutynin Treatment of Patients with Urge Urinary Incontinence." *Journal of Urology* 166 (1): 140–45 (July 2001).

DeMars, Leslie R. "The Impact of Cancer Therapy on Reproductive Function." *Obstetrical & Gynecological Survey* 56 (5): 251–53 (May 2001).

Demello, Ann B. "Uterine Artery Embolization." *AORN Journal* 73 (4): 788–814 (April 2001).

Dickey, R. P. *Managing Contraceptive Pill Patients*, 7th edition. London, Ont.: Emis Canada, 1993.

Dickinson, Jan E., and Sharon F. Evans. "The Optimization of Intravaginal Misoprostol Dosing Schedules in Second-Trimester Pregnancy Termination." *American Journal of Obstetrics & Gynecology* 186 (3): 470–74 (March 2002).

Dittrich, Richard, et al. "Transdermal Contraception: Evaluation of Three Transdermal Norelgestromin/Ethinyl Estradiol Doses in a Randomized, Multicenter, Dose-Response Study." *American Journal of Obstetrics & Gynecology* 186 (1): 15–20 (January 2002).

Donders, Gilbert. "We, Specialists in Vulvovaginitis." *American Journal of Obstetrics & Gynecology* 184 (2): 248 (January 2001).

Drake, Susan, et al. "Improving the Care of Patients with Genital Herpes." *British Medical Journal* 321 (7261): 619–23 (September 9, 2000).

Driscoll, Alisa, and Joel M. H. Teichman. "How Do Patients with Interstitial Cystitis Present?" *Journal of Urology* 166 (6): 2118–20 (December 2001).

Duerr, Ann, et al. "Human Papillomavirus-Associated Cervical Cytologic Abnormalities Among Women with or at Risk of Infection with Human Immunodeficiency Virus." *American Journal of Obstetrics & Gynecology* 184 (4): 584–90 (March 2001).

Eggertson, Laura. "Abortion Services in Canada: A Patchwork Quilt with Many Holes." *Canadian Medical Association Journal* 164 (6): 847–49 (March 20, 2001).

Ellerbrock, Tedd V., et al. "Incidence of Cervical Squamous Intraepithelial Lesions in HIV-Infected Women." *Obstetrical & Gynecological Survey* 55 (6): 361–62 (June 2000).

Enserink, Martin. "The Vanishing Promises of Hormone Replacement." *Science* 297 (5580): 325–26 (July 19, 2002).

Erickson, Deborah R., et al. "Nonbladder Related Symptoms in Patients with Interstitial Cystitis." *Journal of Urology* 166 (2): 557–62 (August 2001).

Farquhar, Cynthia M. "Endometriosis." *British Medical Journal* 320 (7247): 1449–52 (May 27, 2000).

Fedele, Luigi, et al. "Use of a Levonorgestrel-Releasing Intrauterine Device in the Treatment of Rectovaginal Endometriosis." *Fertility & Sterility* 75 (3): 485–88 (March 2001).

Ferris, Daron G, Mark Schiffman, and Mark S. Litaker. "Cervicography for Triage of Women with Mildly Abnormal Cervical Cytology Results." *American Journal of Obstetrics & Gynecology* 185 (4): 939–43 (October 2001).

Fisher, William A., and Richard Boroditsky. "Sexual Activity, Contraceptive Choice, and Sexual and Reproductive Health." *Canadian Journal of Human Sexuality* 9 (2): 79 (summer 2000).

Franz, Rachel. "Common Skin Conditions May Indicate HIV Infection in Women." *Dermatology Nursing* 12 (4): 280 (August 2000).

Fulmer, Brant R., et al. "Acute and Long-Term Outcomes of Radio Frequency Bladder Neck Suspension." *Journal of Urology* 167 (1): 141–45 (January 2002).

Gelbaya, T. A., and H. E. El-Halwagy. "Focus on Primary Care: Chronic Pelvic Pain in Women." *Obstetrical & Gynecological Survey* 56 (12): 757–64 (December 2001).

"Gender Identity in Testicular Feminisation." *British Medical Journal* 308 (6935): 1041 (April 16, 1994).

Gillmer, Michael. "Sexual Chemistry: A History of the Contraceptive Pill." *Nature* 414 (6866): 850 (December 20/27, 2001).

Ginsberg, David A., et al. "Permanent Urinary Retention After Transurethral Injection of Collagen." *Journal of Urology* 167 (2, Part 1 of 2): 648 (February 2002).

Glassberg, Kenneth I. "Gender Assignment and the Pediatric Urologist." *Journal of Urology* 161 (4): 1308–10 (April 1999).

Glazener, Cathryn, et al. "Conservative Management of Persistent Postnatal Urinary and Faecal Incontinence: Randomised Controlled Trial." *British Medical Journal* 323 (7313): 593–96 (September 15, 2001).

Gokhale, Ravindra, Mary Hernon, and Ajit Ghosh. "Genital Piercing and Sexually Transmitted Infections." *Sexually Transmitted Infections* 77 (5): 393–94 (October 2001).

Goldman, Howard B. "Interstitial Cystitis: The Great Enigma." *Journal of Urology* 164 (6): 1921 (December 2000).

Goldman, Howard B., Raymond R. Rackley, and Rodney A. Appell. "The In Situ Anterior Vaginal Wall Sling: Predictors of Success." *Journal of Urology* 166 (6): 2259–62 (December 2001).

Gollub, Erica L., "The Female Condom: Tool for Women's Empowerment." *American Journal of Public Health* 90 (9): 1377–81 (September 2000).

Gonzalez, Dagoberto I., Jr., et al. "Recurrence of Dysplasia After Loop Electrosurgical Excision Procedures with Long-Term Follow-Up." *American Journal of Obstetrics & Gynecology* 184 (3): 315–21 (February 2001).

Gottlieb, Scott. "Abortion Pill Is Approved for Sale in United States." *British Medical Journal* 321 (7265): 851 (October 7, 2000).

Graham, Carol A., and Veronica T. Mallett. "Race as a Predictor of Urinary Incontinence and Pelvic Organ Prolapse." *American Journal of Obstetrics & Gynecology* 185 (1): 116–20 (July 2001).

Grimes, David A. "The Continuing Need for Late Abortions." *Journal of the American Medical Association* 280 (8): 747–50 (August 26, 1998).

———. "Medical Abortion: Public Health and Private Lives." *American Journal of Obstetrics & Gynecology* 183 (2) Supplement: S1–S2 (August 2000).

Gupta, Kalpana, Thomas M. Hooton, and Walter E. Stamm. "Increasing Antimicrobial Resistance and the Management of Uncomplicated Community-Acquired Urinary Tract Infections." *Annals of Internal Medicine* 135 (1): 41–50 (July 3, 2001).

Hader, Shannon L., et al. "HIV Infection in Women in the United States: Status at the Millennium." *Journal of the American Medical Association* 285 (9): 1186–92 (March 7, 2001).

Hallowell, Nina, et al. "Surveillance or Surgery? A Description of the Factors That Influence High Risk Premenopausal Women's Decisions About Prophylactic Oophorectomy." *Journal of Medical Genetics* 38 (10): 683–91 (October 1, 2001).

Harlow, Bernard L., Lauren A. Wise, Elizabeth G. Stewart. "Prevalence and Predictors of Chronic Lower Genital Tract Discomfort." *American Journal of Obstetrics & Gynecology* 185 (3): 545–50 (September 2001).

Harmanli, Ozgur H., et al. "Urinary Tract Infections in Women with Bacterial Vaginosis." *Obstetrical & Gynecological Survey* 55 (8): 489–90 (August 2000).

Harper, Diane M. "Treatment Threshold Probability for Vaginitis." *American Journal of Obstetrics & Gynecology* 183 (2): 517–18 (August 2000).

Harper, Diane M., et al. "Healing Experiences After Cervical Cryosurgery." *Journal of Family Practice* 49 (8): 701–6 (August 2000).

Hartge, Patricia, et al. "Complex Ovarian Cysts in Postmenopausal Women Are Not Associated with Ovarian Cancer Risk Factors: Preliminary Data from the Prostate, Lung, Colon, and Ovarian Cancer Screening Trial." *American Journal of Obstetrics & Gynecology* 183 (5): 1232–37 (November 2000).

Hartmann, Katherine E., et al. "Technologic Advances for Evaluation of Cervical Cytology: Is Newer Better?" *Obstetrical & Gynecological Survey* 56 (12): 765–74 (December 2001).

Hartnett, Nicole M., and Barry G. Saver. "Is Extended-Release Oxybutynin (Ditropan XL) or Tolterodine (Detrol) More Effective in the Treatment of an Overactive Bladder?" *Journal of Family Practice* 50 (7): 571 (July 2001).

Harvey, Marie-Andree, Kevin Baker, and George A. Wells. "Tolterodine Versus Oxybutynin in the Treatment of Urge Urinary Incontinence: A Meta-Analysis." *American Journal of Obstetrics & Gynecology* 185 (1): 56–61 (July 2001).

Hayes, Margaret, and Gail A. Harkness. "Body Piercing as a Risk Factor for Viral Hepatitis: An Integrative Research Review." *American Journal of Infection Control* 29 (4): 271–74 (August 2001).

Helfgott, Andrew, et al. "Vaginal Infections in Human Immunodeficiency Virus–Infected Women." *American Journal of Obstetrics & Gynecology* 183 (2): 347–55 (August 2000).

Henderson, Lesley J. "Diagnosis, Treatment, and Lifestyle Changes of Interstitial Cystitis." *AORN Journal* 71 (3): 525–38 (March 2000).

Hernandez, Enrique. "Relationship Between Postmenopausal Hormone Replacement Therapy and Ovarian Cancer." *Journal of the American Medical Association* 285 (24): 3089–90 (June 27, 2001).

"History of Abortion in Canada." Pro-Choice Action Network: prochoiceactionnetwork-canada.org/history.html. (Retrieved April 6, 2002.)

"HIV/AIDS and U.S. Women Who Have Sex with Women (WSW)." Article distributed by CDC discussing the risks of female-to-female HIV infection transmission.

"HIV and AIDS—United States, 1981–2000." *Journal of the American Medical Association* 285 (24): 3083–84 (June 27, 2001).

Holzman, Claudia, et al. "Factors Linked to Bacterial Vaginosis in Nonpregnant Women." *American Journal of Public Health* 91 (10): 1664–70 (October 2001).

Hopkins, Michael P., Vivian von Gruenigen, and Steven Gaich. "Laparoscopic Port Site Implantation with Ovarian Cancer." *American Journal of Obstetrics & Gynecology* 182 (3): 735–36 (March 2000).

Hubacher, David, and David A. Grimes. "Noncontraceptive Health Benefits of Intrauterine Devices: A Systematic Review." *Obstetrical & Gynecological Survey* 57 (2): 120–28 (February 2002).

Hunskaar, Steinar. "Fluctuations in Lower Urinary Tract Symptoms in Women: Reassurance and Watchful Waiting Can Prevent Overtreatment." *British Medical Journal* 320 (7247): 1418–19 (May 27, 2000).

"International Work: Janesway Condom Acceptability Research." *Soundings* (fall/winter 2000).

Irwin, Barbara, Angela Patterson, and Michael Power. "Management of Urinary Incontinence in a UK Trust." *Nursing Standard* 16 (13–14–15): 33–37 (December 12, 2001).

Jaffe, Robert B. "Estrogen Replacement Therapy and Ovarian Cancer Mortality in a Large Prospective Study of US Women." *Obstetrical & Gynecological Survey* 56 (8): 479–80 (August 2001).

———. "Potential of Norethisterone Enanthate for Male Contraception: Pharmacokinetics and Suppression of Pituitary and Gonadal Function." *Obstetrical & Gynecological Survey* 56 (3): 157–58 (March 2001).

———. "Use of Copper Intrauterine Devices and the Risk of Tubal Infertility Among Nulligravid Women." *Obstetrical & Gynecological Survey* 57 (2): 91–92 (February 2002).

Jakus, Sharon, et al. "Margin Status and Excision of Cervical Intraepithelial Neoplasia: A Review." *Obstetrical & Gynecological Survey* 55 (8): 520–27 (August 2000).

Jarow, J. P., et al. "The Effect of Testosterone Male Contraception upon Intratesticular Testosterone Concentration in the Human Testis." *Fertility & Sterility* 76 (3) Supplement 1: S155 (September 2001).

Jensen, Jeffrey T., et al. "Acceptability of Suction Curettage and Mifepristone Abortion in the United States: A Prospective Comparison Study." *American Journal of Obstetrics & Gynecology* 182 (6): 1292–99 (June 2000).

Joffe, Carole. "Medical Abortion in Social Context." *American Journal of Obstetrics & Gynecology* 183 (2) Supplement: S10–S15 (August 2000).

Johnson, Sandra Marchese, Paula K. Roberson, and Thomas D. Horn. "Intralesional Injection of Mumps or Candida Skin Test Antigens: A Novel Immunotherapy for Warts." *Archives of Dermatology* 137 (4): 451–55 (April 2001).

Jones, Howard W., III. "A Comparison of Bladder Neck Movement and Elevation After Tension-Free Vaginal Tape and Colposuspension." *Obstetrical & Gynecological Survey* 56 (4): 211–13 (April 2001).

———. "A Comparison of the Objective and Subjective Outcomes of Colposuspension for Stress Incontinence in Women." *Obstetrical & Gynecological Survey* 56 (11): 691–92 (November 2001).

———. "Prevalence of Metronidazole-Resistant Trichomonas Vaginalis in a Gynecology Clinic." *Obstetrical & Gynecological Survey* 56 (11): 693–94 (November 2001).

———. "Primary Chemotherapy in Stage IV Ovarian Cancer: A Prospective Phase II Study." *Obstetrical & Gynecological Survey* 57 (2): 87–89 (February 2002).

———. "The Role of Laparoscopy in Second-Look Evaluations for Ovarian Cancer." *Obstetrical & Gynecological Survey* 56 (5): 277–79 (May 2001).

———. "Secondary Cytoreductive Surgery for Localized Intra-Abdominal Recurrences in Epithelial Ovarian Cancer." *Obstetrical & Gynecological Survey* 56 (9): 551–52 (September 2001).

———. "Treatment of Complicated Candida Vaginitis: Comparison of Single and Sequential Doses of Fluconazole." *Obstetrical & Gynecological Survey* 57 (1): 26–27 (January 2002).

———. "Which Women with Stress Incontinence Require Urodynamic Evaluation?" *Obstetrical & Gynecological Survey* 56 (5): 272–74 (May 2001).

Keefe, Kristin A., et al. "Fluorescence Detection of Cervical Intraepithelial Neoplasia for Photodynamic Therapy with the Topical Agents 5-Aminolevulinic Acid and Benzoporphyrin-Derivative Monoacid Ring." *American Journal of Obstetrics & Gynecology* 184 (6): 1164–69 (May 2001).

Khanna, Rakesh, and S. Sathish Kumar. "Pathogen Causing Infection Related to Body Piercing Should Be Determined." *British Medical Journal* 320 (7243): 1211 (April 29, 2000).

Kim, Catherine, et al. "Diabetes and Depot Medroxyprogesterone Contraception in Navajo Women." *Archives of Internal Medicine* 161 (14): 1766–71 (July 23, 2001).

Kjellberg, Lennart, et al. "Regular Disappearance of the Human Papillomavirus Genome After Conization of Cervical Dysplasia by Carbon Dioxide Laser." *American Journal of Obstetrics & Gynecology* 183 (5): 1238–42 (November 2000).

Klam, Stephanie, et al. "Comparison of Endocervical Curettage and Endocervical Brushing." *Obstetrical & Gynecological Survey* 56 (1): 23–24 (January 2001).

Klein, Arnold, and Martin L. Schwartz. "Uterine Artery Embolization for the Treatment of Uterine Fibroids: An Outpatient Procedure." *American Journal of Obstetrics & Gynecology* 184 (7): 1556–63 (June 2001).

Kobashi, Kathleen C., et al. "Pelvic Prolapse." *Journal of Urology* 164 (6): 1879–90 (December 2000).

Koelle, Dieter, et al. "Treatment of Postoperative Urinary Retention by Elongation of Tension-Free Vaginal Tape." *American Journal of Obstetrics & Gynecology* 185 (1): 250–51 (July 2001).

Krissi, Haim, et al. "Fallopian Tube Torsion Laparoscopic Evaluation and Treatment of a Rare Gynecological Entity." *Journal of the American Board of Family Practice* 14 (4): 274–77 (July/August 2001).

Kroll, Gigi L., and Leslie Miller. "Vulvar Epithelial Inclusion Cyst as a Late Complication of Childhood Female Traditional Genital Surgery." *American Journal of Obstetrics & Gynecology* 183 (2): 509–10 (August 2000).

Kruse, Beth, et al. "Management of Side Effects and Complications in Medical Abortion." *American Journal of Obstetrics & Gynecology* 183 (2) Supplement: S65–S75 (August 2000).

Lambert, B., and Y. Lepage. "Endocervical Curettage in Cervical Evaluation." *Obstetrical & Gynecological Survey* 55 (11): 689–90 (November 2000).

Lambert, Erika C. "College Students' Knowledge of Human Papillomavirus and Effectiveness of a Brief Educational Intervention." *Journal of the American Board of Family Practice* 14 (3): 178–83 (May/June 2001).

Lessey, Bruce A. "Medical Management of Endometriosis and Infertility." *Fertility & Sterility* 73 (6): 1089–96 (June 2000).

Lim, Y. T. "Mistletoe Therapy in Endometriosis." *Fertility & Sterility* 77 (2) Supplement 1: S53 (February 2002).

Lipsky, Martin S., Teresa Waters, and Lisa K. Sharp. "Impact of Vaginal Antifungal Products on Utilization of Health Care Services: Evidence from Physician Visits." *Journal of the American Board of Family Practice* 13 (3): 178–82 (May/June 2000).

Lipsky, Martin S., and Theresa Waters. "The 'Prescription-to-OTC Switch' Movement: Its Effects on Antifungal Vaginitis Preparations." *Archives of Family Medicine* 8 (4): 297–300 (July/August 1999).

Liu, Wei-Min, et al. "Laparoscopic Bipolar Coagulation of Uterine Vessels: A New Method for Treating Symptomatic Fibroids." *Fertility & Sterility* 75 (2): 417–22 (February 2001).

Lutgendorf, Susan K., et al. "Stress and Symptomatology in Patients with Interstitial Cystitis: A Laboratory Stress Model." *Journal of Urology* 164 (4): 1265–69 (October 2000).

MacIsaac, Laura, and Philip Darney. "Early Surgical Abortion: An Alternative to and Backup for Medical Abortion." *American Journal of Obstetrics & Gynecology* 183 (2) Supplement: S76–S83 (August 2000).

Manges, Amee R., et al. "Widespread Distribution of Urinary Tract Infections Caused by a Multidrug-Resistant Escherichia coli Clonal Group." *New England Journal of Medicine* 345 (14): 1007–13 (October 4, 2001).

Marciante, Kristin D., et al. "Modeling the Cost and Outcomes of Pharmacist-Prescribed Emergency Contraception." *American Journal of Public Health* 91 (9): 1443–45 (September 2001).

Marrazzo, Jeanne M., et al. "Papanicolaou Test Screening and Prevalence of Genital Human Papillomavirus Among Women Who Have Sex with Women." *American Journal of Public Health* 91 (6): 947–52 (June 2001).

Mayers, Lester B., et al. "Prevalence of Body Art (Body Piercing and Tattooing) in University Undergraduates and Incidence of Medical Complications." *Mayo Clinic Proceedings* 77 (1): 29–34 (January 2002).

McDonnell, Marcia, and Cathy R. Kessenich. "HIV/AIDS and Women." *Lippincott's Primary Care Practice* 4 (1): 66–73 (January/February 2000).

McFarlane, Mary, Sheana S. Bull, and Cornelis A. Rietmeijer. "The Internet as a Newly Emerging Risk Environment for Sexually Transmitted Diseases." *Journal of the American Medical Association* 284 (4): 443–46 (July 26, 2000).

McGaraghan, Amy, and Karen Smith-McCune. "Follow-up of Unsatisfactory Papanicolaou Test Results." *Journal of the American Medical Association* 283 (10): 1290–91 (March 8, 2000).

McGregor, James A., and Janice I. French. "Bacterial Vaginosis in Pregnancy." *Obstetrical & Gynecological Survey* 55 (5) Supplement 1: 1–19 (May 2000).

McIlhaney, Joe S., Jr. "Sexually Transmitted Infection and Teenage Sexuality." *American Journal of Obstetrics & Gynecology* 183 (2): 334–39 (August 2000).

Meyer, Diana. "Body piercing: Old Traditions Creating New Challenges." *Journal of Emergency Nursing* 26 (6): 612–14 (December 2000).

Michael, Yvonne L., et al. "Quality of Life Among Women with Interstitial Cystitis." *Journal of Urology* 164 (2): 423–27 (August 2000).

"Mifepristone (Mifeprex): RU 486 Approved for Abortion." *American Journal of Nursing* 100 (12) (December 2000).

Mindel, Adrian, and Melinda Tenant-Flowers. "Natural History and Management of Early HIV Infection." *British Medical Journal* 322 (7297): 1290–93 (May 26, 2001).

Mitka, Mike. "Promoting Emergency Contraception." *Journal of the American Medical Association* 285 (24): 3080 (June 27, 2001).

Modan, Baruch, and Sholom Wacholder. "Ovarian Cancer, Oral Contraceptives, and BRCA Mutations." *New England Journal of Medicine* 345 (23): 1706–7 (December 6, 2001).

Modan, Baruch, et al. "Parity, Oral Contraceptives, and the Risk of Ovarian Cancer Among Carriers and Noncarriers of a BRCA1 or BRCA2 Mutation." *New England Journal of Medicine* 345 (4): 235–40 (July 26, 2001).

Moniak, Charles W., et al. "Endocervical Curettage in Evaluating Abnormal Cervical Cytology." *Obstetrical & Gynecological Survey* 55 (8): 487–89 (August 2000).

Morin, Jack. "Ten Rules of Anal Sex." Lair.org: lair.org/library/sexuality/analrules.html. (Retrieved March 5, 2002.)

Morris, Bobbi J., Cathy Young, and Kathleen Kearney. "Emergency Contraception." *American Journal of Nursing* 100 (9): 46–48 (September 2000).

Morris, M. C., P. A. Rogers, and G. R. Kinghorn. "Is Bacterial Vaginosis a Sexually Transmitted Infection?" *Sexually Transmitted Infections* 77 (1): 63–68 (February 2001).

Murphy, Sheila T., et al. "Preaching to the Choir: Preference for Female-Controlled Methods of HIV and Sexually Transmitted Disease Prevention." *American Journal of Public Health* 90 (7): 1135–37 (July 2000).

Muzii, Ludovico, et al. "Atypical Endometriosis Revisited: Clinical and Biochemical Evaluation of the Different Forms of Superficial Implants." *Fertility & Sterility* 74 (4): 739–42 (October 2000).

Nanda, Kavita, et al. "Accuracy of the Papanicolaou Test in Screening for and Follow-up of Cervical Cytologic Abnormalities: A Systematic Review." *Annals of Internal Medicine* 132 (10): 810–19 (May 16, 2000).

Narod, Steven A., Ping Sun, and Harvey A. Risch. "Ovarian Cancer, Oral Contraceptives, and BRCA Mutations." *New England Journal of Medicine* 345 (23): 1706–7 (December 6, 2001).

"National Guideline for the Management of Chancroid." *Sexually Transmitted Infections* 75 (1S) Supplement: 43S–45S (August 1999).

"National Guideline for the Management of Lymphogranuloma Venereum." *Sexually Transmitted Infections* 75 (1S) Supplement: 40S–42S (August 1999).

"National Guideline for the Management of Trichomonas Vaginalis." *Sexually Transmitted Infections* 75 (1S) Supplement: 21S–23S (August 1999).

Ness, Roberta B., et al. "Oral Contraceptives, Other Methods of Contraception, and Risk Reduction for Ovarian Cancer." *Epidemiology* 12 (3): 307–12 (May 2001).

Newhall, Elizabeth Pirruccello, and Beverly Winikoff. "Abortion with Mifepristone and Misoprostol: Regimens, Efficacy, Acceptability and Future Directions." *American Journal of Obstetrics & Gynecology* 183 (2) Supplement: S44–S53 (August 2000).

Newton, Edward R., et al. "Predictors of the Vaginal Microflora." *American Journal of Obstetrics & Gynecology* 184 (5): 845–55 (April 2001).

Nguyen, David, and Lili Church. "Are Biannual Papanicolaou (Pap) Tests Useful in Postmenopausal Women? Does Hormone Replacement Therapy (HRT) Affect the Development of Cervical Cytology Abnormalities?" *Journal of Family Practice* 50 (4): 368 (April 2001).

Nothnick, Warren B. "Treating Endometriosis as an Autoimmune Disease." *Fertility & Sterility* 76 (2): 223–31 (August 2001).

Olive, David L., and Elizabeth A. Pritts. "Drug Therapy: Treatment of Endometriosis." *New England Journal of Medicine* 345 (4): 266–75 (July 26, 2001).

Paavonen, Jorma. "Chlamydia Trachomatis and Cancer." *Sexually Transmitted Infections* 77 (3): 154–56 (June 2001).

Paavonen, Jorma, et al. "Vaginal Clindamycin and Oral Metronidazole for Bacterial Vaginosis: A Randomized Trial." *Obstetrical & Gynecological Survey* 55 (11): 691–92 (November 2000).

Parker, Leslie A. "Ambiguous Genitalia: Etiology, Treatment, and Nursing Implications." *Journal of Obstetric, Gynecologic, & Neonatal Nursing* 27 (1): 15–22 (January/February 1998).

Propert, K. J., et al. "Re: A Prospective Study of Interstitial Cystitis: Results of Longitudinal Followup of the Interstitial Cystitis Data Base Cohort." *Journal of Urology* 164 (6): 2030 (December 2000).

Pymar, Helen C., and Mitchell D. Creinin. "Alternatives to Mifepristone Regimens for Medical Abortion." *American Journal of Obstetrics & Gynecology* 183 (2) Supplement: S54–S64 (August 2000).

Randic, Ljiljana, Herman Haller, and Silva Sojat. "Nonsurgical Female Sterilization: Comparison of Intrauterine Application of Quinacrine Alone or in Combination with Ibuprofen." *Fertility & Sterility* 75 (4): 830–31 (April 2001).

Redwine, D., C. H. Mann, and J. T. Wright. "Evidence on Endometriosis: Elitism About Randomised Controlled Trials Is Inappropriate." *British Medical Journal* 321 (7268): 1077–78 (October 28, 2000).

Richards, Lynn A., and Paula Klemm. "An Inpatient Cervical Cancer Screening Program to Reach Underserved Women." *Journal of Obstetric, Gynecologic, & Neonatal Nursing* 29 (5): 465–73 (September/October 2000).

Richardson, Barbra A. "Nonoxynol-9 as a Vaginal Microbicide for Prevention of Sexually Transmitted Infections: It's Time to Move On." *Journal of the American Medical Association* 287 (9): 1171–72 (March 6, 2002).

Richmond, Donna M., et al. "Contraception: Myths, Facts, and Methods." *Dermatology Nursing* Supplement: 19–26 (February 2001).

Ridgway, Geoffrey L. "Laboratory Diagnosis of Sexually Transmitted Diseases." *Sexually Transmitted Infections* 76 (2): 147 (April 2000).

Rivera, Roberto, Irene Yacobson, and David Grimes. "The Mechanism of Action of Hormonal Contraceptives and Intrauterine Contraceptive Devices." *American Journal of Obstetrics & Gynecology* 181 (5, Part 1): 1263–69 (November 1999).

Rodrigues, Isabel, Fabienne Grou, and Jacques Joly. "Timing of Emergency Contraception." *American Journal of Obstetrics & Gynecology* 186 (1): 167–68 (January 2002).

Rodriguez, Carmen, et al. "Relationship Between Postmenopausal Hormone Replacement Therapy and Ovarian Cancer." *Journal of the American Medical Association* 285 (24): 3089–90 (June 27, 2001).

Rofeim, Omid, et al. "Use of the Neodymium: Yag Laser for Interstitial Cystitis: A Prospective Study." *Journal of Urology* 166 (1): 134–36 (July 2001).

Rosenthal, M. Sara. *The Canadian Type 2 Diabetes Sourcebook*. Toronto: Wiley Canada, 2002.

———. *50 Ways Women Can Prevent Heart Disease*. New York: McGraw-Hill, 2000.

———. *The Gynecological Sourcebook*, 3rd ed. New York: McGraw-Hill, 1999.

———. *Managing PMS Naturally*. Toronto: Penguin Books, 2001.

———. *Women Managing Stress*. Toronto: Penguin Books, 2002.

Ross, Jonathan. "Pelvic Inflammatory Disease." *British Medical Journal* 322 (7287): 658–59 (March 17, 2001).

Rothrock, Nan E., et al. "Depressive Symptoms and Quality of Life in Patients with Interstitial Cystitis." *Journal of Urology* 167 (4): 1763–67 (April 2002).

Rouzi, Abdulrahim A., et al. "Epidermal Clitoral Inclusion Cyst After Type I Female Genital Mutilation." *American Journal of Obstetrics & Gynecology* 185 (3): 569–71 (September 2001).

Rushton, A., and Shirley Bond. *Natural Progesterone*. London: Thorsons Publishing, Inc., 1999.

"Safer Sex: How? Safer Sex for Lesbian and Bisexual Women." YouthResource: youthresource.com/health/safersex/lesbian.cfm. (Retrieved March 5, 2002.)

Sarma, A. V., et al. "Epidemiology of Vulvar Vestibulitis Syndrome: An Exploratory Case-Control Study." *Sexually Transmitted Infections* 75 (5): 320–26 (October 1999).

Sawaya, George F., et al. "Current Approaches to Cervical-Cancer Screening." *New England Journal of Medicine* 344 (21): 1603–7 (May 24, 2001).

Schaff, Eric A., et al. "Vaginal Misoprostol Administered 1, 2, or 3 Days After Mifepristone for Early Medical Abortion: A Randomized Trial." *Journal of the American Medical Association* 284 (15): 1948–53 (October 18, 2000).

Schlecht, Nicolas F., et al. "Persistent Human Papillomavirus Infection as a Predictor of Cervical Intraepithelial Neoplasia." *Journal of the American Medical Association* 286 (24): 3106–14 (December 26, 2001).

Schwebke, Jane R. "Asymptomatic Bacterial Vaginosis: Response to Therapy." *American Journal of Obstetrics & Gynecology* 183 (6): 1434–39 (December 2000).

Shah, Keerti V., et al. "Diagnosis of Human Papillomavirus Infection by Dry Vaginal Swabs in Military Women." *Sexually Transmitted Infections* 77 (4): 260–64 (August 2001).

Sibbald, Barbara. "Emergency Contraceptive Pill Hits Ontario Market." *Canadian Medical Association Journal* 165 (3): 328 (August 7, 2001).

———. "Over-the-Counter Emergency Contraception Available Soon Across Country?" *Canadian Medical Association Journal* 164 (6): 849 (March 20, 2001).

———. "Will Canada follow US Lead of RU 486?" *Canadian Medical Association Journal* 164 (1): 82 (January 9, 2001).

Simms, I., et al. "National Assessment of PID Diagnosis, Treatment and Management in General Practice: England and Wales." *International Journal of STD & AIDS* 11 (7): 440–44 (July 2000).

Spinillo, Arsenio, et al. "Effect of Antibiotic Use on the Prevalence of Symptomatic Vulvovaginal Candidiasis." *American Journal of Obstetrics & Gynecology* 180 (1): 14–17 (January 1999).

Stamm, Walter E. "An Epidemic of Urinary Tract Infections?" *New England Journal of Medicine* 345 (14): 1055–57 (October 4, 2001).

Stead, Maxine L., et al. "Communication About Sexual Problems and Sexual Concerns in Ovarian Cancer: Qualitative Study." *British Medical Journal* 323 (7317): 836–37 (October 13, 2001).

Stephenson, Joan. "Genital Herpes Vaccine Shows Limited Promise." *Journal of the American Medical Association* 284 (15): 1913–14 (October 18, 2000).

———. "HIV Risk from Oral Sex Higher Than Many Realize." *Journal of the American Medical Association* 283 (10): 1279 (March 8, 2000).

Stewart, Felicia H., et al. "Clinical Breast and Pelvic Examination Requirements for Hormonal Contraception: Current Practice vs Evidence." *Journal of the American Medical Association* 285 (17): 2232–39 (May 2, 2001).

Sulik, Sandra M., et al. "Are Fluid-Based Cytologies Superior to the Conventional Papanicolaou Test? A Systematic Review." *Journal of Family Practice* 50 (12): 1040–46 (December 2001).

Sun, Yan, et al. "Augmented Stretch Activated Adenosine Triphosphate Release from Bladder Uroepithelial Cells in Patients with Interstitial Cystitis." *Journal of Urology* 166 (5): 1951–56 (November 2001).

Swerdloff, R. S., et al. "Suppression of Spermatogenesis in Man Induced by Nal-Glu Gonadotropin-Releasing Hormone Antagonist and Testosterone Enanthate (TE) Is Maintained by TE Alone." *Obstetrical & Gynecological Survey* 54 (5): 319–20 (May 1999).

Tabnak, Farzaneh, and Richard Sun. "Need for HIV/AIDS Early Identification and Preventive Measures Among Middle-Aged and Elderly Women." *American Journal of Public Health* 90 (2): 287–88 (February 2000).

Tanis, Bea C., et al. "Oral Contraceptives and the Risk of Myocardial Infarction." *New England Journal of Medicine* 345 (25): 1787–93 (December 20, 2001).

Taylor-Robinson, David, and Isobel J. Rosenstein. "Is Mycoplasma Hominis a Vaginal Pathogen?" *Sexually Transmitted Infections* 77 (4): 302 (August 2001).

Teichman, Joel M., et al. "Tic Douloureux of the Bladder and Interstitial Cystitis." *Journal of Urology* 164 (5): 1473–75 (November 2000).

Terrell, Christine L. "Antifungal Agents. Part II. The Azoles." *Mayo Clinic Proceedings* 74 (1): 78–100 (January 1999).

Tomblin, Frankie A., Jr., and Kristy H. Lucas. "Lysine for Management of Herpes Labialis." *American Journal of Health-System Pharmacy* 58 (4): 298, 300, 304 (February 15, 2001).

Trzcianowska, Halina, and Erik Mortensen. "HIV and AIDS: Separating Fact from Fiction: Help Your Patients Manage HIV by Learning What's True and What's Not." *American Journal of Nursing* 101 (6): 53–59 June 2001.

Van Ophoven, Arndt, Frank Oberpenning, and Lothar Hertle. "Long-Term Results of Trigone-Preserving Orthotopic Substitution Enterocystoplasty for Interstitial Cystitis." *Journal of Urology* 167 (2, Part 1 of 2): 603–7 (February 2002).

Vastag, Brian. "Chlamydia Toxin and Chronic Illness." *Journal of the American Medical Association* 286 (23): 2934 (December 19, 2001).

Verhoeven, Veronique, Dirk Avonts, and Lieve Peremans. "Copper Intrauterine Devices and Tubal Infertility Among Nulligravid Women." *New England Journal of Medicine* 346 (5): 376–77 (January 31, 2002).

Videlefsky, Andrea, et al. "Routine Vaginal Cuff Smear Testing in Post-Hysterectomy Patients with Benign Uterine Conditions: When Is It Indicated?" *Journal of the American Board of Family Practice* 13 (4): 233–38 (July/August 2000).

Walker, Gail R., James J. Schlesselman, and Roberta B. Ness. "Family History of Cancer, Oral Contraceptive Use, and Ovarian Cancer Risk." *American Journal of Obstetrics & Gynecology* 186 (1): 8–14 (January 2002).

Watson, Rory. "European Women's Group Calls for Human Papillomavirus Testing." *British Medical Journal* 323 (7316): 772 (October 6, 2001).

Weir, Erica. "Emergency Contraception: A Matter of Dedication and Access." *Canadian Medical Association Journal* 165 (8): 1095 (October 16, 2001).

————. "Female Genital Mutilation." *Canadian Medical Association Journal* 162 (9): 1344 (May 2, 2000).

————. "Navel Gazing: A Clinical Glimpse at Body Piercing." *Canadian Medical Association Journal* 164 (6): 864 (March 20, 2001).

————. "The Public Health Toll of Endometriosis." *Canadian Medical Association Journal* 164 (8): 1201 (April 17, 2001).

Weiss, Barbara. "OTC Emergency Contraception?" *RN* 64 (5): 3ON–5ON (May 2001).

Weiss, Jerome M. "Pelvic Floor Myofascial Trigger Points: Manual Therapy for Interstitial Cystitis and the Urgency-Frequency Syndrome." *Journal of Urology* 166 (6): 2226–31 (December 2001).

Welch, Jan. "Caring for Women with Circumcision: A Technical Manual for Health Care Providers." *British Medical Journal* 320 (7247): 1481 (May 27, 2000).

Westney, O. Lenaine, Cindy L. Amundsen, and Edward J. Mcguire. "Bladder Endometriosis: Conservative Management." *Journal of Urology* 163 (6): 1814–17 (June 2000).

Wiesenfeld, Harold C., et al. "Treatment Threshold Probability for Vaginitis." *American Journal of Obstetrics & Gynecology* 183 (2): 518 (August 2000).

Witkin, Steven S., et al. "Individual Immunity and Susceptibility to Female Genital Tract Infection." *American Journal of Obstetrics & Gynecology* 183 (1): 252–56 (July 2000).

Yamey, Gavin. "Sexuality and Cancer." *British Medical Journal* 323 (7317): 874 (October 13, 2001).

Zanetta, Gerardo, et al. "Survival and Reproductive Function After Treatment of Malignant Germ Cell Ovarian Tumors." *Journal of Clinical Oncology* 19 (4): 1015–20 (February 15, 2001).

# Index